Cultural Psychology
of Immigrants

Cultural Psychology
of Immigrants

Edited by

Ramaswami Mahalingam
University of Michigan

2006

LAWRENCE ERLBAUM ASSOCIATES, PUBLISHERS

Mahwah, New Jersey   London

Copyright © 2006 by Lawrence Erlbaum Associates, Inc.
All rights reserved. No part of this book may be reproduced in any form, by photostat, microform, retrieval system, or any other means, without prior written permission of the publisher.

Lawrence Erlbaum Associates, Inc., Publishers
10 Industrial Avenue
Mahwah, New Jersey 07430
www.erlbaum.com

Cover design by Tomai Maridou

Library of Congress Cataloging-in-Publication Data

Cultural psychology of immigrants / edited by Ramaswami Mahalingam
    p. cm.
Includes bibliographical references and index.
ISBN 0-8058-5314-6 (cloth : alk. paper)
ISBN 0-8058-5315-4 (pbk. : alk. paper)
1. Immigrants—Psychology. 2. Emigration and immigration—Psychological aspects. 5. Assimilation (Sociology) 6. Culture and globalization. I. Mahalingam, Ram
JV6225.C85 2006
305.0'06912—dc22   2005044675
                                       CIP

Books published by Lawrence Erlbaum Associates are printed on acid-free paper, and their bindings are chosen for strength and durability.

Printed in the United States of America
10 9 8 7 6 5 4 3 2

To
my school teachers

Vijaya, Kalyani, Subbulakshmi, Chandra,
Padma, Dalsi, Venkatraman, Karichankunju,
Natarajan, Ramaswami

&
students

Cheri, Eleanor, Hiro, Jan, Jana,
Jennifer, Joel, Mandy, Mark, Melita,
Ravishankar, & Sundari

Contents

Preface

Ramaswami Mahalingam

Two pedagogical moments shaped the genesis of the book. Six years ago, I was teaching an undergraduate course on cultural psychology. I noticed that most of my students were children of immigrants. In the entire course, I allocated one week for the topic of immigration. At the end of the term, several students wrote in their evaluation forms that this course helped them to understand their parents better. Considering how little I covered immigration in my class, I wondered whether cultural psychology could indeed help us to understand the psychology of immigrants. If cultural psychology of immigrants were to be a different discipline, what it might look like? I realized that I needed to ground cultural psychology in an interdisciplinary framework to make it relevant to the study of immigrants. To get my intellectual feet wet, I applied for a Distinguished Faculty Grant at the University of Michigan to develop an interdisciplinary graduate seminar on culture and immigration. As part of the course, I envisioned a "small" speaker series where eminent scholars from the fields of sociology, anthropology and American culture could give talks to the graduate students about their work. In the middle of teaching the course, an exciting idea crossed my mind. Wouldn't it be wonderful to invite all the people we read during the course for a conference to initiate an interdisciplinary dialogue on immigrant research? With the help of generous funding from several units at the University of Michigan, I was able to expand my "small" speaker series into a full-fledged conference on immigrant psychology. Meanwhile, I also managed to develop an undergraduate course on cultural psychology of immigrants. The conference was held at the end of the semester. As part of the course, the undergraduate students attended the conference. Having read the works of all the speakers during the term, the students were among the most well-informed people in the audience.

The conference was as exciting as I thought it would be, and it generated several stimulating conversations. We had speakers from the disciplines of psychology, sociology, anthropology, social work, American culture, and Asian American studies. Although these scholars were familiar with each other's work, this was the first time they were able to get together to share their work. Transcending the disciplinary and methodological boundaries, several themes about the complex dimensions of immigrants' experience emerged. Intersections of race, class, gender, sexuality, and culture shape the cultural psychology of immigrants. Immigrants negotiate their social status in a new culture using a variety of personal, social, and cultural resources. Transnational ties play an important role in the making of immigrant selves. Immigrants are exposed to dual worldviews, cultural practices, and beliefs while negotiating their social positioning in the new cultural context. So far, these complex dimensions of immigrants have not been adequately examined in cultural psychological research.

This volume addresses this gap. Given the importance of immigrant studies to a variety of disciplines, this volume provides a fresh interdisciplinary perspective on understanding the cultural psychology of immigrants. Distinguished scholars from the fields of behavioral ecology, psychology, sociology, American culture, public health, social work, and anthropology examine the various cultural psychological consequences of displacement among different immigrant and refugee communities in the United States, Canada and Europe. There are four sections in the book: (a) Immigration, Globalization, and Transnationalism: Theoretical Perspectives, (b) Immigration and Race, (c) Immigration, Self, Gender, and Narratives, and (d) Immigration and Family.

The chapters in the Immigration, Globalization, and Transnationlism section provide a variety of theoretical perspectives on immigration. Bobbi Low's chapter provides a behavioral ecological perspective to study immigrants. Silvia Pedraza's chapter offers a historical overview of sociological research on immigrants. Using refugee narratives, Valentine Daniel discusses the complex phenomenological predicaments of refugees. Using Caribbean immigrants as an example, Eleanor Murphy's chapter makes a strong case for understanding the significance of transnational ties in shaping immigrant health. Together these four chapters provide diverse theoretical perspectives to study immigrants and refugees.

The chapters in the Immigration and Race section examine racial discrimination of immigrants as well as immigrants' discriminatory attitudes toward African Americans. Thomas Pettigrew's chapter overviews research on anti-immigrant prejudice and discrimination in Europe and in the United States. Victoria Esses, Joerg Dietz, and Arjun

Bhardwaj's chapter investigates the role of prejudice in discounting immigrant skills in Canada. Teceta Thomas Tormala and Kay Deaux's chapter examines the complexities of racial and ethnic identity construction among Black immigrants. Ramaswami Mahalingam, Cheri Philip, and Sundari Balan compare first- and second-generation Indian Americans' attitude toward African Americans. All the chapters in this section examine how racialization and racial positioning of immigrants shape discriminatory attitudes of dominant as well as immigrant groups.

The chapters in the section Immigration, Self, Gender, and Narratives investigate how intersections of race, ethnicity, gender, social class, and sexuality influence the making of self among different immigrant groups. Magdalena Zaborowska investigates the implications of James Baldwin's construction of racial and cultural identities in a transatlantic immigrant context to the study of immigrant narratives. Margaret Abraham examines the social and psychological consequences of model minority myth for South Asian immigrant women who are in a domestic violence situation. Patricia Pessar's chapter probes the complex realities of citizenship making among refugee women. Oliva Espín's chapter highlights the role of language in making sense of gender and sexuality among immigrant women. Ramaswami Mahalingam and Jana Haritatos examine the cultural psychological aspects of gender socialization among second-generation Indian American women. Together, these chapters illustrate the powerful role of narratives in the making of self at the various intersections of immigrant and refugee identities.

The chapters in the section Immigration and Family document the pivotal role of family contexts in shaping various aspects of child development, identity formation, and negotiation. Using Indo-Caribbean families as an example, Jaipaul Roopnarine and Ambika Krishnakumar provide a cultural-ecological framework to study various determinants of child developmental outcomes. Karen Dion's chapter examines the intricate relationship among gender, intergenerational relationships, and identity development in immigrant families. Min Zhou's chapter examines the interaction between social context and family in shaping intergenerational relations and ethnic identity negotiations. Izumi Sakamoto proposes a complex model for understanding the important role of families in identity negotiation among Japanese academic migrants in the United States. All these chapters highlight the pivotal role of families in shaping identity formation, negotiation, and development shaped by the intersections of race, class, gender, and ethnicity.

This volume provides a rich interdisciplinary perspective to further our understanding of cultural psychology of immigrants. Its chapters also exemplify the very interdisciplinary nature of immigrant research. These chapters illustrate the commonalities and differences among ethnic immigrants and refugees in the ways in which they embody, construct, negotiate, and make sense of their newfound selves in the displaced context. Cultural psychology needs to identify different trajectories of such meaning-making processes and their psychological consequences, such as how these trajectories are influenced by intersections of race, class, ethnicity, gender, and sexuality and by the social context of the immigrant and refugee communities. This collection of essays contributes toward developing an interdisciplinary framework to further our understanding of the cultural psychology of immigrants. This volume is limited in that it focuses primarily on immigrants to Western industrialized nations. Future research on the psychology of immigration should include those who immigrate within regions, including those permanently displaced by war or natural disasters, and others who cross borders seeking safety or opportunity.

I thank the following units at the University of Michigan for their generous financial support, without which my intellectual venture would not have been possible: Office of the Vice President for Research, Office of Vice Provost, LSA, Institute for Research on Women and Gender, Women's Studies, Research Center for Group Dynamics, Center for South Asian Studies, Latino/a studies, Asian American Psychology Student Association, Latin American and Caribbean Studies Program, Rackham Graduate School, Culture and Cognition Program, and the Department of Psychology. I thank Joan DeCosta, Sherry Mason, Venece Williams, and Wenda Richmon-Morton for their help with organizing the conference. I also appreciate the secretarial assistance of Kristi Copping and Ken Kuklock.

I greatly appreciate Jennifer Yim's efficiency in coordinating various aspects of the conference. My special thanks to Ann Lin, Abigail Stewart, Jacquelynn Eccles, and Lorraine Gutierrez for their support and encouragement during various stages of this project. I thank the following reviewers for providing additional guidance in developing the project: Glenn Adams, University of Kansas; Anton Allahar, University of Western Ontario; and Fabienne Doucet, University of Connecticut. I thank the following graduate students for their unending enthusiasm and support throughout this project: Mark Akiyama, Sundari Balan, Mandeep Grewal, Jana Haritatos, Janxin Leu, Eleanor Murphy, Cheri Philip, Viswanathan Ravishankar, Joel Rodriguez, Hiro Saito, Melita Vas, and Jennifer Yim. I wholeheartedly thank editor Debra Riegert for her encouragement and perseverance. Finally, I am deeply grateful to Lauren Ungar and Jeeva Muhil for being a perennial source of support and love during many stressful phases of this project.

Contributors

Abraham, Margaret, Professor and Chair, Department of Sociology, Hofstra University

Balan, Sundari, Doctoral Student, Department of Psychology, University of Michigan

Bhardwaj, Arjun, Doctoral Student, Department of Psychology, University of Western Ontario, Richard Ivey School of Business

Daniel, Valentine, Professor, Department of Anthropology, Columbia University, New York

Deaux, Kay, Professor, Department of Psychology, City University of New York, Graduate Center

Dietz, Joerg, Doctoral Fellow, Department of Psychology, University of Western Ontario, Richard Ivey School of Business

Dion, Karen, Professor, Department of Life Sciences (Psychology), University of Toronto at Scarborough

Espin, Oliva, Professor, Department of Women's Studies, San Diego State University

Esses, Victoria, Professor, Department of Psychology, University of Western Ontario

Haritatos, Jana, Postdoctoral Fellow, Center for Health and Community, University of California San Francisco.

Krishnakumar, Ambika, Associate Professor, Department of Family Studies, Syracuse University

Low, Bobbi, Professor, University of Michigan School of Natural Resources and Environment

Mahalingam, Ramaswami, Assistant Professor, Department of Psychology, University of Michigan

Murphy, Eleanor, Postdoctoral Fellow, Department of Epidemiology, Mailman School of Public Health, Columbia University

Pedraza, Silvia, Associate Professor, Department of Sociology, University of Michigan

Pessar, Patricia, Professor, Department of Anthropology and American Culture, Yale University

Pettigrew, Thomas, Professor, Department of Psychology, University of California, Santa Cruz

Philip, Cheri, Postdoctoral Fellow, Howard University

Roopnarine, Jaipaul, Professor, Department of Family Studies, Syracuse University

Sakamoto, Izumi, Assistant Professor, School of Social Work, University of Toronto

Tormala, Teceta, Visiting Professor, Department of Psychology, Indiana University

Zaborowska, Magdalena, Associate Professor, Department of American Culture, University of Michigan

Zhou, Min, Professor, Department of Sociology, and Chair, Department of Asian American Studies, University of California, Los Angeles

Cultural Psychology of Immigrants: An Introduction

Ramaswami Mahalingam
University of Michigan

Cultural psychological research has demonstrated the constituent role of culture in how we think, how we feel, and how we perceive our social experience (Cole, 1996; Markus & Kitayama, 1991; Nisbett, 2003; Rogoff, 2003; Shweder & Sullivan, 1990; Sperber, 1996). The major strands of research in cultural psychology have generally ignored immigrants, with a few exceptions, such as research on psychological acculturation (Berry, 1995), biculturalism (Hong, Morris, Chiu, & Benet-Martinez, 2000), and identity negotiation (Suarez-Orozco & Suarez-Orozco, 2001). Interestingly, cultural psychology, as a discipline, does not generally treat immigrants as an intrinsically interesting or worthy object of study. In fact, most research on cultural psychology treats immigrants as a control group (e.g., Nisbett, 2003). This research places them on a continuum between participants in their "home" culture and their "host" culture. Although this approach has some merit, cultural psychology needs to take into account the distinct aspects of immigrants' social location and its impact on their psychological well-being.

Bhatia and Ram (2001), highlight some major gaps in how cultural context is conceptualized in cultural psychological studies on immigrants. In particular issues of power, transnational ties, and social marginality have not been adequately addressed in cultural psychological research on immigrants. In summary, there are at least two major shortcomings in cultural psychological approaches to the study of immigrants. The first is related to insufficient theorization of how immigrants "represent their culture." The second is inadequate exploration of how power and social marginality shape immigrants' representations of culture. To address these lacune in research on immigrants, this chapter provides a cultural psychology framework to study cultural psychology of immigrants. Integrating current research on social marginality and idealized cultural narratives, I identify the following three interrelated aspects of an immigrant's social experience as the core of the proposed cultural psychology framework: (a) representations of culture, (b) social location and marginality, and (c) idealized cultural identities. In the following sections, I discuss the importance of each of these features in detail before proposing a cultural identities model to study immigrants.

IMMIGRANTS AND REPRESENTATIONS OF CULTURE

Immigrants are exposed to dual worldviews, cultural practices, and beliefs. Immigrants' "home culture" alone may not be sufficient to help us understand the cultural psychology of immigrants. Unlike people in their "home culture," the comparative sociocultural context of immigrants influences how they "represent" their "home culture" while trying to make sense of their "host culture." Immigrants are both *folk anthropologists* and *informants* at the same time. The relational context of their displacement makes them aware of the comparative nature of their cultural identity, and they are challenged to develop a deeper understanding of their own culture. They develop a newer appreciation of culture not merely as a set of practices and shared values, but as something that needs to be reflected on and explained. A new immigrant, like an anthropologist in an "exotic culture," tries to make sense of the host culture—its mores and practices and the meaning and grammar of various social cartographies.

As "aliens," immigrants are constantly asked to explain various aspects of their "culture" to the "natives"—ranging from food customs to foreign policy issues to tips on the best ethnic restaurant in town. In the process, they try to decipher various meanings associated with the new identities that are forced on them. While making sense of the racial and social arrangements of the host society, they also embody the newer forms of racial and ethnic identities that codify their social and historical experiences (Kim, 1999). The dual role of informing and absorbing the new culture uniquely positions an immigrant to be aware of social hierarchies and power among various social groups.

Although there are similarities between immigrants and anthropologists, there are some interesting differences. Immigrants' attitudes toward the dominant culture often remind me of *Annam*, a kind of swan that is believed to have a mythical ability to separate the good from the bad. For instance, if you give Annam a mixture of water and milk, it will drink the milk and leave the water in the bowl. Immigrants often view American cultural experience is a mixture of milk and water, and like Annams, they believe they can take the "milk" (good American values such as independence, hard work) and leave the "water" (the undesirable aspects of the culture, such as dating, violence, and drugs). They also expect their children to imbibe the qualities of Annams. Immigrants often make "value judgments" about their "home" and "host" cultures. As Daniel (this volume) points out, although immigrants share the same predicament as anthropologists in the ways they experience the disruption of their "culture," immigrants do not have the same cultural privileges associated with a Western anthropologist who studies a non-Western culture. Thus, their marginalized social location colors immigrants' representations of "host" as well as "home" culture.

SOCIAL LOCATION AND MARGINALITY

According to Mahalingam (in press), social location refers to intersecting identities such as race, caste, class, gender, and sexuality embedded in a social context, where the power differential among these axes of identities locates an immigrant in a complex field of racial positioning (Kim, 1999). Dominant group members essentialize social categories in order to legitimize existing social hierarchies. In contrast, a marginalized social location heightens one's awareness of social power and of contextual influences on identity (Fiske, 1993; Mahalingam, 2003). Marginalized groups have to contest such essentialist representations, because they become tropes for discriminatory ideologies that justify the marginalized status of immigrants. To negate such hegemonic social representations, people at marginalized locations feel a stronger need to create a positive identity than do members of a dominant group.

Because many immigrants lack the social and cultural capital necessary to successfully negotiate their social status, they are often marginalized (Portes & Rumbaut, 1996). Like other marginalized groups, immigrants seek a positive cultural identity by locating their roots in a mythical past and claiming a legacy as inheritors of a "richer" civilization. As folk anthropologists, immigrants construct a narrative of their cultural heritage in order to develop a reflective understanding, making sense of their cultural practices. Such selective invocation of cultural heritage provides an interesting counterpoint to the denigrating dominant cultural accounts of representations of immigrants—also known as ethnophaulisms (see Mullen, 2001, for a review).

Such idealized identities play a significant role in creating and sustaining an essentialized sense of "community," devoid of internal contradictions (Anderson, 1991). Although much scholarly attention has focused on the historical and social contingencies of such "imagined communities," the discipline of psychology has rarely examined the role of marginalized social location in accentuating our general psychological need to create an "idealized" positive identity (Tajfel, 1981) and the psychological consequences of such idealizations.

CULTURAL NARRATIVES
AND IDEALIZED CULTURAL IDENTITIES

Cultural narratives of those on the social margins often are the communal memory of resilience and resolve under oppressive and marginal locales (Mahalingam, in press). They valorize the triumph of individuals who succeed against all odds and in the face of social discrimination. Three cultural narratives exemplify the valorization of self among marginalized groups. An example from India is the story of Ekalaivya, a Dalit (formerly treated as "Untouchable"). He was a great archer who is valorized for being an ideal student. At the request of his teacher (who was a Brahmin), Ekalaivya gave up his right-hand thumb as *Gurudakshina* (gift to a guru), knowing very well that he could never practice archery again. Ekalaivya is still viewed as the embodiment of an ideal student for giving up all his learning for his teacher (see Mahalingam, in press).

In a study of slave narratives, Sanger (1995) found that slave folk songs revealed that slaves believed that they had a more privileged relationship with God than did Whites.

> Spirituals contained descriptions of the rewards the slaves envisioned as a result of their status as God's chosen ... For instance, in the song, "Hold the wind", the slaves sang 'when I get to heaven, gonna be ease,' 'Me and my God gonna do as we please' and 'gonna chatter with the Father, and argue with the Son Tell them about the world I just come from ...' Slaves implicitly claimed for themselves a relationship with God more personal and more privileged than that experienced by Whites. (Sanger, 1995, pp. 188–189)

Another example is the story of John Henry, an African American sharecropper who worked himself to death while competing with a power drill. His narrative presents an idealized prototype symbolizing strength and persistence of African Americans.

These examples suggest the power of idealized narratives and the acute need for marginalized communities to create such idealized narratives to foster a positive self identity. However, they are also stark and ominous reminders of the heavy cost of asserting agency from an unprivileged location. These costs are both physical and psychological. In studying the health disparities of African Americans, James (1994) found that African Americans who internalize the values signified by the John Henry myth (hard work, excellence), but nevertheless are not economically successful, are more likely to suffer from hypertension, even after controlling for the effects of income and education.

CULTURAL PSYCHOLOGY OF IMMIGRANTS:
AN IDEALIZED CULTURAL IDENTITIES MODEL

These three examples of narratives of idealized selves of marginalized groups such as Dalits and African Americans suggest the acute need to create and believe in such idealizations because these idealizations help them to negate dominant groups' view that they lack "culture" (e.g., "deficit cultural" models; for a review, see Ogbu, 1981). As empirical research on John Henryism suggests, there are costs and benefits associated with such idealized views of self. Such ideals could help individuals to cope, to assert and to feel proud of their identity. Their salience in defining self-worth also becomes especially significant as these cultural narratives play a vital role in the construction of idealized group identities.

Extending the research on social marginality and idealized cultural identities to the study of immigrants and refugees, I argue that immigrants may feel the need to idealize their identities. The dual role of immigrants in a new cultural milieu—as folk anthropologists and as informants—also forces them to rethink their assumptions about their culture and identity. Such rethinking profoundly influences their need to "imagine" or "project" an idealized cultural identity in order to assert, negotiate and make sense of their social positioning.

In summary, marginalized status contributes to the idealization of one's identity. Internalization of such idealizations has positive and negative consequences. Intersections of race, class, gender, and sexuality (Stewart & McDermott, 2004) and transnational ties (Foner, 2002; Murphy & Mahalingam, 2004) also play a critical role in the appropriation of these ideals.

Intersections of Race, Class, Gender, and Idealized Cultural Identities

Intersections of ethnicity, class, gender, and sexuality play a critical role in the production and appropriation of these ideals. Idealized cultural identities serve multiple functions. Because gender is a major site for inscribing idealized cultural identities, engendered idealized cultural identities affect ethnic women's lives in complex ways. Several cultural theorists have pointed that in many cultures women are believed to embody the essence of their culture and group identity and are thought to be repositories of family honor (Dube, 2001: Ortner, 1974). Research on gender socialization among immigrants indicates that immigrants view women as the purveyors of "culture" (Dasgupta & Dasgupta, 2000; Dion, this volume; Espiritu, 2001; Gill & Vasquez, 1996). There is more pressure on first-and second-generation women than there is on men to uphold idealized cultural identities. Gender-specific cultural ideals valorize ethnic women as more "chaste" and "family-oriented" than

"White" women (Espiritu, 2001; Mahalingam & Haritatos, this volume). Several variants of female ideals are culture specific. For instance, the notion of Pativirda (the devoted wife) has a strong influence in how first- and second-generation immigrants view how an Indian American woman "ought" to behave, and their everyday lives are influenced by such ideals (Abraham, this volume). Similarly Gil and Vasquez (1996) argued that the notion of *Marianismo* has a major impact on Latina women's mental health. Based on their clinical work, they describe some specific Marianista beliefs:

> (a) a good wife must always provide her husband and children with a good meal which she prepares herself (b) a good mother should not argue with her husband before her children (c) a good wife must put up with her husband's relatives, no matter how offensive or inconsiderate they are (d) a good wife must have an impeccable home and preferably must keep it that way herself (e) a good Latina must obey traditions *al pie de la letra*, to the letter of the law (f) a good mother should take care of her children herself or with the help of very trustworthy relatives. (Gil & Vasquez, 1996, p. 184)

Thus, engendered cultural ideals not only constrict ethnic women's lives but also imply that they should strive to achieve these ideals in order to be different and superior to "White women" (Mahalingam & Leu, 2005). In addition, the first- and second-generation immigrant women are expected to be morally, academically, and professionally better than White women (Mahalingam & Leu, in press).

Internalization of idealized cultural identities has several consequences. An idealized cultural identity may positively contribute to a positive sense of self, but it may also become a source of stress (Mahalingam & Haritatos, 2005). In a study conducted in India, Mahalingam and Jackson (2005) found that Indian women from caste groups that commit female infanticide (where the sex ratios can be as dramatic as 614 girls for every 1000 boys) tend to valorize their gender identity and strongly believe in the power of chaste women and macho men (Mahalingam & Jackson, 2005). Such essentialist beliefs about gender ideals, although contributing to strong self-esteem, also contribute increased feelings of shame and depression. Mahalingam and Haritatos (2005) examined the relationship between internalization of a model minority myth and psychological well-being among Asian Americans. They found that internalization of Asian American women ideals contributed both to pride in being a model minority and to pressure to be a model minority. Individual differences might play a role in how people negotiate the pride and pressure associated with believing to be part of an idealized group.

Idealized cultural identities also help immigrants to feel that they occupy a higher social position within the racial hierarchies in the United States. Kim (1999) argued that idealized cultural identities, such as model minority myth, triangulate Asian American identities vis-à-vis a White–Black continuum and positioning Asian Americans above African Americans in terms of achievement. According to Prashad (2000), Indian immigrants also seek an "authentic" identity to feel closer to White Americans.

> Desis [Indians] seek out an "authentic culture" for complex reasons, among them the desire not to be seen as fundamentally inferior to those who see themselves as "white" and superior. To be on a par with or at least not beneath these people, desis, like other subordinated peoples, revel in those among them who succeed in white terms. There is a *sotto voce* knowledge among nonwhites of their various forms of greatness. Parents instruct their children to recognize all kinds of people valued by Europe. (p. 157)

In a study of second-generation Indian American professionals, Dhingra (2003) found that many of them felt that they were not model minorities but "model Americans." Thus, immigrants may at times use idealized identities to distance themselves from other marginalized groups by assigning themselves in an intermediate status within the racial hierarchy.

Another important factor that contributes to the production and the salience of idealized cultural identities is transnational ties. Several sociologists have pointed to the increasingly transnational nature of the immigrant experience (Foner, 2002; Portes, Guarnizo & Landolt, 1999). Transnational ties help immigrants to maintain cultural and social links with their home countries. Often, they also lobby for their home country with the U.S. government (Foner, 2002). Transnational ties can make immigrants value their ethnic identity, which might lead to new forms of idealizations.

In summary, the cultural psychology of immigrants is shaped by their marginalized social location and by how they represent their culture and idealized cultural identities (see Fig. 1.1). Intersections of ethnicity, gender, and class and transnational ties also influence the various ways in which cultural ideals are appropriated.

The following hypothesized relationships need to be further examined. Idealized cultural identities relate positively to pride and pressure but they will also positively relate to individual difference factors, such as resilience. Pride in being part of an ideal group will be positively related to pressure to live up to the expectations of being a model minority. Pride will positively relate to resilience, and pressure will negatively relate to personal resilience (Luthar, Cicchetti, & Becker, 2000). Resilience will positively relate to mental and physical health and negatively relate to perceived stress and perceived discrimination (Barry, 2002; Barry & Grilo, 2003; Mossakowski, 2003). Resilience will also positively relate to achievement (Suarez-Orozco & Suarez-Orozco, 2001). These hypothesized relationships may differ by gender, by generational status, and by the gendered nature of idealized identities. Hence it is critical to identify the culture-specific nature

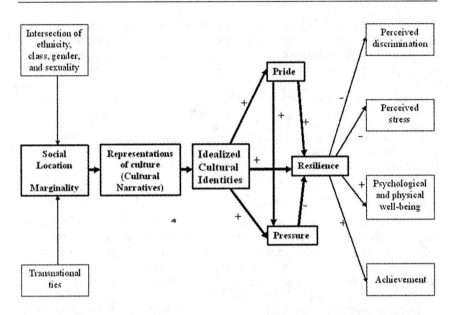

FIG. 1.1.   Cultural psychology of immigrants: An idealized cultural identities model.

and salience of cultural ideals (e.g., Marianismo, Pativirda, model minority) so that the psychological impact of endorsement of these ideals can be ascertained.

IMPLICATIONS AND FUTURE DIRECTIONS

I proposed a framework for a cultural psychology of immigrants that suggests idealized cultural identities have dual effects. Whether "self-imagined" or "imposed" by the dominant culture, idealized cultural identities affect immigrants' lives in complex ways. It is critical to identify what aspects of culture are salient to an immigrant and how they become an integral part of an idealized ethnic identity. Ethnic organizations and religious institutions play an important role in affirming certain aspects of ethnic identities (Kurien, 1999, 2003). In addition, cultural mythologies in the form of myths and literary or personal narratives might also contribute to the creation of new cultural ideals. Participation in religious and ethnic institutions and exposure to ethnic literature will highlight unique aspects of one's "cultural roots" that might lead to a greater acceptance of idealized cultural identities.

The salience of idealized cultural identities might also change over one's lifetime. Longitudinal studies are needed to examine the shifts in endorsement of idealized cultural identities and their psychological consequences and the mediating role of various life events. In addition, social contexts (e.g., group composition or family context) may also prime various aspects of idealized cultural identities. For instance, a specific immigrant context (e.g., ethnic enclaves vs. predominantly White suburbs) might intensify or weaken the salience of idealized identities. Perhaps ethnic enclaves and suburbs may lead to different ways of internalizing cultural ideals, because they offer different vantage points for social comparisons between and within social groups. In addition, it is critical to examine the role of various family and parental practices in the socialization of these idealized beliefs about ethnic identity in these divergent immigrant settings.

Different kinds of transnational ties, such as cultural, political, and financial contacts with the home culture, also signal the power and authority of cultural identities (Murphy & Mahalingam, 2004). Cultural contacts in the form of touring ethnic music or dance groups might remind the immigrants of the richness of their cultural heritage. Such contacts open up possibilities for developing a deeper understanding of culture, which might lead to internalization of idealized cultural identities. Political ties may help immigrants to recognize the cultural capital of their ethnic identities. Many first- and second-generation immigrants offer financial help to their relatives back home. Helping extended families may strengthen cultural bonds. Hence it is critical to understand the mediating role of transnational contacts in the endorsement of idealized cultural identities.

The process of idealization of cultural identities might also be affected by transnational migratory experience. For example, Indo-Caribbeans in New York are "twice" removed from their "culture." Most of them are descendents of early Indian migrants who came to the Caribbean as indentured labors during the colonial period (Roopnarine & Krishnakumar, this volume). The Indo-Caribbean vision of Indian culture is tempered by their diasporic experience and their desire to be distinguished from Afro-Caribbeans. This complex social context may contribute to an intense need to idealize Indian culture. After being "twice removed" from their "original" culture, they are for the first time in direct contact with a large number of Indian immigrants and financially can afford to make a trip to their "motherland," India. In contrast, direct immigrants from India believe that their conception of Indian culture is more "authentic" than the representations of Indo-Caribbeans (Roopnarine, personal communication, 2005). However, both groups deploy a narrative of an "ancient and glorious" Indian culture to negate the dominance of "American" culture. A comparison of Indian immigrants and

Indo-Caribbean immigrants in the United States will help us to understand whether the salience of idealized cultural identities is stronger for Indo-Caribbean immigrants than it is for Indian immigrants.

Future research should investigate the complex consequences of internalization of idealized cultural identities at the intersections of social identities and social contexts:

1. How do intersecting marginalized identities such as gender, social class, and immigrant status affect the psychological costs and benefits of negotiating idealized cultural identities?
2. Do idealized cultural identities help marginalized groups to cope with various forms of social discrimination and life stressors?
3. Does pressure from idealized identities adversely affect academic achievement?
4. Are there changes across life span in the internalization of cultural ideals?
5. Do different kinds of transnational ties influence internalization of idealized cultural identities?
6. Do twice-removed immigrants (e.g., Indo-Caribbeans) idealize their identity in a way different from other immigrants?

An interdisciplinary approach is necessary to answer these questions. In addition, a combination of qualitative and quantitative methods should be used to investigate the complex relationship of narratives, social marginality, and idealization of identities.

CONCLUSIONS

The cultural psychology of immigrants foregrounds the unique social positioning of immigrants and how they represent their "culture" in order to project an idealized self and ethnic identity. Various social intersections influence the production, internalization, and appropriation of these ideals while immigrants try to negotiate their status within the social hierarchy. Developing a deeper understanding of cultural psychology of immigrants necessitates an interdisciplinary approach integrating insights from disciplines such as sociology, anthropology, and ethnic studies (Foner, Rumbaut, & Gold, 2000). Although cultural psychology has a productive intellectual engagement with anthropology, its ties to sociology or ethnic studies have been tenuous or virtually nonexistent. Study of immigrants provides an exciting opportunity for cultural psychology to draw from the rich sociological and ethnic studies literature on immigration. The proposed idealized cultural identities model provides a framework to look at how cultural, historical, and sociological factors shape how immigrants represent, produce, and appropriate idealized selves and ethnic identities and the impact this has on immigrants' mental and physical well-being. The cultural psychology of immigrants has great potential to contribute to our understanding of culture, power, and social location and how intersections of various identities affect immigrants' lives.

REFERENCES

Anderson, B. (1991). *Imagined communities.* New York: Verso.

Barry, D. T. (2002). An ethnic identity scale for East Asian immigrants. *Journal of Immigrant Health, 3,* 87–94.

Barry, D. T., & Grilo, C. M. (2003). Cultural, self-esteem, and demographic correlates of perception of personal and group discrimination among East Asian immigrants. *American Journal of Orthopsychiatry, 73*(2), 223–229.

Berry, J. W. (1995). Psychology of acculturation. In N. R. Goldberger (Eds.), *The culture and psychology reader* (pp. 457–488). New York: New York University Press.

Bhatia, S., & Ram, A. (2001). Rethinking 'acculturation' in relation to diasporic cultures and postcolonial identities. *Human Development, 44*(1), 1–17.

Cole, M. (1996). *Cultural psychology: A once and a future discipline.* Cambridge: Harvard University Press.

Dasgupta, S., & Dasgupta, S. D. (2000). Women in exile: Gender relations in the Asian American community in the United States. In J. Yu-wen Shen & M. Song (Eds.), *Asian American studies: A reader* (pp. 324–337). New Jersey: Rutgers University Press.

Dhingra, P. H. (2003). Being American between Black and White: Second-generation Asian American professionals' racial identities. *Journal of Asian American Studies, 6*(2), 117–147.

Dube, L. (2001). *Anthropological explorations in gender: Intersecting fields.* Thousand Oaks, CA: Sage.

Espiritu, Y. (2001). "We don't sleep around like White girls do." Family, culture and gender in Filipina American lives. *Signs, 26*(2), 415–440.

Fiske, S. T. (1993). Controlling other people: The impact of power on stereotyping. *American Psychologist, 48*(6), 621–628.

Foner, N. (2002). *From Ellis Island to JFK: New York's two great waves of immigration.* New Haven, CT: Yale University Press.

Foner, N., Rumbaut, R. G., & Gold, S. J. (Eds.). (2000). *Immigration research for a new century.* New York: Russell Sage.

Gil, R. M., & Vasquez, C. S. (1996). *Maria paradox: How Latinas can merge Old World traditions with New World self esteem.* New York: Putnam.

Hong, Y., Morris, M. W., Chiu, C., & Benet-Martinez, V. (2000). Multicultural minds: A dynamic constructivist approach to culture and cognition. *American Psychologist, 55*(7), 709–720.

James, S. A. (1994). John Henryism and the health of African-Americans. *Culture, Medicine, and Psychiatry, 18,* 163–182.

Kim, C. J. (1999). The racial triangulation of Asian Americans. *Politics and Society, 27*(1), 105–138.

Kurien, P. (1999). Gendered ethnicity: Creating a Hindu Indian identity in the United States. *American Behavioral Scientist, 42*(4), 648–670.

Kurien, P. (2003). To be or not to be South Asian: Contemporary Indian American politics. *Journal of Asian American Studies, 6*(3), 261–288.

Luthar, S.S., Cicchetti, D., & Becker, B. (2000). The construct of resilience: A critical evaluation and guidelines for future work. *Child Development, 71*(3), 543–562.

Mahalingam, R. (2003). Essentialism, culture and power: rethinking social class. *Journal of Social Issues, 59*(4), 733–749.

Mahalingam, R. (in press). Culture, essentialism, and psychology of marginality. A developmental perspective. In A. Fuligni (Ed.), *Social identity and academic achievement.* New York: Russell Sage.

Mahalingam, R., & Haritatos, J. (2005). *Cultural psychology and gender: A cultural ecological intersectionality perspective.* Manuscript submitted for publication.

Mahalingam, R., & Jackson, B. (2005). *Idealized cultural beliefs, self-appraisals, and mental health: The idealized cultural identities model.* Unpublished manuscript.

Mahalingam, R., & Leu, J. (2005) Culture, essentialism, immigration and representations of gender. *Theory and Psychology, 15*(6), 841–862.

Markus, H., & Kitayama, S. (1991). Culture and self: implications for cognition, emotion and motivation. *Psychological Review, 98,* 224–253.

Mossakowski, K. N. (2003). Coping with perceived discrimination: Does ethnic identity protect mental health? *Journal of Health and Social Behavior, 44*(3), 318–331.

Mullen, B. (2001). Ethnophaulisms for ethnic immigrant groups. *Journal of Social Issues, 57*(3), 457–475.

Murphy, E. J., & Mahalingam, R. (2004). Trnasnational ties and mental health of Caribbean immigrants. *Journal of Immigrant Health, 6*(4), 167–178.

Nisbett, R. (2003). *Geography of thought: How Asians and Westerners think differently ... and why.* New York: Free Press.

Ogbu, J. U. (1981). Origins of human competence: A cultural-ecological perspective. *Child Development, 52,* 413–429.

Ortner, S. (1974). Is male to female as nature is to culture? In M. Rosaldo & L. Lamphere (Eds.), *Woman, culture, and society* (pp. 67–88). Stanford, CA: Stanford University Press.

Portes, A., Guarnizo, L. E., & Landolt, P. (1999). The study of transnationalism: Pitfalls and promise of an emergent research field. *Ethnic and Racial Studies Review, 22*(2), 217–237.

Portes, A., & Rumbaut, R. G. (1996). *Immigrant America: A portrait.* Berkeley: University of California Press.

Prashad, V. (2000). *The karma of brown folk.* Minneapolis: University of Minnesota Press.

Rogoff, B. (2003). *The cultural nature of human development.* New York: Oxford University Press.

Sanger, K. (1995). Slave resistance and rhetorical self-definition. *Western Journal of Communication, 59,* 177–192.

Shweder, R. A., & Sullivan, M. A. (1990). The semiotic subject of cultural psychology. In L. A. Pervin (Ed.), *Handbook of personality: Theory and research* (pp. 399–416). New York: Guilford.

Sperber, D. (1996). Anthropology and psychology: Towards an epidemiology of representations. In D. Sperber (Ed.), *Explaining culture: A natrualistic approach* (pp. 57–76). Cambridge, MA: Blackwell.

Stewart, A. J., & McDermott, C. (2004). Gender in psychology. *Annual Review Psychology, 55,* 519–544.

Suarez-Orozco, C., & Suarez-Orozco, M. M. (2001). *Children of immigrants.* Cambridge, MA: Harvard University Press.

Tajfel, H. (1981). *Human groups and social categories: Studies in social psychology.* New York: Cambridge University Press.

Part I

Immigration, Globalization,
and Transnationalism:
Theoretical Perspectives

2

Whither Thou Goest: An Evolutionary Perspective on Migration

Bobbi S. Low
University of Michigan

THE "WHAT AND WHY" OF MIGRATION

Anthropologists, biologists, and sociologists are all interested in the patterns, causes, and effects of migration. The focus of each of these groups of scholars differs, and they identify varied causes and effects, at different levels. However, their findings are not contradictory, but rather complementary. Here I hope to connect the understanding of several of these fields, looking at migration at several levels, perhaps to spark some interdisciplinary cross-fertilization.

There is something of a gap in the literature. In part, most of the sociological literature on migration in humans concerns immigrants' fates *after* migration—but biologists, for example, are interested primarily in the precipitating factors that *lead to* migration. And some studies look at aggregate patterns, whereas much remains to be learned from studying individual variation (e.g., sex, or birth order patterns in migration). Here I suggest that a new perspective, behavioral ecology, may help connect existing studies in two ways. First, behavioral ecology has been very fruitful in analyzing migration in other species, helping us understand and test predictions about the roles of predictability and variation in the environment as they foster different kinds of migration. Second, when we ask about human migration, we often care about very subtle issues—but unless we understand the very basic, shared patterns, we may misinterpret what we see. Finally, behavioral ecology focuses on the reproductive costs and benefits of behaviors, including migration; and although many studies do not examine these aspects, for many modern disputes (e.g., conflicts over migrant versus native fertility, support systems for migrants), we need to understand the relationships between migration and reproductive patterns. Perhaps behavioral ecology can add new dimensions to our understanding of migration in our own species.

We use the term *migration* to mean a number of different things, whether we are discussing human or non-human patterns. At the largest scale, we sometimes mean the *dispersal of populations over evolutionary time*. Thus, Cavalli-Sforza and colleagues (Cavalli-Sforza, Menozzi, & Piazza, 1996) mapped the long-term patterns of human dispersal over the globe, using genetic analyses. Most uses of the term *migration* concern a smaller scale, in both time and space; there are three main such uses. We may mean regular movement of individuals or populations between areas that repeatedly and regularly differ in habitat quality (*seasonal migration*)—like African wildebeest, and people in a number of traditional societies. We may mean much less defined, but still repeated, movement (e.g., *nomadic* movement), as among the Cree people, and some Arctic caribou. Finally, we may mean simply leaving one's birth area (*natal migration*)—as Belding's Ground squirrels, wolves, and women in many societies do.

All of these kinds of migration occur in both nonhumans and humans, but for some species, and in some parts of the globe, certain kinds of migration may be more common, or less. One advantage to adding a behavioral ecological perspective is that it both points out similarities (usually of ecological and resource conditions) between studies on nonhumans and studies on humans, and serves to link them. At its most basic level, migration is shaped by ecological conditions, and how these affect survival and reproduction. But our individual costs and benefits in migrating or not depend not only on ecological conditions, but on our age, our sex, our socioeconomics condition, our conspecific competitors, our resources ... and more.

Biologists, who are perhaps more sanguine than other scholars about humans as biological creatures, argue that the same basic rules that apply to other species also apply to the costs and benefits of human migration. Along with the generalities of "being a mammal" and the ecological variation we encounter, we also have some traits that are particularly human; these help set the stage for the things we can do in our lives, and for the specific patterns of migration we see. Sociologists, demographers, and geographers (e.g., Grigg, 1977; Moffitt, 2003, 2005) have "push versus pull" theories, which analyze "proximate" drivers (described later) of all three kinds of migration. The pushes and pulls may be resources, family connections—there can be many quite different drivers—and this is part of what I want to explore here. Analyses of human migration rarely make explicit the relationships between individual survival and fertility, and the most important driver of migration in all other species: ecological conditions. From an evolutionary perspective (e.g., behavioral ecology and evolutionary anthropology), all of the meanings of "migration" reflect ecological influences of *better* versus *worse* conditions for individual survival and reproduction (e.g., Clarke & Low, 2001).

Natal, seasonal, and nomadic migration all occur today in both human and nonhuman species; as noted earlier, from an evolutionary and ecological view, all three are prompted by similar (ecological) conditions. Evolutionary/behavioral ecology approaches to the study of migration, looking at very basic ecology, complement sociological and psychological approaches that analyze more specifically human migration factors.

WHAT EVOLUTIONARY BIOLOGY
AND BEHAVIORAL ECOLOGY CAN ADD

All approaches ask "why migrate?" or "under what conditions is migration more likely, and by whom?" but there is diversity in focus beyond these issues. Social scientists, like most of us informally, tend to think about how we *feel* and *think* about migrating, about our conscious decisions. Yet underneath the almost endless possible conscious opinions about why you or I decide to migrate, to what place, and when, there are ecological influences, as well. And these are more patterned; looking carefully at a wide spectrum of species for these correlates can be useful.

The famous ethologist Niko Tinbergen (1963) noted decades ago that there are many ways to ask "why?" Until we connect the various approaches, we can miss important patterns. Consider: Why do some individuals in some bird species migrate regularly? There are four biological kinds of answers (Holekamp & Sherman, 1989; Tinbergen, 1963), and they can easily be grouped, for our purposes, into two main categories: *ultimate* answers (explaining why a particular migration pattern is reproductively advantageous—helps the individual survive or reproduce better), and *proximate* answers (explaining the actual "how it happens"—the trigger).

So, why do some birds migrate? One answer might be "because of changing day length," another "because of changing hormone levels" (Charnov, 1980). Both of these answers are, like most sociological and psychological explanations, *proximate* explanations; they deal with discovering the immediate "trigger" for migration. They do not explain, in terms of reproductive costs and benefits, why migrating bird species have *evolved to respond* to changes in daylength by changing hormonal levels and migrating. Proximate answers do not explain why, in many species, some individuals migrate but others do not, or why some individuals move earlier or later than others. Those questions are the focus of behavioral ecology, which deals with ultimate causes: Under what circumstances will migrating individuals profit genetically? And why is migration costly for some individuals, in some circumstances, but beneficial for others?

The *ultimate* cause of seasonal migration, as with other behaviors, always concerns reproductive success. Whenever we see seasonal geographic shifts in foraging and nesting areas, for example, we understand that individuals that seek the (predictably timed) better conditions, shifting seasonally, leave more descendants than those who remain in one area. This is why we expect nectar-eating birds, like hummingbirds, to migrate in many environments, but we expect that seed-eating birds (many finches) and some insect-eating birds (woodpeckers) may remain in northern climates over the winter.

The logic about ultimate causation does not vary, but the proximate triggers may vary. When day length is the most reliable predictor of seasonal shifts, for example, individuals who use day length as a cue will do much better than those who use some other proximate cue, or who fail to migrate. We also expect variation in which individuals of a population migrate, because the benefits and costs of migration (in terms of survival and reproduction) typically differ for older, prime-age birds, compared with yearlings. Proximate and ultimate (selective) approaches complement each other because they ask "why?" at two very different levels—and if we wish fully to understand "why," we need both levels.

Importantly, such ecological predictions are *statistical*, not universal, and different kinds of individuals may experience different costs and benefits to migration. That is, not only would we predict that hummingbirds should migrate while seed eaters are less likely to, but we also recognize that older, better nourished individuals may have different migration options than adolescent, not-yet-established individuals, for example.

Finally, nothing prevents individuals from making suboptimal, personally (reproductively) costly choices; this is especially true in an intelligent, complex, highly social species like humans. A student once asked me, when we were talking about migration, how evolutionary theory would explain her choice to serve overseas in the Peace Corps, for example. There are many subtle answers, ways in which such an experience, in our highly social species, might actually have a positive effect on her survival and reproduction—but in fact the simplest possibility is that she, as a conscious human, can make any choice she desires, independent of its likely impact in our evolutionary past. All that ecological, behavioral, and evolutionary theory can tell us is this: Behaviors that are reproductively costly (like celibacy, for example) will never become and remain over generations the most common form of behavior in any population. No population will evolve to be comprised primarily of people like Mother Teresa, who remained celibate throughout her life, and cared exclusively for (nonrelated) others, with no return to her family for this sacrifice.

THE BEHAVIORAL AND EVOLUTIONARY ECOLOGY OF MIGRATION

What, then, do we know about the ecology, and reproductive impact, of migration? For other species, we can make testable predictions about key questions. What are the conditions that will foster or depress migration? What kind of migration do we expect to see under particular conditions? What kinds of migration will be common or rare? For humans, as I already noted, we also are concerned with the consequences of migration: how older, younger, male, female, wealthy, poor, well-educated and poorly educated, migrants are likely to fare. Figure 2.1 summarizes the general principles; I return to it later to examine particular cases.

Even if we focus only on "ultimate" causes (impact on reproductive success of ecological better-versus-worse conditions), there are com-

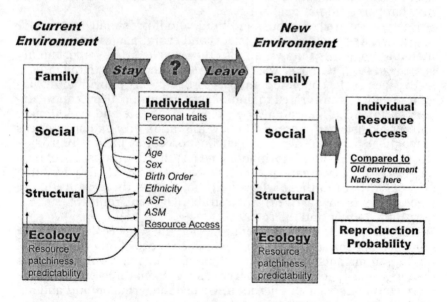

FIG. 2.1. Human migration is a dynamic process. An individual's costs and benefits of staying versus leaving an area are influenced by family, social, societal, and ecological conditions. For an emigrant, the important patterns in the new location must be compared not only to nonemigrants, but to natives of the new area.

plications. "Migration" is not a singular phenomenon. The most common kinds of migration in other species are natal migration (leaving home to disperse and find a mate) and seasonal migration. Both have strong ecological correlates. Very few species are fully nomadic wanderers, with no pattern to their movement.

These patterns in other species probably have a familiar ring; they should, because until relatively recently, these were also the most common types of human migration. We add additional layers of complexity. Migration pattern and type have ecological influences, but differ across traditional hunter-gatherer societies, historical societies (e.g., nineteenth-century European agricultural and proto-industrial societies), and modern nation-states. Seasonal migration, for example, is more common in traditional hunter-gatherers than in the other two cases—an entire group may move seasonally (discussed later), whereas in both historical agricultural and modern societies, only a subgroup (migrant agricultural workers) regularly moves. And modern nation-states show another kind of migration: individuals forced to move for what appear to be structural reasons, unrelated to individual costs and benefits. We have political immigrants, for example, who may have crossed national borders.

Because we are conscious, and think about proximate reasons for migration, we consider the ecological and evolutionary aspects of human migration less than we do for other species. How important are structural (e.g., political, warfare) versus "micro" (e.g., familial: sex, birth order, socioeconomic status) factors? How are individuals in various societies acculturated to think about migration? How can we understand political migration? Behavioral ecologists and evolutionary anthropologists are interested in how migration may influence access to marriage partners, degree of genetic inbreeding, lifetime reproductive patterns (e.g., family formation and fertility), and subsequent population growth. We care not only about migrant family formation (compared both to those who stayed home, and those native to the place migrants have arrived), but also about how migrants think about migration, family, and life roles.

It is worth exploring the extent to which the same ecological forces influence our migratory patterns as well as those of other species. In traditional and historical societies, natal dispersal (which includes leaving home specifically to marry) and seasonal migration are the more common forms of migration. We use the terms *nomad* and *nomadic* primarily for societies that must depend on resources that do show fluctuations in time and space—but for which the fluctuations are unpredictable, rather than seasonal (e.g., Low, 1990a).

Traditional society data come primarily from societies that still existed when Europeans made contact. Such societies seem far removed from today's complexities—and in some ways, they are. Historical societies provide a link. Most were a mix of agriculture and manufacturing (or proto-manufacturing); several are well documented; and particularly in the case of nineteenth-century data, we can look at how migration and family-formation patterns changed with industrialization. Historical demographic data are particularly useful in part because the movements of individuals either can be reconstructed from a variety of population sources (Towner, 2001) or are explicitly recorded within original records (e.g., Clarke & Low, 1992; Low, 1989; 1990b; Voland & Dunbar, 1997). A small number of studies have focused on dispersal patterns from an evolutionary perspective. Although there are some differences across the populations studied, important generalities emerge.

MIGRATION PATTERNS IN NONHUMANS, TRADITIONAL AND HISTORICAL SOCIETIES

Natal Migration

Most vertebrate species show natal migration—offspring leave the family in which they were born to establish and breed elsewhere. In a number of species, whether and when offspring leave home depends in large part on whether/when ecological conditions are favorable for family formation (e.g., resource-rich), or stressed. Resource distribution and the particular utility of resources thus strongly affect natal migration.

Either both sexes or only one sex may leave the natal group. Biologists have suggested this that pattern lowers the potential for inbreeding, and may reduce local resource competition (Devillard, Allainé, Gaillard, & Pontier, 2004; McNutt, 1996; Negro, Hiraldo, & Donazar, 1997; Perrin, 2000; Taylor, Morley, Rico, & Balshine, 2003). In some species, particularly when leaving is risky or dangerous and conditions are highly competitive (i.e., territories or mates are hard to find; it is difficult to get established), a phenomenon known as "helpers at the nest" occurs: Previous offspring remain with their parents and help raise their parents' current offspring (Emlen, 1991, 1997; Koenig & Dickenson, 2004).[1] Variations in ecological conditions affect how likely potential helpers are to stay and help or to disperse (e.g., Koenig & Dickenson, 2004; also see Emlen, 1984, 1995, 1997). Interestingly, in some human societies (including, e.g., several nineteenth-century European ones), the "helper" phenomenon occurred; usually an older daughter stayed.

Among our closest relatives, the primates, there is patterned variation in whether males, or females, or both, disperse. With notable exceptions, dispersal is male biased in polygynous species: Males leave to find new territories, or new groups in which to compete for mates.

---

[1]Often helpers are the full siblings of the current offspring, but the degree of relatedness may vary. The more closely related helpers are to the current offspring, typically the more they help (e.g., Reyer, 1980).

In contrast, in monogamous primates, both sexes typically disperse (Pusey & Packer, 1987). Among the prosimians (lemurs, lorises, tarsiers, and galagos), there are no confirmed examples of male philopatry: Males, or both sexes, disperse, but males do not remain in the natal group (Strier, 2003). Among the Cercopithecines (Old World monkeys with cheek pouches, like macaques), dispersal is male biased, and female matrilines remain together. In the other major group of Old World monkeys, the Colobines (colobus mokeys and their kin), both sexes disperse. In the cebids (New World monkeys) and the Great Apes (hominoids, like chimpanzees, orangutans, and gorillas), about half of the taxa show female-biased dispersal. In the other half, both sexes disperse.

In all hominoids, and all but one group of New World monkeys (capuchins), it is females who leave their natal group, and males who stay (male philopatry). Thus it is not surprising that human societies, in which natal dispersal is common, tend to follow the hominoid pattern: Most human societies are patrilocal or male-philopatric. Of the 563 traditional societies included in the *Ethnographic Atlas* (Murdock, 1967), more than 300 are primarily patrilocal: A couple resides with or near the husband's patrilineal relatives, or they are virilocal (equivalent to patrilocal, except that the husband's patrikin are not aggregated in patrilocal, patrilineal kin groups). Thus, women leave home to live away from their own kin, with or near their husband's kin, in most traditional societies. In Fig. 2.1, we would see a path with influences of "individual characteristics" (being female), and perhaps "family" (in many societies, a woman is destined to marry a man of a certain relationship—e.g., father's brother's son—so that family relationships would dictate).

Most traditional societies are sedentary (*n* = 364) or semisedentary (66), so that women, after leaving home, have few to no opportunities to move back and forth to their own matrilineal kin. Evolutionary anthropologists suggest that this influences the strength of some sex differences in coalition-building and resource behaviors (Low, 1989, 1990a, 1990b, 1993, 1994, 2000; Low, Clarke, & Lockridge, 1992).

This combination of female-biased natal dispersal and polygyny has implications for women's status in many traditional societies. In many societies, co-wives are not related (nonsororal polygyny), and a woman's interests coincide neither with those of her husband nor with those of her co-wives. Nonetheless, despite these inherent potential conflicts of interest in polygyny, women sometimes can do well in terms of finding other women allies (Yanca & Low, 2004). In part this appears to arise from the differential ability of women to find allies and form coalitions in different systems. Dan Sellen and his colleagues (Sellen, Borgerhoff Mulder, & Seiff, 2000) found that among Datoga pastoralists of East Africa, women in marriages with a single co-wife produced fewer surviving offspring than women with more co-wives; further, their children grew more poorly during their first 3 years. Resources play a part in this pattern; Sellen et al. noted that among the rich, number of co-wives is irrelevant, but that in other marriages, women's direct access to critical resources is crucial. Among the swidden agriculturalist Yanomamö of the Orinoco valley in South America, there is little in the way of wealth or heritable resources. Here, a man of high status (who also is likely to have more wives and more children than other men) would receive more food gifts from others in the village than poorer men. His wives thus have more food available (Hames, 1996).

Cross-culturally, women can sometimes have significant allies in traditional polygynous systems (Yanca & Low, 2004), more often when the polygyny is sororal (wives are sisters). When co-wives are sisters, female coalitions can exert considerable influence in the kin group; when women live close to their natal families, as well, they have nearby allies. Thus, the relationship between women's interests and polygynous/non-polygynous systems is not a obvious one; as Borgerhoff Mulder (1992) noted, women adopt strategies in the face of conflicts of interest and female–female competition, and there is a hierarchy of questions that need to be addressed.

In historical societies, natal migration remained common. Not surprisingly, in 19th-century Sweden and Ireland, people were most likely to leave areas in which the quantity, quality, or dependability of resources was poor (Clarke & Low, 1992; Low, 1989, 1990a, 1990b; Low & Clarke, 1991; Strassmann & Clarke, 1998). Migration also varied with individual access to resources, and here the pattern is more complex; for example, both sons and daughters of poor men were likely to leave the parish of their birth looking for employment (review in Low, 2000); sons and daughters of wealthier men tended to remain in the birth parish, where they were well-situated in term of resource access. In Fig. 2.1, both "ecology" and "family" would be important drivers.

The stream of natal migrants was composed of two tiers in both nineteenth-century Sweden (Clarke & Low, 1992) and nineteenth-century New England (Towner, 2001). The upper classes possessed resources and skills that were in themselves mobile, allowing these people to take advantage of opportunities elsewhere, especially in comparison to the land-based resources of farmers. However, poor people left to find employment and mates. For the wealthy, migration was probably more often a matter of choice than for the poor.

Although both men and women left their place of birth, a higher proportion of women migrated in both Sweden (Clarke & Low, 1992) and New England (Towner, 2001). Men tended to dominate long-distance migration, such as from Sweden to the United States (Clarke, 1993; Clarke & Low, 1992). Although unmarried people dominated the migrant stream in 19th-century Sweden (Clarke & Low, 1992), the opposite was true during the same time period in New England (Towner, 2001). We can understand dispersal best in this case as a facultative demographic response to social, ecological, and reproductive options in the local area and beyond (Fig. 2.1; Clarke, Saether, & Roskaft, 1997).

Migration introduces uncertainty with regard to family formation and eventual fertility; successful migrants to a new place, if it is richer in resources, may have more children than comparable "stayers" (Fig. 2.1)—but it is also true that in many cases, a higher proportion of migrants, compared to stayers, fail to marry and establish families, and fertility may be delayed. Fertility and number of surviving children decreased with an increase in the number of lifetime moves made in the Skellefteå region of 19th-century Sweden (Clarke, 1993; Clarke & Low, 1992, 2001). Women who moved delayed their first birth by more than three-quarters of a year. Similarly, women movers in 18th- and 19th-century Krummhörn, Germany, married about 1 year later than nonmovers (Voland & Dunbar, 1997). The uncertain outcomes of migration lead to increased variance in family formation (discussed later).

Seasonal Migration

Seasonal migration is always associated with a predictable alternation of better and worse environmental conditions. Some migrations can be quite dramatic; consider the fall southward migration of ruby-throated hummingbirds, which despite their size (4 inches long, 1/100 ounce) have one of the longest migration paths of any hummingbird. They breed as far north as parts of Canada, but winter in Central America. Early researchers concluded that migrants could not cross the Gulf of Mexico because the energy demands of a 500-mile journey were beyond the capabilities of such a small bird. It now appears that at least some of the population makes the flight directly from Florida to Yucatán, although most birds migrate around the Gulf of Mexico through Texas and northern Mexico to winter in Central America as far south as Panama.

In traditional human societies, seasonal migration follows patterns similar to those in other species: Hunters follow seasonal migrations of prey species, for example. In historical data, frequently class (resource access) differences are evident in seasonal migration. Farm workers, with no right to land, often had little choice: They had to move in search of better working conditions (review in Low, 2000), sometimes seasonally, sometimes simply in repeated moves with no clear temporal pattern.

MODERN SOCIETIES

In other species, and in traditional and historical societies, most migrations fall into a limited number of categories, and most are influenced by the ecology of resources. Most migration patterns fall into natal migration (leaving the natal area to marry and reproduce) and seasonal migration (following predictable, seasonal fluctuations in important resources like food). Today, however, we have added new causes, and produced new patterns, of migration; analyzing migration for modern conditions is complicated. Sometimes migration is the result of intention: We produce what we intend. Sometimes, however, policy or exigencies produce unexpected patterns of migration.

In the modern equivalent of internal warfare (among groups within political boundaries, e.g., Somalia, Rwanda), some people become political emigrants. Local impacts can produce ripple effects, as when political emigrants manage to leave their home country and move to, for example, Sweden or Germany. Economic downturns also prompt people to move, seeking jobs, and there may be resulting impacts on areas not originally affected. Here, the line is blurred between "purely" ecological factors (e.g., plant productivity) and economic factors; both are functionally similar, because they both concern access to resources. Here is an important area for future research.

Structural Causes of Migration in Modern Societies

Migration patterns and rates are of growing concern in the modern world, yet migration is extremely difficult to study in modern populations, because although for many things we have excellent records, in the cases of most interest, our ability to track individuals may be least developed. In this regard, historical data sets (described earlier) offer the rare opportunity to study correlates and consequences of migration. But we do have current and recent examples with relatively good data; here I review three cases. In each, political decisions, not even necessarily aimed at creating migration, were extrinsic structural forces (Ogbu, 1981) that had huge impacts on people's movements and sometimes their fertility.

Indonesia

In response to increasing population pressure, developing countries around the world are encouraging population redistribution, often through government-sponsored resettlement programs such as the well-publicized programs in Brazil and Indonesia (Desbarets, 1990; Ilchman, Lasswell, Montgomery, & Weiner, 1975). O'Connor (2004) analyzed the situation in Indonesia. Indonesia's population, currently around 235 million (CIA, 2003), is quite unevenly distributed. Indonesia's population policy has focused on redistribution—moving people around. This well-intentioned program interacts with another policy, intended to increase forest production for economic reasons. As a result, increasing population pressures and cultural displacement have led to environmental degradation (Fearnside, 1997; Lumbranraja et al., 1998) and ethnic conflicts throughout transmigrant areas. Here is a case in which two centrally planned policies, separately aimed at efficient logging and population redistribution, have negative affected ecological conditions, ethnic conflict levels, and people's family formation (O'Connor, 2004).

Mao's China

In Mao's cultural revolution and the later "One Child" Policy, we are more aware of central decisions about people's fertility than about migration, but in fact forced (extrinsic or involuntary; e.g., Ogbu, 1981) migration had significant impacts on people's family formation, and even survival (Fig. 2.1; Ting, 2004b). The particularly violent first phase of the Cultural Revolution (CRI) spanned from 1966 to 1969 (Schoppa, 2002; review in Ting, 2004a, 2004b). Mao used the Red Guards to shatter the party organization, to rekindle revolutionary enthusiasm, and to destroy so-called counterrevolutionary values (Worden, Savada, & Dolan, 1987). Established cadres and professionals were removed from their positions and replaced with workers, peasants, and soldiers (Lin & Xie, 1988). A new "sent down" movement drafted intellectuals and scholars for manual labor in order to reeducate them. Large numbers of urban youth were sent away for "reeducation." A countering rural-to-urban migration, by an estimated 16 million people, supplied military support and factory workers in cities. The results were dramatic crossovers in social stratification and mobility, with little correlation between education and occupational attainment during 1966–1976 (e.g., Lin & Xie, 1988).

Over 20 million university, high school, and middle school students were sent to the countryside and border regions (Lin & Xie, 1988), causing tremendous disruption in the lives of young urban people. Some disruptions affected not only how people felt, but how their life histories proceeded. For example, Shanghai women who were in their early twenties during the early phase of the Cultural Revolution had lower martial fertility at age 20–24 years than women in the older cohorts, including those who went through the Great Leap Forward Famine at the same age (Ting, 2004b).

Despite the egalitarian *aims* of Mao's China, the "cultural capital" of the parents—the nonmaterial benefits parents could give their children (knowledge, connections to powerful people; "social" in Fig. 2.1; Ting, 2004a, 2004b)—was an important factor. White-collar couples tended to have fewer, but better educated, children than blue-collar couples in the urban areas (common in many societies). This meant that, despite state policies aimed at moving people about specifically to interrupt the intergenerational inheritance of cultural capital, parents' education and occupation *still* affected the attainments of their children. Academic achievement still exerted significant impacts on the life course of the youth. During the time of economic constriction (beginning in the early 1960s, right after the Great Leap Forward), children of blue-collar background with poor academic performance were the first sent to the countryside by the government, in hopes of alleviating the growing unemployment problems in urban China.

The Soviet Collapse and the Kamchatkan Penninsula

Finally, in three areas of the central valley of the Kamchatkan Peninsula (in the east of the ex-Soviet Union), Hitztaler (2004a, 2004b) found striking responses in fertility and migration to resource changes precipitated by the collapse of the Soviet Union in 1991. This was an area in which the Soviets had subsidized forestry efforts; people (particularly young men and young couples) migrated there with the intent of making good money, then returning to Moscow, for example, able to afford good housing.

With the collapse, subsidies disappeared. The removal of subsidies for forestry reduced people's resource access; reduced fertility, increased mortality, and out-migration followed. Out-migration increased not only in central Kamchatka, but also throughout the Russian Far East. This loss of subsidy interacted with local socioeconomic, ecological, and historical conditions in the three (rural and resource-dependent) localities Hitztaler examined. Villages facing a local natural resource crisis (e.g., where forestry had removed most easily-harvested timber) showed earlier and greater net negative migration than those with a relatively intact resource base.

People's decisions to migrate are clearly complex, and affected by socio-economic, political, ecological, and historical conditions. More dramatic fertility declines, mortality increases, and out-migration occurred where the socio-economic crisis coincided with a local natural resource crisis. Further, migration responses of indigenous and nonindigenous women differed: indigenous women were less likely to migrate.

In summary, structural factors are an important contributor to the additional complications of migration patterns in today's world. Structural forces, such as political shifts, may combine with other causes: we have "ecological refugees" and "political refugees" and can produce unforeseen and undesirable consequences. In many cases, although both ecology (aspects of resource destruction and availability) and political pressures and actions are combined, we are less aware of the ecological factors—yet they are often the result of the structural changes.

AFTER MIGRATION

Once a person has migrated, then what? Much of our interest, and much of what we must understand if we are to influence conditions for the better, arises from this question. Migration represents trade-offs—which differ for different kinds of individuals. Most studies that consider both migrants and comparable groups that did not migrate find that migrants' success is more *variable* (whether on average better or worse) than the success of those who stayed home. Resource access is a key determinant, both for *proximate* success (e.g., getting a good job) and for *success in evolutionary terms* (forming successful families). Although these tend to correlate, for migrants, the variation in family formation can be considerable, and should be of interest to many scholars.

The trade-offs shown in Fig. 2.1, both before and after migration, are central. Having migrated, is an immigrant better off than before in terms of resource access and job opportunities (e.g., Boyle, 2001), health, and familial and social support? How does the migrant fare, compared to natives of the new area, after we control for age, gender, education, and skill? What affects immigrant fertility, and dependence on welfare? How do the children of migrants fare (Van Hook, Brown, & Kwenda, 2004)? Are there structural phenomena (e.g., political policies about migrants, entrenched racism) that affect migrants, or are the influences largely those of individual familial and social support network (Fig. 2.1)? These are complex, and often politically charged, questions. Many of the following chapters explore these important concerns—with welcome new data and analysis.

Whether migration is *voluntary* or *forced* clearly matters (e.g., Laliberte, Benoit, & Piche, 2003). A graduate student, from perhaps the Indian subcontinent, in engineering in the United States may decide to stay in the United States rather than return. His or her employment options, once the legal requirements are satisfied, are relatively good. Contrast this with the situation facing almost any forced migrant: likely abrupt transition to a place not of his or her own choosing, perhaps no ability to take fungible resources useful in the new location, and with skills only accidentally relevant to the new conditions. These two individuals would be most strongly influenced by different segments in Fig. 2.1.

Gender matters. Although women have been the majority of natal migrants in human evolutionary history, this fact does not mean that today they would find migration easier than men. How do men versus women, and boys versus girls, handle the process of fitting in to a new and different society? How does their sense of self, their identity, change? In many cases, it matters how close the *societal values* are, when the area of origin and the area of resettlement are compared. Consider a young girl having moved to the United States with her family from a society in which female clitoridectomy is common, and preferred. In the United States, this is not a legal operation; the family's social values may come into sharp conflict with U.S. legal and social norms.

How life proceeds for immigrants develops from the interaction of these constraints. From the sociological literature we know that the deliberate fertility of couples is influenced by how well they perceive themselves to be doing, compared to their parents, and whatever peer group is relevant. Couples who see themselves as "doing well" tend to begin, and continue, families. For migrants, who is the relevant peer group? People back in their place of origin? People in their new home? Immigrant families may be better off than the former group, and less well off than the latter—but here perception, rather than reality, appears to matter.

In summary, human migration is a complex and dynamic phenomenon that we are only beginning to understand—and we must understand it, for its implications are huge, and may go well beyond our current understanding of "acculturation." There are ecological complexities: changes, perhaps imposed changes, of resource availability. There are gender issues. There are social and societal complications, and immigrants' responses, as immigrants must define (or redefine) themselves in light of their self-generated social identity and whatever social identity is superimposed on them.

FUTURE DIRECTIONS

Most prior research has looked at broad patterns (e.g., aggregate patterns in transnational migration, analysis of structural factors). Yet research at a finer scale reminds us that individual resources (physical, social, and educational) and individual strategies can make a huge difference in outcomes. What we need now is migration research that begins to tease apart the important factors—ecological, structural, community, familial, personal—that shape human migration patterns in all their complexity, and to follow carefully the consequences of migration on individual attitude, psychology, reproduction, and demography. Only then can we understand the depth of complexity in human migration. The chapters in this book offer us an excellent interdisciplinary and integrative start, taking ecological considerations and individual variation seriously.

BOBBI LOW

I grew up during a period of internal migration in the United States, after the Second World War; my grandfather was an economic internal migrant during the Great Depression, when the school for which he was principal closed. Later, I settled with a second-generation American of Lithuanian descent; he came from a family with an iconic family legend of forbidden love across class and wealth lines, midnight elopement, and migration to the United States. I was always drawn to the stories and feelings of internal and transnational immigrants, and these interacted with my formal training as an ecologist and evolutionary biologist, to create a focus on the ecology of migration, and the ways in which we humans, as well as other species, are shaped and moved by their environments: physical, biotic, and social.

REFERENCES

Borgerhoff Mulder, M. (1992). Women's strategies in polygynous marriage: Kipsigis, Datoga, and other East African cases. *Human Nature, 3,* 45–70.

Boyle, P. (2001). A cross national comparison of the impact of family migration on women's employment status. *Demography, 38*(2), 201–213.

Cavalli-Sforza, L., Menozzi, P., & Piazza, A. (1996). *The history and geography of human genes.* Princeton, NJ: Princeton University Press.

Charnov, E. L. (1980). Vole population cycles: A case for kin-selection? *Oecologia, 45,* 1–2.

CIA. (2003). *The world factbook, United States Central Intelligence Agency.* Retrieved March 6, 2004, from http://www.cia.gov/cia/publications/factbook/geos/id.html

Clarke, A. L. (1993). Women, resources, and dispersal in 19th-century Sweden. *Human Nature, 4*(2), 109–135.

Clarke, A. L., & Low, B. (1992). Ecological correlates of human dispersal in 19th century Sweden. *Animal Behaviour, 44,* 677–693.

Clarke, A. L., & Low, B. (2001). Testing evolutionary hypotheses with demographic data. *Population and Development Review, 27*(4), 663–660.

Clarke, A. L., Saether, B. E., & Roskaft, E. (1997). Sex biases in avian dispersal: A reappraisal. *Oikos, 79*(3), 429–438.

Desbarets, J. (1990). *Population resettlement programs in comparative perspective: A review.* Australian National University, Canberra.

Devillard, S., Allainé, D., Gaillard, J.-M., & Pontier, D. (2004). Does social complexity lead to sex-biased dispersal in polygynous mammals? A test on ground-dwelling sciurids. *Behavioral Ecology, 15*(1), 83–87.

Emlen, S. T. (1984). Cooperative breeding in birds and mammals. In J. R. Krebs & N. B. Davies (Eds.), *Behavioural ecology: An evolutionary approach* (2nd ed., pp. 305–335). Oxford, UK: Blackwell Scientific.

Emlen, S. T. (1991). Evolution of cooperative breeding in birds and mammals. *Behavioral Ecology: An Evolutionary Approach* (3rd ed., pp. 301–337).

Emlen, S. T. (1995). An evolutionary theory of the family. *Proceedings of the National Academy of Sciences USA, 92*(18), 8092–8099.

Emlen, S. T. (1997). Predicting family dynamics in social vertebrates. In J. R. Krebs & N. B. Davies (Eds.), *Behavioural ecology: An evolutionary approach* (4th ed., pp. 228–253). Oxford, UK: Blackwell Scientific.

Fearnside, P. (1997). Transmigration in Indonesia: Lessons from its environmental and social impacts. *Environmental Management, 21,* 553–570.

Grigg, D. B. (1977). E. G. Ravenstein and the "laws of migration." *Journal of History and Geography, 3,* 41–54.

Hames, R. (1996). Costs and benefits of monogamy and polygyny for Yanomamö women. *Ethology and Sociobiology, 17,* 181–199.

Hitztaler, S. (2004a). Changing human populations in post-Soviet Kamchatka: An integrated study of shifts in fertility and net population. *Population and Environment, 25*(4), 335–354.

Hitztaler, S. (2004b). The relationship between resources and migration patterns in central Kamchatka during the post-Soviet period. *Population and Environment, 25*(4), 355–375.

Holekamp, K. E., & Sherman, P. W. (1989). Why male ground squirrels disperse. *American Scientist, 77*, 232–239.

Ilchman, W., Lasswell, H., Montgomery, J., & Weiner, M. (Eds.). (1975). *Policy sciences and population.* Lexington, MA: Lexington Books.

Koenig, W. D., & Dickenson, J. L. (Eds.). (2004). *Ecology and evolution of cooperative breeding in birds.* Cambridge, UK: Cambridge University Press.

Laliberte, D., Benoit, L., & Piche, V. (2003). The impact of forced migration on marital life in Chad. *European Journal of Population, 19,* 413–435.

Lin, N., & Xie, W. (1988). Occupational prestige in urban China. *American Journal of Sociology, 93,* 793–832.

Low, B. (1989). Occupational status and reproductive behavior in 19th century Sweden: Locknevi parish. *Social Biology, 36,* 82–101.

Low, B. (1990a). Sex, power, and resources: Ecological and social correlates of sex differences. *International Journal of Contemporary Sociology, 27*(1–2), 49–74.

Low, B. (1990b). Occupational status, landownership, and reproductive behavior in 19th-century Sweden: Tuna parish. *American Anthropologist, 92*(2), 457–468.

Low, B. (1993). Ecological demography: A synthetic focus in evolutionary anthropology. *Evolutionary Anthropology, 2,* 176–187.

Low, B. (1994). Human sex differences in behavioral ecological perspective. *Analyse und Kritik, 16,* 38–67.

Low, B. (2000). *Why sex matters: A Darwinian look at human behavior.* Princeton, NJ: Princeton University Press.

Low, B., & Clarke, A. L. (1991). Family patterns in 19th-century Sweden: Impact of occupational-status and landownership. *Journal of Family History, 16*(2), 117–138.

Low, B., Clarke, A. L., & Lockridge, K. A. (1992). Toward an ecological demography. *Population and Development Review, 18*(1), 1–31.

Lumbranraja, J., Syam, T., Nishide, H., Mahi, A., Utomo, M., Kimura, S., & Kimura, M. (1998). Deterioration of soil fertility by land use changes in South Sumatra, Indonesia from 1970–1990. *Hydrological Processes, 12,* 2003–2013.

McNutt, J. W. (1996). Sex-biased dispersal in African wild dogs, Lycaon pictus. *Animal Behaviour, 52,* 1067–1077.

Moffitt, R. (2003). Causal analysis in population research: An economist's perspective. *Population and Development Review, 29*(3), 448–458.

Moffitt, R. (2005). Remarks on the analysis of causal relationships in popoulation research. *Demography, 42*(1), 91–108.

Murdock, G. P. (1967). *Ethnographic atlas.* Pittsburgh: University of Pittsburgh Press.

Negro, J. J., Hiraldo, F., & Donazar, J. A. (1997). Causes of natal dispersal in the lesser kestrel: inbreeding avoidance or resource competition? *Journal of Animal Ecology, 66*(5), 640–648.

O'Connor, C. (2004). Effects of central decisions on local livelihoods in Indonesia: Potential synergies between the programs of transmigration and industrial forest conversion. *Population and Environment, 25*(4), 319–333.

Ogbu, J. U. (1981). Origins of human competence: A cultural-ecological perspective. *Child Development, 52,* 413–429.

Perrin, N. (2000). Local Competition, Inbreeding, and Evolution of Sex-Biased Dispersal. *The American Naturalist, 155*(1), 116–127.

Pusey, A. E., & Packer, C. (1987). Dispersal and philopatry. In B. B. Smuts, D. L. Cheney, R. M. Seyfarth, R. W. Wrangham, & T. T. Struhsaker (Eds.), *Primate societies* (pp. 250–266). Chicago: University of Chicago Press.

Reyer, H.-U. (1980). Flexible helper structure as an ecological adaptation in the pied kingfisher. *Behavioral Ecology and Sociobiology, 6,* 219–227.

Schoppa, R. (2002). *Revolution and its past: Identities and change in bodern Chinese history.* Englewood Cliffs, NJ: Prentice Hall.

Sellen, D., Borgerhoff Mulder, M., & Seiff, D. (2000). Fertility, offspring quality, and wealth in Datoga pastoralists: Testing evolutionary models of intersexual selection. In L. Cronk, N. Chagnon, & W. Irons (Eds.), *Adaptation and human behavior: An anthropological perspective* (pp. 91–114). Hawthorne, NY: Aldine de Gruyter.

Strassmann, B. I., & Clarke, A. L. (1998). Ecological constraints on marriage in rural Ireland. *Evolution and Human Behavior, 19*(1), 33–55.

Strier, K. B. (2003). *Primate behavioral ecology* (2nd ed.). Boston: Allyn and Bacon.

Taylor, M. I., Morley, J. I., Rico, C., & Balshine, S. (2003). Evidence for genetic monogamy and female-biased dispersal in the biparental mouthbrooding cichlid *Eretmodus cyanostictus* from Lake Tanganyika. *Molecular Ecology, 12*(11), 3173–3177.

Tinbergen, N. (1963). On the aims and methods of ethology. *Zeitschrift fur Tierpsychologie, 20,* 410–463.

Ting, T.-F. (2004a). Resources, fertility, and parental investment in Mao's China. *Population and Environment, 25*(4), 281–297.

Ting, T.-F. (2004b). Shifts in reproductive patterns in China. *Population and Environment, 24*(4), 299–317.

Towner, M. C. (2001). Linking dispersal and resources in humans: Life history data from Oakham, Massachusetts (1750–1850). *Human Nature, 12*(4), 321–349.

Van Hook, J., Brown, S. L., & Kwenda, N. (2004). A decomposition of trends in poverty among children of immigrants. *Demography, 41*(4), 649–670.

Voland, E., & Dunbar, R. I. M. (1997). The impact of social status and migration on female age at marriage in an historical population in North-West Germany. *Journal of Biosocial Science, 29,* 355–360.

Worden, R., Savada, A., & Dolan, R. (1987). *China: A country study* (4th ed.). Washington, DC: Library of Congress.

Yanca, C., & Low, B. (2004). Female allies and female power: A cross-cultural analysis. *Evolution and Human Behavior, 25,* 9–23.

3

Assimilation or Transnationalism? Conceptual Models of the Immigrant Experience in America

Silvia Pedraza
University of Michigan

Americans are immigrants—people whose origins are various but whose destinies made them American. Immigration—voluntary or involuntary—is what created all multiracial and multicultural nations. The United States is a prime example. Sometimes the migrants moved freely from the area of origin to the area of destination. Such was the experience of the European immigrants. Sometimes their movement was coerced and resulted from processes not of their own making. This was the experience of enslaved Africans, as well as of Mexicans, Native Americans, and Puerto Ricans, whose history began with conquest and annexation. Sometimes their movement was semicoerced and semifree—the experience of indentured servants (whether Japanese, Chinese, Irish, or German) in the 19th century and of refugees, such as Jews at the turn of the 20th century and Cubans, Cambodians, Guatemalans, and Salvadorans in the latter part of the 20th century.

The major questions in immigration research can be summarized briefly as follows: What led people to make the decision to move—what "push" and "pull" factors impelled them to displace and uproot themselves (see Lee, 1966)? What is the nature of the crossing—not only literally but also, more abstractly, the policies of two governments that can, in societies that have developed long histories of emigration and immigration, result in their developing systems of economic and political migration (see Burawoy, 1976; Pedraza-Bailey, 1985)? and, What can people attain afterward? A recurrent question in studies of immigration is: How do we best describe that process—as assimilation, adaptation, integration, incorporation, or transnationalism and diasporic citizenship? This chapter traces the development of these concepts overtime as social scientists struggled to explain these important social processes. Before doing so, we turn to a brief history of immigration to America.

HISTORY OF IMMIGRATION

As Philip Martin and Elizabeth Midgley (2003, p. 11) underscored, European colonization of the New World entailed three processes—colonization, coercion, and immigration—that superimposed a new population on the native peoples of the Americas. Colonization took place in the 17th and 18th centuries when English colonists established the cultural and institutional foundations of what became the United States. They also seized control of various Dutch, French, and Spanish settlements, and established English as the public language and English common law as the basis for the legal system. In addition, Martin and Midgley underscored, two types of coercion were involved in the peopling of America: the importation of slaves from Africa (19% of the population in 1790) and the incorporation of American Indians, French, Mexican, Puerto Ricans, and other populations "through political deals, war settlements, or purchase of territory as the United States expanded westward," such as the Louisiana Purchase (1803), the Treaty of Guadalupe Hidalgo at the end of the war between Mexico and the United States (1848), and the Spanish-American War (1898). The third source of Americans, and the largest, was immigration. Over the course of several centuries, immigrants to the United States came in waves—an image that denotes that the number of immigrants could be seen to start, rise, peak, decline, and eventually disappear onto our shores.

Four waves of migration transformed America over the course of history (Muller & Espenshade 1985). In the first wave, northwestern Europeans immigrated to the United States up until the mid-19th century; in the second, southern and eastern Europeans arrived at the end of the 19th and the beginning of the 20th centuries; in the third, precipitated by two world wars, African Americans, Mexicans, and Puerto Ricans moved from the South to the North; and in the fourth, immigrants mostly from Latin America and Asia arrived, from 1965 into the present. Each wave has been characterized by a different racial or ethnic composition and coincided with profound changes in the nature of American society. The immigrants of the first wave came to an essentially colonial, agrarian society; those of the second and third waves came to an urban society where they supplied the cheap labor essential to industrialization and expansion; and those of the fourth wave are coming to an increasingly postindustrial, service-oriented society. Because immigration is American history, yesterday as well as today, immigration is central to the identity of its people as hyphenated Americans; it is also central to America's identity as a nation of immigrants. This is what is distinctive about the American experience.

In 1890, 86% of the foreign-born in the United States came from European countries—Great Britain, Ireland, Germany, Scandinavia, and France being the lead countries—plus 11% came from Canada (U.S. Bureau of the Census, 2001). In 1910, at the peak of immigration from southern and eastern Europe, there were 13.5 million foreign-born residents, nearly 15% of the total population of the United States. In 2002, of the total population of over 281 million, the foreign-born population reached an all-time high of 32.5 million, according to the Current Population Survey (CPS), but they also constituted around 15%. Most notable was the shift in origins, as now most come from Latin America and Asia (Martin & Midgley, 2004). This large number of immigrants at the turn of both centuries mostly settled in California, New York, Florida, Illinois, and Texas. In the early 1900s, nativism was expressed in cartoons in leading magazines, such as *Life*, that depicted Irish men as brutes and drunkards and Jews as vulgar social climbers and also expressed anti-Catholic prejudice (see Higham, 1955). In 1994, the same nativism was expressed in California's Proposition 187, which sought to deny schooling and the use of social services to undocumented workers and their children. Faced with deteriorating economic conditions and natural disasters, such as earthquakes, the people of California attributed their social ills to the presence of a large number of illegal aliens.

High rates of immigration, coupled with the high birth rates of many minority groups, such as African Americans and Hispanic Americans, are also changing the composition of the United States. At the dawn of the 21st century, Hispanics surpassed African Americans as the largest minority population. Forecasts put the proportion of White Americans at less than half of the population by the middle of the century. At that point, the traditional "minorities" will, together, constitute the majority (Martin & Midgley, 2003). Hence, the United States is once again being transformed. Such profound demographic shifts can be expected to generate conflict and resistance, which will be most keenly felt in the areas where "minorities" are most concentrated: California, the southwestern states, Texas, Florida, Illinois, and New York.

The First Wave

The first wave of immigration consisted of those who arrived prior to 1880, when the nation was predominantly a colonial, agricultural society. In 1790, the English constituted 60% of the population. Entries began to be recorded only in 1820. Between 1820 and 1880, over 10 million immigrants arrived, mostly from northwestern European nations such as England, Scotland, Germany, the Netherlands, France, Spain, Norway, Sweden, and Ireland. In 1890, of the 7.3 million in the United States who were born in northern and western Europe, 1.25 million came from Great Britain (England, Scotland, and Wales), 1.87 million came from Ireland, 2.8 million came from Germany, and close to half a million came from Scandinavia (U.S. Bureau of the Census 2002). These immigrants were motivated by political, economic, and religious factors.

The involuntary migrations of Africans from West Africa as slaves, the subordination of the American Indians, and the annexation of a large part of Mexico's territory, what is today the American Southwest (California, Arizona, Texas, and parts of New Mexico, Colorado, and Utah), also shaped the people of the United States. In addition, the free movement of Mexicans to *"el Norte"* began as a seasonal labor trek (Corwin, 1978). Because travel was expensive and entailed a long, precarious voyage, many European immigrants indentured themselves to pay for the passage.

Few immigrants were as impelled to move as the Irish, who were "pushed" not only by the displacement of the peasantry that was the result of the transition from feudalism to capitalism taking place throughout western Europe then (cf. Bodnar, 1985), but also by the famine that resulted from the potato blight at midcentury. It is estimated that one-third of the total population of Ireland emigrated throughout the 19th century, about 4 million people. In 1914, the population of Ireland was half what it had been in 1840 (Diner, 1984).

Most of the early immigrants came looking for land—for security, for work, to support their way of life as farmers. The Homestead Act of 1862 that President Lincoln signed made it possible for them to obtain the deed to the land they had worked. It also promoted the settlement of the West, the frontier expansion that Frederick Jackson Turner (1893/1920) argued was what shaped the American experience of substantial upward mobility; it also forged the core American value of rugged individualism. Both constituted an American exceptionalism.

The Second Wave

Between 1880 and 1924, during the second major wave of immigration, over 27 million immigrants arrived in the United States; about 81% were from the southern and eastern European nations, such as Italy, Greece, Austria-Hungary, Poland, and Russia. In 1910, of the 4.5 million people who had been born in southern and eastern European countries, over 1.3 million came from Italy, 1.2 million from the Soviet Union (mostly Jews), nearly 1 million from Poland, and close to half a million from Hungary. Due to the severe restrictions imposed on Asian immigration—the Chinese Exclusion Act (1882) and the Japanese

Gentleman's Agreement (1906)—only 124,500 came from China and Japan (U.S. Bureau of the Census 2002).

To this day, the peak number of immigrants to the United States arrived in the years 1907–1908. As these groups passed through the processing center that was largely a welcoming center at Ellis Island, New York, significant numbers of immigrants from China and Japan were arriving on the West Coast, where they were processed through the detention center at Angel Island, California. On both coasts, most of these migrants were rural, with very low levels of literacy, and unskilled—peasants whose identification was, first and foremost, with their village and their parish.

By the early 1900s, the frontier was closed, and most newcomers found jobs in Eastern and Midwestern cities. Many became the industrial working class that fueled the economic growth that attended industrialization and the growth of capitalism. Immigrants made up more than half of the operatives in the key industries of steel, mining, and meatpacking (Martin & Midgley, 2003).

Among the European immigrants were the Jews, who fled Europe because of the anti-Semitic violence they encountered in the *pogroms*—anti-Jewish riots—at the end of the 19th century. Contrary to most of the other immigrants at the time, the Jews were already urban and very often literate and skilled, particularly in the needle trades. It is estimated that approximately one-third of all Jews in Eastern Europe migrated to the United States between 1880 and 1924. Pushed by circumstances beyond their control, they fled violence and persecution and came searching for personal and religious liberty. Their story in the United States was clearly a story of success, particularly in comparison to the other immigrant groups who came at the same time (Gold & Phillips, 1996). Clearly, they were refugees, although immigration law at this time did not recognize refugees as a separate type of immigrant. The legal category of refugee did not begin to develop until after World War II, with the 1948 Displaced Persons Act and a series of Refugee Relief Acts and Refugee Assistance Acts in the 1950s and 1960s that were largely brought about by the Cuban exodus and under which the Vietnamese and other Indochinese refugees were admitted. Only in 1980 did the United States finally pass a Refugee Act, shortly before the arrival of 125,000 *Marielitos* from Cuba's Mariel harbor and 10,000 Haitians who washed ashore onto the beaches of Florida and its Keys (Pedraza, 1996b).

In the beginning, U.S. immigration law had barred the entry of only those persons considered unfit, such as prostitutes, convicts, lunatics, idiots, and the very ill. But partly because of World War I, nativism peaked in the 1920s. Nativism involves the fear many feel of the threat—cultural and economic both—that immigrants pose. This led to further restrictions. With the 1924 Immigration and Nationality Act, the door to further immigration was closed. National-origins quotas were set that favored immigration from northern and western European nations while curtailing immigration from southern and eastern European nations. At the same time, all immigration from Asia was banned. These quotas remained in place until they were abolished by the 1965 amendments to the 1952 Immigration and Nationality Act.

Yet even as immigration from southern and eastern Europe was being curtailed, an exception was made for Mexico. Agricultural growers successfully argued to Congress that they needed Mexican workers because World War I had caused a labor shortage. The Western Hemisphere Exemption constituted an enormous "pull" to Mexican immigrants. But although growers expected the Mexicans to return home, "like a homing pigeon," many did not go back but instead put down roots and created communities on this side of the border (Pedraza-Bailey, 1985).

The Third Wave

After the closing of the door to European immigration in 1924, the third major wave of migration was mostly internal. The migration of African Americans, Mexicans, Native Americans, and Puerto Ricans from the South to the North transformed rural people into urban dwellers. This entailed a dramatic social transformation, as large as the one of immigrants who crossed the oceans. For example, at the beginning of the 20th century most African Americans lived in the agricultural South; by 1960, about half were living in the industrial North. They were attracted by the employment opportunities generated by the industrialization of the North and by World War I. Between 1940 and 1960, when agriculture in the South declined further and World War II created yet more economic expansion, particularly in the Northeast and the Midwest, it is estimated that millions of African Americans, Mexicans, Native Americans, and Puerto Ricans left the rural areas of the South to look for work in cities and in factories. This urbanization set the stage for the Civil Rights Movement (Piven & Cloward, 1979). The Civil Rights Movement inspired other social movements, such as the Mexican American movement *La Causa*. These social movements broke down the systematic exclusion imposed by "Jim Crow" legal segregation.

World War II also gave rise to the Bracero Program (from the Spanish word *brazos*, arms), which was initiated through the influence of agricultural growers, who once again argued to Congress that instituting this contract-labor program was absolutely necessary, given the wartime shortage of labor in California's fields. During the course of more than 22 years, approximately 4.7 million *braceros* came to work in California, then the leading agricultural state. What was supposed to be an emergency, wartime measure lasted a full generation, until substantial labor displacement of American workers led to its termination (Galarza, 1964; Massey et al., 1987). The Bracero Program also gave rise to substantial illegality (cf. Samora, 1971). A renewal of this plan has now been proposed by President George W. Bush as a way of curbing excessive undocumented migration from Mexico and of providing for the orderly, administered importation of temporary help. In the 1940s and 1950s, approximately 30 to 40% of immigration came from the Western Hemisphere (Martin & Midgley, 2003), although a substantial number of Jewish refugees from the holocaust perpetrated by Nazi Germany also arrived.

The Fourth Wave

The fourth wave of migration began in the immediate post-World War II period. It gained particular impetus from the 1965 amendments to the McCarran–Walter Immigration and Nationality Act of 1952 that abolished the national origins quotas of 1924. In so doing, it reopened the door to immigration to the United States. The major criteria for legal admission to the United States in this period are still the ones in place at the beginning of the 21st century: occupational certification (giving preference to immigrants whose occupations were in a "relative shortage" in the United States) and family reunification (giving preference to immigrants whose immediate family had been divided by the migration). In 2002, more than half of the foreign-born residents were born in Latin America—30% from Mexico alone—whereas 26% were born in Asia, 14% in Europe, and 8% in Africa and other regions (Martin & Midgley, 2004). In 1990, of the 8.4 million immigrants who were born in Latin America, 4.3 million came from Mexico, 1.9 million from the Caribbean (Cuba and Haiti leading), 5.4 million from Central America (El Salvador and Nicaragua leading), and 1 million from South America (Colombia and Peru leading), with Canada contributing an additional three-fourths of a million. Among the 5 million immigrants who were born in Asia, China and India were the leading sources, each contributing close to half a million (U. S. Bureau of the Census, 2002). There have always been two immigrant Americas—a working-class immigrant America and a middle-class immigrant America (cf. Bodnar, 1985). Our present-day admissions criteria contribute to the development of both. In recent decades, occupational preference has been given both to very poor immigrants, such as Mexicans, Puerto Ricans, Dominicans, and Jamaicans, who were often contracted to work in the fields, in construction, and in other menial service jobs, and to very skilled immigrants, such as Colombians, Filipinos, Asian Indians, Koreans, Taiwanese, and Ecuadorians, who were often contracted to work as doctors, accountants, computer technicians, and nurses.

The European immigrant struggle at the turn of the 20th century was shaped by the transition from feudal, agrarian societies to industrial manufacturing capitalist societies in the Old World and the New. John Bodnar (1985) underscored that "transplanted by forces beyond their control," the immigrants were "indeed children of capitalism." At the turn of the 20th century, the artisans, craftsmen, and illiterate, unskilled peasants from the feudal societies of Germany, Ireland, Poland, Italy, and Mexico went on to become the American working class and to supply the cheap labor that made possible the enormous economic growth of this developing, industrial, capitalist society. At the turn of the 21st century, the immigrant struggle is not only the child of capitalism but also the child of communism, in the case of Cubans, Vietnamese, Cambodians, Chinese, and Soviet Jews. It is estimated that over the course of 45 years of Cuba's communist revolution, more than 12% of the Cuban population left the island, turning their backs on the land of their birth. Most of these emigrants went on to live in the United States.

To undocumented workers of working-class origin from Latin America, the 1986 Immigration Reform and Control Act (IRCA) brought a fresh start, as it both offered amnesty for illegal aliens who had lived and worked in the United States as upright contributors to this nation's economy, and placed the brunt of the problem on employers who knowingly hired illegal aliens. The Mexican community especially benefited from IRCA, as did many workers from Central and South America. Many of the new immigrants who come to the United States bring substantial social resources with them (of social class, capital, education, institutional know-how). As a result, these new immigrants can quickly insert themselves at rather high levels in this society—what Ivan Light (1983) called "leapfrog migration." At the same time, the prospects for working-class immigrants grow increasingly dim. These bear the brunt of the economic restructuring of America, of the declining number of good jobs in manufacturing industries, as well as of persistent and growing poverty. Clearly, there are two Americas. In fact, a more accurate image may be that of a third America, as Jorge Ramos (2004) recently argued. The third America encompasses the undocumented workers—not only Mexican but also Central and South American, Caribbean, Asian, at times even European—who are the most vulnerable and powerless inhabitants of our nation yet do much of the labor others do not want to do.

ASSIMILATION

The study of immigrants was closely wedded with the beginnings of social science in America at the turn of the 20th century (Portes 1978). Immigrants and their plight were the focus of vivid studies from the early days of "the Chicago school," whose work on immigration, ethnic, and urban studies laid the very foundations of American sociology (e.g., Park & Burgess, 1921; Park, 1950, 1928; Thomas & Znaniecki, 1927). Despite varying emphases, they shared the expectation that the outcome to the process of integrating those who arrived at its shores would be a process of assimilation. Yet from the outset there was an ambiguity in the idea that Park himself (1913/1950) underscored. That ambiguity remained until Milton Gordon (1964) distinguished between types of assimilation: cultural versus structural. But the fundamental characteristic of assimilation theory was already evident: Assimilation was expected to be a one-way process that would also be natural and evolutionary, which as time passed would yield the inevitable outcome of the adaptation of minority ethnic groups to the mainstream culture. A very different concept—transculturation—arose in Cuba, the peopling of which through conquest and immigration resembled that of the United States. Fernando Ortiz (1963/1983), one of Cuba's leading social scientists, proposed the notion of transculturation to signify how one culture comes to express itself in another, as was the case of *Santería*, the popular religious expression in Cuba that blended West African beliefs with Spanish Catholicism. Even in the United States, another important text of the time, Nathan Glazer and Daniel Patrick Moynihan's (1963) *Beyond the Melting Pot*, examined the incorporation of Blacks, Puerto Ricans, Jews, Italians, and Irish in New York City and found substantial ethnic malleability and persistence. But the leading influence was that of the assimilation school, a major exponent of which was Glazer (1971), who argued that while Blacks did not seem to be assimilating to the mainstream, due to the Southern experience of slavery and "Jim Crow," in the North their experience more closely resembled that of other immigrants, and, in due time, they would also achieve assimilation.

As Gordon (1964) defined it, cultural assimilation entailed a process of acculturation on the part of the immigrants, of becoming "like" in cultural patterns, such as language, behavior, and values; while structural assimilation resulted only when the immigrants had been "taken up and incorporated" and entailed the full integration of the immigrants and their descendants into the major institutions of the society (educational, occupational, political) and into the social cliques, clubs, and institutions of the core society that lead to intimate primary relationships, including intermarriage. This distinction aimed to provide a more exact conceptual tool to gauge the reality of the assimilation of immigrants and racial minorities in America.

The Chicago school in the early part of the century also emphasized the "natural history" of ethnic relations, as best expressed in Park's race relations cycle. Park (1913/1950) evolved his theory of the race relations cycle as stages of interaction through which immigrant or racial groups progressed irreversibly: contact, competition, and accommodation, culminating in eventual assimilation (pp. 138–158). Because at the root of his thinking was the ecological emphasis on race relations as spatial relations that defined the Chicago school of urban sociology, Park expected that the notion of assimilation and the stages of the race relations cycle could be extended to immigrants and racial minorities alike. From his point of view, both European immigrants and American Blacks came from rural, peasant backgrounds and, on migration to the urban ghetto, confronted a similar clash of cultures.

Thus, immigration and race and ethnic relations could both be viewed within the same frame of reference.

This perspective was clearly apparent in another of the classics of the Chicago school: W. I. Thomas and Florian Znaniecki's *The Polish Peasant in Europe and America* (1927). Drawing from the work of Thomas, Park also was responsible for disseminating the theory of the "marginal man." Park (1928) stressed that marginal human beings—those who, as a result of migration, ended up living simultaneously in two separate worlds—were not only marginal, never fully belonging to one world or the other, but also enormously creative and intelligent, as experiencing more than one social world had sharpened their vision and sensibilities. Again Park extended the concept of the marginal man from its origins in the notion of the human being caught between two cultures—the immigrant, the mixed-blood person (Eurasian, mestizo, or mulatto), the outcast and stranger (the Jew)—to encompass the experience of American Blacks who shared the same national culture but lived at the margins of society in social, rather than cultural or ethnic, marginality. Thus, it was left to E. Franklin Frazier (1957), student of the Chicago school and Black sociologist, to demarcate the difference between race relations and ethnic relations. He underscored that American Blacks had experienced successive forms of economic subordination (slavery, the plantation society, "Jim Crow") with the outcome of extensive cultural assimilation but, rather than final structural assimilation, complete social and institutional segregation. Sociologists, then, in the early part of the 20th century were concerned with what the experience of immigration had done to the immigrants' lives themselves and with the outcomes to the process of integrating those who arrived at its shores, outcomes that were usually conceptualized as acculturation and assimilation—becoming like the dominant population, which at the turn of the century clearly meant conformity to Anglo-Saxon ways (Gordon, 1964).

Research on immigrants and the eventual outcomes of the processes of immigration, therefore, was at the very foundations of American sociology. But that emphasis began to wane until, in the 1960s, it all but disappeared. Several different trends promoted its disappearance. First, the Immigration and Nationality Act of 1924 cut the massive waves of European immigration to the United States. Second, under the pressures of Anglo-conformity, the children of those European immigrants went on to assimilate in American society at a time when the price of success was often one's ethnicity and identity. Like Paul Cowan (1982), writer for *The Village Voice* whose real name should have been Saul Cohen, many successful Americans became orphans in history, having lost their ethnic legacies. This can be seen in how often the old immigrants had to change their names, to Anglicize them. Looking at the first generation of Hollywood movie stars, for example, Kirk Douglas (father or our Michael Douglas today) was really the Eastern European Jewish Issur Anielovitch; Rita

Hayworth, the love goddess, was really Spanish—Margarita Carmen Cansino; and Dean Martin was really Dino Crocetti (Baltzell, 1964). And third, as Portes (1978) stressed, the research focus on immigrants and immigration was also lost as a result of the arrival of the racial demands and militancy of the Civil Rights Movement, so that the analytical focus shifted to that of racial and ethnic relations. In the process, what is really distinctive about immigrants was lost. What is distinctive about immigrants? At the micro level, it is that they have experienced another whole life in another country and culture, which they bring with them and which decisively continues to influence them; at the macro level, it is that the state in two societies permits the immigrants to exit and enter. As gatekeeper, the state regulates and directs migration through a body of law.

From the theoretical vantage point, immigrants are also distinct in that they bring with them a whole host of social resources (their social class, education, occupation, culture, values) from another society, and their outcomes in American society will be partly a function of those initial resources, partly a function of the nature of their migration (whether they are political or economic immigrants, victims of genocide, settlers or sojourners), and partly a function of the social context that greeted them, of the amount of opportunity available to them in their new society (in the particular cities and industries where they became concentrated, and in the nature of the discrimination or exclusion they afterward faced).

INTERNAL COLONIALISM

In sociology the major challenge to assimilation theory came from the proponents of the internal colonialism model, the theoretical effort to delineate in what ways the experiences of the racial minorities (Blacks, Puerto Ricans, Mexicans, Native Americans—some of its oldest immigrants and most indigenous native sons and daughters) differed significantly from the experiences and eventual assimilation of the White European immigrants at the turn of the century. The internal colonialism model underscored that the experience of these groups was different in that they had suffered a process of internal colonization due to their place and role in the system of production, place and role they came to occupy because of their color, their race (Barrera, 1979; Blauner, 1969). Proponents of the internal colonialism model underscored that the European migration had been voluntary, the result of decisions the immigrants themselves had taken, whereas the migration of the racial minorities had been involuntary, the result of slavery, annexation, conquest—processes that involved substantial violence. Moreover, they stressed, the European immigrants had changed their cultural patterns at will, gradually over the course of generations, while cultural change had been imposed on the racial minorities. Even more, the ghetto had been only a one- or two-generation phenomenon for the European immigrants and their descendants, whereas for the racial minorities it had become a nearly permanent condition. Last, they stressed, the European immigrants had substantial control of their own communities, through teachers, police officers, small business owners, and social workers, whereas the racial minorities' communities had been manned and controlled by outsiders. Hence, the racial minorities had suffered from a process of colonization unlike anything experienced by the European immigrants.

An important corrective to the assimilation model, the internal colonialism model itself suffered from stretching the colonial analogy overly far, not recognizing the essential differences between the domestic situation of race relations in the United States and what happened in Africa and Asia. Thereafter, Joe Feagin (1978) sought to transcend the shortcomings of both the assimilation and internal colonialism models by focusing on the varying ways in which different ethnic groups were incorporated, became a part of the society, by paying attention to the initial and continuing placement and access of various groups within the economic, political, and educational institutions of the society.

Still, as a central concept that guided research, incorporation, like its predecessor, assimilation, assumed a one-way process, failing to take into account that immigrants not only become incorporated into a new society, they also transform it. Immigrants did not just become incorporated into American society; they made and remade America and are fashioning her still.

Despite the challenges the concept of assimilation and acculturation received from other concepts, such as internal colonialism, incorporation, and more recently transnationalism and diasporic citizenship, Richard Alba and Victor Nee (2003) argued in *Remaking the American Mainstream* that it is still a necessary concept. In their view, assimilation is a grand narrative that served to describe well the experience of the southern and eastern European immigrants, as well as the Asian immigrants who arrived at the turn of the 20th century and, over the course of several generations, went on to join the mainstream of American life in terms of their levels of educational attainment, patterns of suburbanization, and intermarriage. As Alba and Nee emphasized, the process by which they achieved parity in terms of their life chances was partly historically contingent—dependent on two World Wars, the GI Bill, and the like. It was also racialized—that is, exclusive to those who had become "White" in the process. Banks, other credit lenders, and real estate developers kept Blacks, Mexicans, Puerto Ricans, and Native Americans from joining the mainstream of life in suburbia due to their race. Still, even for those formerly excluded groups, there has been progress. Reynolds Farley and Richard Alba, in "The New Second Generation in the U.S." (2002), examined the pattern of occupational distribution for older immigrants and for the new second generation in the United States in

1998–2000. They showed that even for those groups dominated by low-wage labor immigrants in the first generation (such as Mexicans, Central Americans, and Afro-Caribbeans), there has been considerable improvement in the average occupational position in the second generation, although not to the point of parity with native-born whites, as is the case for Asians and South Americans, immigrants who arrived with high levels of human capital. Hence, it would seem that for all the challenges to the concepts of assimilation and acculturation over time, the concepts are still useful in exactly the way Gordon intended them to be: as a conceptual yardstick with which to measure the extent to which various groups have joined the American mainstream over the course of time.

TRANSNATIONALISM

As a result of the fourth wave of American immigration that we are still living through, sociology refocused its research on immigrants as a social category distinct from racial and ethnic minorities and on immigration as an international process that reshuffles persons and cultures across nations, until we now find ourselves amid a veritable explosion of immigration research as well as a search for new concepts such as those of transnationalism and diasporic citizenship with which to describe the new realities.

The concept of transnationalism arose when social scientists noticed that under the impact of changes in the nature of modern communications at this century's end, many immigrants failed to shed their old identities and totally assimilate. Instead, they developed new bicultural identities and lived their lives and were quite involved in more than one nation, more than one world—in effect, making the home and adopted countries both one lived social world. In his study of Mexican working-class immigrants living in Redwood City, California, Roger Rouse (1992) found that "while they lived in Redwood City, they were also living deep in western Mexico" (p. 45) and were obliged to balance two quite different ways of life, which resulted in "cultural bifocality," as he expressed it.

Basch and colleagues (Basch, Schiller, & Blanc, 1994, p. 7) formalized the definition of transnationalism now in use: the process by which immigrants "forge and sustain multi-stranded social relations that link together their societies of origin and settlement." Thus, they underscored, immigrants "take actions, make decisions, and develop subjectivities and identities embedded in networks of relationships that connect them simultaneously to two or more nations" (Basch et al., 1994, p. 7). Like all social processes, this has economic, political, and social dimensions, both in its causes and consequences. However, soon thereafter the cry arose that transnationalism is not new, although much of the literature sounds as if it is (Foner, 1997; Moya, 2004; Waldinger, 2004). Comparing immigrants at the turn of the century with contemporary immigrants to New York—the quintessential immigrant city—Foner (1997) showed that many transnational patterns actually have a long history. At the turn of the last century, many immigrants were involved in what is now called transnationalism. For example, Italian and Russian immigrants also kept ties of sentiment and family alive with those back home by living in what today are called "transnational households" with members scattered across households; by sending remittances back home; and by making political contributions for particular causes, such as the Irish support for the nationalist cause back home. Moreover, with the exception of Russian Jews who fled from political and religious persecution, the return rates for many immigrant groups, like the Italians, were extremely high, around one-third, even higher than today's.

Although these critiques are valid, my own view is that, nonetheless, much is distinctive about our current transnationalism. In today's global economy, changes in the technologies of transportation and communication (jet air travel, faxes, electronic mail, the Internet, videos) have changed the qualitative experience of immigration. These modern communications (or are they post-modern?) have enabled immigrants to maintain more frequent and closer contact with their home country and to participate regularly—both actually and vicariously—in the life they once left behind. Based on substantial participant observation in various immigrant communities, as well as observing the changes over time in my own transnational relationship to my country of origin, I argue that although immigrants in the past also led transnational lives, there is a qualitative difference in the transnational experiences immigrants live today. Because the new technologies allow immediate communication, immigrants can experience the world they left behind as if they were still there. For example, today Costa Ricans can easily and rapidly travel between "home" and "host" societies, rather than spending many months at sea, as was the voyage that Italians took to return to Italy in the 19th century; likewise, cable television has brought Greece, with its colorful festivals and Olympics, right into the living room of Greek immigrants. Moreover, although in the past communication was not reliable and was painfully slow, today it is nearly certain and fast. For example, the "overseas Chinese" that lived scattered throughout the Southeast Asian nations in the early part of the 20th century often paid a "letter writer" to write the letter they could not, so as to send their messages back to their families in China. However, the letter often did not reach those in the rural areas, or it took a month or two to reach them, so that the news had grown old, whereas today a fax sent to a temple or a benevolent association will penetrate deep in China and arrive immediately. Even Cuban Americans, whose travel is so restricted by the perennial conflicts between the United States and Cuban governments, now communicate regularly with relatives and friends back in the island through electronic mail, since a friend who works for a state corporation with access to e-mail can invariably be found. Although Irish immigrants in the early part of the 19th century heard that a new baby had been baptized in Ireland long after the event, today Mexican immigrants can quickly see the baptism that just took place back in their village on video. Rather than being substantially cut off from the past, today's immigrants live—existentially speaking—both in the past and the present at once. A strong emotional thread now ties the two realities, as never before.

Immigrants today are there not just in their memories and imaginations, but vicariously, in that very moment; they are able to participate—economically, politically, socially, emotionally—in a regular, constant way, often creating two "homes" that rest on the pillar of an identity (or identities) that incorporate two or more nations, social worlds, at the same time. This is true even when, as Waldinger (2004) pointed out, dual loyalties can be conflicting. My point is not to emphasize a past/present divergence, as Waldinger put it, but to emphasize that we do now live in a brave new world that is both vastly more impersonal and personal at once. We know the ways in which our new world is more impersonal—for example, telephone menus now answer most of our questions automatically, without our hearing a human voice; clothing is bought and sold online via the computer without our ever touching the cloth in our hands for its feel. But our new world is also far more personal across very great distances than it once was, as the new technology allows us immediate intellectual and emotional communication with those we love that remained behind. Those sustained affective, emotional linkages also constitute a form of transnationalism, as Elizabeth Aranda and Elena Sabogal (2004) argued. They give evidence of the social networks across various nations that immigrants are embedded in, even though they do not entail sustained cross-border exchanges, as Portes et al. (Portes, Guarnizo, & Landolt, 1999) insisted on. For many immigrants in their new "home," this communication with their families and friends back in their old "home" represents the foundation of their emotional and economic well-being. As Waldinger (2004) concluded, "History involves change, which is why any particular historical constellation is distinct from other like developments encountered before." Thus, we do want to know how and why "now" differs from "then." However, as both David Hollinger (1995) and Jose Moya (2004) stressed, the major differences are not necessarily between "then" and "now," but between groups who show remarkable variation in the development of diasporic identities and political and social involvement.

Like all social forms, transnationalism can have both positive and negative impacts—economically, politically, and socially. Transnationalism is not only salutary for the mental health of immigrants, but is also salutary for the economic health of the underdeveloped nations they came from. A recent survey of remittance senders conducted by Bendixen and Associates for the Inter-American Development Bank (2001), based on 1,000 interviews done with Latin American immigrants in the United States, asked them whether they had ever sent money to their family in their home country. The results showed that 65% of Mexicans had done so, as had 67% of Cubans, 74% of South Americans, 78% of Dominicans, and 82% of Central Americans. That in itself constitutes a good measure of the extent to which immigrants today are involved in transnationalism. In many Latin American countries today, immigrant remittances represent millions, even billions of dollars a year—the second or third largest source of foreign exchange, quite critical to the survival of those societies (Lora, 2003). This is true with respect to not only Mexico, Guatemala, El Salvador, Dominican Republic, and Venezuela, but also Cuba. Despite the insistence of a very vocal part of the Cuban American exile community, whose political task is to insist that no dollars be sent back to Cuba because that props up Fidel Castro's regime, another sizable part of the Cuban American exile community insists on putting their families back in Cuba first—and quietly sends dollars back to their families left behind, who need it—a moral task in which women are centrally involved (cf. Pedraza, 1991).

Not only does migration result in remittances, but remittances also result in migration. In her study of the cumulative causation of migration from Costa Rica, the Dominican Republic, Nicaragua, Mexico, and Puerto Rico to the United States, Elizabeth Fussell (2004) found that in all communities in these countries, except Puerto Rico, larger amounts of remittances sent to households in a given year were associated with higher migration prevalence ratios the following year, especially in places with older migration streams, such as Mexico and the Dominican Republic. As Fussell underlined, immigrants who send back remittances demonstrate the rewards to migration, thus enticing more members of the sending community to go to the United States. Puerto Rico was an exception because, as U.S. citizens, Puerto Ricans migrate freely to and fro—so much so that Jorge Duany (2000) investigated how a "nation on the move" constructs its identity in Puerto Rico (where 61% of Puerto Ricans live) and the diaspora (where fully 39% of Puerto Ricans now live). Although language (Spanish) and culture (Latin American) used to be the cultural markers of the Puerto Rican identity, such a large diaspora, many of whom do not speak Spanish and are rather American, challenges the very markers of that identity.

Moreover, although overall the impact of immigrant remittances is positive for buoying the sinking economies back home, it can also create certain imbalances. Sarah Blue's (2004) survey of Cuban families in Havana who received remittances from their relatives abroad showed that the remittances were relinking the family that both the Cuban government and the exile community had torn asunder, and that they certainly provided some measure of material comfort for those left behind, improving their lives; however, they also served to exacerbate racial inequality. Because the first two waves of the Cuban exodus (from 1959 to 1974) were predominantly White (cf. Pedraza, 1996a), Black and Mulatto Cubans in the island have fewer immigrant networks abroad they can rely on to send remittances to improve their household consumption or to sponsor their emigration.

Transnationalism has class as well as racial dimensions. Harriett Romo's (2004) study of the transnational lives of the Mexican elite in San Antonio, Texas, described the major influence they had on the cultural and artistic life in the city of San Antonio itself, as well as the role of "broker" they played between the Mexican community, on the one hand, and the Anglo elite, on the other, on behalf of the Mexican community.

DIASPORIC CITIZENSHIP

It is also important to recognize that yesterday as well as today, the immigrants' return migration and their involvement with life in the countries they left was due not only to their bonds of love and loyalty for the family and nation left behind, but also to their lack of acceptance in America. Michel Laguerre (1998) proposed the broader concept of diasporic citizenship—"a set of practices that a person is engaged in, and a set of rights acquired or appropriated, that cross nation-state boundaries and that indicate membership in at least two nation states" (p. 190). Laguerre underlined that thereby Haitian immigrants in the United States today "escape complete minoritization since the link with the homeland allows one to enjoy the majority status one cannot exercise in the adopted country" (p. 192). Thus Laguerre underscored the difference that race—being Black and immigrant—makes.

Moreover, as a social practice, diasporic citizenship is ahead of its legal expression. Laguerre argued that a new conception of dual citizenship is developing that is dual in two senses: first, in the sense it has always been for many immigrants—that while they are in the home country (Italy, Haiti) they are its citizens, while when they are in the United States they are Americans; second, in the new sense that the diaspora—those who are, as the etymology of the word indicates, scattered asunder like seeds—can now participate fully in the social and political life of both countries, exerting quite an influence on the course of the political life in the home country. Foner provides a telling example. In the last Dominican presidential election, many Dominicans residing in New York quickly flew to the island to vote. In the next elections, the trip will be unnecessary because, due to electoral reforms, it will be possible to vote while remaining in New York. This gives the diaspora (whether Haitian, Dominican, Mexican) a role in homeland politics that is much larger than ever before. Moreover, as Laguerre underscored, it removes the future of citizenship from its modern-day location in the nation-state. With Haiti's long history of political repression, the diaspora may well be playing the role of the missing political center—between the army and the government, siding with the people, thus helping the development of civil society and democracy in Haiti. Incidentally, that is precisely the role that the Cuban diaspora has never been able to play with respect to Cuba, at least in part because both the American and Cuban governments have drastically curtailed its involvement with life in Cuba, its transnationalism, much less its diasporic citizenship. As David Hollinger (1995) underscored, the new immigration, like the old, "displays a variety of degrees of engagement with the United States and with prior homelands, and it yields some strong assimilationist impulses along vivid expressions of diasporic consciousness" (p. 153). Governments will try to restrict the flows of communication involved in transnationalism. As of the Summer of 2004, President George W. Bush drastically curtailed the involvement of Cuban-Americans with their family and friends in the island by restricting their travel (only once every 3 years now) and the amount of money they may send back as remittances through formal channels, such as Western Union, as well as the goods they may send to the island. These restrictions will only temporarily reduce the flow of people, goods, and money, however. Cuban immigrants, like all other immigrants, will find a way to get around the government's restrictions. Try as governments might to stop the immigrants' transnationalism, however, they will not be able to do so. Transnationalism is a fact of the modern (or postmodern) world in which we live, it is a result of the spread of the new forms of communication.

Laguerre (1998) underscored that transnational Haitian Americans developed loyalty to their new country as well as to their homeland, loyalties that give rise "to a fragmented bi-polar identity that transcends national boundaries and is central to the social construction of the transnational citizen" (p. 173). He also saw such an identity as the result of transnationalism. Here I disagree with Laguerre, for to me such an identity (preferably called a bicultural identity) is not only fragmented but also sharper in its sensibility—not unlike that of Park's "marginal man" at the beginning of the 20th century. It is also both cause and consequence of transnational practices. To my mind, a bicultural identity not only is the result of transnationalism but also is that on which transnationalism first depends and ultimately (over the course of time and further investments) cements. Precisely because transnationalism depends on such a bicultural identity, it is unclear at present whether the second generation, the children of immigrants, can or will participate in such a transnational social field. Although that is the subject of future research, I believe that they can or will do so only to a rather delimited extent. However, it is possible for even a small group of the second and third generations to play an influential role, as they can transfer ideas and resources that can have important impacts in both places.

Last, participation in transnational practices and the exercise of a diasporic citizenship has consequences for the extent to which immigrants can engage in ethnic politics in American life. The emotional health the new transnationalism gives us may well come at the price of domestic political engagement, of creating institutions and lobbies that can improve their lives as immigrants, workers, ethnics. Transnationalism has consequences for the extent to which immigrants can assimilate—both culturally and structurally—in America. In the end, it may still be up to the second and future generations to play the ethnic politics game. Such, indeed, was the role the descendants of the old immigrants played in the past, when city-level political "machines" built on the support of various ethnic groups traded votes for city jobs and contracts. Hence, it is quite likely that the shift in concepts—from assimilation to transnationalism—will only be useful to describe the lived experience of the immigrant generation. That, however, is a necessity at a time like now when America is not only a "nation of immigrants"—whose history was written by immigrants—but is also an immigrant nation—whose present relies on immigration. Perhaps in the brave new world of this 21st century most nations will also become immigrant nations.

ABOUT THE AUTHOR

I was a child of the Cuban refugee exodus. As a child, I lived through both a dictatorship and a revolution, both of which left a mark in my research. An immigrant at a very young age, I consider myself to be a member of the 1.5 generation—that is, at the time of immigration I was old enough to have acquired Cuban values, culture, and history, and also young enough to have become American in values, culture, and history. This hybrid, bilingual and bicultural identity allows me to both feel a sense of belonging to both nations but also to distance myself. Moreover, I am the child of a family that became deeply divided over the revolution, where I often played the role of the "go-between" between those who left and those who stayed. All these experiences have driven me to study immigration not only as a historical, political, and economic process, but also as a social psychological process, in both its causes and consequences.

ACKNOWLEDGMENTS

I wish to express my gratitude to Steven Gold for his comments on an earlier draft of this chapter.

REFERENCES

Alba, R., & Nee, V. (2003). *Remaking the American mainstream: Assimilation and contemporary immigration.* Cambridge, MA: Harvard University Press.

Aranda, E., & Sabogal, E. (2004, October). *Transnational capital and emotional livelihoods.* Paper presented at the meetings of the Latin American Studies Association, Las Vegas, NV.

Baltzell, E. D. (1964). "The immigrant's progress and the theory of the establishment." In E. O. Laumann, P. M. Siegel, & R. W. Hodge (Eds.), *The logic of social hierarchies*. Chicago: Markham.

Basch, L., Schiller, N. G., & Blanc, C. S. (1994). *Nations unbound: Transnational projects, postcolonial predicaments, and deterritorialized nation states*. Langhorne, PA: Gordon and Breach.

Barrera, M. (1979). *Race and class in the Southwest*. South Bend, IN: University of Notre Dame Press.

Blauner, R. (1969). Internal colonialism and ghetto revolt. *Social Problems, 16*, 393–408.

Blue, S. A. (2004, October). *The social cost of remittances: Race and income equality in contemporary Cuba*. Paper presented at the meetings of the Latin American Studies Association, Las Vegas, NV.

Bodnar, J. (1985). *The transplanted: A history of immigrants in urban America*. Bloomington: Indiana University Press.

Burawoy, M. (1976). The functions and reproduction of migrant labor: Comparative material from Southern Africa and the United States. *American Journal of Sociology, 81*, 1050–1087.

Corwin, A. F. (1978). *Immigrants—And immigrants: Perspectives on Mexican labor migration to the United States*. Wesport, CT: Greenwood.

Cowan, P. (1982). *An orphan in history: Retrieving a Jewish legacy*. New York: Doubleday.

Diner, H. R. (1984). *Erin's daughters in America: Irish immigrant women in the nineteenth century*. Baltimore, MD: Johns Hopkins University Press.

Duany, J. (2000). Nation on the move: The construction of cultural identities in Puerto Rico and the Diaspora. *American Ethnologist, 27*, 5–30.

Farley, R., & Alba, R. (2002). The new second generation in the U. S. *International Migration Review, 36*(Fall), 669–701.

Feagin, J. R. (1978). *Racial and ethnic relations*. Englewood Cliffs, NJ: Prentice Hall.

Foner, N. (1997). What's new about transnationalism? New York immigrants today and at the turn of the century. *Diaspora, 6*, 355–376.

Frazier, E. F. (1957). *Race and culture contacts in the modern world*. New York: Alfred A. Knopf.

Fussell, E. (2004, October). *Migration from central America and the Caribbean to the U. S.: The Role of cumulative causation*. Paper presented at the meetings of the Latin American Studies Association, Las Vegas, NV.

Galarza, E. (1964). *Merchants of labor: The Mexican Bracero story*. Santa Barbara, CA: McNally and Loftin.

Glazer, N. (1971). Blacks and ethnic groups: The difference, and the political difference it makes. *Social Problems, 18*, 444–461.

Glazer, N., & Moynihan, D. P. (1963). *Beyond the melting pot: The Negroes, Puerto Ricans, Jews, Italians, and Irish of New York City* (2nd ed.). Cambridge, MA: MIT Press.

Gold, S. J., & Phillips, B. (1996). Mobility and continuity among Eastern European Jews. In S. Pedraza & R. G. Rumbaut (Eds.), *Origins and destinies: Immigration, race, and ethnicity in America* (pp. 182–194). Belmont, CA: Wadsworth Press.

Gordon, M. M. (1964). *Assimilation in American life*. New York: Oxford University Press.

Higham, J. (1955). *Strangers in the land: Patterns of American nativism, 1860–1925.* New Brunswick, NJ: Rutgers University Press.

Hollinger, D. (1995). *Postethnic America.* New York: Basic Books.

Inter-American Development Bank. (2001). "Survey of Remittance Senders: U.S. to Latin America." Bendixen & Associates. Washington, DC: Inter-American Development Bank.

Laguerre, M. S. (1998). *Diasporic citizenship: Haitian Americans in transnational America.* New York: St. Martin's Press.

Lee, E. S. (1966). A theory of migration. *Demography, 3,* 47–57.

Light, I. (1983). *Cities in world perspective.* New York: Macmillan.

Lora, E. A. (2003). Changing patterns in the supply of labor. In *Economic and social progress in Latin America 2004* (chap. 3). Washington, DC: Inter-American Development Bank.

Martin, P., & Midgley, E. (2003). Immigration: Shaping and reshaping America. *Population Bulletin, 58,* 1–44. Washington, DC: Population Reference Bureau.

Martin, P., & Midgley, E. (2004). Number of foreign-born reaches all-time high in the U. S. *Population Reference Bureau.* Retrieved January 30, 2005, http://www.prb.org

Massey, D. S., Alarcón, R., Durand, J., & González, H. (1987). *Return to Aztlan: The social process of international migration from western Mexico.* Berkeley and Los Angeles: University of California.

Muller, T., & Espenshade, T. J. (1985). *The fourth wave: California's newest immigrants.* Washington, DC: Urban Institute.

Moya, J. (2004, November). *Diaspora studies: New concepts, approaches, and realities?* Paper presented at the meeting of the Social Science History Association, Chicago.

Ortiz, F. (1983). *Contrapunteo Cubano del Tabaco y el Azúcar.* La Habana, Cuba: Editorial de Ciencias Sociales. (Original work published 1963)

Park, R. E. (1928). Human migration and the marginal man. *American Journal of Sociology, 33,* 881–893.

Park, R. E. (1950). *Race and culture.* New York: Free Press. (Original work published 1913)

Park, R. E., & Burgess, E. W. (1921). *Introduction to the science of sociology.* Chicago: University of Chicago Press.

Pedraza, S. (1991). Women and migration: The social consequences of gender. *Annual Review of Sociology, 17,* 303–325.

Pedraza, S. (1996a). Cuba's refugees: Manifold migrations. In S. Pedraza & R. G. Rumbaut (Eds.), *Origins and destinies: Immigration, race, and ethnicity in America* (pp. 263–279). Belmont, CA: Wadsworth Press.

Pedraza, S. (1996b). American paradox. In S. Pedraza & R. G. Rumbaut, (Eds.), *Origins and destinies: Immigration, race, and ethnicity in America* (pp. 479–491). Belmont, CA: Wadsworth Press.

Pedraza-Bailey, S. (1985). *Political and economic migrants in America: Cubans and Mexicans.* Austin: University of Texas Press.

Piven, F. F., & Cloward, R. A. (1979). *Poor people's movements: Why they succeed, how they fail.* New York: Random.

Portes, A. (1978). Immigrant aspirations. *Sociology of Education, 51,* 241–260.

Portes, A., Guarnizo, L. E., & Landolt, P. (1999). Introduction: Pitfalls and promise of an emergent research field. *Ethnic and Racial Studies, 22,* 463–478.

Ramos, J. (2004, July 19). The three Americas. *The Miami Herald.*

Romo, H. (2004, October). *First class: Transnational lives of the upper middle class in San Antonio, Texas.* Paper presented at the meetings of the Latin American Studies Association, Las Vegas, NV.

Rouse, R. (1992). Making sense of settlement: Class transformations, cultural struggle, and transnationalism among Mexican immigrants in the United States. *Annals of the New York Academy of Sciences, 645,* 25–52. Special issue in N. G. Schiller, L. Bash, & C. Blanc-Szanton (Eds.), *Towards a transnational perspective on migration.*

Samora, J. (1971). *Los Mojados: The wetback story.* Notre Dame, IN: University of Notre Dame Press.

Thomas, W. I., & Znaniecki, F. (1927). *The Polish Peasant in Europe and America* (2 Vols.). New York: Alfred A. Knopf.

Turner, F. J. (1920). The significance of the frontier in American history. In *The significance of the frontier in American history.* New York: Holt. (Original work published 1893)

U.S. Bureau of the Census. (2001). *Region and country or area of birth of the foreign-born population, with geographic detail shown in decennial Census publications of 1930 or earlier: 1850 to 1930 and 1960 to 1990.* Retrieved January 30, 2005, http://www.census.gov/population/www/documentation/twps0029/tab04.html Last revised January 18, 2001.

Waldinger, R. (2004, November). *Immigrant transnationalism and the presence of the past.* Paper presented at the meeting of the Social Science History Association, Chicago.

4

The Dialectic of Recognition and Displacement in a Globalized World

E. Valentine Daniel
Columbia University

This chapter is less about a warrantable class of people named refugees whom we study than it is about persons who are in a discourse that is best represented by the label *the refugee problem*. Refugee studies as a field captured anthropology's attention when the discipline itself began its dynamic transformation, which continues to this day. In this transformation, some saw a discipline in crisis, others, a fecund change. In this apparent contradiction, this chapter finds its justification in being both descriptive and prescriptive. Written for anthropologists as well as nonanthropologists, not everything I have to say will rise up to the standards of adequacy or even necessity for all its readers, but I hope that there is something here that will engage and inform all readers, regardless.

ANTHROPOLOGY AND REFUGEE STUDIES: A BRIEF HISTORY

The origin of the term *refugee* can be traced to its use as a descriptive label applied to the Huguenots who sought refuge in Protestant England from the religious persecution they suffered in Roman Catholic France (Zolberg, Suhrke, & Aguayo, 1989, p. 2). Like most concepts, its connotations have changed over the years. Its current use, denoting an official, international, bureaucratic, and politico-legal category of persons, may be traced back to no earlier than the immediate post-World War II years. In its current sense, the first refugees were Europeans—especially European Jews—who were displaced by Nazism in particular and the ravages of World War II in general. Its Euro-genesis and consequent Euro-centrism was made vivid by the international community's failure to even register, on its official radar screen, the displacement of more than 15 million persons during the partition of the Indian subcontinent into India and Pakistan in 1947. Those were the early days. With time, no continent was to be spared its "refugee problem"; it was to become truly global (Malkki, 1995b).

Anthropology's formal entry into refugee studies was marked in 1982 by the founding of the Center for Refugee Studies at Oxford (CRSO), whose first director was the anthropologist, Barbara Harrell-Bond. That same year, CRSO also inaugurated the publication of its journal, *The Journal of Refugee Studies* (Oxford University Press, Oxford), which has had a robust life since then. Five years later, "The Committee on Refugee Issues ... was established ... [under] the General Anthropology Division, a unit of The American Anthropological Association" (Malkki, 1995a, p. 24). With this, the "refugee problem" had finally moved into the bioscope of anthropology's field of inquiry.

The refugee problem was seen either as one of "national development," and therefore part of development studies, or as a social and politico-legal problem regarding admission and settlement of asylum seekers in Western countries, making it a concern of sociology, political science, and legal studies. Both sides of the "problem" entailed Euro-American goals and concerns. These developed nations' goal was to develop underdeveloped countries along the lines of capitalist democracies of Europe that had successfully stemmed their outflows of refugees or of North America, which never had such emigration to deal with. The question of settling (physical and sociocultural) asylum seekers spawned by postcolonial effects was to become part of Euro-American anxieties.

Contrary to common assumptions, underdeveloped countries of Asia and Africa have borne a disproportionate share of giving refuge to those escaping violence, compared with the developed countries of North America, Europe, and Japan. The anxieties of these underdeveloped nations over settling refugees within their borders, however, are far less polymorphous as they are in the developed ones. In Africa, asylum seekers were seen as fellow tribesmen in misfortune or as bothersome neighbors putting a strain on limited food resources. In Pakistan, the Afghanis were seen as refugee-warriors or Muahjirin, engaged in a holy war (Shaharani, 1995).

In the mid-1990s, anthropology—thanks to its own evolution as a discipline—turned a critical eye on the whole subject of refugees. Anthropologists began to see refugees as part of a discourse. Politicians had spun it, scholars theorized it, and asylum seekers found themselves in it. Ethnographers continued to do field research among groups of people at close quarters, intensively and for sustained periods of time, as is their wont. Battered it was, and yet the culture concept predisposed anthropologists to approach universal claims with caution, making them more alert to differences in discourses and discursive practices. The "field," however, was not necessarily a place, but a movement of people through spaces that shared a common discourse. By the mid-1980s, the displacement of peoples from their places of domicile increased dramatically and refugee discourse itself became a global phenomenon. This discourse, as anthropologists were to soon find out, was a significant part of "displacement."

TWO KEY TERMS

Displacement

The movement of peoples from one place to another, as groups or as individuals, is not new. Thanks to national boundaries, nomadism has become an aberration, and migrants, refugees, and asylum seekers have been made conspicuous by their displacement (or being out of place). Indeed, in late modernity, the refugee has become the displaced person *par excellence*. The polysemy in the "dis" in "displacement" is so fecund that their perfusion throughout refugee discourse is worthy of remarkable scrutiny.

When "place" in "displace" functions as a verb, the prefix *dis* is a morpheme that plays an adverbial function. According to the *Oxford English Dictionary*, its Indo European etymon is *dwis*, which means two. It implies an act of making twain, separating, drawing apart or drawing away. Even though "displacement" is not a widely recognized word in the non-English-speaking world, its paradigmatic exemplum—"refugee"—with its near-universal currency carries with it the connotations of "displacement" that encompass it. In the following lament of Kavitha, a Canadian asylee from Sri Lanka, one can see "dis" at work:

The air force dropped their bomb right in the middle of the street. Those on this side of the street ran one way; those on that side ran that way. My uncle and his family lived on that side. They ran into the sea and were arrested by the Navy. We ran into the jungle. The LTTE took us. After that day we never saw my uncle and his two older sons. Before we left for Canada, we found my aunt and my "cousin sisters" and their youngest brother in a camp. After my father paid some money, the officer "dismissed" them: "Go to Canada, go to Africa, go anywhere. Don't come back here." All three cousins are married. One in Sweden. One in Germany. The youngest is in Vancouver. The youngest brother—he was only nine when we left—nobody knows where he is. He was arrested in Seattle for not having a Canadian visa. He was in detention for one year. The last letter we received from him was from Canada. When the Immigration and Refugee Board there interviewed him he forgot what he had said earlier, to the Immigration officers in the U.S. At the Canadian border, he

changed his story, and was accused of being mixed up with Tiger activities. So Canada refused him asylum. When he was first interviewed (at
the ports of entry by Immigration officers), he was a little boy. What did
he know? He told them what we asked him to say. Here, we adults can't
remember exactly what we told them. So how could he? He was a child
only. He even went to school in Canada for awhile. He has "behavioral
problems," they told. The school doctor told that he had anti-social behaviors. My aunt, she never liked Canada anyway. She used her son's not
getting a visa as an excuse and went back to live with my other uncle in
Colombo. She said that she was going to make a home for her son for
when he returned. That's what she said. But we know she didn't like Canada anyway. Too cold. Hated the food. Jaffna vegetables, like drum
sticks, came only in cans. She died last year. They cremated her right
there in Kanattha.[1] She wasn't even cremated in Jaffna. Now, Tigers occupy their house, our house, two other two-story houses on the street.
No one is left there. We are everywhere. We do everything and anything.
Look at father, a barrister. Now he is a bank cashier. He can't practice law
here. Mother? A Tamil Literature teacher. Who wants to learn Tamil literature here? That is why she is like this. There, if she were not teaching at
school, she would be tutoring students privately, at home. You could
never see her like this, seated all by herself, all day. Busy, busy, busy.
Thin as a stick. But busy. Now she is like this. Puffed up like a bomb. The
doctor calls it clinical depression. Because of her condition father is always in a bad temper. I have to see my friend secretly. Father will kill me if
he knew. For him, white boyfriends are forbidden. He wants me to marry
a "good Tamil." "Good Tamil!" Joke! Show me one, I'll marry him. We argue about this.[2]

The English *dismiss* that Kavitha uses is quite appropriate. Note
the splitting up (of the family) and the separation (from the land of
one's birth). Not just been divided, the family has been scattered or
dispersed. The dividing and the dispersal were not done voluntarily; they entailed the use of direct or indirect force. In the life of an
asylum seeker, displacement is an act of force, of separation by
force, a wrenching.

The morpheme *dis* also means to deprive, to take away. Her aunt
was deprived of the customary right to be cremated in her *urkadu
sudalai* (the cremation grounds of her *ur*). Instead, she was cremated
in Kanattha, "where all kinds of people"—irrespective of caste, class or
ethnicity are cremated or buried—are *dis*posed of. The right to practice law has been taken away from her father; he has been *dis*barred.
Her mother can no longer teach Tamil. She was a woman of words, a
teacher, and now she is a woman of silence, a brooder; was active, now
inactive—"just sits around"—was thin, is fat; was powerful, is *disem*-

---

[1]The largest public cemetery in the island, located in Colombo.

[2]September 1998. Interview of Kavitha Rasanayagam in Seattle, WA. She spoke in a
mixture of English and Tamil, which has, for the purpose of this essay, been glossed entirely into English.

powered. In so many ways, she has been transformed into the opposite of what she once was. She has been truly *dis*abled.

There are more adverbial functions of *dis*. The youngest boy has *dis*appeared. Here it bears the connotation of failure: the failure to appear. He has failed in yet another way; adjectivally, he is a profound *dis*appointment. The youngest boy's privilege of staying in Canada was *dis*allowed because he was *dis*honest. Although the charge of dishonesty threatens every displaced person from without the community, *dis*satisfaction is the most common sentiment directed at them from within. Kavitha's aunt was dissatisfied with the weather and the food in Canada; her father was dissatisfied with and disappointed in the man she had chosen to befriend. As a prefix for acts of undoing, we find the displaced persons *dis*pleasing (Kavitha's dating an American displeases the father, the father's displeasure displeases the daughter, the therapist's ethnocentrism displeases Kavitha, and her mother, by isolating herself in depression, literally *dis*joins her self from the rest causing *dis*union in the family. And then there is *dis*ease and *dis*integration. Disintegration's opposite, integration, is the most important "un*dis*sed" state sought by those who have the right and privilege of granting asylum. But Western psychology expects integration to be found principally in the individual, to which we now turn.

The Individual

The ideal refugee or asylum seeker, as defined by the United Nations and whose definition has been adopted and adapted by the various member nation-states, is, like these very same nation-states, imagined as bounded and sovereign. The United Nations Protocol on Refugees defines a refugee as:

> An individual who owing to a well-founded fear of being persecuted for reasons of race, religion, nationality, membership of a particular social group or political opinion, is outside the country of his nationality and is unable, or unwilling, to avail himself of the protection of that country; or who, not having a nationality and being outside the country of his former habitual residence, is unable or, owing to such fear, is unwilling to return to it.

This definition is intended to help Immigration and Naturalization Service (INS) officials to recognize a refugee. Recognition plays no small part in the granting of asylum. It is central. In this protocol definition, displacement may be tacitly acknowledged, but the word as such is not used, and "displacement" itself is not posed as the issue at hand. In fact, most litigation, controversies, and casebook entries pertain to the "individual." "Fear" itself is seen as an individual emotion and the narrative of the asylum seeker as a unique narrative. Group membership may be indicated, but most cases founder on questions of the justification of the *individual's* fear of persecution and the individual's qualifications to assume new citizenship. In short, displacement is not at issue, but the refugee as an individual is.

An individual is expected be well integrated, not someone whose very being is so multiply "*dis*"-sed. In court hearings all over North America and Europe, the asylum seeker, must prove that he or she, as a *sovereign* individual, has a well-founded fear of persecution. The first test of this ideal is to examine the asylum seeker's narrative itself. What INS officials expect is an "integrated" narrative. It matters little how disintegrated the person's life may be, as long as the narrative conceals the latter. An integrated narrative promises, if not an integrated individual, then at least a person with a real potential for integration. Indeed, in a fundamental sense, it would be redundant to call someone an integrated individual. The semantic import of the word, in-"dividual" (that which cannot be divided), is strongly assumed although mostly hidden from reflective awareness of most Westerners. The assumption that all selves are by definition *in*dividual selves goes unquestioned. The myriad ways in which the covert meaning of *in*dividual causes overt confusion and misunderstandings may be witnessed in every legal forum in Europe and North America where petitions for asylum seekers are adjudicated. The applications by many Third World refugees founder on the point of the applicant trying to prove that he or she has reason to fear persecution, as an individual, not merely because his or her kinsman was tortured by the state of the country from which he or she had fled, or because his or her ethnic group or village had been threatened by a terrorist group. For instance, just being a Mayan in Guatemala, where the persecution of Mayan Indians in general is as ubiquitous as it is well documented (Manz, 1995), is insufficient reason for granting asylum to a Mayan Indian. The asylum seeker must show why he or she, personally and individually, has a well-founded fear of persecution. The killing of a close relative by agents of the state may not be reason enough for granting him or her asylum. Quite often, the U.S. State department or its equivalent in other Western countries determines whether a group in a certain state need fear persecution by that state. The determination is based on interstate and international interests rather than on human interests.

At a culturally subtler level, take the case of a Tamil mother from Sri Lanka seeking asylum in Canada. Her only son, a refugee in Canada, dies and is cremated. Many years later, even after her two daughters married and sought and received refuge in Australia, this mother seeks permanent residence in Canada. Why? Because she wishes to live on the soil with which her son's ashes have combined and of which, when she dies, she wishes her own ashes to become a part. Attempts by attorneys to persuade her to make her case on other, more "acceptable" grounds (e.g., she had witnessed her husband's murder by the armed forces and was a potential witness against these armed forces in a future investigation, and therefore had reason to fear that she might be killed were she to return) failed to impress her. What was culturally "truest" to her was the sense of self that did not end at the boundary of the skin but extended to a relationship with the soil—but no longer the soil of her land of birth, but the soil in which her only male progeny was buried.[3] This represents a *dividuated*[4] rather than an "individuated" sense of self, as well as the cultural need to recover a deeply disequilibriated sense of self by rejoining a part of her that died along with her son.

It is easy to forget that a person who seeks asylum is above all else a human being whether or not s/he is an *individual*, sovereign or otherwise. There are many ways of being human. Being an individual is just one of them.[5] The juridico-political definition of an individual is a product of Western modernity, arguably only as old as the modern nation-state itself, and by no means universal. These elements of presentism and Eurocentrism are of no concern to the officials who determine the future of the asylum seeker, nor is the reduction of personhood to individuality, regardless that such a reduction may undermines some people's sense of what it is to be human. The human sciences should help facilitate the appreciation of this fact and the cost of failing to do so. Such an intervention would be an instance of local knowledge being brought to bear on the dictates of supralocal knowledge in a courtroom, which, in the best of all possible worlds, should be both a local and a translocal site. Anthropologists have only recently begun to understand and execute in practice such an appreciation. The very juridico-political definition—itself intended to be bounded and sovereign—of a "refugee" is, like the individual, inherently unstable.

ANTHROPOLOGY'S PLACE IN REFUGEE STUDIES: DEVELOPING PROSPECTS

Even so brief a sketch of the range of discursive practices that constitute the refugee phenomenon reveals the complexity of the field, the dense microlegitimations *in situ*, its misrecognitions and misunderstandings. What is or might be the place of anthropology in such a field? An anthropologist begins by observing at the level of tiny local events. He or she asks the little question that engages with multiple levels of the discursive field. Such local events may be encountered in a Red Cross-run refugee camp in Uganda, a drunken brawl in a halfway house in Denmark, an INS detention center in Seattle, a court hearing in London, a little church in the Netherlands, an Internet chat group discussing Kosovo, or a chance discussion among fellow travelers on a

---

[3]See Daniel (1984, chap. 1) for a discussion of the relationship between one's body and soil among Tamils.

[4]See McKim Marriott (1976) for a detailed discussion of "dividuality."

[5]See Raymond Williams (1976, pp. 161–165) for a discussion of the 17th- and 18th-century origins of the modern notion of the individual.

train. It is at the level of local events that refugees discourse takes content and shape, and eventually determines truth, justice, the deserving and the underserving. Such local events reveal global prejudices, but to one who is deeply steeped in the life of a community and is at ease with its language—in the widest sense—they also reveal local prejudices, embedded in barely articulated sentiments. Life in such sites is a continuous process of the universalization of the parochial and the parochialization of the universal. It becomes the ethnographer's task to understand, interpret, and convey to a wider world the full import of this "life," for displaced individuals and communities.

However, as soon as we invoke the notions of "community" and "field," new questions are generated. For we can no longer—especially in refugee studies—take the meaning of community for granted, with such a community fixed in time or place. A community of refugees is quite often a community in motion, presenting the kind of field site and field work that until recently was not part of the anthropological imagination, with the qualified exception of the study of nomads.[6] Such a community expands and contracts, concentrates and dissipates, adjusts and adapts, all the while redefining itself demographically and culturally according to the times, places, and spaces through which it moves and relative to the moving generations. Children tend to take displacement in stride; young adults take it on as a challenge to be overcome; the elderly either resist or surrender because they see no alternative. Likewise, members of the working class may adapt to displacement much more successfully than might professionals (Knudsen, 1995). The anthropologist, as field-worker, commentator, translator, and—if called on to be one—advisor, cannot harbor an essentialized and static notions of community, culture, or person. He or she must be attuned to their shifts and shift accordingly, unremittingly questioning and reevaluating one's "ethnographic authority" in light of this dynamic community and shifting field (Clifford, 1981). Over the last two and a half decades, field work and the attendant claim to ethnographic authority by anthropologists has come under much criticism. Much of the criticism was justified and its significant effects on the discipline sobering, whereas some of it has merely had the effect of throwing out the baby of unsubstitutable aspects of ethnography with the bath water of ethnographic conceit. Were we to preserve the best of the conceivable consequences of ethnographic field work as the *sine qua non* of the discipline—even though the concept of "the field" in field work itself has undergone major changes—then it should be noted that in no other human science, including journalism, can one find the importance given to the injunction to observe and listen painstakingly, closely, sympathetically, critically, and whenever possible, repeatedly, and always to interpret in context. Add to this in-

---

[6]In Evans-Pritchard's ethnographic classic (1940) on the Nilotic tribe, the Nuer, we see the tension between the tribe's nomadism and the ethnographer's impulse to situate in place, time, and structure.

junction the value given to participation in the life of a community to the fullest extent possible, and you have in a nutshell the distinctiveness of ethnographic field research. Calling such fieldwork "ethnographic" is not to limit its use to card-carrying anthropologists but to make it available to whoever in the human sciences is willing to practice the method of participant observation to the fullest extent possible. For it is in such a "field" that one has the possibility of witnessing the formation of the refugee in his or her nascent state and the process of his or her displacement and reemplacement.

Reading the Field

If one of the effect of the critique of ethnographic authority was to prod ethnographers into becoming more reflective about writing—its authority, veracity, style, responsibility, and so on—then an accompanying, although unintended, consequence has been the cultivation of keener ways of reading (Dirks, 1996). The primary reading material for the ethnographer is not literature in the conventional sense of that term but the text and texture of social and cultural contexts, called the *field*, in which he or she immerses him- or herself just as a reader of a riveting novel might immerse himself in his book. Refugee discourse is such a text. But the text—here, refugee discourse—is most productively read if it is read as "genealogy": gray, meticulous, patiently documentary, scribbles on a field of entangled and confused parchments, on documents that have been scratched over and recopied many times, a site wherein one encounters the union of erudite knowledge and local memories of historical struggles, dissentions, and disparities (Foucault, 1971/1977, p. 139). The psychiatric social worker, the embassy official, or the immigration judge looks for a coherent autobiographical narrative from the refugee—the testament to an integrateable if not integrated individual self. Deviation from this ideal is seen as indicating untruthfullness and its speaker as unworthy of refuge. The life of a refugee, following the moment of the first involuntary and unwelcome displacement, is almost never a simple narrative that leads to a single truth. It too is a genealogical: gray, scribbled over by a mess of memories and experiences, differently valued and variously arranged, and shaded over by a range of emotions that keep shifting as twilight shadows in the woods. Genealogy cannot be diagramed as a neat descent of ancestors (causes) and progeny (effects) as in a kinship diagram or as a straightforward history. Rather, genealogy is more akin to the combined working out of genetics—with all its internal complexities, environmental factors, and more than a touch of pure chance (Hacking, 1990, pp. 200–215; Peirce, 1891–1893/1992). In genealogy, events are selectively remembered and forgotten and interpretations selected out and selected in. The agent that does the selecting is rarely the individual; culture, history, or "governmentality" does it (Foucault, 1994, pp. 74–76, 299—300).

Refugee narratives are presented as stories. But to read one as a story would be to "read" the narrative poorly. The keener way of reading it is to read against the grain of the text, and that is also one way of reading genealogically. From poststructuralism—and deconstruction in literary study in particular—anthropologists may learn to read against the grain, yet with pragmaticist restraint so as to avoid descending into silliness (Margolis, 1995). How far can we push the analogy of text and reading? The text that the field-worker encounters is not a text made up of words on paper—although it may include that, too—but a complex admixture of signs that are embodied in and surround human being in people's ordinary and extraordinary lives. These signs are not empty signifiers paired with floating signifieds. Rather, they are signals of alternately anchored and disanchored lives (Daniel, 1995).

Reading against the grain of refugee discourse is to read the formations, forms and transformations of displacement, not as dispensed for us by the idea and reality of the nation-state alone but also as revealed to us in the tiny local events and sideshows of history. To read against the grain is to be able to simultaneously read along the grain. It is only through such readings that one discovers the following: (a) Many of the statutes pertaining to refugees, established and enforced by nation-states and the United Nations, serve states' rights over human rights. (b) All refugees are not victims in their self-understanding. (c) Some refugees consider the decentering and denationalizing of their lives and identities liberating. (d) Age, gender, and class play a significant role in the self-definition of self and the cultivation of one's life in the host-country. (e) The ideal-typical refugee is neither ideal nor typical.

The formula used to be simple in anthropology: With respect to other cultures and societies, read sympathetically, along the grain of their context; in reading official discourse in one's our own society, read against the grain. The world is far more complex now and so is refugee discourse itself. It implicates power of nations, states, races, classes, ethnes, religions, and more. This calls for a habit change in our own disciplinary methodology. If there be a rule of thumb to be used, but with caution, it would be to read against governmentality, and to be suspicious of all effortless readings. Even as we recognize the will to inquiry in field work—a highly localized art—it cannot be practiced without the acknowledgment of the reality of a thoroughly globalized world. To acknowledge this is to realize that "context" is as much trans-local as it is local, trans-present as it is present in the here and now. For how can one understand a Kosovar refugee without knowing the history of empire, the history of World War II, UN politics and Yugoslavian politics, Balkan geography, world geography, the Serbs' religion and Slav religion, Christianity and Islam? The greater part of official discourse on refugees has been written by the pen of power dipped in the ink of statist interests (Aleinikoff, 1995). The fuller text is, however, thick not only with words that constitute definitions and protocols but also with human suffering and triumphs that defy words or are expressed in nonverbal signs that may range from a gesture to the organization of space, a tick to a talent, a pathology to a poem, a stutter to the composing of a song. The critical anthropologist studies the formation of a refugee in the context of the dialectic conjunction of locally and globally shaped, power-shot-through, human experiences.

DISPLACEMENT AND PRODUCTIVE HOMELESSNESS

A displaced person can also be a decentered one. Displacement and decentering are spatial orientations relative to a place called "home." Home in the case of displacement connotes something physical, whereas in the case of decentering, it connotes something psychological, moral, and even spiritual. When refugees are repatriated, they may find "home," in both senses of the term, unavailable[7] or missing. Even if a change of party, policy, or heart on the part of the government or the intervention of an international organization may remedy displacement, it may be much harder for a refugee to recover his or her center and home, in the moral sense. The deficiencies in the juridico-political definition are exposed only when the presence of both these senses of "home" is realized. There is, however, another, more self-affirming side to displacement, decentering, and "homelessness." In the extreme instance, the only "home" known to the asylum seeker or refugee could be "hell" for which no nostalgia could be stirred up, and the movement toward, or the settling in, any civil society would be "heaven" by comparison. One cannot be interested only in the homesick refugee as a victim of displacement or in the complaisant[8] individual, profoundly grateful for being rescued from a hell of a home. Much more common is the displaced person who finds in displacement the strength to overcome debilitating "homesickness," and in decenteredness a privileged perspective on the blind spots at the centers of power, wherever they happen to be. Such displacement and decentering become catalysts of critical creativity. Refugees are also creators of new worlds and new possibilities, and, as such, they embody the "quickened kernel" for a more interesting world (Fischer, 1995).

In conventional field work, most anthropologists spent a year or two of intense research work with a community that belonged to a place, from where they would return home and write a monograph. Some would make one or more return visits to the same "field." Few (but a steadily increasing number) retain close links with their friends, acquaintances, and contacts in the field, and return fre-

---

[7]In Heidegger's *Zuhandenheit* (usually translated as "readiness to hand" but rendered as as "unavailableness," by Dreyfus, 1991, pp. 60–87).

[8]In *Leviathan*, Hobbs defined his fifth law of nature as "Compleasance." Also see George Etherege (1979).

quently in order to keep in touch with the place and the persons in place. In this newer kind of field research, where the interest in a people persists over space, time, and generations, one finds an unprecedented depth of commitment to inquiry that also serves as a stay against premature claims to expertise on a place or people. Such studies can no more hope to essentialize a "villager," a "tribesman," or a typical "ethnic," than they could reduce a refugee into a "thing." All one could do is persist in sketching out their perpetual motion, positioning oneself as a dialectical realist (Hacking, 2002, p. 13).

If "homelessness" and the resulting state of *unheimlich* of the refugee can be productive, so can those of the anthropologist. In a little under two and a half decades, anthropology itself has undergone a certain measure of displacement and decentering. It has been forced to give up the comfort and conceit of working in a sequestered place among relatively sequestered peoples and stable communities in a distinctly demarcated elsewhere called "the field." In giving up the conceit of its own "center(s)" of comfort and expertise, it too has experienced a certain decentering. Two main factors brought about this change. First is the realization that all peoples of the world have always been part of the trans-local—even if not global—and have never been exclusively local, and now only less so. Second, as the century comes to a close, global flows—be they of peoples, goods, or information—have dramatically increased in volume and frequency. The marginal—peoples and places—that served as anthropology's centers of interest for over a century are just as likely to be found in the interstices of the metropolises and cosmopolitan capitals of the world. The refugee has become the quintessential "marginal" in the center.

The refugee and the anthropologist are held together, although in very different ways, by what Max Weber called, an "elective affinity" of displacement, decenteredness and homelessness. The recognition of globalization, the translocation of "the field," the transformation of "community," and the discovery of the marginal in the center are some of the factors that have contributed to a productive homelessness in anthropology.

DISPLACEMENT AND THE DIALECTIC
OF SPACE AND PLACE

More than one song refers to a "place called home." Its counterpart would be a "space called house." Some anthropologists who began their work among settled communities witnessed their internal displacement by war, their flight out of the country to escape terror and transient lives in refugee camps, and their eventual resettlement in foreign lands. In a refugee's life, space supplants place. A detention center is an interstitial space where tiny local events tend to happen; a UNHCR camp is a space where one can find the dialectic between the local and the trans-local at work. A refugee camp is a space that could serve as an "instruction manual" for how to "read" a text or a life according to official dictats and witness their coming into contradiction with alternate readings offered by traces of place: local voices, local experiences, and local truth claims. There are those who came to a host country as adults but whose formative years were in their native lands, and those who left their native countries as children but had grown up in the host country. For many in the first group, "home" remains their place of birth and their adopted country a mere safe space. For most of the young, neither country is a place called home; nor are these mere spaces of habitation. Thanks to the Internet and ease of travel in this highly globalized world, they live amid the traffic of information between their countries of birth and of adoption, and thereby experience space–place not as a difference in kind, but as loci of degree, in an ever shifting landscape, in reality and imagination. To them, home will always remain an uncanny place.

Anthropologists working among refugees have also found it necessary to do ethnographies of the state in spaces such as the U.S. INS or the British Home Offices, spaces that are privileged domains of refugee discourse production (Fuglerund, 1999). Such studies are still in their infancy. Economists, political scientists, and sociologists—in decreasing order—have a much longer history of working in such spaces where they have come to feel more or less at home. Being "at home," however, can be both a liability and an asset. The assets are obvious. As for liabilities, such social scientists are more disposed to reading refugee discourse along the grain of habit, scored over by the centers of power housed in such spaces.

In such spaces of discourse production, numerous kinds of human beings and human acts come into being hand in hand with our invention of the ways to name them. Ian Hacking (2002) called this doctrine "dynamic nominalism" (p. 2). Foucault, in several books, documented the workings of dynamic nominalism in history. Alan Young's (1996) wonderful account of the birth of PTSD (post-traumatic stress disorder) is another potent illustration of the power of dynamic nominalism, closer to our time and theme. By "being out of place," in such spaces, anthropologists are better positioned to see the asymmetries between the name and the named that are brought together into nominalistic symmetries by such force-fields of normalization (Dreyfus & Rabinow, 1983, pp. 257–261). The human beings named *refugees* may not only be asymmetrical to the names given them but may in fact be significantly different; the failure to expose such differences is not only an epistemological flaw, it is an ethical failure.

THE DISPLACED: SEEKER OF RECOGNITION?

Refugee discourse—the paradigmatic discourse of displacement—is produced in a variety of sites: in parliaments and Congress, at embassies and government offices, at airport customs and in detention centers, in laws courts and academic conferences, in pubs and in editorial rooms. In all such spaces of official and nonofficial discourse on refugees and asylum seekers, "recognition" is the gavel.

Recognition is also the centerpiece of one of the greatest philosophical parables of modernity, Hegel's "Lord and Bondsman" (Hegel, 1977). This parable appears in chapter IV of his *Phanomenologie des Geistes* (henceforth, *PhG*), translated into English as *The Phenomenology of Spirit/Mind*. *PhG* is an attempt to answer the question: What is it to know or what is knowing? Its significance in the present analysis lies in the claim that knowledge is power (Foucault, 1994). The answer tracks the dialectical journey of thought from knowledge claims based on sense certainty via many intermediary stages and culminates in absolute knowledge or knowledge based on a well-worked-through scientific philosophy. It is a phenomenological account based on European history. Not all the noted phases of knowledge are universal, either historically or psychologically. However, several of the phenomenological stages worked on and through by Hegel, with minor modifications, are recognizable and are contemporaneous to our own experiences in late modernity. Although my main interest is in the phase marked by the Lord and Bondsman parable—the stage at which one becomes a self-conscious, *socially* aware being—one encounters clear flashes of previously sublated[9] phases in far less extra-ordinary circumstances. Consider the following snippet from a conversation between two customs officers and me[10]:

Ms. Q: I'd know, right away, can tell, if one of them were to enter this room. Nobody has to tell me a thing. Don't need to have known anything about this person.

EVD: No previous knowledge?

Ms. Q: None.

EVD: You're not saying that someone doesn't have to have any previous knowledge, say, not even know what or who a refugee is.

Ms. Q: In a way I am saying that. All that past knowledge doesn't matter really. Each time one of them comes before me—or comes into the room even, as I said—I know it's one of them.

EVD: By just looking at him or her.

Ms. Q: I don't even have to look at them.

EVD: You mean from the person's English. His accent, I mean.

Ms. Q: They need not say one word. They need not open their mouth.

EVD: [Light-heartedly, but also goading] It has to be by the smell, then. You are not telling me that, like now, you are facing me with your

---

[9]The English translation of *aufheben*. It means to both cancel and retain, lift up, as in lifting up ("deposing") a rider from his horse. The best colloquial analogy is to kick someone upstairs.

[10]Ms. Q is a retired customs officer and Mr. Z is a recent recruit to customs. The occasion is a reception given to me after I delivered an invited lecture on the Sri Lankan civil war to customs officers at their Queens Branch, in New York. Ellipses indicate words that have been edited out.

Ms. Q: back to the door. Let's say one of them walks in that door. Are you saying you will immediately know that an illegal alien has just entered the room?

Ms. Q: No. I don't mean the smell or the English or the clothes or anything like that. I just know.

Mr. Z: [Having eavesdropped on our conversation, as he joins us jovially, with the coment] Are we being racist here? Smell of refugees?

Ms. Q: [Defensively] I am not being racist. For Christ's sake, my grandparents were immigrants. On both sides. [Laughing] I didn't say "smell. [Pointing at me] He said it.

EVD: No, no. What I mean is that you must be able to tell that an "illegal alien" is present only by one of your five senses. Correct? How else ...?

Ms. Q: Yeah.

EVD: Then, which is it? Sight, hearing, smell, touch ... What's the other?

Mr. Z: Taste.

Ms. Q: Just a feeling. That's all. Just a simple feeling.

Mr. Z: It's the sixth sense.

Ms. Q: You might say that. It comes from thirty years of experience.

Mr. Z: The same is true of asylum seekers. Like, I can smell a lie from a mile.

EVD: You mean it metaphorically I hope. Otherwise tell me what aroma a lie has because I would certainly like to use it when my students come to me with excuses for why their papers are late.

Mr. Z: [Laughing] You are big into smells today, Professor.

EVD: You are the one who said you could smell a lie from a mile away. You don't mean, smell smell. Right? Now, just wanted to be sure. I am an anthropologist and we are not allowed to take anything for granted. I am out here to learn. We have heard stranger stories and some true too.

Mr. Z: Inconsistencies, you know. Like the beginning, the middle and the end don't match up. That's what I mean. By the time they stand like before a judge; that's another story. By then, they are like well coached by their lawyers.

Ms. Q: The same thing. Sixth sense. Even when the story is straight. Trust your sixth sense. Sixth sense.

Ms. Q presents her consciousness as the sensor. The extraordinary length to which she goes in order to avoid naming any particular sense appears to indicate the high value she places on immediate knowledge.[11] To her, it seems that even to name a particular sense is to risk conceding that knowledge is mediated. Note even Hume was that fastidious.[12] Having decided to base her knowledge claim on sensation, however (even if only the sixth sense), she has based her knowledge claim on sense certainty.

---

[11]The history of valorization of unmediated knowledge in dominant Western epistemology would take us too far afield at this time. Its link to "individualism" deserves exploration.

[12]Hume considered the apprehension by the senses to qualify as immediate knowledge.

EVD: I am really interested in this sixth sense.

Ms. Q: What else do you call it? Some of these guys are just like Americans. They speak American, they dress American, they look American but they are illegal refugees. You just know it.

EVD: Let's leave refugees for a moment. Generally you guys must be trained to look for certain signs that mark an illegal. From training, experience or a training manual, perhaps? If you see an individual with those signs, you then think, that person is likely to be an illegal. Yeah?

Then came the priceless sentence which, I am sure, the officer did not mean to have come out the way it did—as a *non sequitur*—and probably did not mean it either. But it turns out to be a perfect illustration of Hegel's point about sensory-certainty and perceptual knowledge.

Ms. Q: Dr. Daniel. Let me tell you this. Even if I did not know anything about a refugee, even if I did not know that this person was a refugee, I can tell you that he is a refugee.

EVD: You mean "illegal," not a "refugee."

Ms. Q: That's right. Illegal alien.

Mr. Z: What she means is. OK, yes, we have books and manuals—these keep changing—and we must keep up. These tell us what to look for .... And we look for these ... signs. We have to write up our reports. In the report or in court we can't say we had a feeling .... Lawyers ... they are out there .... By the rules .... Always by the book.

Ms. Q: That is worth our jobs.

Ms. Q and Mr. Z: We play by the law.

Mr. Z: But an experienced officer ... like Ms. Q, will be able to pick out an illegal, long before .... [W]e don't even have to get to that point, asking questions or say, search the luggage or look at the papers. None of that. That's what she means. Not that we don't make mistakes. Everybody make mistakes. God makes mistakes, for cryin' out loud.

Ms. Q: We learn from our mistakes.

Mr. Z: But an experienced officer rarely makes a mistake. So yes. You can say that. You can. An experienced officer can sense an illegal. It is hard to say how. But he can, without any of that other stuff.

EVD: Other stuff?

Ms. Q: Rules, signs, tip-offs and stuff that...

EVD: I want to be sure. We were talking about illegal aliens, right? Not about those from other countries who are seeking asylum legally. Because earlier, as we were talking, I noticed that refugees and asylum seekers were also thrown in there, into the same category.

Ms. Q   Illegal aliens.
& Mr. Z:

Ms. Q: We mean illegal aliens.

EVD: "Sixth sense!" Now that is what I would like to know about. You say, it's not smell, ... none of those.

Mr. Z: In a sense, it is like all of them working together. It is like pulling the string on the Basmati rice bag like you mentioned in your lecture. If you pull the right end of the string, and the right first stitch, then all the other stitches come lose; the bag opens.

EVD: You should've been a writer, Mr. Z. You have a good mind for metaphors and images.

Ms. Q: He is a Columbia man.

Mr. Z: No, NYU. The trick is to pull the right knot. Spot the right signal.

Ms. Q: That is right. If you see something unusual, you will find it to be unusual. So what? It's unusual. Nothing more. If a trained customs officer sees something unusual with his eyes, then all his other senses kick in; they open up; they hear, they smell, ... they sense, everything. If you ask me, which sense raised my suspicion? I don't know. I couldn't tell. Most of the time ... I don't know ... I wouldn't be able to tell you. I might just pick any one thing and tell you. There, this is what made me suspicious. Do I know for sure? No. As I said, it is not one sense. You can't even say which sense. As he said, all of them. And more. That's the sixth sense we are telling you about.

EVD: Very interesting. But you sense so many things all at once. Take the eye. At a glance you see so many, probably thousands of things: a red blouse, a blue shirt, faded denim jeans, an earring perhaps, a backpack, black hair, white complexion, you name it. You know what I mean?

Mr. Z: I know what you mean. We see millions of things but we don't notice them all. We register only five or ten things that we see. *They* matter. The others are things that everybody or anybody has. Don't mean a thing.

EVD: You got it! Exactly! So you select from all these millions of things you see just the five or ten you mentioned.

Mr. Z: Exactly. Things that we use to tell that marks a refugee, I mean illegal.

In passing, let us note that Ms. Q's and Mr. Z's tendency to conflate illegal aliens, immigrants, refugees, and asylum seekers. This "error" that arises from ignorance and/or prejudice is common enough among the general American public. For even INS officers to slip up in this manner is indicative of the depth of ingrained cultural habits of thought that it even overrides official knowledge of legal categorical distinctions.

How Ms. Q and Mr. Z Come to Know Their Objects

At some point in this three-way conversation Mr. Z realizes that the senses convey to consciousness congeries—not a coherence—of unrelated sensory qualities. Unrelated sense data, as Mr. Z came around to admitting, tell us nothing. The INS officer's trained consciousness picks out some of those sensory stimuli, puts them together, and discards the rest. Behold! They reveal to him an object, and he knows that it is an "illegal." With this acknowledgment, Mr. Z has begun to submit to the authority of what Hegel called *perception*. In perception we grasp the same sense data that were fed to consciousness but as related to one and the same object, a particular. Now, perceptive consciousness is aware that what is present to it at this level is no mere collection but a coherence of sense data that constitute a thing, a particular. But a particular what? If this account of perceptual knowledge were to be sustained, it is not enough for the agent to claim that the object sensed is an individual "thing," a selective bundle of properties with which she or he has become directly acquainted. As Mr. Z concurs, his identification of a bare particular sensory object—a particular "illegal"—is only possible if there is a simultaneous acquaintance with a second object, the universal "illegal" of which the particular is an instantiation: a particular illegal. Perception, therefore, is based on the nexus of two different objects combined into one. Ms. Q and Mr. Z may not have perceived the nexus, but they did perceive the percipient that results from the union of two distinct "objects."

Thus, perception turns out to be the awareness of two types of representations of objects: representations of particulars and representation of universals. But perception cannot explain this combination by basing it on what is simply given to perception. It can only be explained by something other than perception. Hegel calls this the force of reflective "understanding." Understanding is based on the realization that what was taken to be immediate objects of perception are only our *representation* of particulars and universals. These representations cannot be explained by either one of them, but only by something nonperceptible. The latter, we tend to attribute to some "supersensible essence,"[13] as Ms. Q attempted to do right away in her claim about "knowing" when an "illegal" enters a room.

The supposed true essence of a thing is not directly available to consciousness but as mediated by reflective understanding. "A curtain of sorts [is drawn] between us and the world, and the 'understanding is capable of getting behind the curtain and gaining the knowledge of [the essence of things]. If this conception is sustainable, then the knowledge that would be thus gained would be independent of history and social practice" (Pinkard, 1994, p. 38). Sense certainty survives sublation, as a necessary but hardly sufficient aspect in this more complex form of knowing. In reflective understanding, there is the dawning of an awareness of one's own consciousness playing a part in the knowing of the object.

Self-consciousness thus formed, however, remains sealed within self certainty. In the three-way conversation, there is no acknowledgment that the object of knowledge, the displaced person, is also a knowing subject in his or her own right. As such, knowledge claims seem limited to the three stages of Hegel's phenomenology of knowing: sense certainty, perception, and understanding. It is at this stage that

---

[13]Hegel calls it the "unconditional universal."

Hegel uses the lord–bondsman dialectic to move the phenomenology of knowing forward where a self-conscious subject is confronted by another self-conscious subject.

THE DIALECTIC OF RECOGNITION

Hegel's parable of the Lord and Bondsman is an abstraction, a fiction, and "intolerably involuted" (Lauer, 1993, p. 89). It is but one phase in the long journey from sensory consciousness to absolute knowledge, although a very important phase. The parable raises many questions; some will be answered, some left unanswered; some deemed unanswerable even in the context of the whole of *PhG*. In Hegel's parable there are no mediating social institutions involved when the lord-to-be and the bondsman-to-be first meet. This makes the implied analogy between the master–slave and the refugee–official both simpler and more difficult. Like an algebraic equation or an architect's floor plan, a parable represents by simplifying reality, and like them it also foregrounds certain significant features that would have otherwise been lost. A page limit prevents me from supplying the ethnographic analogues in the parable. Those who have worked with displaced persons will, however, recognize the master–slave in many official–refugee interactions. Such "masters" may be found among detention-center guards, customs officers, prosecutors, judges, UNHCR and Red Cross workers, nongovernmental organizations (NGOs), and citizens of the host country.

Briefly, this parable is about the confrontation of two independent, self-conscious agents. Let's call them C-1 and C-2. Prior to facing each other, their encounters had been only with sensuous objects; each of which was, as object *qua* object, in-itself and for-itself, indifferent to all else. None existed *for* another, not even for C-1 and/or C-2, and each agent's relation to these objects was primarily practical, not theoretical. Each had relied on his own cognitive activity—acquired through sensory, perceptual, and reflective understanding—to know how the world was and how it accommodated to his needs. Being subjects, however, these agents had used these objects to fulfill their own desires by *negating* (killing, consuming, recognizing, or transforming) them. The objective worlds that they incorporated into consciousnesses became, thereby, mere extensions of themselves that did not challenge their private, self-consciousnesses-assured, self-certainties.

Their self-certainties were adequate as long as they were isolated self-conscious monads; they were shaken, however, when each faced the other, equally self-conscious being, with its own truth claims and worldview. The encounter ushers the two into *social space*. The subject cannot negate this new "other," which is no longer a disinterested object but an equally willful, independence-seeking, interested subject. C-1 can no longer make C-2 an extension of itself and vice versa. At stake is each being's independence. To be sure, the master-to-be (say, C-1) does not seek the recognition of his *existence* by the slave-to-be (C-2)—that was already assured by sense certainty, perception, and understanding—but the recognition of his *independence* from all determinations, especially the determination of C-2.

Before the encounter, as an organism, C-1 acted on the principle that he was to satisfy desires and his desires were given to him in life. What was authoritative for him was not any desire determined by an object but by *his* overall desires about what *he* wished to accomplish. He was free to act or not to act on any given desire. He could have even chosen death over life. After the encounter, C-1 has no say in C-2's self-certainties; the former has no control of what the latter thought of him. At this stage, given no conventions of negotiation and compromise, the only way to recover his independence from any possible determination by this incomprehensible other was to kill him. The other's predicament, sentiments, and options were symmetrical. Thus became available the sole option to "battle unto death" to settle the question of who was the determiner and who the determined. The decision to battle unto death throws into clear relief life's ultimate desire, life itself. By his willingness to risk his very life in battle for honor, dignity, and freedom, C-1 established his independence from all external determinations, including life. The paradox is that were C-2 to have died in battle, C-1 would have lost all possibilities of winning the very recognition from the self-conscious being that he risked his life for. The only recognition he would have received would have been the recognition of a corpse. But insofar as C-2 chose life over honor and dignity, signified by his willingness to recognize C-1's authority, he had become C-1's slave.

Paradoxically, C-2's slave-consciousness was no longer a self-determining consciousness and his recognition—a slave's recognition—could not be a freely willed one. Therefore, C-1's triumph did not assure the certainty that comes from true independence or freedom. A slave is property, a virtual object. From C-2's perspective, had he died fighting for freedom, he would have only become the slave of the ultimate master, death.

The asylum seeker is in C-2's position. He has chosen life over death in escaping the persecution at the hands of the regime of his native land. At the series of "gates" of the host country, he chooses life over honor, dignity, and self-determining freedom. The gatekeepers themselves may be slaves to their own governments and truth regimes to which they have uncritically or unavoidably submitted. Their submissions may have, in their own equivalents, been a choice of life over death. Consider, for instance, an immigration judge who told me, after I had described in well-documented detail the circumstances in Sri Lanka that had threatened the defendant who stood before him pleading asylum: "Thank you for educating the court on the conditions in Sri Lanka. I found the facts quite persuasive. But under the circumstances I must act on the assertion by our own State Department that Tamils have no fear of persecution in Sri Lanka because of their ethnicity." Vis-à-vis the U.S. government, the judge was in the position of C-2.

When facing the asylum seeker, however, the gatekeeper, as a representative of the government, becomes the master. The asylum seeker, by trying to tell a consistent narrative rather than an inconsistent but honest one about his experience, is submitting to the gatekeepers' certainties about the world in order to live, in order to prevent himself from being deported back to literal or figurative death.

The major apparent difference between Hegel's master/slave and the government/its official or the gatekeeper/asylum seeker is that Hegel's self-conscious agents first encounter each other as equals; the other two are unequal pairs. However, if viewed at a level of a higher moral order, C-1, the gatekeeper's choices aren't encouraging ones either. Denying C-2 asylum carries its own risks for C-1. There is that risk in deporting C-2 to his death. What kind of victory would that be for C-1? The other risk lies in the consequences of winning the battles of wills, narratives, truth claims, and self-certainties: the risk of his own moral death.

The master–slave parable does not end there, nor does *PhG* end with the end of the parable. But I must end here for now, leaving behind a final point worth pondering by interrogating Hegelian modernity itself.

Do all cultures give "recognition" so important a place in the life of a person, a people, or a nation? Recognition, in the final analysis, is about truth claims and hence truth. Hegel's *Phenomenology* as a view of history is shot through with Christian presuppositions, among which the most important one is the status of truth. Christianity is paradigmatic of the single-truth ideology. Where the truth is one, different-truth claims have no place, and in the face of difference, the conditions are ripe only for conquest, conversion, or "colonization." Imagine a world in which what is sought after is not primarily recognition but to be left alone, to be let be. Recognition may well be of practical importance when it comes to the gates guarded by governmentality. But many who are given asylum find themselves, as minorities, for instance, confronting gates and gatekeepers where recognition is made into the issue repeatedly when what is asked for by the asylees and minorities is to be let be.

REFERENCES

Aleinikoff, T. A. (1995). State-centered refugee-law. From resettlement to containment. In E. V. Daniel & J. C. Knudsen (Eds.), *Mistrusting refugees* (pp. 257–78). Los Angeles: University of California Press.

Clifford, J. (1981). On ethnographic authority. *Representations, 2*(Spring), 132–143). Berkeley: University of California Press.

Daniel, E. V. (1984). *Fluid signs: Being a person the Tamil way.* Berkeley: University of California Press.

Daniel, E. V. (1995). *Charred lullabies: Chapters in an anthropography of violence.* Princeton, NJ: Princeton University Press.

Dirks, N. (1996). Reading culture: Anthropology and the textualization of India. In E. V. Daniel & J. F. Peck (Eds.), *Culture and contexture* (pp. 275–295). Berkeley: University of California Press.

Dreyfus, H. L. (1991). *Being-in-the-world: A commentary on Heidegger's being and time.* Cambridge, MA: MIT Press.

Dreyfus, H. L., & Rabinow, P. (1983). *Michel Foucault: Beyond structuralism and hermeneutics.* Chicago: University of Chicago Press.

Etherege, G. (1979). The art of complaisance. In J. Barnard (Ed.), *The man of mode* (pp. 1–24). London: Methuen.

Evans-Pritchard, E. E. (1940). *The Nuer.* New York: Oxford University Press.

Fischer, M. J. (1995). Starting over: How, what and for whom does one write about refugees? The poetics and politics of refugee film as ethnographic access in a media-saturated world. In E. V. Daniel & J. C. Knudsen (Eds.), *Mistrusting refugees* (pp. 126–150). Los Angeles: University of California Press.

Foucault, M. (1977). Nietzsche, genealogy, history. In D. F. Bouchard (Ed.), *Language, counter-memory, practice* (pp. 139–164). Ithaca, NY: Cornell University Press. (Original work published 1971)

Foucault, M. (1994). *Ethics, subjectivity and truth.* Ed. P. Rabinow. New York: New Press.

Fuglerund, O. (1999). *Life on the outside: The Tamil diaspora and long distance nationalism.* London: Pluto Press.

Hacking, I. (1990). *The taming of chance.* Cambridge: Cambridge University Press.

Hacking, I. (2002). *Historical ontology.* Cambridge, MA: Harvard University Press.

Hegel, G. W. F. (1977). *Phenomenology of spirit.* Trans. A. V. Miller. New York: Oxford University Press.

Knudsen, J. C. (1995). When trust is on trial: Negotiating refugee narratives. In E. V. Daniel & J. C. Knudsen (Eds.), *Mistrusting refugees* (pp. 13–35). Los Angeles: University of California Press.

Lauer, Q. (1993). *A reading of Hegel's phenomenology of spirit.* New York: Fordham University Press.

Malkki, L. H. (1995a). Refugees and exile: From "refugee studies" to the national order of things. In W. H. Durham, E. V. Daniel, & B. Schieffelin (Eds.), *Annual review of anthropology* (Vol. 24). Palo Alto, CA: Annual Reviews.

Malkki, L. H. (1995b). *Purity and exile: Violence, memory, and national cosmology among Hutu refugees in Tanzania.* Chicago: University of Chicago Press.

Manz, B. (1995). Fostering trust in a climate of fear. In E. V. Daniel & J. C. Knudsen (Eds.), *Mistrusting refugees* (pp. 151–167). Los Angeles: University of California Press.

Margolis, J. (1995). *Interpretation radical but not unruly.* Berkeley: University of California Press.

Marriott, M. (1976). Diversity without dualsim. In B. Kapferer (Ed.), *Transactions and meaning: Directions in the anthropology of exchange and symbolic behavior* (pp.109–42). Philadelphia: Institute for the Study of Human Issues.

Peirce, C. S. (1990). The *monist* metaphysical series. In N. Houser & C. Klosel (Eds.), *The essential peirce* (pp. 285–371). Bloomington: Indiana University Press. (Original work published 1891–1893)

Pinkard, T. (1994). *Hegel's phenomenology: The sociality of reason.* Cambridge: Cambridge University Press.

Shaharani, N. M. (1995). Afghanistan's Muhajirin (Muslim "refugee warriors"): Politics of mistrust and distrust of politics. In E. V. Daniel & J. C. Knudsen (Eds.), *Mistrusting refugees* (pp. 187–206). Los Angeles: University of California Press.

Williams, R. (1976). *Keywords: A vocabulary of culture and society.* New York: Oxford University Press.

Young, A. (1996). Bodily memory and traumatic memory. In P. Antze & M. Lambeck (Eds.), *Tense past: Cultural essays in trauma and memory* (pp. 89–102). New York: Routledge.

Zolberg, A. R., Suhrke, A., & Aguayo, S. (Eds). (1989). *Escape from violence.* New York: Oxford University Press.

5

Transnational Ties and Mental Health

Eleanor J. Murphy
Columbia University

The psychological well-being of immigrants has consistently evoked scholarly investigation in various forms—from the earlier works on European immigrants to the United States to contemporary analyses of Latin American, Asian, and African immigrants. With immigration conceptualized as a unique and profound stressor, rapid and uncomplicated assimilation into the host society has been traditionally viewed as the epitome of psychological adjustment (Berry, 1995). Consequently, researchers have paid much attention to factors that enhance or deter assimilation. Recently, however, the assimilation model has encountered a tweaking of sorts, with the contrasting of earlier modes of incorporation into the new country, to that of more recent forms of migration patterns. Among the newer modes of assimilation, transnationalism—the maintenance of social ties across national borders—has been increasingly featured by immigration scholars, who have demonstrated the necessity and importance of transnational activities among recent immigrants. Although much of the previous research has emphasized social and economic outcomes, very little attention has been paid to mental or psychological health as a function of transnational ties. In this chapter, by drawing on findings from a recent study of West Indian immigrants, in addition to incorporating works from theorists who study transnationalism, I highlight the role of transnational activities in their psychological adjustment. Furthermore, I emphasize the need for further empirical and theoretical inquiry into transnationalism as it relates to mental health among immigrants in general.

In studying immigrants' social adjustment, researchers have focused on general patterns and factors that may enhance or hinder assimilation in a particular immigrant group (Berry, 1995). A common definition of assimilation is the gradual incorporation into the new society via the adaptation of the customs and values of that society with a simultaneous relinquishment or modification of traditional customs and values of the sending society. This construct has also been utilized by many analysts in developing frameworks for understanding immigrants' patterns of general settlement, their modes of incorporation into the host society, and the social, economic, political, and psychological outcomes for these immigrants (Berry, 1995; Foner, 2001; Portes & Zhou, 1994; Waters, 1999). More recently, however, researchers have noted that the assimilationist model is significantly limited in view of the fact that current immigration and settlement patterns are deviating from the traditional ways in which previous immigrant groups might have been incorporated in the United States (Portes & Rambaut, 1990, 1997). Although assimilation may have been conceptualized as a linear process at one time, within the last decade or so, many researchers have begun to address the notion of a more complex and globalized form of immigrant adaptation and integration. For example, many recent immigrants have been observed to retain extensive ties to their home countries while attempting to settle and develop in the new country (Furnham, 1987). Consequently, various constructs are now emerging, and these relatively newer expressions have been broadened to accommodate the contemporary forms of migration and settlement.

A highly salient concept that has emanated from this discourse is transnationalism, or transnational ties (Glick Schiller, Basch, & Szanton Blanc, 1995; Goldring, 1996; Mahler, 1998; Portes, Guarnizo, & Landolt, 1999; Smith & Guarnizo, 1998). Among the major transnational theorists, Portes and colleagues have defined transnationalism as the maintenance of occupations or activities that *necessarily* require regular social contacts over time across national borders and/or across cultures (Portes et al., 1999). Foroun and Glick Schiller (2001) advanced the concept of transnationalism as a constant movement developed and sustained by immigrants who build extensive networks linking the new country and the country of origin.

These definitions convey the idea that transnationalism occurs on a variety of levels, from familial and community to economic and political. Instances of transnationalism can be found with the Salvadorians living in New York, who send remittances and write letters to friends and family back home (Mahler, 2001); the Dominicans who establish political parties with offices that span the United States and the Dominican Republic (Graham, 2001); the West Indians who feature the largest annual ethnic and cultural parade in New York (Foner, 2001); the Asian Indians who promote investments in business ventures in India (Lessinger, 1992); and so forth.

Indeed, research analysts have begun to develop theoretical and empirical bodies of literature that take into account these forms of interactions. Although transnational practices have always occurred, even among the earliest waves of immigrants, recent technological advances (both in the home countries and in America) have facilitated the movement between nation-states, thereby making the study of this construct now more accessible than ever (Foner, 2001). For example, prepaid phone cards along with decreasing rates have allowed immigrants to indulge in more frequent and longer contact with loved ones, or to conduct business transactions via telephone. Rapid transformations in the media like television, videotapes, and, most recently, the Internet have exponentially broadened the range and intensity of transnational ties. Consequently, virtually every recent immigrant group features many different forms and levels of transnationalism. In describing transnational activities, an important caveat is that some of the activities are not immediately apparent as transnational activities, because they may seem routine, unnecessary, and common to immigrants and nonimmigrants alike. However, even the same activity may warrent completely different interpretations depending on whether the individual doing the activity is a recent immigrant or not. For example, a third- or fourth-generation Mexican American who visits Mexico might view the visit as a more leisurely or symbolic activity, whereas for a first-generation Mexican, this activity may be necessary to maintain contact with immediate family members, or otherwise have a direct impact on his or her current life circumstances.

TRANSNATIONAL TIES AND MENTAL HEALTH

The task of settling into a new country can place an immigrant at increased of anxiety due to constant pressures and worries about being able to "make it," depression around unrealized expectations, and decreased satisfaction with life as a result of a host of concurrent stresses associated with readjustment (Baptiste, Hardy, & Lewis, 1997; Gopaul-McNicol & Brice-Baker, 1997; Murphy & Mahalingam, in press). However, immigrants have been shown to rely on various strategies that enable them to be relatively resilient amid uncertainty and other difficult circumstances. For example, the maintenance of informal networks of friends and kin has been shown to be a common denominator in ensuring instrumental and emotional security for West Indians and other new immigrants (Foner, 2001). The social implications of transnationalism at the community, familial, and individual levels have been recognized, despite the relative ambiguousity around its definition (Foner, 1987; Pessar, 1999). Immigration literature has begun to focus on transnational ties and practices among new immigrants, with the recognition that they may serve to socially enhance the immigrants' lives by directly or indirectly promoting and maintaining valuable social networks. In fact, current bodies of work stress the findings that transnational ties can produce desirable social and economic among immigrant groups, including West Indians (Bobb, 2001; Foner, 2001; Rogers, 2001). Although transnationalism has rarely been studied in mental health, it has been implicitly linked to certain factors such as social support, ethnic identity, and perceived discrimination—all of which have been associated with psychological health. To date, there are few, if any, studies that examine the ways in which the maintenance of transnational ties plays a role in mental health outcomes for immigrants.

THE INFLUENCE OF TRANSNATIONAL ACTIVITIES ON PSYCHOSOCIAL OUTCOMES

One of the basic ways in which immigrants maintain ties with their home countries is through contact with close relatives and/or friends whom they have left behind (Foner, 2001). This type of contact usually involves communication and the provision of money and goods by the immigrant to the people left at home. For instance, in West Indian families, a pattern of immigration called serial migration occurs, usually when the head of a household, usually a mother or father, leave the Caribbean to seek employment in the United States. Occasionally the family may migrate as one unit, but in the majority of families, at least some of the children are left behind to continue schooling, while the parent gets established in the new country. This phenomenon necessitates continuous contact between the parent and the children across borders, or between the parent and the person(s) left in charge of the children. Thus parents may continue to provide financial support by sending remittances, or by sending material goods to those left behind (Crawford-Brown & Rattray, 2001; Foner, 2001). In addition, relatives may communicate with each other via telephone, airmail, or even e-mail. Sending remittances and communicating via letters have been shown to be common transnational activities of Salvadorian immigrants in suburban New York (Mahler, 2001).

Another way of achieving contact is by traveling back to the home country to visit friends and relatives, or providing assistance for friends and relatives to visit. The frequency and nature of this may depend on several factors such as affordability of vacations, immigration status, and conditions in home country (Foner, 2001; Kasinitz, 2001). Due to the increasing availability of affordable airline tickets, traveling back and forth on a regular basis has become relatively easy even for the less affluent immigrants. The ease of travel in turn facilitates business and economic transactions between borders. The question remains whether traveling to visit should be classified as a transnational activity, because almost everyone who can afford to travels at some point in his or her life. Again, this might be somewhat difficult to tease apart, because only a subjective appraisal by the immigrant may dictate just what type of travel and visitation is taking place. Another form of transnational travel occurs when immigrants come to the United States seeking temporary employment, work in the United States for a few months, and then return home. This cyclical employment pattern may continue over a period of several years, until the immigrant may decide to stay permanently in the United States (Henke, 2001). Examples of such can be found with housekeepers, nurse's aides, and manual laborers.

For many immigrants who are unable to travel frequently, the presence of a vibrant cultural arena in the host country may ward off feelings of alienation and facilitate adjustment. Most immigrants tend to reside in niches or enclaves for that reason (Foner, 2001; Henke, 2001). Among Caribbeans, for example, many of the cultural activities take place in the form of leisurely and informal get-togethers, parties, and social outings. Other activities such as club meetings, church services, and concerts may be more formerly planned and attended. Cultural ties not only maintain emotional affirmation, but also may lead to instrumental support through contact with other immigrants (Foner, 2001).

Although some cultural activities may be pursued on a largely individual and informal basis, with the view that they are purely social and leisurely outlets, others may be seen as vehicles for further agency and developments and thus require more organized planning, in the form of group solidarity and leadership. Some of these cultural practices may have further implications for economic and other social conditions in the lives of immigrants as well as those remaining in the home countries. Thus a broad array of political activism may emerge from what started as cultural pursuits

Individuals who have achieved a certain degree of economic autonomy may use their economic success in the United States to generate and maintain further economic activity in their homelands (Foner, 2001; Lessinger, 1992). Furthermore, they may start businesses in the United States that rely on the importing of commodities from their home countries. Because of the desire to continue traditional customs, immigrants create a local market for these goods and services that can be obtained from resources in their home countries. Conversely, there may be immigrants who send remittances and products from the United States back to their home countries to maintain grocery stores and other businesses there. Other immigrants may see opportunities for investment in real estate back home, while establishing the United States as their primary residence.

TRANSNATIONAL TIES AND SOCIAL SUPPORT

Transnationalism has been shown to solidify social networks among immigrants (Bobb, 2001), which in turn has implications for psychological well-being. This is because the social networks may produce tangible resources, social capital and emotional support that may off-set some of the alienating and stressful effects of immigration. A cor-pus of research devoted to investigating the impact of social support has resulted in a large number of empirical studies that provide evi-dence for the postulation that social support serves to directly de-crease emotional distress, and also functions as a buffer against the stress brought about by trying events (Ritsner, Modai, & Ponizovsky, 2000). Allen (1987) maintained that most first-generation and even some second-generation West Indians tend to have a kind of "so-journer" status. Consequently, they keep in close contact with other West Indians by residing in ethnic enclaves (Regis, 1988), participating in social organizations such as sports, taking regular trips to the Ca-ribbean, funding relatives, and sponsoring social and political events in the Caribbean (Foner, 1987).

Most bodies of social support literature tend to advance the general view that social support and social interactions are highly beneficial to psychological well-being (Sarason, Levine, Bhasham, & Sarason, 1983). Nonetheless, some studies have yielded mixed findings on this issue, and point to the paradoxical nature of such social activities that may serve to increase, rather than decrease, everyday stress (Antonucci, 1998). Some studies, for instance, have elucidated the fact that because of their migration patterns, some Caribbean immigrants are obliged to operate transnationally (Pessar, 1999). Under those con-ditions, transnational ties may not necessarily yield positive conse-quences. For example, children may remain in the Caribbean for schooling, while their parents are in the United States; women may travel back and forth to obtain temporary domestic work, and so forth (Foner, 1987). Although these activities may help them to achieve so-cial cohesion, by forcing them to retain contact with certain networks or people, it might also place a burden on those in the provider role. In addition, it can be speculated that a certain type of frustrating nostal-gia may be induced via prolonged but distant contact with loved ones. Besides relational burdens, it has been debated that relying solely on transnational connections might be a poor professional and economic strategy in the long run, keeping immigrants in low-paying, low-status occupations and enhancing suspicion and mistrust of fellow immigrants (Nee & Sanders, 2001).

TRANSNATIONAL TIES AND ETHNIC IDENTITY

Besides enhancing social cohesion and a sense of social support, transnational ties may also help immigrants to consolidate their eth-nic identity at a time when they may find a number of different identi-ties suddenly thrust on them. Ethnic identity has been defined as a person's subjective sense of belonging to a certain group or culture (Phinney, 1990). This construct has received a great deal of attention among social psychologists. Given the multiethnic society that America has become, largely because of immigration, it is apparent that ethnic identity has important implications for the way in which people see themselves, and their perception of how society responds to them, both of which impact psychological well-being (Phinney, Horenczy, Liebkind, & Vedder, 2001). For Caribbean immigrants of African descent, ethnic identity comes into play for a number of reasons. Like their European-descended immigrant counterparts, West Indians arrive in the United States with the hope to integrate and assimilate into the larger society (Waters, 1999). However, unlike the former group, the latter group's ability to assimilate is restricted along racial lines (Gopaul-McNicol & Brice-Baker, 1997), like other minority immigrants of color. If and when they do assimilate, their assimilation, by and large, is limited to the larger group of African Americans.

In the United States, African Americans have been among the most disparaged groups, even compared to other ethnic minority groups, having a historical legacy of slavery and oppression (Phinney & Onwughalu, 1996; Waters, 1999). Caribbean immigrants are racially similar to African Americans and share certain historical elements of being forcibly removed from their homeland and brought to another country to work as slaves. However, immigrants from the Caribbean have been able to enjoy relative autonomy in their home countries due to the absence of the colonizers who initially enslaved them. There, Blacks are in the majority and the everyday racial persecution and harassment encountered by African Americans is largely absent in the Caribbean (Gopaul-McNicol, 1993; Waters, 1999). Hence, the immigrants enter the United States with an outlook similar to that of other immigrant groups—one that encourages them to believe that hard work, education, and determination can overcome all obstacles—including racism (Portes & Rumbaut, 1990). Phinney and Onwughalu (1996) conducted a study comparing the effects of racial identity on the attitudes toward American values, among African Americans and African immigrants. They found that for African Americans, a racial identity was strongly associated with a negative attitude toward American ideals, but positively correlated with self-esteem, whereas for the African immigrants there was no correlation between racial identity, attitudes, and self-esteem.

It has been argued that West Indian immigrants have an identity that stresses their country of origin, and although they do have a Black racial identity, it is produces a different kind of consciousness than that of African Americans (Rogers, 2001). Furthermore, immigrants with stronger transnational ties tend to have a stronger ethnic identity, which serves as a potential buffer against racial prejudice (Rogers, 2001). This "identity" offers them psychological protection in a number of ways: First, maintaining the idea that they came from a culture where they are valued and accepted, and second, that they have the option to go back there if things don't work out in the host country, can be very comforting to immigrants who feel a sense of alienation (Rogers,

2001). It has also been suggested that this immigrant identity may be tested and threatened as they spend more time in the United States and become more aware of the pervasive nature of racial discrimination (Phinney & Onwughalu, 1996; Rogers, 2001; Waters, 1999). This may lead to increased frustration and dissatisfaction with life.

As research suggests, ethnic identity may also influence the perception of and stress associated with racial discrimination (Waters, 1994). Afro-Caribbeans with an immigrant identity may understand that racism exists; they may have the psychological option of not viewing it as the most determinative factor in their lives. Instead, the emphasis is placed on opportunities and rewards for ambition and hard work. Even though the ability to bypass racism as an explanation for poor treatment in society may decline as the immigrant spends more time in the United States (Bobb, 2001; Waters, 1999), it may afford some protection during the initial years of settlement.

THE TRANSNATIONALISM SCALE

In order to examine the relationship between transnational activities and psychological well being among first-generation West Indians, a self-report questionnaire was administered to a convenience and venue sample of 137 adults aged 18 to 54 in urban New York. The questionnaire included a measure that was constructed to assess the types and frequency of transnational activities, such as regularly participating in cultural events, and active engagement in political transactions (Transnationalism Scale). Twenty-one items for the scale were developed by drawing on previous qualitative research that described the nature and extent of transnational activities among various immigrant populations including West Indians. The items were grouped into four domains (family ties, cultural ties, economic ties, and political ties) for face validity. Each item described an activity and the respondents were required to indicate on a 6-point Likert scale (0 = *have not done* to 5 = *very often*), the extent to which they participated in the activity within the past 2 years. This scale, with its psychometric properties and factor loadings for each domain, along with the sample on which it was validated, has been described extensively elsewhere (Murphy & Mahalingam, 2004). Once the scale had been evaluated for reliability and validity, the sample size was increased to 200 participants (77 males and 123 females).

Although the factor-analytic structure of the scale was generally consistent with the original grouping of domain items, we were able to further classify and refine some of the domains. For instance, the domain of family ties showed two main groupings of activities: communication, and travel. In addition, family-related communication received the highest score from the respondents. This was contrasted with political activism, which received the lowest score of all the domains (Murphy & Mahalingam, 2004). Interestingly, the overall composite score for the scale was lower than the midpoint of the range—an unanticipated finding. However, based on the way that the scale was constructed, it was possible that the transnational activities of the respondents was not particularly varied, even though they engaged in frequent social and family-related communication and movement across borders. This may be true of West Indians in general, but might be different for other groups. Further research might help to elucidate whether it would be of superior utility to measure transnational activities within separate domains, such as political ties versus familial and social ties, versus having a monolithic scale that lumps the various domains together.

Among the drawbacks of the scale was that it assessed respondents' subjective perception of their participation in various activities, and was not held against any external or objective observation. There can be significant differences between people's appraisals and their actions, due to social desirability that is elicited by broad surveys. This limitation might be addressed through other concurrent and/or qualitative assessments used in conjunction with the scale.

TRANSNATIONAL TIES AND MENTAL HEALTH: FURTHER DIRECTIONS

Indices of psychological well-being, such as anxiety, depression, and life satisfaction, were measured and correlated with scores on the transnationalism scale. Although transnationalism was related to higher life satisfaction, it was also related to higher depression. Depression and anxiety have been shown to go hand in hand with various types of loss. For many immigrants, leaving their home countries represents loss on several different levels, and consequently the immigrants may go through a period of mourning (de Dellarossa, 1978; Lijtmaer, 2001; Marlin, 1994). This mourning may be associated with negative affect states such as depression, but it may also motivate immigrants to try to hold on to whatever they can of their past. Therefore, they may engage in a wide range of transnational activities, or engage in a few activities with a high frequency. This effect may also be bidirectional, for instance, with immigrants who call home more often being at higher risk of feeling depressed. Studies have shown that immigrants who are in this phase begin to idealize their home countries, and speak of "back home" in glowing terms (Lijtmaer, 2001). This may actually represent an important step in acculturation, the necessity of grieving a loss, before moving on to further stages in the process. Although theorists have justifiably cautioned against conceptualizing the nostalgic sentiments and associated activities of immigrants as transnationalism (Foroun & Glick Schiller, 2001), it is still possible that these sentiments might propel action on an individual basis, which may result in a mass organizational-level undertaking. For instance, on the transnationalism scale, political activism was shown to be significantly correlated with depression. Political and economic activism might be viewed as functional activities, which may not necessarily yield the emotional rewards that social communication does. Hence West Indians who are very active politically may be at risk of burnout and other factors that lead to depression. They may be also more aware of and less insulated from the harsher realities of overcoming cultural and economic barriers that plague many immigrant groups. It therefore appears that transnationalism might be used as a coping mechanism when people are anxious or depressed, but it might also bring about depressive and anxious symptoms, depending on the modality through which it operates. In other to address issues of causality between activities and psychological factors, it would be necessary to conduct further ethnographic research to generate additional theories, as well as to conduct longitudinal research exploring precisely what factors motivate immigrants to participate in such activities.

Demographic factors including socioeconomic status (SES) and other constructs such as ethnic identity and social support were further examined. The primary results from the study revealed that transnational ties were positively related to ethnic identity, although weaker than expected. Transnsationalism encompasses activities that are done and therefore represent a more functional aspect of keeping in touch with one's culture, whereas ethnic identity involves ideas and attitudes—intellectual abstractions that may or may not mirror actual activities. More specifically, respondents who endorsed more frequent social and family related communication also endorsed higher ethnic identity. Although this was not surprising for first-generation immigrants, it would be interesting to know whether this relationship holds for second-generation West Indians, who are less likely to have remaining relatives and/or friends living in their parents' home countries. Additionally, it would be of interest to examine whether other immigrant groups with different ethnic and racial identities necessarily derive any particular benefit or drawback from transnational ties, where their ethnic identity is concerned. Further, longitudinal research might reveal changes, as immigrants spend more time in the new country, in the patterns of the relationships between transnational ties and ethnic identity.

Transnationalism was also positively related to SES—another finding that was expected. Although the availability and affordability of communication devices such as cellular phones are not as restricted to the financially well off as might have been once the case, there are nonetheless limitations on the resources of less affluent individuals. SES may also dictate the backdrop under which transnational activities are conducted—for instance, having to send remittances and necessary goods to family has a different meaning than sending goods to maintain a store back home. Consequently, transnationalism may be stressful, depending on the way in which it is contextualized. For example, sending money and supplies to friends and relatives in the home country could result in financial strain, thereby producing anxiety and depression.

Transnationalism was also shown to be significantly related to social support. More specifically, the domains of social and cultural ties, family and social-related communication, and financial and commercial ties were positively related to social support. West Indians rely heavily on family members and informal social networks among friends and acquaintances. On the other hand, they appear less likely to rely on government funded community resources. A notable result was that social support was positively related to life satisfaction, but also *positively* related to anxiety. Given that much research on social support has demonstrated the positive side of receiving familial support, it is obvious that there are psychological benefits derived from having such connections. It may be harder to understand how reliance on family members can actually maintain a certain level of stress that could have been reduced, were other sources of support tapped into. Research nonetheless has shown that opportunities for family tensions and disappointments do exist, and these factors may offset some of the stress-reducing benefits that come from familial support. This notion is supported by Antonucci's (1998) work on the stressful effects of social support.

The complex pattern of association between transnationalism and the social and psychological factors suggests that this phenomenon comprises important activities, some of which might be the result of current circumstances that immigrants find themselves in, and others of which help to bring about and maintain improvements in the lives of West Indians. Moreover, it is clear that different forms of transnational ties are differentially related to psychosocial outcomes. Although the study described in this chapter highlighted a form of transnationalism that seemed to occur primarily at the family and community level, other major forms of transnational ties, such as larger economic undertakings and political organizations, should be investigated and statistically measured as well.

Another point of interest would be to examine what role, if any, gender plays in the relationship between transitional ties and psychological outcomes. Previous research has shown that there are gendered patterns of transnational operations, especially with regard to certain types of economic and social activities (Ho, 1991; Hondagneu-Sotelo, 1994). In this study, although there were no significant gender differences on overall scores for the scale, the relative distribution of scores across domains for men and women were not assessed. That may be an area that requires deeper probing.

The transnationalism scale is a preliminary step in linking transnationalism with broader adaptation and integration strategies. Although it remains to be seen whether such a scale can be fitted into a more generic template and used among other immigrant groups, the transnational scale has already demonstrated some reliability and validity for use among English-speaking Caribbean immigrants. It is necessary to conduct further research that would be instrumental in refining this measure, thereby increasing its overall utility in social and behavioral science fields.

REFERENCES

Allen, E. (1987). *West Indians. Clinical guidelines in cross-cultural mental health.* New York: John Wiley & Sons.

Antonucci, T. (1998). The negative effects of close social relationships. *Family Relations: Interdisciplinary Journal of Applied Family Studies: Special Issue: The family as a context for health and well-being.* 47(4), 379–384.

Baptiste, D., Jr., Hardy, K., & Lewis, L. (1997). Family therapy with English Caribbean immigrant families in the United States: Issues of emigration, immigration, culture and race. *Contemporary Family Therapy, 19*(3), 337–359.

Berry, J. W. (1995). Psychology of acculturation. In N. R. Goldberger (Eds.), *The culture and psychology reader* (pp. 475–488). New York: New York University Press.

Bobb, V. (2001). Neither ignorance nor bliss: Race, racism and the West Indian immigrant experience. In H. Cordero-Guzman, R. Smith, & R. Grosfoguel (Eds.), *Migration, transnationalization & race in a changing New York* (pp. 211–238). Philadelphia, PA: Temple University Press.

Crawford-Brown, C., & Rattray, J. (2001). Parent–child relationships in Caribbean families. In *Culturally diverse parent-child and family relationships: A guide for social workers and other practitioners* (pp. 107–130). New York: Columbia University Press.

De Dellarossa G. S. (1978). The professional of immigrant descent. *International Journal of Psychoanalysis, 59*(1), 37–44.

Foner, N. (1987). *New immigrants in New York.* New York: Columbia University Press.

Foner, N. (2001). West Indian migration to New York: An overview. In *Islands in the city* (pp. 1–22). Berkeley: University of California Press.

Foner, N. (2001). Transnationalism then and now: New York immigrants today and at the turn of the twentieth century. In H. Cordero-Guzman, R. Smith, & R. Grosfoguel (Eds.), *Migration, transnationalization & race in a changing New York* (pp. 35–57). Philadelphia, PA: Temple University Press.

Foroun, G., & Glick Schiller, N. (2001). The generation of identity: Redefining the second generation within a transnational social field. In H. Cordero-Guzman, R. Smith, & R. Grosfoguel (Eds.), *Migration, transnationalization & race in a changing New York* (pp. 35–57). Philadelphia, PA: Temple University Press.

Furnham, A. (1988). The adjustment of sojourners. In Y. Kim & W. Gudykunst (Eds.), *Cross-cultural adaptation: Current approaches* (pp. 42–62). Newbury Park, CA: Sage.

Glick Schiller, N., Basch, L., & Szanton Blanc, C. (1995). From immigrant to transmigrant: Theorizing transnational migration. *Anthropological Quarterly, 68*(1), 48–63.

Graham, P. (2001). Political incorporation and reincorporation: simultaneity in the Dominican migrant experience. In H. Cordero-Guzman, R. Smith, &

R. Grosfoguel (Eds.), *Migration, transnationalization & race in a changing New York* (pp. 87–108). Philadelphia, PA: Temple University Press.

Goldring, L. (1996). Blurring Borders: Constructing transnational community in the process of Mexico–US migration. *Research in Community Sociology, 6,* 69–104.

Gopaul-McNicol, S. (1993). *Working with West Indian families.* New York: Guilford Press.

Gopaul-McNicol, S., & Brice-Baker, J. (1997). Caribbean Americans. In S. Friedman (Ed.), *Treatment of anxiety disorders across cultures* (pp. 81–98). New York: Guilford Press.

Henke, H. (2001). *Patterns of migration to the United States in the twentieth century. The West Indian Americans.* Westport, CT: Greenwood Press.

Ho, C. (1991). *Salt-water Trinnies: Afro-Trinidadian immigrant networks and non-assimilation in Los Angeles.* New York: AMS Press.

Hondagneu-Sotelo, P. (1994). *Gendered transitions* (pp. 98–147). Berkeley: University of California Press.

Kasinitz, P. (2001). Invisible no more? West Indian Americans in the social scientific imagination. In N. Foner (Eds.), *Islands in the city. West Indian migration to New York* (pp. 257–275). New York: Columbia University Press.

Lessinger, J. (1992). Investing or going home? A transnational strategy among Indian immigrants in the United States. In N. Glick Schiller, L. Basch, & C. Blanc-Szanton (Eds.), *Towards a transnational perspective on migration* (pp. 53–80). New York: New York Academy of Sciences.

Lijtmaer, R. (2001). Splitting and nostalgia in recent immigrants: Psychodynamic considerations. *Journal of the American Academy of Psychoanalysis, 29*(3), 427–438.

Mahler, S. (1998). Theoretical and empirical contributions toward a research agenda for transnationalism. In M. P. Smith & L. E. Guarnizo (Eds.), *Transnationalism from below* (pp. 64–100). New Brunswick, NJ: Transaction Press.

Mahler, S. (2001). Suburban transnational migrants: Long Island's Salvadorans. In H. Cordero-Guzman, R. Smith, & R. Grosfoguel (Eds.), *Migration, transnationalization & race in a changing New York* (pp. 109–130). Philadelphia, PA: Temple University Press.

Marlin, O. (1994). Special issues in the analytic treatment of immigrants and refugees. *Issues in Psychoanalytic Psychology, 16*(1), 7–16.

Murphy, E. J., & Mahalingam, R. (2004). Transnational ties and mental health of Caribbean immigrants. *Journal of Immigrant Health, 6*(4), 167–178.

Murphy, E. J., & Mahalingam, R. (In press). Perceived congruence between expectations and outcomes: Implications for mental health among Caribbean immigrants. *American Journal of Orthopsychiatry.*

Nee, V., & Sanders, J. (2001). Trust in ethnic ties: Social capital and immigrants. *Trust in society. Russell Sage Foundation series on trust* (Vol. 2, pp. 374–392). New York: Russell Sage Foundation.

Pessar, P. R. (1999). Engendering migration studies. *American Behavioral Scientist, 42*(4), 577–600.

Phinney, J. S. (1990). Ethnic identity in adolescents and adults: Review of research. *Psychological Bulletin, 108,* 499–514.

Phinney, J. S., Horenczy, K., Liebkind, K., & Vedder, P. (2001). Ethnic identity, immigration, and wellbeing: An interactional perspective. *Journal of Social Issues, 57*(3), 493–510.

Phinney, J. S., & Onwughalu, M. (1996). Racial identity and perception of American ideals among African American and African students in the United States. *International Journal of Intercultural Relations, 20*(2), 127–140.

Portes, A. (1997). Immigration theory for a new century: Some problems and opportunities. *International Migration Review, 31*(4), 799–825.

Portes, A., & Rambaut, R. (1990). *Immigrant America: A portrait.* Berkeley: University of California Press.

Portes, A., Gurarnizo, L. E., & Landolt, P. (1999). The study of transnationalism: Pitfalls and promise of an emergent research field. *Ethnic and Racial Studies Review, 22*(2), 217–237.

Portes, A., & Zhou, M. (1994). Should immigrants assimilate? *Public Interest, 16,* 18–34.

Regis, H. (1988). A theoretical framework for the study of the psychological sense of community of English-speaking Caribbean immigrants. *Journal of Black Psychology, 15*(1), 57–76.

Ritsner, M., Modai, I., & Ponizovsky, A. (2000). The stress support patterns and psychological distress of immigrants. *Stress Medicine, 16,* 129–147.

Rogers, R. (2001). "Black like who?" Afro-Caribbean immigrants, African Americans, and the politics of group identity. In *Islands in the city* (pp. 163–192). Berkeley: University of California Press.

Sarason, I., Levine, H., Basham, R., & Sarason, B. (1983). Assessing social support: The Social Support Questionnaire. *Journal of Personality and Social Psychology, 44*(1), 127–139.

Smith, M., & Guarnizo, L. (1998). *Transnationalism from below.* New Brunswick, NJ: Tansaction Press.

Waters, M. (1994). Ethnic and racial identification of second-generation Black immigrants in New York City. *International Migration Review 28*(4, 108), 795–820.

Waters, M. (1999). *Black identities: Immigrant dreams and American realities..* Cambridge, MA: Harvard University Press.

Part II

Immigration and Race

6

A Two-Level Approach to Anti-Immigrant Prejudice and Discrimination

Thomas F. Pettigrew
University of California, Santa Cruz

Many of us writing in this volume are first-, second-, or at least third-generation North Americans. In my case, my mother emigrated from Scotland with my grandmother to the United States a century ago. The problems of winning acceptance in a strange land were central themes of my family's legends and dynamics. Let me share four vivid examples of these themes.

1. The immigration officer at Ellis Island tried to misspell their simple four-letter name of Gibb. My fiery grandmother interpreted this as an unprovoked humiliation and caused a scene over the slight. My then 6-year-old mother was badly frightened for fear they would not be allowed to enter the country. Indeed, she never forgot the trauma.

2. My grandmother steadfastly refused to become a citizen. But she became extremely anxious each January when I accompanied her to a required annual visit to register with immigration authorities.

3. My mother also remembered the intense teasing she endured in school concerning her strong Scottish accent. She quickly adapted, and later developed the thickest Virginian accent one could imagine.

4. Finally, my mother came to identify passionately with the United States. Indeed, she would not tolerate any criticism of her

adopted country—a not uncommon first-generation response. "If you don't like America," she would bluntly tell a critic, "go back to where you came from!" I would gently remind my mother that most Virginians were not immigrants; they *were* where "they came from."

But this family history had little immediate meaning for me. As a White citizen of "British" extraction in the Anglophilic and racist Virginia of the 1930s and '40s, I had no problems of acceptance. The blatant injustice that surrounded me involved the extreme prejudice and discrimination endured by Black Virginians. Consequently, I have spent most of my life combating racism and studying what social science euphemistically calls "Black–White relations."

This personal introduction explains why I long regarded racism and the problems faced by immigrants as markedly different phenomena in both intensity and form. This erroneous view grew naturally out of my special experience growing up in a Scottish-American immigrant family in the racist southern United States. It was not until the 1980s that I questioned this misconception. Starting in 1984, I began to conduct systematic research with Dutch and German colleagues on the reactions of western Europeans to the millions of new immigrants (e.g., Meertens & Pettigrew, 1997; Pettigrew, 1997, 1998b, 2000a, 2000b; Pettigrew & Meertens, 1995, 1996, 2001; Pettigrew et al., 1998; van Dick et al., 2003; Wagner, van Dick, Pettigrew, & Christ, 2003). It was clear from this work that prejudice and discrimination against racial and immigrant minorities are not nearly as different as I had thought.

TWO RESEARCH TRADITIONS
ON ANTI-IMMIGRANT ATTITUDES

A rapidly growing North American and European research literature in the social sciences focuses on prejudice and discrimination against new immigrants. (See, for example, an entire issue of the *Journal of Social Issues* devoted to immigration, edited by Esses, Dovidio, & Dion, 2001.) Findings from this work divide into two reasonably distinct categories.

1. At the individual and intergroup levels of analyses, social psychologists show that forms of anti-immigrant prejudice and discrimination closely resemble the general literature on these subjects for nonimmigrant targets (e.g., Jackson, Brown, Brown, & Marks, 2001; Pettigrew & Meertens, 1995; Pettigrew et al., 1998). In basic outline, these anti-immigration findings track most of the phenomena documented by Gordon Allport (1954) in his classic volume *The Nature of Prejudice*.

At this level, anti-immigrant prejudice and discrimination share many features in common with outgroup prejudice and discrimination in general. We note that prejudice against outgroups—whether immigrant or nonimmigrant—is typically patterned in similar ways from Australia and South Africa to North America and Europe. Thus, correlations between prejudice and demographic, political, and psychological variables at the individual level of analysis are remarkably similar across the globe.

2. At the cultural and structural levels, however, anthropologists, political scientists and sociologists demonstrate that resistance to immigrants often reveals sharply different patterns from prejudice and discrimination against other outgroups. For example, societies treat new immigrants in contrasting ways as a function of such variables as prior history with immigration, prior relationship with the immigrant group, laws regarding citizenship, the employment situation, the speed of entry of the newcomers, and the size and spatial distribution of the immigrant group.

Interestingly, several apparent discrepancies emerge in the results of the two research traditions. These ostensible inconsistencies can lead to conflicting predictions and policy implications. This chapter traces briefly each of these research traditions. Then it attempts to bring the two research literatures together and offers suggestions for resolving their apparent conflicts in results.

THE SOCIAL PSYCHOLOGICAL STUDY
OF ANTI-IMMIGRANT PREJUDICE AND DISCRIMINATION

Social psychology has shown repeatedly that the basic dynamics of prejudice are similar across a broad range of outgroup targets and outgroup situations. Of course, there are unique aspects of each type of intergroup prejudice related to different histories and situations. But the overarching disciplinary finding documents the comparability across a wide range of targets and areas. Moreover, starting with the classic research on the authoritarian personality in the 1940s (Adorno, Frenkel-Brunswik, Levinson, & Sanford, 1950), social psychologists also have found that prejudice against one outgroup typically correlates positively with prejudices against other outgroups. At the individual level of analysis, anti-immigrant prejudice is no exception to these general findings.

Western Europe's reactions to the new immigrants in their midst are best documented by one of the largest survey studies of ethnic prejudice ever conducted with probability samples. In 1988, the European Union's Eurobarometer survey (number 30) asked seven probability samples in four nations a wide range of prejudice measures about a variety of minorities (for details, see Reif & Melich, 1991). In what was then West Germany, the survey asked 985 majority respondents about Turks. In France, it asked 455 majority respondents about North Africans and 475 about southeastern Asians. In the Netherlands, it asked

462 majority respondents about Surinamers and 476 about Turks. And in Great Britain, it asked 471 majority respondents about West Indians and 482 about Asians (largely Pakistanis and Indians; Pettigrew et al., 1998; Zick, 1997).

Two key measures distinguished between blatant and subtle types of prejudice (Pettigrew & Meertens, 1995). Blatant prejudice is the traditional form; it is hot, close and direct. The 10 items that tap it involve open rejection of minorities based on presumed biological differences. Subtle prejudice is the more modern form; it is cool, distant, and indirect. The 10 items that measure it are not readily recognized as indicators of prejudice. They tap the perceived threat of the minority to traditional values of the majority, the exaggeration of cultural differences with the minority, and the absence of positive feelings toward the minority. American researchers have studied similar distinctions (Pettigrew, 1989; Sears, 1988). And, as various European writers had proposed earlier (Barker, 1982; Bergmann & Erb, 1986; Essed, 1990), the subtle prejudice measure proves equally useful in Europe.

Thus, these extensive data involve seven independent samples, four different European nations, six diverse target minorities, and two measures of prejudice. We can now look at these 14 (7 samples × 2 prejudice scales) tests of the correlates of European prejudice against immigrants (Pettigrew & Meertens, 1995) and compare them with the standard findings of North American survey data (Allport, 1954; Hood & Morris, 1997, 1998; Schuman, Steeh, Bobo, & Krysan, 1997).

In addition, the International Social Survey (ISS) of 1995 provided relevant data on 17 countries throughout Europe (Kunovich, 2002). Nine of the countries are in Western Europe, and eight are in Eastern Europe. It used as the dependent variable for a 6-item scale that directly measures attitudes toward immigrants and refugees. It asks if respondents believe immigrants "increase crime," "take jobs away from people," and are "bad for the economy." The scale also taps policy issues by asking if "the number of immigrants should be reduced" and if "refugees should not be allowed to stay."

Demographic Correlates of Prejudice: Age and Education

North American studies of prejudice routinely show that prejudice increases with the age of the respondents. These consistent patterns occur whether the target group is African Americans (Schuman et al., 1997) or Latino-American and Asian-American immigrants (Hood & Morris, 1997). This near-linear effect also emerges in the Western European data in all but one of our 14 tests. The measures of both blatant and subtle prejudice against immigrants reveal this trend (Pettigrew, 2000a; Pettigrew & Meertens, 1995). In the ISS data of 1995, age is significantly and positive associated with anti-immigrant attitudes in both Western and Eastern Europe, but not in all countries (Kunovich, 2002).

Similarly, North American research consistently finds that measures of social class, particularly education, relate negatively to prejudice against Blacks, Latinos, and Asians. An exception occurred more than a half-century ago when some surveys showed greater anti-Semitism among the better educated (Allport, 1954). This finding suggests that we will find greater prejudice among those in the social structure who perceive the greatest threat from the outgroup in question. For all but upper status immigrants (such as Hong Kong immigrants to Vancouver, Canada), the perceived threat posed by immigrants is greatest at the lower socioeconomic levels of the host society.

Once again, this pattern emerges in Europe. The 1988 Eurobarometer survey showed that for both blatant and subtle prejudice the well-educated were more tolerant of immigrants and more often favored greater rights for the new arrivals (Pettigrew, 2000a; Pettigrew & Meertens, 1995; Pettigrew et al., 1998). And the 1995 data from throughout Europe show the same trend for education in both Western and Eastern Europe (Kunovich, 2002).

Political Correlates of Prejudice: Political Conservatism, Nationalism, Group Relative Deprivation, and Interest in Politics

North American surveys consistently show that political conservatism, nationalism, and a sense of group deprivation relative to target outgroups are positively correlated with prejudice of many types (Pettigrew, 2000a, 2001b; Pettigrew & Meertens, 1995). Moreover, general interest in politics is associated with outgroup tolerance. Each of these predictors operates in the same manner in the Eurobarometer results in all seven samples for both blatant and subtle prejudice (Pettigrew, 2000a; Pettigrew & Meertens, 1995). These variables are not tested in the report on the ISS data (Kunovich, 2002).

Personality Correlate of Prejudice: Authoritarianism

Ever since the classic study of authoritarianism at the University of California at Berkeley (Adorno, et al., 1950), research in North America has consistently found a strong positive relation between this personality syndrome and prejudice. Not surprisingly, the same relationship holds in European data on prejudice against immigrants (Pettigrew, 2000b).

Experiential Correlate of Prejudice: Contact With the Outgroup

Optimal intergroup contact is one of the reliable means of reducing prejudice in the social psychological research literature (Pettigrew,

1998a; Pettigrew & Tropp, 2000, in press). Research around the globe reveals its value, and research on attitudes toward immigrants is no exception. Hood and Morris (1997) found that living in areas with Asian and Latino immigrant populations relates to significantly reduced levels of prejudice. Similarly, the Eurobarometer 30 data show that contact with immigrants throughout Western Europe—especially contact that involves friendship—is a major indicator of lowered prejudice (Pettigrew, 1997; Pettigrew & Meertens, 1995).

Research on the discriminatory behavior of individuals is less prevalent, but it also uncovers comparable findings. In a famous review, Crosby, Bromley, and Saxe (1980) summarized the research literature on subtle forms of interpersonal discrimination often committed by White Americans on black Americans. Guided by this early work in the United States, Klink and Wagner (1999) demonstrated essentially the same phenomena of interpersonal discrimination by native Germans against immigrant minorities.

THE CULTURAL AND STRUCTURAL STUDY OF ANTI-IMMIGRANT RESPONSES

At the cultural and structural levels of analysis, however, anthropologists, political scientists, and sociologists demonstrate that resistance to immigrants often reveals sharply different patterns of prejudice and discrimination against other outgroups. Consider 11 such cultural and structural examples.

Prior National Experience With Immigration. The New and Old Worlds have different experiences with immigration. For the New World, in-migration from throughout the world is a centuries-long pattern. To question the belongingness of another group can raise questions about your own group. For instance, even the most intense American racists, such as George Wallace, never question the belongingness of African Americans. In Western Europe, by contrast, the belongingness of the new immigrant groups—from the Turks to the Vietnamese—is often the first barrier for immigrants to overcome. Although there has been far more immigration into Western Europe in earlier eras than current popular thinking recognizes (Poles to Germany, Russians to France, etc.), there remains a vast difference between North America and Western Europe in prior experience with immigration.

Diverse Conceptualizations of Immigration and Citizenship Among Host Countries. Related to the belongingness issue are the contrasting ways host societies conceptualize ethnicity, citizenship, and immigration. Different frames for viewing immigration shape different receptions of immigrants (Pratto & Lemieux, 2001).

Thus, in striking contrast to North America, the Germans and British have an informal "blood" notion of their national identities. This conceptualization makes it difficult for immigrants to gain citizenship in Germany and for immigrants even with citizenship to gain full entry into the dominant group in Great Britain. It also means that ideologies of assimilation and segregation held by the host population closely relate to attitudes toward immigrants (Zick, Wagner, van Dick, & Petzel, 2001).

Prior History of Host Country With the Outgroup. There is a sharp difference between French attitudes toward Vietnamese and Algerian immigrants. France lost colonial wars to both peoples, but the French harbor far greater prejudice against the Algerians (Pettigrew & Meertens, 1995; Pettigrew et al., 1998). One possible explanation is that the French considered Algeria a *départment*—an integral part of France itself. They did not regard Indochina in this manner. By violently breaking from the motherland, Algerians became a special target of abuse for Jean-Marie Le Pen and his Nationalist Front.

Multiple Distinguishing Characteristics. Native European minorities, such as the Basques of Spain, the Scots of Great Britain, or the Frisians of the Netherlands, typically share a language, religion, and even physical appearance with their national majorities. But new immigrants often differ on a multiplicity of such traits. These differences make the new immigrants appear conspicuous and far more numerous than they actually are.

The Employment Situation. Times of mass unemployment are clearly not optimal for the arrival of immigrants. Both the United States and Canada cut back severely on in-migration during the Great Depression of the 1930s. But the European situation of recent years presents almost the opposite picture. According to Eurostat, the European Union (EU) statistical office, there were in 2001 more deaths than births in 43% of the 211 regions that comprised the EU. Even when the new immigrants are included, one-fourth of the European Union's regions lost population in 2001 (Fuller, 2002). Moreover, Western Europe's native populations are rapidly aging. Rather than a general picture of unemployment, the absence of young workers severely threatens European prosperity. In fact, Western Europe requires immigration to compensate for the decline and aging of its labor force (Staubhaar & Zimmerman, 1993).

Germany and other Western European nations recognized this problem in the 1950s when the loss of men in World War II was a major factor. The so-called "guest worker" and other programs to encourage in-migration were direct results of this mounting problem. Indeed, the dramatic rise in Western Europe's economic fortunes in the last third of the 20th century would not have been possible without the arrival of the millions of new immigrants (Thraenhardt, 1992). Their labor proved essential for the industrial expansion and the German "economic miracle."

To be sure, this economic fact is not widely recognized in Europe. The costs, rather than gains, of immigration receive primary attention. Hence, when recessions come and unemployment rises, Le Pen, Heider, and other anti-immigrant politicians have aroused employment fears among their native populations. "Two million unemployed," shouted Le Pen in a famous remark, "that's two million immigrants too many" (Gunn, 1998, p. 23). Such xenophobic appeals are especially effective among those in the host society who hold zero-sum beliefs about how resources are allocated to groups (Esses, Dovidio, Jackson, & Armstrong, 2001).

Imagine the counterfactual. What might have been the degree of resistance to the new immigrants of Western Europe had the shortage of young workers not been so acute? European governments would not have initiated the guest worker programs. And immigrants who would have arrived would have faced even more hostility.

The Speed of Entry. Perceived threats—to jobs, housing, education, and social benefits—underlie prejudice against many minorities (Stephan & Stephan, 1996). An immigrant group arriving suddenly in the host country can increase such threats dramatically. Italy witnessed this phenomenon in the years between 1989 and 1992 (Pettigrew et al., 1998). Immigration into Italy spiked during these years, closely followed by a sudden rise in anti-immigrant opinions.

The Cultural Affinity Between the Host Society and the New Immigrants. Cultural conflicts, or the absence of such conflicts, between the host and immigrant populations is also important. In his study of ethnic slurs, Mullen (2001, p. 472) concluded "that smaller, less familiar, and more foreign ethnic immigrant groups tend to be cognitively represented in a simplistic and negative manner."

Espenshade and Calhoun (1993) studied the attitudes of southern Californians to undocumented workers in their midst. They found only weak support for a labor market competition explanation. Rather, cultural affinity proved to be an important predictor of attitudes toward illegal immigrants. Latino Americans, who share cultural ties with the majority of the illegals in southern California, were considerably more accepting of the new arrivals.

Language is an especially important component of cultural affinity. Eastern European immigrants to Germany, for example, have an advantage over Turkish immigrants in often having had some prior experience with the German language. Clement, Noels, and Deneault (2001) demonstrated the central role of second-language communication for shaping the effects of intergroup contact, ethnic identity, and psychological communication.

The Political Structures of the Receiving Countries.

Koopmans (1995) investigated the substantial differences in violence directed at immigrants across Western European nations. Using social movement theory, he shows the importance of political elites in legitimizing the violence by portraying the new immigrants as "unbearable burdens." Koopmans argued that extreme-right political parties act as safety valves by providing alternatives to violence for the expression of anti-immigrant feelings. Thus, he maintained, violence rates are lowest in countries with strong anti-immigration parties (France, Denmark, and Norway) and highest in countries where such parties have failed to develop strength (Germany and the United Kingdom).

But Koopmans's thesis is problematic. Europe's experience between the World Wars provides counterexamples. Fascist parties and political violence developed together during these turbulent years. A rival explanation easily fits his data on differential violence across Europe. The right-wing parties of Germany (the Christian Democrats) and the United Kingdom (the Conservatives) incorporated the anti-immigrant agenda. This action had three results. It allowed these conservative parties to wrest working-class votes away from their left-wing opposition (Thraenhardt, 1996). It also stunted the growth of the far-right Republicaners in Germany and the National Front movement in the United Kingdom. Finally, the racist stands of these established right-wing parties lent far greater legitimization to anti-immigrant violence than the extreme parties of France, Denmark, and Norway could manage. This last effect helps to explain the greater violence directed against immigrants in Germany and Great Britain. In any event, the unique political party alignment of each host nation is an important structural element in the reception accorded new immigrants.

The Opportunities for Optimal Intergroup Contact Across Housing, Work, Educational, and Recreational Settings.

Opportunities for intergroup interaction are an obvious structural prerequisite for optimal intergroup contact (Pettigrew, 1998a). Segregation and discrimination in housing, employment, and schools are widespread in Western Europe, yet there is wide variance in these factors across nations (Pettigrew, 1998b).

The Potential for and Actual Existence of Integrative Associations of Immigrants and Nonimmigrants.

Darby (1986), Varshney (2002) and others have emphasized the importance of multiethnic associations with common interests in reducing intergroup violence. This literature has developed in economics and political science, and it largely ignores intergroup contact theory in social psychology. But these two quite separate theoretical domains neatly dovetail with one another.

The Size and Concentration of the Immigrant Group. In aggregate analyses, the size of the immigrant population is typically positively related to anti-immigrant attitudes—especially in poorer countries. Hence, Quillian (1995) found that the interaction of high non-European Union minority percentage and low gross national product accounts for 70% of the variance in anti-immigrant prejudice means across 12 European Union nations (see also Fuchs, Gerhards, & Roller, 1993). The concentration of immigrants in particular urban areas—such as Frankfurt, Marseilles, and Rotterdam—enhances this effect. This result coincides with similar aggregate findings concerning anti-Black prejudice, discrimination, and voting across counties in the American South (e.g., Pettigrew & Campbell, 1960; Pettigrew & Cramer, 1959). However, there are, we shall note, significant exceptions to this trend in areas where the immigrant minorities constitute small percentages of the population.

COMBINING THE TWO RESEARCH TRADITIONS

Each of these research literatures offers invaluable insights, and both are essential to obtain a rounded perspective on the problem of anti-immigrant responses of native populations. Note how each research tradition supplies what the other lacks. Aggregate data on structural and cultural factors require links with intergroup and individual data to avoid the ecological fallacy of assuming microprocesses from aggregate data alone. Similarly, individual and intergroup data require links with the broader aggregate data tapping cultural and structural contexts to avoid the compositional fallacy of assuming macro-processes from individual data alone.

This two-level perspective applied to immigration attitudes is, of course, a special case of the broader issue for social science generally in combining structural (or contextual) effects with individual effects. There is an extensive literature throughout the social sciences addressing this central issue—especially among political scientists (e.g., Forbes, 1997; Glaser, 1994; Hood & Morris, 1997; Stein, Post, & Rinden, 2000) and sociologists (e.g., Blau, 1960; Davis, Spaeth, & Huson, 1961; Tannenbaum & Bachman, 1964; Taylor, 1998, 2000). Psychological social psychologists have rarely considered the issue in depth. This chapter does not attempt to summarize this methodological literature. Instead, it draws on this work to help with our application of this fundamental issue to the specific topic of attitudes toward immigrants and immigration.

Investigators have employed a great variety of methods to bear on this problem. One of the most direct and ambitious techniques involves the development of a data file that merges both census and other structural data with survey data on individuals (Glaser, 1994; Kunovich & Hodson, 2002; Taylor, 1998, 2000). This approach requires knowledge of the precise geographic sampling points of the survey data.

Taylor (1998, 2000) provides a pointed example of such an analysis. Using hierarchical regression, she tested the effect of racial compositions of local populations on white Americans' racial attitudes. Consistent with the results of earlier and less elegant designs, Taylor (1998, p. 512) found for an array of dependent variables that "white negativity swells as the local black population share expands." This structural effect is sizable. A mere 10% increase in the black populations leads to a larger increase in white prejudice than 3 years of education decreases prejudice. Moreover, controlling for this compositional variable reduces by about half the South/non-South regional difference in White racial attitudes.

Using the same approach and similar hierarchical regression software, Kunovich and Hodson (2002) searched for the correlates of ethnic bigotry in Bosnia and Croatia just before the breakup of the old Yugoslavian republic. Unlike Taylor's racial results for the southern United States, they found ethnic diversity was associated with decreased prejudice across areas.

Mediational analyses using structural equation models offer another approach (Baron & Kenny, 1986). Here cultural and structural variables act as distal predictors of anti-immigrant attitudes and behavior whose effects are mediated by individual and intergroup variables acting as proximal predictors. Across diverse European societies, social psychological variables act in similar ways as they mediate the effects of contrasting cultural and structural components on attitudes toward immigrants (Pettigrew, 2001a).

Apparent Divergences in Findings of the Two Approaches

The most interesting and important feature of the two-level approach is that it allows us to seek reasons for apparent discrepancies in findings across the two levels. Indeed, the two levels of analysis often arrive at what first appear to be strikingly different conclusions. These differences lead to contrasting implications for effective public policy. Consider the apparent discrepancy between the two research literatures concerning the differential effects of the size of the minority population on majority prejudice. On the one hand, as Taylor's work indicates, political science and sociological theory and research have long held that the larger a minority's population ratio, the *greater* the threat to and prejudice of the majority (e.g., Pettigrew & Campbell, 1960; Pettigrew & Cramer, 1959; Fuchs, Gerhards, & Roller, 1993; Taylor, 1998, 2000).

But greater numbers of immigrants also should lead to more contact between the host population and the new arrivals. Thus, this aggregate finding seems at variance with the research results at the individual level. It conflicts with the standard social psychological finding that more intergroup contact typically leads to *reduced* prejudice (Pettigrew & Tropp, 2000, in press). How can we explain this apparent theoretical conflict?

To start, we should note that the discrepancy does not always emerge. There are numerous instances where, just as contact theory would predict, *smaller* population ratios of the target group are actually associated with increased prejudice against them. The states that formerly constituted East Germany, for example, have significantly smaller percentages of immigrants but consistently more anti-immigrant prejudice than the former West Germany. And restricted intergroup contact in the East explains the difference (Wagner et al. 2003). Similarly, Zick (1997) found that German cities (as opposed to states) with larger immigrant populations tended to have on average less prejudice. We noted that the same effect was found for areas within Bosnia and Croatia (Kunovich & Hodson, 2002).

In North American results, Taylor (1998), using the same two-level methods noted earlier, found that large local concentrations of Asian and Latino Americans did not engender heightened White antipathy toward these groups. Similarly, Hood and Morris (1997) reported that European Americans who live in areas with more Asian and Latino immigrants have more favorable attitudes toward immigration and these immigrant groups. Their later work showed that this finding held only for documented, legal immigrants (Hood & Morris, 1998). For the undocumented illegals, however, larger proportions were associated with greater Anglo prejudice. Hood and Morris (1998) theorized that this difference reflected the contrasting types of interactions that legal and illegal immigrants were likely to have with Anglos.

As is often the case, we can glean a clue to our puzzle from these apparent "error cases." These exceptions typically involve relatively small numbers of the minority target group. East Germany, for example, has only about 2% foreigners, compared with West Germany's 10% (Wagner et al., 2003). This situation also typifies most situations for Bosnia and Croatia. Similarly, in the United States with few exceptions, Asian and Latino American concentrations are smaller than African American concentrations in the South. Where this is not the case, the dominant threat pattern often returns. Thus, Hood and Morris (1997) found that European Americans residing in California, which receives a lion's share of all Asian and Latino immigration to the United States, harbor more critical views of both immigration and immigrant groups.

At this point, a simple and straightforward solution to the puzzle suggests itself. It appears as if intergroup contact and threat are *competing* influences on attitudes toward immigrants. In low-density areas, maximized contact gains acceptance for immigrants. In high-density areas, heightened threat overcomes contact effects and triggers increased prejudice against immigrants.

But further exploration reveals this trade-off view between contact and threat is too simple. The interplay of the two predictors is far more complex for at least two reasons—one at the macro level of analysis, the other at the micro level.

At the macro level, the degree of group separation governs the boundaries of possible intergroup interaction. Segregation severely restricts the operation of intergroup contact processes. An area may have a large minority percentage—such as the Black Belt counties of the Deep South—and still have reasonably little intergroup contact if there is strict group segregation in work, residential, and educational settings.[1] The cross-group interaction that does occur is unlikely to occur under optimal conditions. Such areas help to account for the apparent inconsistency of the findings between the two levels of analysis. This segregation factor also explains in large part why structural-level studies of White Southern attitudes toward Black Americans often differ in their results from similar studies involving attitudes toward Asian and Latino Americans, whose segregation indices from Whites are considerably smaller (Massey & Denton, 1993). This structural explanation is more parsimonious than the standard theory in political science that cultural differences between minority groups cause these diverse results (Forbes, 1997; Gurr, 1993; Hechter, 1975).

Results from a statewide telephone survey of Texas adults suggest a micro factor (Stein et al., 2000). This study uncovered a strong *interaction* between contact and Latino population percentages in Texas counties. Defining contact as "how many days during last week did you speak with a Hispanic person," these investigators noted, as expected, that contact and minority context were positively correlated ($r = +.30$). They also showed that contact correlated with more positive attitudes toward Latinos, whereas high-density Latino counties provided more negative attitudes than low-density areas.

What is most noteworthy is the highly significant interaction between the two variables. This interaction reflects the fact that those European Americans who resided in heavily populated Latino areas *and* had the most contact were especially favorable in their views of Latinos. This led the investigators to conclude that the two predictor variables—contact and context—"complement rather than compete with each other" (Stein et al., 2000, p. 290) The converse of this interaction is that those who live in high-density areas but who have scant contact with the target group are the most hostile.

From these interesting findings, we can deduce that both individual and structural factors are critically important. In addition, the sharp bifurcation in the attitudes found in high-density counties suggests the relevance of a theoretical contribution by Tesser (1980) that has never received the attention it deserves (see also Back, 1992; Flay, 1978; Stewart & Peregoy, 1983). Using catastrophe theory from mathemat-

---

[1]Exceptions to this principle sometimes occur in those instances where a particular ethnic group carves out a segregated and specialized occupational niche. For an example from Bosnia and Croatia, see Kunovich and Hodson (2002).

ics, Tesser modeled the behavior of individuals who are caught in conflict between their individual dispositions and social pressure. This is precisely the situation of tolerant, equalitarian Anglo-Texans living in high-density Latino counties with anti-Latino normative structures. Tesser's model predicts that this conflict between personal dispositions and social pressure will result in bimodal responses—and this fits the Texas survey findings. The model furthers holds that shifts in dispositions in situations with high social pressure will result in sudden, discontinuous, "catastrophic" changes in behavior. And when there are increases in social pressure with high dispositional orientations toward tolerance, bimodality in responses will emerge.

Applied to the Texas data, we postulate, then, that low-density Latino counties lack strong pressures to conform to anti-Latino norms. This allows their Anglo residents to follow their dispositions toward prejudice or tolerance. But in high-density Latino areas, anti-Latino Anglos receive normative support for their dispositional tendencies. They are joined by some with less prejudicial orientations who simply avoid Latino contact and bend to the normative pressures of the counties in which they reside. But some tolerant Anglo Texans in these counties deviate from the norms, exploit the opportunity for increased contact with Latinos afforded by their counties, and emerge as the most tolerant group of all. Such a possibility fits the Texas survey data of Stein, Post, and Rinden (2000). And it adds to the present author's contentions advanced a half century ago that conformity is a critical part of antiminority prejudice in areas with high concentrations of minority population (Pettigrew, 1958, 1959, 1961).

A FINAL WORD

I have explored in detail this apparent discrepancy in findings between the two levels for several reasons. First, it is important both theoretically and empirically to untangle this puzzle. Second, the suggested solutions are of considerable practical and social policy significance. Finally, this exercise underlines the significance of the central contention of this chapter: namely, that theoretical and practical advances in understanding resistant responses to the world's new immigrants can best be made by focusing future research on the links between the macro and micro levels of analysis.

REFERENCES

Adorno, T. W., Frenkel-Brunswik, E., Levinson, D. J., & Sanford, R. N. (1950). *The authoritarian personality*. New York: Harper, 1950.
Allport, G. W. (1954). *The nature of prejudice*. Reading, MA: Addison-Wesley.
Back, K. W. (1992). This business of topology. *Journal of Social Issues, 48*(2), 51–66.
Barker, M. (1982). *The new racism: Conservatives and the ideology of the tribe*. Frederick, MD: Aletheia.

Baron, R., & Kenny, D. A. (1986), The moderator-mediator variable distinction in social psychological research: Conceptual, strategic, and statistical considerations. *Journal of Personality and Social Psychology, 51,* 1173–1182.

Bergmann, W., & Erb, R. (1986). Kommunikationslatenz, Moral und oefentliche Meinung [Latent communication, moral and public opinion]. *Koelner Zeitschrift fuer Soziologie und Sozialpsychologie, 38,* 223–246.

Blau, P. M. (1960). Structural effects. *American Sociological Review, 25,* 178–193.

Clement, R., Noels, K. A., & Deneault, B. (2001). Interethnic contact, identity, and psychological adjustment: The mediating and moderating roles of communication. *Journal of Social Issues, 57,* 559–577.

Crosby, F. J., Bromley, S., & Saxe, L. (1980). Recent unobtrusive studies of black and white discrimination and prejudice: A literature review. *Psychological Bulletin, 87,* 546–563.

Darby, J. (1986). *Intimidation and the control of conflict in Northern Ireland.* Dublin, Ireland: Gill and McMillan.

Davis, J. A., Spaeth, J. L., & Huson, C. (1961). A technique for analyzing the effects of group composition. *American Sociological Review, 26,* 215–225.

Espenshade, T. J., & Calhoun, C. A. (1993). An analysis of public opinion toward undocumented immigration. *Population Research and Policy Review, 12,* 189–224.

Essed, P. (1990). *Everyday racism: Reports from women of two cultures.* Claremont, CA: Hunter House.

Esses, V. M., Dovidio, J. F., & Dion, K. L. (Eds.). (2001). Immigrants and immigration. *Journal of Social Issues, 57,* 375–631.

Esses, V. M., Dovidio, J. F., Jackson, L. M., & Armstrong, T. L. (2001). The immigration dilemma: The role of perceived group competition, ethnic prejudice, and national identity. *Journal of Social Issues, 57,* 375–387.

Flay, R. R. (1978). Catastrophe theory in social psychology: Some applications to attitudes and social behavior. *Behavioral Science, 23,* 335–350.

Forbes, H. D. (1997). *Ethnic conflict: Commerce, culture, and the contact hypothesis.* New Haven, CT: Yale University Press.

Fuchs, D., Gerhards, J., & Roller, E. (1993). Wir und die Anderen. Ethnozentrismus in den zwölf Ländern der europäischen Gemeinschaft [Us and the others: Ethnocentrism in the 12 countries of the European Community]. *Kölner Zeitschrift für Soziologie und Sozialpsychologie, 45,* 238–253.

Fuller, T. (2002, December 12). Low birthrates pose challenge for Europe. *International Herald Tribune.*

Glaser, J. M. (1994). Back to the black belt: Environment and white racial attitudes in the South. *Journal of Politics, 56,* 21–41.

Gunn, S. (1989). *Revolution of the right: Europe's new conservatives.* London: Pluto.

Gurr, T. R. (1993). Why minorities rebel: A global analysis of communal mobilization and conflict since 1945. *International Political Science Review, 14,* 161–201.

Hechter, M. (1975). *Internal colonialism: The Celtic fringe in British national development, 1536–1966.* Berkeley: University of California Press.

Hood, M. V., & Morris, I. L. (1997). Amigo o enemigo? Context, attitudes, and Anglo public opinion toward immigration. *Social Science Quarterly, 78,* 309–323.

Hood, M. V., & Morris, I. L. (1998). Give us your tired and your poor, ... but make sure they have a green card: The effects of documented and undocumented migrant context on Anglo opinion toward immigration. *Political Behavior, 20*, 1–15.

Jackson, J. S., Brown, K. T., Brown, T. N., & Marks, B. (2001). Contemporary immigration policy orientations among dominant-group members in Western Europe. *Journal of Social Issues, 57*, 431–456.

Klink, A., & Wagner, U. (1999). Discrimination against ethnic minorities in Germany: Going back to the field. *Journal of Applied Social Psychology, 29*, 402–423.

Koopmans, R. (1995). *A burning question: Explaining the rise of racist and extreme right violence in Western Europe.* Berlin: Wiss. Zentrum, Soz-Forsch.

Kunovich, R. M. (2002). Social structural sources of anti-immigrant prejudice in Europe: The impact of social class and stratification position. *International Journal of Sociology, 32*, 39–57.

Kunovich, R. M., & Hodson, R. (2002). Ethnic diversity, segregation, and inequality: A structural model of ethnic prejudice in Bosnia and Croatia. *Sociological Quarterly, 43*, 185–212.

Massey, D. S., & Denton, N. A. (1993). *American apartheid: Segregation and the making of the underclass.* Cambridge, MA: Harvard University Press.

Meertens, R. W., & Pettigrew, T. F. (1997). Is subtle prejudice really prejudice? *Public Opinion Quarterly, 61*, 54–71.

Mullen, B. (2001). Ethnophaulisms for ethnic immigrant groups. *Journal of Social Issues, 57*, 457–475.

Pettigrew, T. F. (1958). Personality and socio-cultural factors in intergroup attitudes: A cross-national comparison. *Journal of Conflict Resolution, 2*, 29–42.

Pettigrew, T. F. (1959). Regional differences in anti-Negro prejudice. *Journal of Abnormal and Social Psychology, 59*, 28–36.

Pettigrew, T. F. (1961). Social psychology and desegregation research. *American Psychologist, 16*, 105–112.

Pettigrew, T. F. (1989). The nature of modern racism in the United States. *Revue Internationale de Psychologie Sociale, 2*(3), 291–303.

Pettigrew, T. F. (1997). Generalized intergroup contact effects on prejudice. *Personality and Social Psychology Bulletin, 23*, 173–185.

Pettigrew, T. F. (1998a). Intergroup contact theory. *Annual Review of Psychology, 49*, 65–85.

Pettigrew, T. F. (1998b). Responses to the new minorities of Western Europe. *Annual Review of Sociology, 24*, 77–103.

Pettigrew, T. F. (2000a). Systematizing the predictors of prejudice. In D. O. Sears, J. Sidanius, & L. Bobo (Eds.), *Racialized politics: The debate about racism in America* (pp. 280–301). Chicago: University of Chicago Press.

Pettigrew, T. F. (2000b). Placing authoritarianism in social context. *Politics, Groups and the Individual, 8*, 5–20.

Pettigrew, T. F. (2001a). Intergroup relations and national and international relations. In R. Brown & S. Gaertner (Eds.), *Blackwell handbook of social psychology: Intergroup processes* (pp. 514–532). Oxford, UK: Blackwell, 2001.

Pettigrew, T. F. (2001b). Summing up: Relative deprivation as a key social psychological concept. In I. Walker & H. Smith (Eds.), *Relative deprivation:*

Specification, development and integration (pp. 351–373). New York: Cambridge University Press.

Pettigrew, T. F., & Campbell, E. Q. (1960). Faubus and segregation: An analysis of Arkansas voting. *Public Opinion Quarterly, 24,* 436–447.

Pettigrew, T. F., & Cramer, M. R. (1959). The demography of desegregation. *Journal of Social Issues, 15,* 61–71.

Pettigrew, T. F., Jackson, J., Ben Brika, J., Lemain, G., Meertens, R. W., Wagner, U., & Zick, A. (1998). Outgroup prejudice in Western Europe. In W. Stroebe & M. Hewstone (Eds.), *European review of social psychology* (Vol. 8, pp. 241–273). Chichester, UK: Wiley.

Pettigrew, T. F., & Meertens, R. W. (1995). Subtle and blatant prejudice in Western Europe. *European Journal of Social Psychology, 57,* 57–75.

Pettigrew, T. F., & Meertens, R. W. (1996). The *verzuiling* puzzle: Understanding Dutch intergroup relations. *Current Psychology, 15,* 3–13.

Pettigrew, T. F., & Meertens, R. W. (2001). In defense of the subtle prejudice concept: A retort. *European Journal of Social Psychology, 31,* 299–309.

Pettigrew, T. F., & Tropp, L. (2000). Does intergroup contact reduce prejudice? Recent meta-analytic findings. In S. Oskamp (Ed.), *Reducing prejudice and discrimination: Social psychological perspectives* (pp. 93–114). Mahwah, NJ: Lawrence Erlbaum Associates..

Pettigrew, T. F., & Tropp, L. (in press). A meta-analytic test of intergroup contact theory. *Journal of Personality and Social Psychology.*

Pratto, F., & Lemieux, A. F. (2001). The psychological ambiguity of immigration and its implications for promoting immigration policy. *Journal of Social Issues, 57,* 413–430.

Quillian, L. (1995). Prejudice as a response to perceived group threat. *American Sociological Review, 60,* 586–611.

Reif, K., & Melich, A. (1991). *Euro-Barometer 30: Immigrants and outgroups in western Europe, October–November 1988.* Ann Arbor, MI: Inter-University Consortium for Political and Social Research.

Schuman, H., Steeh, C., Bobo, L., & Krysan, M. (1997). *Racial attitudes in America: Trends and interpretations* (rev. ed.). Cambridge, MA: Harvard University Press.

Sears, D. D. (1988). Symbolic racism. In P. A. Katz & D. A. Taylor (Eds.), *Eliminating racism: Profiles in controversy* (pp. 53–84). New York: Plenum.

Staubhaar, T., & Zimmerman, K. F. (1993). Towards a European migration policy. *Population Research and Policy Review, 12,* 225–241.

Stein, R. M., Post, S. S., & Rinden, A. L. (2000). Reconciling context and contact effects on racial attitudes. *Political Research Quarterly, 53,* 285–303.

Stephan, W. G., & Stephan, C. W. (1996). Predicting prejudice: The role of threat. *International Journal of Intercultural Research, 20,* 409–426.

Stewart, I. N., & Peregoy, P. L. (1983). Catastrophe theory modeling in psychology. *Psychological Bulletin, 94,* 336–362.

Tannenbaum, A. S., & Bachman, J. G. (1964). Structural versus individual effects. *American Journal of Sociology, 69,* 585–595.

Taylor, M. C. (1998). How white attitudes vary with the racial composition of local populations: Numbers count. *American Sociological Review, 63,* 512–535.

Taylor, M. C. (2000). The significance of racial context. In D. O. Sears, J. Sidanius, & L. Bobo (Eds.), *Racialized politics: The debate about racism in America* (pp. 118–136). Chicago: University of Chicago Press.

Tesser, A. (1980). When individual dispositions and social pressure conflict: A catastrophe. *Human Relations, 33*, 393–407.

Thraenhardt, D. (Ed.). (1992). Europe—A new immigration continent: Policies and politics since 1945. In D. Thraenhardt (Ed.), *Europe: A new immigration continent* (pp. 47–92). Muenster, Germany: LIT Verlag.

Thraenhardt, D. (1996). The political uses of xenophobia in England, France and Germany. *Party Politics, 1*, 323–345.

Van Dick, R., Wagner, U., Pettigrew, T. F., Christ, O., Jackson, J. S., Petzel, T., Castro, V., & Wolff, C. (2003). The role of perceived importance in intergroup contact. *Journal of Personality and Social Psychology, 87*(2), 211–227.

Varshney, A. (2002). *Ethnic conflict and civic life: Hindus and Muslims in India*. New Haven, CT: Yale University Press.

Wagner, U., van Dick, R., Pettigrew, T. F., & Christ, O. (2003). Ethnic prejudice in East and West Germany: The explanatory power of intergroup contact. *Group Processes and Intergroup Relations, 6*, 22–36.

Zick A. (1997). *Voruteile und Rassismus: Eine sozialpsychologische Analyse* [Prejudice and racism: A social psychological analysis]. Muenster, Germany: Waxmann.

Zick, A., Wagner, U., van Dick, R., & Petzel, T. (2001). Acculturation and prejudice in Germany: Majority and minority perspectives. *Journal of Social Issues, 57*, 541–557.

7

The Role of Prejudice in the Discounting of Immigrant Skills

Victoria M. Esses
Joerg Dietz
Arjun Bhardwaj
University of Western Ontario

Attitudes toward immigrants and obstacles to their successful integration into receiving societies have emerged as important areas of investigation for the 21st century. Immigration rates have risen to unprecedented levels globally, and Western countries increasingly depend on immigrants to maintain their population size and labor force (UN Department of Economic and Social Affairs, 2004). As a result, the reactions of members of receiving societies to immigrants and immigration are of importance both for the achievement and well-being of immigrants, and for the economic and social well-being of the receiving societies.

In North America, some negative beliefs and attitudes toward immigrants are evident. Previous research indicates that immigrants are at times seen as competing with members of the host nation for economic resources and for cultural dominance, and as a threat to the host society (e.g., Esses, Hodson, & Dovidio, 2003; Esses, Jackson, & Armstrong, 1998; Stephan, Renfro, Esses, Stephan, & Martin, 2005; Stephan, Ybarra, & Bachman, 1999). Such beliefs can lead to negative attitudes toward immigrants and immigration that have important implications for the treatment of immigrants. In this chapter, we focus on one domain in which attitudes toward immigrants may play a particularly important role—the integration of immigrants into the host country's labor force. In particular, we examine the role of attitudes toward immigrants in the devaluation or discounting of immigrants' skills (e.g., educational credentials and work experience).

The chapter is organized as follows: Following an overview of immigrant participation in the North American labor force, we review analyses of census and survey data that have provided evidence of the discounting of immigrants' skills and that have suggested that racial minority immigrants may be particularly likely to experience skill discounting. Next, we describe the context in which the assessment of foreign credentials takes place and suggest a framework for examining the role of prejudice in this process. We then present our experimental research that has begun to investigate the role of prejudice in immigrant skill discounting. We conclude by discussing the practical and theoretical implications of this research.

IMMIGRANT PARTICIPATION
IN THE NORTH AMERICAN LABOR FORCE

The successful integration of immigrants into a host country's labor force is of considerable importance. From the perspective of immigrants, success in the labor market is crucial for economic and psychological well-being. Unemployment and underemployment can lead immigrants to experience poverty, frustration, and poor psychological well-being (e.g., Aycan & Berry, 1996; Reitz, 2005). From the perspective of the host society, it is essential to take advantage of immigrants' skills and experience so that they contribute to the economic base within a nation and contribute to the nation's ability to compete successfully in the global economy. In Canada, immigrants have recently accounted for over 70% of labor force growth, and comprise approximately 20% of the total work force (Statistics Canada, 2004). Similarly, in the United States, immigrants accounted for approximately 60% of labor force growth in the last 4 years, and currently comprise approximately 15% of the total labor force (Sum, Fogg, Khatiwada, & Palma, 2004; see also Dietz & Pugh, 2004).

Despite the importance of immigrant participation in the labor force, there is evidence that immigrants to Canada and the United States experience lower levels of earnings and of labor-force participation than do native-born individuals (e.g., Li, 2001; Reitz, 2001a, 2001b, 2003a, 2003b). One important factor contributing to this gap in earnings and employment for immigrants is the lack of recognition of foreign credentials. That is, the foreign-acquired educational and experience-based skills of immigrants tend to be discounted relative to those of locally trained employees (e.g., Li, 2001; Reitz, 2003a, 2003b, 2005). This phenomenon has been termed *skill discounting*. Skill discounting may involve the devaluation of foreign education (e.g., degrees and diplomas), foreign professional training (e.g., apprenticeships), foreign work experience, and other work-related skills that immigrants may bring with them (see Reitz, 2005) .

Skill discounting has negative consequences for immigrants in material and psychological terms, and also limits the extent to which a country can benefit from immigrants' knowledge and experience. It results in suboptimal productivity of the immigrant work force in the economy (the so-called brain waste). For example, in Canada, Reitz indicated that "the Canadian economy is losing up to $2.4 billion because immigrants' skills are underutilized and up to $12.6 billion because they are underpaid" (quoted in Toye, 2002).

It has been demonstrated that skill discounting is especially likely to occur for immigrants who are racial minorities (e.g., Baker & Benjamin, 1997; Hum & Simpson, 1999; Li, 2001; Metropolis Conversation Series, 2001; Reitz, 2003b, 2005; Swidinsky & Swidinsky, 2002). Because of increasing proportions of new immigrants who are racial minorities, the negative effects of skill discounting can be expected to become even more severe in North America in the coming years (Citizenship and Immigration Canada, 2004; Hanson, 2004). In addition, the fact that racial minorities are particularly likely to experience skill discounting suggests that prejudice may play an important role in the process. Before turning to this possibility, however, we briefly review survey and census-based evidence of skill discounting.

PREVIOUS EVIDENCE OF SKILL DISCOUNTING

Analyses of census and survey data in Canada have provided consistent evidence of the discounting of immigrant skills. In his analyses of census data, Reitz (2001a, 2001b, 2003a, 2003b, 2005) demonstrated that recently arrived immigrants consistently experience lower rates of labor-force participation and lower levels of earnings relative to the native-born population. Further analyses indicate that a significant proportion of these differences can be attributed to the lower value in the Canadian labor market of immigrant skills obtained outside the country (e.g., years of education, university degree) relative to the value of the skills of native-born individuals obtained in Canada (Reitz, 2001a, 2001b, 2003a, 2003b, 2005). In addition, as education and knowledge-based skills have become increasingly emphasized in employment, the extent of this discounting has also increased, such that Canadian employers seem to be making sharper distinctions between skills obtained outside the country and those obtained locally (see Reitz, 2005). Indeed, the analyses suggest that the current labor-market value in Canada of immigrants' foreign work experience is virtually zero (Reitz, 2001a). That is, Canadian employers place little or no value on work experience obtained outside the country.

The employment experiences of skilled immigrants to the United States seem to be similar (Reitz, 2003a). In the United States, immigrant education is also discounted. In addition, as in Canada, as the value of education has increased in the United States, this has benefited primarily the native-born population, increasing the disparities between immigrants and nonimmigrants (Reitz, 2003a). Also of note, in both Canada and the United States, skill discounting is particularly evident for racial minority immigrants (Reitz, 2001a, 2003a, 2003b).

One might assert, of course, that some of the devaluing of foreign skills might be attributed to their true lower quality relative to skills obtained in North America. However, as Reitz (2001a) argued, economic development in many areas outside Europe, particularly in parts of Asia, has advanced considerably in recent years and, at least in some of these places, professional standards are quite high, and comparable to those of Canada. Nevertheless, the earnings disadvantage for immigrants from those areas has changed little. The director of World Education Services, the authorized credential evaluation service of the Government of Ontario, stated, "The fact is that over 75% of foreign credentials in the engineering, health care and IT fields we evaluated in the past year are equivalent to or exceed Canadian standards" (Owen, 2002, as quoted in Human Resource Management, 2002). This suggests that factors other than the true value of skills are operating. Indeed, immigrants may bring quite distinctive qualities with them to their new country, such as knowledge of foreign languages, which may increase their skills base (Reitz, 2001a).

In summary, prior research has provided significant evidence of skill discounting, particularly for racial minority immigrants. There is a lack of knowledge, however, about the processes that drive skill discounting. Complementing the research conducted by other social scientists that examines economic and sociological implications of skill discounting, we take a psychological approach to understanding *why* skill discounting occurs. We use experimental methods to disentangle why individuals who make personnel decisions may attach less value to foreign qualifications than they do to domestic qualifications, particularly for racial minority applicants. We focus on the psychological and organizational factors that may play a role, particularly the role of prejudice and the context in which the skills of foreign-trained workers are evaluated.

PREJUDICE AND SKILL DISCOUNTING

Skill discounting is by its nature an ambiguous phenomenon with multiple antecedents. The evaluation of the skills of foreign-trained workers is associated with greater ambiguity than that of locally trained workers because the evaluation of the quality of skills obtained elsewhere is often difficult, forcing decision makers to make judgement calls (Reitz, 2003a, 2003b, 2005). Decision makers may not have sufficient information about foreign skills to make informed decisions. In addition, even in the presence of such information, decision makers may still feel less confident of their decisions about foreign-trained workers than about locally trained workers. This allows room for subjective factors to play a significant role, including prior beliefs and prejudices about immigrants, particularly racial minority immigrants (see also Reitz, 2003b, 2005).

Figure 7.1 presents a model for understanding the role of prejudice in immigrant skill discounting. This model is based on the justification–suppression model of the expression of prejudice proposed by Crandall and Eshleman (2003) and on related theories of modern prejudice (e.g., Dovidio & Gaertner, 1998). According to these theories, prejudice against racial minorities still exists in modern society but is often suppressed by societal and personal values and norms. As a result, prejudice is typically not openly expressed. That is, in North American society today, individuals are taught that it is not appropriate to hold or act on prejudicial attitudes. As individuals comply with or internalize these norms, they try to suppress their prejudicial attitudes (e.g., Monteith, Sherman, & Devine, 1998). As shown in Fig. 7.1, these suppression factors interrupt the direct relation between prejudice and discrimination. Nonetheless, the prejudicial attitudes still remain, although in a more latent form (Dovidio & Gaertner, 1998). Research on aversive racism and the justification–suppression model of the expression of prejudice suggests, however, that individuals will act on their prejudicial attitudes under certain circumstances. These circumstances include situations (a) for which social norms about appropriate behavior are not clear or (b) in which justifications for the behavior other than prejudice are readily available (e.g., Crandall & Eshleman, 2003; Dovidio & Gaertner, 1998; Dovidio, Gaertner, &

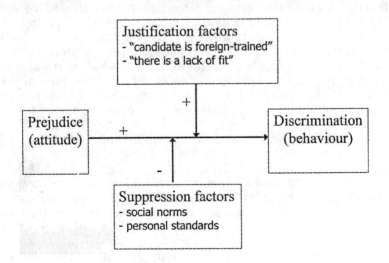

FIG. 7.1.   A justification–suppression model for explaining the role of prejudice in immigrant skill discounting (based on Crandall & Eshleman, 2003).

Bachman, 2001; for employment discrimination examples, see Brief, Dietz, Cohen, Pugh, & Vaslow, 2000; Petersen & Dietz, 2005). As shown in Fig. 7.1, justification factors increase the likelihood that prejudicial attitudes will lead to discrimination because the discriminatory behavior can then be explained away as due to factors other than prejudice.

In the current context, although individuals who make hiring decisions and who assess the quality of applicants for a position may consciously attempt to avoid bias and discrimination in decision making, their attitudes and beliefs may influence assessments and decisions nonetheless. The assessment of immigrant skills is likely to be influenced by latent prejudice for several reasons. First, in many cases, rules (i.e., organizational policies) or norms do not exist for the assessment of foreign-based skills. The resulting ambiguity may lead to weaker suppression effects on the expression of prejudice. In other words, the assessment of foreign skills often takes place in a vacuum of explicit rules and norms, which otherwise might have counteracted prejudicial tendencies to discount foreign skills.

Second, and related to the previous reason, the foreignness of immigrants and of their foreign-acquired skills may lead to concerns about a "lack of fit" with local work environments and demands. The notion of "fit" is commonly evoked as an antecedent of business performance, and it may have its validity if it is well defined (e.g., fit on specific organizational values). In the treatment of immigrants, however, the fit argument is often thoughtlessly and generically applied—"immigrants are simply culturally different" (i.e., the mere categorization as an immigrant becomes grounds for declaring a lack of fit). Even if fit criteria are defined (e.g., friendliness with customers), immigrants may be judged as not having the right fit on the basis of stereotypes about immigrants rather than substantive and explicit assessments of fit criteria. For example, attributing values to an individual based on group membership is stereotyping. Thus, "lack of fit" arguments can become seemingly but not substantively legitimate rationalizations or justifications for the discounting of immigrant skills and the resulting employment discrimination against immigrants.

Taken together, the ambiguity of the assessment of foreign skills (which is significantly greater than the ambiguity surrounding the assessment of domestic skills) and fit arguments make it easier to attribute discrimination against racial minority immigrants to motives other than prejudice. As a result, prejudiced individuals can rationalize their discriminatory behavior as being motivated by seemingly legitimate concerns rather than by prejudice. In the next section, we describe an initial experiment that sought to examine the role of prejudice in the assessment of racial minority immigrant job applicants.

EXPERIMENTAL WORK ON THE ROLE OF PREJUDICE IN SKILL DISCOUNTING

The goal of this study was to examine the potential role of prejudice in the discounting of immigrant skills. To examine this issue, we asked our participants to complete measures of attitudes toward immigrants in a first session, and then in a second session, several weeks later, asked them to evaluate a job candidate who was born and trained in Canada, the United Kingdom, or India. Based on the previous literature on foreign skill discounting, and the literature on aversive racism and justification–suppression of prejudice, we predicted that participants would discount the skills of the immigrant candidates relative to the skills of the Canadian candidate, especially when participants held more negative attitudes toward immigrants. That is, we expected to obtain an interaction between attitudes toward immigrants and the applicant's location of birth/training on the evaluation of the applicant. We also expected that this discounting would be most likely to occur for the immigrant applicant born and trained in India because the "foreignness" of the applicant's qualifications and culture would provide an easy and seemingly legitimate justification for skill discounting.

Attitudes Toward Immigrants

In the first session, we assessed attitudes toward immigrants in two ways. First, we used a rather straightforward measure that asked participants to rate their attitudes toward immigrants and immigration on several scales (Esses, Dovidio, Jackson, & Armstrong, 2001; e.g., "How positive or negative do you feel toward immigrants"; alpha = .92). In addition, we adapted the modern racism scale to assess modern prejudice toward immigrants (McConahay, 1986; e.g., "Immigrants are getting too demanding in their push for equal rights"; alpha = .79). In both cases, the scales were scored so that higher numbers indicated more *negative* attitudes. These scales were embedded in a larger questionnaire that was administered to several hundred participants. The correlation between the more straightforward attitude toward immigrants scale and the more subtle modern prejudice scale was significant ($r = .62$). By using both measures, we were able to determine whether only the more subtle modern prejudice scale would predict ratings of the foreign-trained job applicant, or both the straightforward and subtle measures would do so.

Presentation of Resumé

In the second session, 89 participants who were all Canadian citizens (72 women, 17 men) were told that the study was assessing differences between recruiters' and potential job applicants' perceptions of job résumés. They were further informed that they would be asked to read through a job posting and then evaluate the résumé of one of the applicants for the position. Both the job posting and the résumé were adapted from "real-world" materials. Participants were then presented with a job posting for the position of a full-time psychometrist who would work closely with adult patients, conducting neuropsychological tests. The required qualifications were described as including a Bachelor's degree in psychology or related discipline, previous experience with the administration and scoring of psychological tests within a hospital environment, and demonstrated ability to develop effective interpersonal relationships with patients, families, and multidisciplinary team members.

Participants were then asked to evaluate the résumé of one of the applicants for this position. The résumé contained information indicating that the applicant was born and trained either in Canada, in the United Kingdom, or in India. For the applicants born and trained in the United Kingdom or in India, it was indicated that the applicant was a landed immigrant, eligible to seek employment in Canada, and the dates for the most recent employment abroad indicated that she had arrived in Canada within the last year. The qualifications of the applicant were held constant across conditions and met but did not exceed the required qualifications described in the job posting. In addition, the name of the applicant (Anita Singh) and the language proficiency of the applicant (English, French, and Hindi) were held constant. The applicant's name and proficiency in Hindi indicated that she was of Asian Indian descent. We held applicant race constant to avoid a potential confound of the applicant's country of birth/training and her assumed race. In particular, we suspected that most participants would assume that the applicant who was born and trained in India would be of Indian descent. Thus, we ensured that all applicants were of the same race.

Manipulation checks were included in the study to ensure that participants noticed the birthplace and location of training of the applicant as a function of the manipulation of this information. We found that 92% of participants correctly identified the citizenship of the applicant and that 97% of participants correctly identified whether the applicant was trained in Canada or elsewhere. The accuracy of these responses did not differ significantly among conditions. In addition, a subset of participants was asked to specifically indicate the country of education and work experience of the applicant, if not in Canada. Ninety-eight percent of these participants provided correct responses.

Assessment of Person–Job Fit
and of Person–Organization Fit

Following their examination of the applicant's résumé, participants were asked to respond to items assessing two qualities considered important in the personnel selection process: person–job fit and person–organization fit (Bowen, Ledford, & Nathan, 1991; Kristof-Brown, 2000). As mentioned earlier, person–job fit and person–organization fit may be particularly susceptible to the effects of latent prejudice because those who make personnel decisions may view fit arguments as seemingly legitimate "business justifications" for the discounting of immigrant skills, and not as prejudicially based rationales that would contradict antidiscrimination norms (Frazer & Wiersma, 2001; Petersen & Dietz, 2005). We assessed person–job fit and person–organization fit separately because they are distinct, although related, constructs (r = .52 in the current study), as Kristof-Brown (2000) showed, and likely produce a double barrier for immigrant employees in the personnel selection process.

Person–job fit addresses the question of whether an applicant's skills and motivation are seen as matching the requirements of a specific job and allowing for high job performance. Typically, organizations in Canada and the United States view locally obtained skills as the preferred standard and benchmark for judging qualifications, forcing decision makers to make judgment calls about the equivalency of foreign-obtained skills. Although services are increasingly available for evaluating skills obtained elsewhere (e.g., World Education Services, 2005), as discussed earlier, the assessment of foreign skills is still an ambiguous process, potentially susceptible to various forms of bias. The five items we used to assess person–job fit were designed to assess the extent to which the applicant was seen to have suitable education, employment experience, and social skills for the position, and would be a good fit for the job and demonstrate strong job performance (alpha = .81).

Person–organization fit assessments are based on the extent to which applicants are seen to match the broader attributes of the organization, in terms of such factors as culture and personality. Because foreign-trained employees may be seen as not fitting the profile of other organizational members or clients, their skills may be devalued on the basis of arguments such as potential for communication difficulties, or difficulties working with other organizational members and clients due to cultural differences. The four items designed to assess person–organization fit in the current study included perceptions of the extent to which the applicant would be well liked by coworkers and clients, and the commitment and overall organizational fit of the applicant (alpha = .85).

The Effect of Attitudes Toward Immigrants and Location of Birth/Training on Evaluations of Person–Job Fit and of Person–Organization Fit

Person–Job Fit.   In order to examine the joint effect of attitudes toward immigrants and location of birth and training on evaluations of the applicant, hierarchical multiple regression analyses (e.g., Cohen & Cohen, 1983) were conducted. We first looked at the effect of attitudes toward immigrants and location of birth and training on perceptions of person-job fit.

The variable negative attitudes toward immigrants was entered in the first step, yielding a significant R^2 of .05, $p < .05$. Location of birth/training was entered in the second step with two dummy-coded variables, yielding a nonsignificant R^2 change of .02. In the third step, we entered the interactions between negative attitudes toward immigrants and the dummy-coded variables of location of birth/training (as the products of these variables), and obtained an R^2 change of .12, $p < .005$. As shown in Fig. 7.2, when the applicant was born and trained in Canada or in the United Kingdom, negative attitudes toward immigrants did not affect evaluations of person–job fit. When the applicant was born and trained in India, however, individuals with more negative attitudes toward immigrants evaluated the applicant as lower in person–job fit.

We obtained similar effects using the measure of modern prejudice toward immigrants, instead of attitudes toward immigrants. Modern prejudice was entered in the first step, yielding a significant R^2 of .05, $p < .05$. Location of birth/training was entered in the second step with two dummy-coded variables, yielding a nonsignificant R^2 change of .02. In the third step, we entered the interactions between modern prejudice and the dummy-coded variables for location of birth/train-

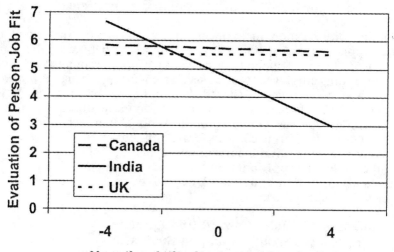

FIG. 7.2.   Evaluations of person–job fit as a function of negative attitudes toward immigrants and the location of birth and training of the applicant.

ing. This step yielded an R^2 change of .05, $p < .089$. As shown in Fig. 7.3, when the applicant was born and trained in Canada or in the United Kingdom, modern prejudice toward immigrants did not play a role in evaluations of person–job fit. When the applicant was born and trained in India, however, individuals higher in modern prejudice evaluated the applicant as lower in person–job fit.

Person–Organization Fit.   We next looked at the effect of attitudes toward immigrants and location of birth and training on perceptions of person–organization fit. Negative attitudes toward immigrants was entered in the first step, and yielded a nonsignificant R^2 of .02. The dummy-coded variables for location of birth/training were entered in the second step, and yielded a nonsignificant R^2 change of .02. In the third step, we entered the interactions between negative attitudes toward immigrants and the dummy-coded variables for location of birth/training, and obtained an R^2 change of .17, $p < .001$. As shown in Fig. 7.4, when the applicant was born and trained in Canada, negative attitudes toward immigrants did not play a role in evaluations of person–organization fit. When the applicant was born and trained in the United Kingdom, there was a tendency for individuals with more negative attitudes toward immigrants to rate the applicant as higher in person–organization fit. Of greatest interest, when the applicant was born and trained in India, individuals with more negative attitudes toward immigrants evaluated the applicant as lower in person–organization fit.

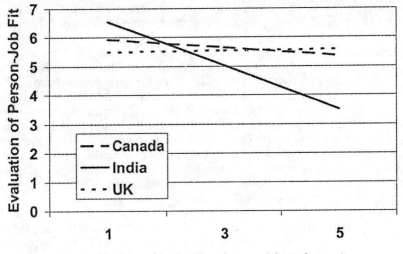

FIG. 7.3.   Evaluations of person–job fit as a function of modern prejudice toward immigrants and the location of birth and training of the applicant.

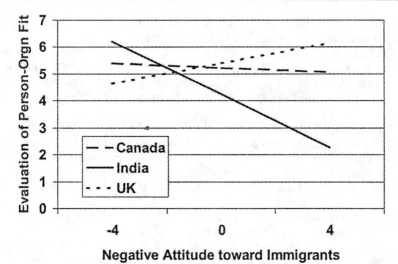

FIG. 7.4. Evaluations of person–organization fit as a function of negative attitudes toward immigrants and the location of birth and training of the applicant.

We again obtained similar results using the measure of modern prejudice toward immigrants, instead of negative attitudes toward immigrants. Modern prejudice was entered in the first step, and yielded a nonsignificant R^2 of .01. The dummy-coded variables for location of birth/training were entered in the second step, and yielded a nonsignificant R^2 change of .02. In the third step, we entered the interactions between modern prejudice and the dummy-coded variables of location of birth/training. This step yielded a significant R^2 change of .11, $p < .01$. As shown in Fig. 7.5, when the applicant was born and trained in Canada, modern prejudice toward immigrants did not play a role in evaluations of person–organization fit. When the applicant was born and trained in the United Kingdom, there was a tendency for individuals higher in modern prejudice to rate the applicant as higher in person–organization fit. Of greatest interest, when the applicant was born and trained in India, individuals higher in modern prejudice toward immigrants evaluated the applicant as lower in person–organiza-tion fit. It should be noted that all of these findings did not change appreciably when we controlled for participant gender.

Several aspects of these findings are of note. First, despite the fact that the applicant's ethnicity was held constant, with the applicant of Indian descent, negative attitudes and modern prejudice toward immigrants predicted less favorable evaluations of the applicant only when the applicant was born and trained in India. This sug-gests that latent prejudice is operating such that prejudiced partici-

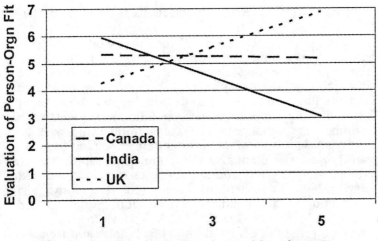

FIG. 7.5.   Evaluations of person–organization fit as a function of modern prejudice toward immigrants and the location of birth and training of the applicant.

pants are hesitant to rate the Indian job applicant as lacking in person–job fit and in person–organization fit unless there is a justification other than prejudice for doing so, namely, qualifications from India and potential for greater cultural differences. Relatedly, for person–organization fit only, individuals who were higher in negative attitudes and modern prejudice toward immigrants showed a tendency to evaluate the applicant born and trained in the United Kingdom more favorably. Perhaps, then, these individuals are "bending over backward" not to appear biased, unless there is a ready justification for their negative evaluations, as is the case when the applicant is born and trained in India. Person–organization fit assessments may be seen as particularly subjective, and thus may be especially susceptible to this "overcorrection" for applicants born and trained in the United Kingdom.

In addition, it is interesting to note that similar, if not stronger, effects were obtained using the measure of negative attitudes toward immigrants versus the measure of modern prejudice toward immigrants. Thus, although the findings suggest that subtle bias may be operating in evaluations of the Indian applicant trained in India, the initial assessment of prejudice did not have to be subtle in order to demonstrate these effects. This is reassuring for the assessment of attitudes toward immigrants, as the more straightforward items are routinely utilized in national surveys of public attitudes (e.g., Environics, 2000).

THEORETICAL AND PRACTICAL IMPLICATIONS

Understanding the processes underlying immigrant skill discounting has both theoretical and practical importance. At a theoretical level, research on prejudice and skill discounting advances knowledge of the ways in which subtle bias may operate in the everyday treatment of racial minority immigrants. This contributes to our understanding of subtle bias and the relation between prejudice and behavior. The current findings suggest that prejudice against immigrants, whether measured in a straightforward or more subtle way, results in a subtle behavioral manifestation of discrimination. That is, only when the applicant was an immigrant from a non-Western country was skill discounting evident. Consistent with research on aversive forms of prejudice and the justification–suppression model (Crandall & Eshleman, 2003; Dovidio & Gaertner, 1998; Dovidio et al., 2001), this suggests that a prejudiced person must feel that a nonprejudicial rationale for discrimination exists before that prejudice is put into action. Our research also has the potential to inform theory in the areas of personnel selection and skill discounting. With regards to theories of personnel selection, our research may form the basis for theoretically driven designs of selection procedures that reduce the likelihood of the enactment of prejudicial attitudes. With regard to skill discounting, by utilizing a psychological perspective to investigate an issue previously addressed by other social scientists such as sociologists and economists, this research has the potential to contribute to the development of theory that bridges disciplinary boundaries.

At a practical level, as we discussed earlier, Western nations such as Canada and the United States need immigrants to maintain a strong and globally competitive economy, and it is essential that these nations "attract, retain, and better utilize the skills of immigrants" (Citizenship and Immigration Canada, 2003, p. 26). Public awareness of immigrant skill discounting means, however, that these nations may have greater difficulty attracting and retaining skilled workers in the future (Human Resources Development Canada, 2002). In addition to the economic implications for the host nation, skill discounting has enormous negative effects on the well-being of immigrants (e.g., Aycan & Berry, 1996). A first step toward eliminating skill discounting is identifying and understanding its antecedents. Our research does so by disentangling the complex interplay of foreign versus domestic qualifications, and prejudicial attitudes held by those who make personnel decisions.

It is easy to overlook the role of prejudice because of its subtle nature. As shown in our research, prejudicial attitudes do not always lead to discrimination toward racial minorities (e.g., the participants in our study did not discriminate against racial minority applicants born and trained in Canada or the United Kingdom). We suggest that this is the case because such discrimination would be difficult to justify. When seemingly nonprejudicial justifications are available, however, prejudicial attitudes do play a role. This was the case in our research when the applicant was born and trained in India. In this case, discrimination could be justified on the basis of unfamiliar qualifications and potential for greater cultural differences. This highlights the importance of the psychological perspective for pinpointing the causes of skill discounting. For example, a recent report on immigrant skill discounting in Canada (Finnie, 2005) found that although the foreign-acquired work experience and education of immigrants, particularly racial minority immigrants, are heavily discounted, the work experience and education earned in Canada by immigrants, including racial minority immigrants, are not. On the basis of this finding, the author concluded that "the low valuation of foreign education and work experience, rather than racial discrimination, represents the main obstacle to immigrants' full participation in the Canadian economy" (Finnie, 2005, p. A14). What the author failed to consider, however, is that the low valuation of foreign education and work experience itself may be subject to the influence of racial prejudice. Thus, the failure to devalue Canadian skills held by racial minority immigrants does not demonstrate that prejudice has no role to play. Rather, our findings suggest that prejudice only leads to discrimination when it can be easily justified by the seemingly legitimate factor of foreign qualifications.

Knowledge that skill discounting can be a manifestation of subtle prejudice and legitimizing justifications suggests the types of interventions that may be profitably implemented. In particular, our results suggest that in addition to attempting to change attitudes in order to reduce prejudice, interventions have to be designed that delegitimize the use of foreign qualifications as a reason for not hiring qualified racial minority immigrants. This may involve awareness training for organizational decision makers, standardized and enforceable organizational policies on the evaluation of foreign qualifications, and the more widespread use of international credential evaluation services that provide "legitimacy" to the skills that immigrants bring with them to their new country.

REFERENCES

Aycan, Z., & Berry, J. W. (1996). Impact of employment-related experiences on immigrants' psychological well-being and adaptation to Canada. *Canadian Journal of Behavioural Science, 28*, 240–251.

Baker, M., & Benjamin, D. (1997). Ethnicity, foreign birth and earnings: A Canada/US comparison. In M. G. Abbott, C. M. Beach, & R. P. Chaykowski (Eds.), *Transition and structural change in the North American labour market* (pp. 281–313). Kingston, Canada: John Deutsch Institute for the Study of Economic Policy.

Bowen, D. E., Ledford, G. R., Jr., & Nathan, B. R. (1991). Hiring for the organization, not the job. *Academy of Management Executive, 5*(4), 35–51.

Brief, A. P., Dietz, J., Cohen, R. R., Pugh, S. D., & Vaslow, J. B. (2000). Just doing business: Modern racism and obedience to authority as explanations for employment discrimination. *Organizational Behavior and Human Decision Processes, 81*(1), 72–97.

Citizenship and Immigration Canada. (2003). *Annual report to parliament on immigration: 2003*. Ottawa, Canada: Government of Canada.

Citizenship & Immigration Canada. (2004). *Annual report to parliament on immigration: 2004*. Ottawa, Canada: Government of Canada.

Cohen, J., & Cohen, P. (1983). *Applied multiple regression/correlational analysis for the behavioral sciences*. Hillsdale, NJ: Lawrence Erlbaum Associates.

Crandall, C. S., & Eshleman, A. (2003). A justification–suppression model of the expression and experience of prejudice. *Psychological Bulletin, 129*, 414–446.

Dietz, J., & Pugh, S. D. (2004). I say tomato, you say domate: Differential reactions to English-only workplace policies by persons from immigrant and non-immigrant families. *Journal of Business Ethics, 52*(4), 365–379.

Dovidio, J. F., & Gaertner, S. L. (1998). On the nature of contemporary prejudice: The causes, consequences, and challenges of aversive racism. In J. L. Eberhardt & S. T. Fiske (Eds.), *Confronting racism: The problem and the response* (pp. 3–32). Thousand Oaks, CA: Sage.

Dovidio, J. F., Gaertner, S. L., & Bachman, B.A. (2001). Racial biases in organizations: The role of group processes in its causes and cures. In M.E. Turner (Ed.), *Groups at work: Theory and research* (pp. 415–444). Mahwah, NJ: Lawrence Erlbaum Associates.

Environics. (2000). Attitudes toward immigration. *Focus Canada, 3*, 118–125.

Esses, V. M., Dovidio, J. F., Jackson, L. M., & Armstrong, T. L. (2001). The immigration dilemma: The role of perceived group competition, ethnic prejudice, and national identity. In V. M. Esses, J. F. Dovidio, & K. L. Dion (Eds.), *Immigrants and immigration. Journal of Social Issues, 57*, 389–412.

Esses, V. M., Hodson, G., & Dovidio, J. F. (2003). Public attitudes toward immigrants and immigration: Determinants and policy implications. In C. M. Beach, A. G. Green, & J. G. Reitz (Eds.), *Canadian immigration policy for the 21st century* (pp. 507–535). Montreal, Canada: McGill Queen's Press.

Esses, V. M., Jackson, L. M., & Armstrong, T. L. (1998). Intergroup competition and attitudes toward immigrants and immigration: An instrumental model of group conflict. *Journal of Social Issues, 54*, 699–724.

Finnie, R. (2005, February 9). Bringing immigrants up to speed. *The National Post*, p. A14.

Frazer, R. A., & Wiersma, U. J. (2001). Prejudice versus discrimination in the employment interview: We may hire equally, but our memories harbour prejudice. *Human Relations, 54*, 173–191.

Hanson, G. H. (2004). *Immigration policy*. Retrieved January 5, 2005 from http://irpshome.ucsd.edu/faculty/gohanson/immigration_policy.pdf

Hum, D., & Simpson, W. (1999). Wage opportunities for visible minorities in Canada. *Canadian Public Policy, 25*, 379–394.

Human Resource Management Guide Canada. (2002). *Ignoring foreign talent costs billions*. Retrieved January 4, 2005, from http://www.hrmguide.net/canada/jobmarket/foreign_credentials.htm

Human Resources Development Canada. (2002). *Knowledge matters: Skills and learning for Canadians.* Ottawa: Government of Canada.

Kristof-Brown, A. L. (2000). Perceived applicant-fit: Distinguishing between recruiters' perceptions of person–job and person–organization fit. *Personnel Psychology, 53,* 643–671.

Li, P. S. (2001). The market worth of immigrants' educational credentials. *Canadian Public Policy, 27,* 23–38.

McConahay, J. B. (1986). Modern racism, ambivalence, and the modern racism scale. In J. F. Dovidio & S. L. Gaertner (Eds.), *Prejudice, discrimination, and racism* (pp. 91–125). Orlando, FL: Academic Press.

Metropolis Conversation Series. (2001). *Economic and social performance outcomes of recent immigrants: How can we improve them?* Retrieved August 17, 2004, from http://canada.metropolis.net/research-policy/converation/conversation_5.html

Monteith, M. J., Sherman, J. W., & Devine, P. G. (1998). Suppression as a stereotype control strategy. *Personality and Social Psychology Review, 2,* 63–82.

Petersen, L.-E., & Dietz, J. (2005). Enforcement of workforce homogeneity and prejudice as explanations for employment discrimination. *Journal of Applied Social Psychology, 35*(1), 144–159.

Reitz, J. G. (2001a). Immigrant skill utilization in the Canadian labour market: Implications of human capital research. *Journal of International Migration and Integration, 2*(3), 347–378.

Reitz, J. G. (2001b). Immigrant success in the knowledge economy: Institutional change and the immigrant experience in Canada: 1970–1995. In V. M. Esses, J. F. Dovidio, & K. L. Dion (Eds.), *Immigrants and immigration. Journal of Social Issues, 57,* 579–613.

Reitz, J. G. (2003a). Educational expansion and the employment success of immigrants in the United States and Canada, 1970–1990. In J.G. Reitz (Ed.), *Host societies and the reception of immigrants* (pp. 151–180). San Diego, CA: Center for Comparative Immigration Research.

Reitz, J. G. (2003b). Occupational dimensions of immigrant credential assessment: Trends in professional, managerial, and other occupations: 1970–1996. In C. M. Beach, A. G. Green, & J. G. Reitz (Eds.), *Canadian immigration policy for the 21st century* (pp. 469–506). Kingston: John Deutsch Institute, Queen's University.

Reitz, J. G. (2005). Tapping immigrants' skills: New directions for Canadian immigration policy in the knowledge economy. *Choices, 11*(1).

Statistics Canada. (2004). *The changing profile of Canada's labour force.* Retrieved January 17, 2005, from http://www12.statcan.ca/engish/census01/Products/Analytic/companion/paid/canada.cfm

Stephan, W. G., Renfro, L., Esses, V. M., Stephan, C. W., & Martin, T. (2005). The effects of feeling threatened on attitudes toward immigrants. *International Journal of Intercultural Relations, 29,* 1–19.

Stephan, W. G., Ybarra, O., & Bachman, G. (1999). Prejudice toward immigrants: An integrated threat theory. *Journal of Applied Social Psychology, 29,* 2221–2237.

Sum, A., Fogg, N., Khatiwada, I., & Palma, S. (2004). *Foreign immigration and the labor force of the U.S.: The contributions of new foreign immigration* to the growth of the nation's labor force and its employed population, 2000–2004. Retrieved January 17, 2005, from http://www.nupr.neu.edu/7-04/immigrant_04.pdf

Swidinsky, R., & Swidinsky, M. (2002). The relative earnings of visible minorities in Canada: New evidence from the 1996 census. *Relations Industrielles, 57,* 630–659.

Toye, S. (2002). *Immigrant "brain waste" weakening economy, says professor.* Retrieved September 7, 2004, from http://www.news.utoronto.ca/bin2/020318a.asp

UN Department of Economic and Social Affairs. (2004). *World economic and social survey 2004: International migration.* New York: United Nations Publications.

World Education Services. (2005). Retrieved January 5, 2005, from http://www.wes.org

8

Black Immigrants to the United States: Confronting and Constructing Ethnicity and Race

Teceta Thomas Tormala
Indiana University

Kay Deaux
City University of New York

African American identity (i.e., the meanings surrounding being a Black American, generated both by Blacks and by outgroup members) has gone through continuous construction and revision over the past 400 years, a consequence of the economic, social, political, and psychological outcomes afforded Blacks in the United States since the country's beginnings. More recently, changes in immigration patterns have challenged the definitions of African American identity. During the past 40 years, West Indian and African Blacks—groups with different sociocultural and historical relationships to race than Black Americans—have immigrated to the United States in increasing numbers. These immigrants are broadening the social construction of blackness in the United States. In this chapter we address the ways in which immigrant status, ethnicity, and race intersect for Blacks living in the United States, and how the very meaning of the African American or Black identity is changing in the process.

The history of immigration in the United States is significantly shaped by the images and realities of race (Deaux, 2004). In a country in which the discourse of Black versus White has had a long and pervasive presence, reactions to new arrivals are perhaps inevitably framed in a dialogue of race.[1] This conjunction of immigration and race relations complicates the study of ethnic relations, of stereotyping, prejudice and discrimination, of the role of social identity on outcomes, and of interpersonal interactions. Black immigrants,[2] in particular, challenge us to consider the influence of culture and ethnicity on the one hand, and the stigmatized "master identity" (Waters, 1999a) of blackness on the other. In parsing out these various influences, we may gain a fuller understanding of the ways in which immigration is causing shifts in the parameters and meaning of race.

In this chapter, we describe the patterns of Black immigration to the United States and consider the implications of those patterns for our understanding of the immigrant experience and our understanding of race and ethnicity more generally. Several questions and themes guide our analysis. First, we present some general statistics on immigration to the United States of people of African descent. Recognizing the diversity that this label represents, we note similarities and differences between the countries of origin that highlight the importance of the cultural context of origin to an understanding of adaptation to the culture of entry. With reference to the culture of entry, we look at the context that Black immigrants encounter, specifically in terms of the beliefs and stereotypes held by native-born citizens. We then turn to the behavior of immigrants themselves, describing research that explores how Black immigrants negotiate situations in which their race and/or ethnicity is potentially relevant and the role that ethnic identification plays in performance, beliefs, and attitudes. Finally, we assess our own involvement in these issues and raise a number of questions for future investigation in the hopes of more fully understanding the complex ways in which culture, ethnicity, and race intertwine.

PATTERNS OF BLACK IMMIGRATION

The arrival of large numbers of Black immigrants to cities such as New York, Washington, DC, and Miami has changed the dynamics of interactions both within the Black community, and between Blacks and outgroup members. Black immigrants constitute about 7% of the foreign-born population living in the United States and about 6% of the Black population in the United States (U.S. Census, 2000). Tables 8.1 and 8.2 present percentages, information on countries of

---

[1]We use the term race to denote differences between groups based on socially constructed categories; we do not assume any biological basis of difference.

[2]Black immigrants are a heterogenous group; the term primarily refers to Blacks immigrating from the Caribbean or African countries. When we use the term *Black immigrants*, we mean any Black who has immigrated to the United States (first generation) or the child of an immigrant (second generation).

TABLE 8.1

Comparison of Immigrants From the Caribbean and From Africa

	West Indian/ Caribbean Immigrants	African Immigrants
Percentage of total U.S. population	0.5%	0.2%
Percentage of Black population in the United States	4.6%	1.6%
Top sending countries of origin, with the number of nationals living in the United States	Jamaica (553,827) Guyana (211,189) Trinidad and Tobago (197,398)	Nigeria (134,940) Egypt (113,396) Ethiopia (69,531)
Metropolitan areas of highest concentration	New York Miami Ft. Lauderdale, FL	Washington, DC New York Atlanta

Note. From Logan and Deane (2003) and U.S. Census (2000).

TABLE 8.2

Foreign-Born Black population, 1900–2000

Year	Population	Percent of total Black population
2000	2,155,443	6.1%
1990	1,154.181	4.0%
1980	815,720	3.1%
1970	253,458	1.1%
1960	125,322	0.7%
1950	113,842	0.8%
1940	83,941	0.7%
1930	98,620	0.8%
1920	73,803	0.7%
1910	40,339	0.4%
1900	20,336	0.2%

Note. Data from U. S. Census (2000).

origin, and the distribution of Black immigrants within the United States, as of the year 2000.

The increasing number of Black immigrants has begun to shift intraracial politics and interactions with American Blacks and has served to refocus the meanings around the Black/African American identity. The presence of West Indians in departments of African American Studies has sparked considerable debate (Hintzen, 2001). Two recent articles in the *New York Times* (Rimer & Arenson, 2004; Swarns, 2004), as examples, discussed how the increasing presence of Black immigrants is affecting who can claim the label of African American (and, as one social consequence, who is entitled to affirmative action funds set aside for that group).

The growing diversity within the Black community in the United States affects not only relations between American and immigrant Blacks, but also the perceptions and attitudes toward the two groups by non-Blacks. Perceptions of the groups are driven in part by the percentages of the groups in the population: As the percentage of a minority group increases, intergroup conflict and misperceptions also rise (Massey & Denton, 1993). Underlying the increase in prejudice and discrimination triggered by a numerical increase of a group is the perception of that group as a threat to economic livelihood (realistic or economic threat) and/or a threat to values and mores (symbolic threat). This process has been shown to occur both for increasing numbers of Blacks (Taylor, 1998) and immigrants (Esses, Jackson, & Armstrong, 1998; Zárate, Garcia, Garza, & Hitlan, 2003). Thus, the low percentages of Black immigrants in the majority of American cities may be (at least temporarily) protecting them from some of the negative evaluation, stereotyping, and discrimination that can affect Black Americans, at both the interpersonal level (e.g., harassment) and the institutional level (e.g., housing).

The demographics of different groups within city populations are also important in determining the ease with which Black immigrants are incorporated into the area. Not only is the percentage of Black immigrants important; also important is the percentage of Black Americans, minorities, and immigrants in any given city. The experience of a West Indian immigrant in New York City, a metropolitan area that has both a large Black (27%) and a large immigrant population (indeed, 26% of the Black population are immigrants), is different from the experience of a West Indian in Los Angeles, where there are high numbers of Asians and Latinos (57% combined), but a smaller percentage of Blacks (11%), or in a city like Montpelier, Vermont, which is 97% White.

The degree to which Black immigrants are categorized into, and group themselves along with, a larger Black or minority group or a larger immigrant group affects both reactions toward Black immigrants by outgroup members and the identities adopted by the group members themselves (as immigrant or Black immigrant, as minority, and/or as Black). Perceptions of threat affect not only Whites' level of prejudice, but also the prejudice level other minority group members as well (Bobo & Hutchings, 1996). The interpersonal dynamics at all levels—intracial (with Black Americans), intragroup (with other minorities), or intergroup (with Whites)—affect the psychology and day-to-day lives of Black immigrants. The dynamics of inter- and intragroup relations can aid or impede the adjustment of Black immigrants. On the one hand, social and economic adjustment is facilitated by having the social capital, ethnic networks, and financial support of other co-ethnics. On the other hand, the presence of Black Americans may have positive or negative outcomes for Black immigrants. The existence of the much more numerous group of American Blacks can serve to absorb societal focus, buffering the experience of immigrant Blacks from the bulk of negative treatment facing U.S.-born Blacks (Foner, 1998). At the same time, large numbers of Black Americans may increase the potential for intraracial tensions, as well as the effects of categorization into the larger stigmatized group.

COMPARING CULTURES OF ORIGIN

Black immigrants have great cultural and linguistic diversity. Both between and within the regions of the Caribbean and Africa, differences in language, traditions, ethnicity, religion, and history exist (see Table 8.3 for a more detailed description of these patterns). As just one ex-

TABLE 8.3
Contemporary Cultures of Origin for First- and Second-Generation Black Immigrants and Native-Born Black Americans, Showing Cultural Context in Country of Birth

Foreign countries of origin: First-generation black immigrants	The United States context: Second-generation immigrants and Black Americans
Blacks are numerical majority[a]	Blacks are numerical minority[b]
Blacks hold significant positions of power[a]	Blacks lack political and social power[a]
Race is not a dimension of stratification[e]	Race is a dimension of stratification[c]
Absence of racialization within societal institutions (e.g., housing, education system, legal system)[a]	Racialized according to the cultural racial hierarchy[d]

[a]Waters (1999a).
[b]U.S. Census (2000).
[c]Crocker, Major, and Steele (1998).
[d]Omi and Winant (1994).

ample, Nigeria in itself is a multilingual and multiethnic nation containing between 250 and 350 ethnic groups that are stratified in society, with different access to resources, wealth, power, and status (Oyewole & Lucas, 2000). Both in Africa and in the Caribbean, the divisions between strata are as fixed and hierarchical as those based on race in the United States (Waters, 1999a). Among most predominantly Black nations, however, certain parallels of history, social structure, and current social hierarchy result in comparable psychological processes among those who immigrate to the United States. These similarities allow the diverse peoples of Africa and the Caribbean to have common ways of perceiving and interpreting American society. The sociohistorical and cultural dimensions that are often comparable among foreign-born Blacks are distinct from those of Black Americans, whose present status and power within the U.S. social system reflects the particular history of race in the United States.

Two main forces have made the experience of Black immigrants to the United States distinct from that of Blacks who have lived in the country for many generations. Although both the United States, on the one hand, and African and Caribbean countries, on the other, have histories of European colonization and domination, the legacy of these periods has been different for the two groups. In the majority of Caribbean and African nations, Blacks are the numerical majority and hold positions of social and political power. In the United States, in contrast, Blacks have never held positions of power in percentages proportional to the group in the United States as a whole. The social, political, and legal institutions of the United States have developed along racial lines since the beginning, and race-based hierarchies continue into the current day (Omi & Winant, 1994).

In addition (and, some theories would posit, consequently; see Jost & Banaji, 1994), race-based stereotyping and bias are fairly infrequent in predominantly Black societies. The association between race and socioeconomic outcomes is low, as is the existence of stereotypes that link particular racial groups with specific negative traits or behaviors. In the United States, blackness is a highly stigmatized category (Crocker, Major, & Steele, 1998); the stereotype about Black Americans is widely held and predominantly negative (Devine & Elliot, 1995; Levy, Stroessner, & Dweck, 1998; Plous & Williams, 1995) (see Table 8.4 for a comparison).

Thus, race has not had the equivalent consequence in the majority of African and Caribbean nations as it has had in the United States.[3] The relative superfluity of the construct of race in the social and

---

[3]Two of the three countries of highest emigration to the United States (Guyana and Trinidad) are nearly evenly divided between East Indian and Black nationals, with 50% and 40% East Indian, respectively. This diversity (and the conflicts that arise between the racial groups) may have implications for the ways in which these immigrants experience race in the American context. Because of the distinctions made between races in their countries of origin, Blackness as a construct may hold meaning in ways that it does not for other Caribbean immigrants, or for African immigrants, who come from greater racial homogeneity.

power structures of Black societies, as compared to the U.S. system, is evident (Bashi, 2001). Similar to the low consensual meaning of White identity in American consciousness (Perry, 2002), where Whites make up the numerical majority, racial identity for Blacks raised in predominantly Black cultures means little until they are exposed to a society with a racial hierarchy vastly different from their own. These immigrants are entering the United States and becoming Black (see Stepick, Stepick, Eugene, Teed, & Labissiere, 2001, for a description of the racialization of Haitian immigrants), in a country where the meanings surrounding their racial identity are much stronger and far more negative than the social representations about blackness in their countries of origin.

HOW BLACK IMMIGRANTS ARE VIEWED IN THE UNITED STATES

For Blacks, skin color activates the stereotypes tied to the group (Maddox & Gray, 2002); at automatic and nonconscious levels, Black immigrants and Black Americans are perceived in the same way. Whether by passersby, customers walking around a store, or drivers in an upper-class neighborhood, Black immigrants will be categorized as Black and subjected to the same kinds of race-based bias and discrimination as American Blacks.

Racial homogenization is not always the rule, however, where perceptions of White Americans are concerned. In situations in which individuating information is available, Black immigrants are often positively distinguished from native-born African Americans. Waters (1999b) described the preference of some White employers for West Indian workers over African American workers. This preferential treatment results from the employers' beliefs that immigrant Blacks are more hardworking and less difficult than African Americans (a belief that is echoed in other research showing favoritism for immigrant workers over Americans; Shih, 2002).

This preference in hiring has also been tested empirically (Eberhardt & Deaux, unpublished data). White participants in an experiment viewed a videotaped interview of a Black man, who was identified by his spoken accent as either African American or Caribbean, but who gave the identical script in both conditions. In the latter condition, participants rated the candidate more favorably, saw him as having better interpersonal skills, and believed he had performed better in the interview than did participants who viewed the African American interviewee (when, in fact, the same person played both roles).

These documented preferences for Black immigrants over native-born African Americans in job-related contexts may be due to differences in stereotypes and general representations about the two groups in U.S. society. In a recent study, Tormala (2005) found that the stereotype traits used by more than one third of participants to describe Black Americans were broad and far more negative than positive. Traits such as *criminal*, *lazy*, and *tough/aggressive* were generated as descriptive of the Black American stereotype, with *athletic* being the only positive trait that was as frequently generated. The stereotype about Black immigrants, in contrast, was far narrower; only a single descriptor—*hardworking*—was generated by more than one third of study participants.

The Tormala data also suggest that the stereotype of Black immigrants may be differentially distributed among different racial groups. White students had a highly underdeveloped stereotype about Black immigrants, both in comparison to their knowledge of the stereotype about Black Americans and in comparison to the stereotypes held by Black American and by Black immigrant students (Tormala, 2005). The degree to which this result holds true across various geographical regions remains to be tested. It is possible that in metropolitan areas with a high percentage of Black immigrants, like New York, Miami, or Washington, DC, the stereotype about Black immigrants is more developed among Whites than it was for the California students in the Tormala (2005) study.

As the findings from Eberhardt and Deaux (unpublished data) suggest, the difference in the content of the stereotype about Black immigrants and Black Americans has consequences for the groups' outcomes. Job hiring is only one domain in which a preference for Black immigrants might result in a more positive outcome for that group over Black Americans. In education, a perception of immigrants as hardworking could lead teachers to favor a first- or second-generation Jamaican or Nigerian student over a Black student of native heritage, leading to differential rates of success. The disproportionate percentage of Black immigrants in elite colleges and universities was highlighted by Rimer and Arenson (2004) in a recent *New York Times* article, along with the turmoil that has arisen within the Black community on campus between immigrants and "the descendants."

The comparison of Black immigrants and Black Americans is only one comparison of interest; another is the distinction between how Black immigrants are viewed and how immigrants in general are perceived. This comparison allows us to examine whether Black immigrants are seen as *immigrants*, or whether their racial designation affords them representations distinct from those of immigrants as a group. American nativism, ethnocentrism, and perceptions of economic competition all underlie the current representations of and attitudes toward immigrants (Esses, Dovidio, Jackson, & Armstrong, 2001; Sánchez, 1999; Stephan, Ybarra, & Bachman, 1999; Zárate, Garcia, Garza, & Hitlan, 2003). Approximately half of the people responding to a recent U.S. survey indicated that immigration should be decreased (Mizrahi, 2005).

Furthermore, attitudes toward immigrants differ by the nationality of the immigrant: Chinese, Korean, and Polish immigrants are more highly regarded than are Cubans, Haitians, and Mexicans (Lapinski, Peltola, Shaw, & Yang, 1997). Native-born Americans believe that immigrants should take on American culture and language rather than maintain their own (Taylor & Lambert, 1996). In general, perceptions of immigrant groups are fairly negative, although mitigated by the size and familiarity of the immigrant group (Mullen, Rozell, & Johnson, 2001) and perception of the group as a symbolic versus economic threat (Stephan et al., 1999).

From the limited research that has been conducted to this point on stereotypes and perceptions of Black immigrants, it appears that they are not being perceived in the same ways as are immigrants more generally. As immigration from the Caribbean and Africa continues to increase—and with it, intergroup conflict and perceptions of threat—an important issue for further study is whether the valence of the stereotypes about members of those nations will become more negative, in line with those about Black Americans.

NEGOTIATING THE U.S. CONTEXT

How do Black immigrants fare in a society in which negative stereotypes and representations about Blacks are pervasive? At a group level, they are performing relatively well. In higher education, there are differences in the matriculation levels of immigrant and American Blacks. At selective colleges and universities, Black immigrants make up 25% of the Black student population although they comprise only about 6% of the total Black population in the United States (Massey, Charles, Lundy, & Fischer, 2002). In other socioeconomic indices as well, demographic analyses show a slight but consistent first-generation Black immigrant advantage over native-born Black Americans. The advantage exists in educational attainment (Butcher, 1994), labor force participation (Model, 1995), occupational distribution (U.S. Census, 2000), employment (Logan & Deane, 2003), and income (Kalmijn, 1996).

How are immigrant Blacks faring on a micro level, as they negotiate situations in which their racial identity is visible and stigmatized, while their ethnic identity is invisible until it is made salient? Waters (1999a) discussed the phenomenon of immigrants' strategic exposure of ethnic or national identity through speech and accent, particularly among the second generation, who often have an American accent that is not identifiable as being of immigrant heritage. In interpersonal situations, this ability to broadcast a distinct ethnic identity may serve as a buffer for Black immigrants against some of the negative effects of their racial identity (Cross & Strauss, 1998). Other situations, such as testing domains, typically do not provide an opportunity for the person to express a distinct ethnic identity. An understanding of both visible and invisible identity as an immigrant is important in determining how Black immigrants negotiate the American context.

Social identities—be they racial, ethnic, gender, social class, or religious—guide thoughts, beliefs, and expectations within varying social contexts and can affect behavior in those situations (Ashmore, Deaux, & McLaughlin-Volpe, 2004; Deaux, 1996). Threats to social identities (and the increased salience of the meanings and representations associated with them) have important consequences on attitudes, behavior, and performance (see Branscombe, Ellemers, & Spears, 1999, for a review). Among American Blacks, stereotype threat is one form of social identity threat that has been shown to affect academic performance, leading African Americans to underperform relative to Whites when under threat conditions (although showing equivalent performance when threat is absent; see Steele, 1997; Steele & Aronson, 1995).

Although the stereotype of Black intellectual inferiority is ubiquitous in the U.S., the same stereotype does not pervade African and Caribbean countries. Accordingly, reasoned Deaux and her colleagues (Deaux et al., 2005), first-generation Black immigrants, who have not been raised with the stereotype of Black underachievement, would not be expected to show underperformance in a stereotype threat situation. In contrast, second-generation Black immigrants, who have had more exposure to the stereotype and more experience with being categorized as African American, are apt to be more vulnerable to stereotype threat effects. Consistent with this theorizing, second-generation immigrants from the West Indies showed a significant decrement in performance relative to first-generation immigrants when stereotype threat conditions were invoked, although performing equally when the situation did not invoke the stereotypes of Black inferiority.

This effect was mirrored in another study showing that first-generation immigrants in a high-threat situation expressed higher expectations for performance on a test than those in a low-threat situation, whereas the reverse pattern was true for second-generation immigrants and Black Americans (Tormala, Steele, & Davies, 2006). The variable or variables underlying these group differences in the effects of identity threat are still being explored, but several possibilities exist. One potential interpretation of the increased performance of first-generation Black immigrants is that the activation of the stereotype by the high threat context engenders a social comparison process between one's own Black immigrant group and the less positively evaluated African American group. This comparison may lead to an attempt to distance oneself positively from the negative stereotype (i.e., "African Americans tend not to do well on high-stakes tests, but I'm not African American, so I'll do well"). Alternatively, performance pressure may make more salient the positive images that one has of one's immigrant group, leading to enhanced performance ("Black immigrants are smart/do well on high-stakes tests").

The first interpretation implies an explicit consideration of the contrast between the Black immigrant and Black American stereotype of achievement or perceived values about education. This degree of active thought is unlikely, given that stereotype threat effects often occur automatically (see Wheeler & Petty, 2001, for a review). We think the second explanation is more likely, based on an observed positive relationship between perceptions of the favorability of one's own group and actual performance in the Deaux et al. (2005) results.

Another question regarding the generational difference is whether Black immigrants perceived racial identity-threatening situations as such. First-generation immigrants may not perceive race-related situational cues to the same degree as Blacks who are born in the United States. Some recent research (2003; Tormala et al., 2006) supports this possibility. In two studies conducted with California college students, first-generation Black immigrants showed lower stigma consciousness than did second-generation immigrants and Black Americans (Thomas, 2003; Tormala et al., 2006). These data imply that foreign-born Blacks are less likely to perceive—or to acknowledge—the role of race in interpersonal interactions and perceptions. However, data collected by Deaux et al. (2005) in the more ethnically diverse locale of New York City found no difference between first- and second-generation West Indian students on a measure of sensitivity to race-based rejection (Mendoza-Denton, Downey, Purdie, Davis, & Peitrzak, 2002). Further work is needed to determine whether the differences between the two sets of finding are due to scale variations or to more complicated issues of context and geographical location.

ETHNIC IDENTIFICATION AND NEGOTIATION

Thus far our discussion has considered Black immigrants in demographic terms, distinguished on the basis of country of origin or generational status. Yet for the psychologist, these externally assigned categories are only part of the story. Black immigrants (and other immigrants as well) who arrive in the United States must redefine themselves in a new context and negotiate their identity vis-à-vis those who would choose to define them. The identification process is thus a multifaceted one, influenced by the history of the immigrant's culture of origin, by the labeling of others whom they encounter, and then translated into a subjective pattern of ethnic identification that serves to define the self across varying contexts (see Fig. 8.1 for a schematic of this process).

Upon arrival to the United States, Black immigrants are generally positive in their view of their group and in their attitudes toward their new country of residence. In comparison to Black Americans, first-generation Black immigrants are more likely to interact with outgroup members (Phelps, Taylor, & Gerard, 2001), more likely to endorse American ideologies of economic opportunities and rights (Phinney & Onwughalu, 1996), less likely to mistrust American cul-

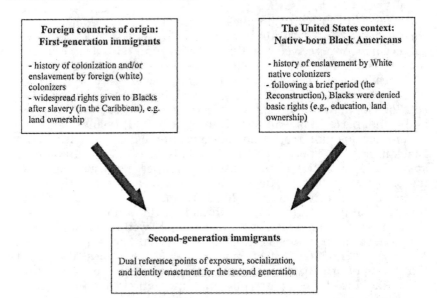

FIG. 8.1.   Sources of influence for second-generation Black immigrants.

ture and society (Biafora, Taylor, Warheit, Zimmerman, & Vega, 1993), and less likely to believe that parents should talk to their children about racism (Thomas, 2002). These data suggest a difference in the ways that the two groups perceive race and the role of race within American society. For the first generation, the absence of a racialized social structure in their countries of origin appears to continue to influence perceptions after initial immigration into American society. In contrast, Black Americans, and to a large extent second-generation Black immigrants, are more influenced by the sociohistorical meanings around Blackness that are embedded in U.S. culture (see Table 8.4 for a description of these and other processes and cultural practices).

These meanings of Blackness, often negative in content, can impact on the immigrant in a process that has been termed *social mirroring* (Suárez-Orozco & Suárez-Orozco, 2001). In this process, the negative views of one's group that are expressed by others are reflected back and may be incorporated in the self-image. (Alternatively, as work by Crocker, Luhtanen, Blaine, and Broadnax [1994] suggests, one may be acutely aware of the negative views of others but not incorporate them into the self-image.) The existence of these kinds of processes makes the assimilation story of immigration a much more complicated one than has previously been told. Recent theorizing by sociologists proposes a model of *segmented assimilation*, in which two alternatives to classic upward assimilation are postulated (Portes & Zhou, 1993). Segmented assimilation holds that immigrants do not necessarily move into an up-

TABLE 8.4
Psychological Processes and Cultural Practices
for First-Generation, Second-Generation, and Native-Born Blacks

	First-generation black immigrants	Second-generation black immigrants	Black Americans
Psychological processes and cultural practices	More likely to interact with outgroup members[a]	Have possibility of strategic use of accents[b]	Less likely to interact with outgroup members[a]
	Belief that American ideals apply to self[a]	Salience of an American identity causes heightened perceptions of prejudice and owered expectation for success than a salient immigrant identity[c]	Belief that Blacks are often over-looked in U.S. policy
	Unwilling/unlikely to view race as a barrier to success[b]	Personal experience with race as a barrier; willing to acknowledge possibility[b]	Personal and historical experiences with race as a barrier; willing to acknowledge possibility
Collective identity	Maintenance of ethnic identity can serve as buffer from stereotypes and prejudice associated with African Americans[b]	Neighborhood demographics have large effects on self-identification[b]	Identity is stigmatized and devalued in U.S. society[e]
	Collective identity tends to be high[d]	Those who identify as African American show greater belief that race affects future outcomes than those who identity as immigrants[b]	Collective identity tends to be high[d]
Negotiation withing U.S. society	Fewer experiences with racial prejudice in countries of origin[b]	Experience with instances of racial prejudice[b]	Experience with instances of racial prejudice[b]

[a]Phelps, Taylor, and Gerard (2001); [b]Waters (1999a); [c]Tormala, Steele, and Davies (2006); [d]Thomas (2003); [e]Crocker, Major, and Steele (1998).

143

wardly mobile middle class, but instead assimilate into different segments of society depending on several class- and culture-based factors. *Downward assimilation* is characterized by integration with the existing underclass and a fall in status position. Groups that follow this path are those more likely to face discrimination on the basis of race. In a third pattern, *ethnic maintenance*, ethnic identification and community are maintained, whereas occupational status rises.

For the Black immigrant, and particularly the second-generation immigrant, the choice is often between these latter two paths (without implying that choice is unconstrained by situational and structural realities). The straight-line, traditional theory of upward assimilation and acculturation can no longer explain the trajectory of groups whose racial status links them to stereotypes already in place within society (Sánchez, 1999; Suárez-Orozco, 2000). As Vickerman (1999) has noted, "The attitudes exhibited by West Indian immigrants in this country derive from the conflict between a strong desire for upward mobility that is implied in the immigrant ethos, and the existence of an entrenched ethnic hierarchy which tends to tightly constrain individuals of African ancestry" (p. 5).

Ethnic identification by second-generation Black immigrants is influenced by the ethnic and immigrant composition of the neighborhood in which they live, as they align themselves with the group whose practices are most prevalent in their daily lives (Gibson, 2001; Hao & Bonstead-Bruns, 1998; Portes & Zhou, 1993). Second-generation immigrants who live in integrated or predominantly White neighborhoods tend to be middle-class or above, and also tend to self-identify as an ethnic American (distinct from Black Americans). This group shows a fairly weak endorsement of the belief in an association between race and success (Waters, 1994). In contrast, second-generation immigrants who live in predominantly Black American neighborhoods, which are often characterized by lower income and poorer schools, tend to self-identify as Black American, show a stronger belief in the association between race and future success, and believe more strongly in the ubiquity of racial prejudice.

Personal experience influences ethnic identification as well. Portes and Rumbaut (2001) noted the role that negative interactions with outgroup members can play, describing a process that they termed *reactive ethnicity*, whereby ethnic identity is strengthened in direct and explicit opposition to the negative feedback from others. As they concluded, "Groups subjected to extreme discrimination and derogation of their national origins are likely to embrace them ever more fiercely; those received more favorably shift to American identities with greater speed and less pain" (p. 187). For the immigrant from the Caribbean or Africa, it is interesting to consider whether the same forces would be at work. Are there different views of these two sites of origin that might lead to different experiences, or are both groups equally lumped together with the native-born African American, effectively constraining their options?

Relatively stable identification patterns can coexist with situationally influenced saliency of a particular aspect of ethnic identity. Thus many immigrants may have access to more than one view of self, views that can be triggered by different situational contingencies. Research has shown, for example, that manipulating identity salience through priming one social identity versus another leads to differences in academic performance (Shih, Pittinsky, & Ambady, 1999), self-appraisals (Ross, Xun, & Wilson, 2002), and attributions for behavior (Benet-Martínez, Leu, Lee, & Morris, 2002). Among Black immigrants, it may be the second generation that has more access to varied representations and hence would be more sensitive to situational variation. Consistent with this notion, Tormala and her colleagues found that second-generation Black immigrants who were primed with an American identity showed greater perception of prejudice and lowered expectancy for success than those primed with an immigrant identity (Tormala et al., 2006).

CONCLUDING THOUGHTS

Immigration adds an important dimension to the exploration of the parameters of race and of Blackness in U.S. society, and stands as an element of increasing importance as the number of immigrants from Africa and the West Indies continues to rise. We ourselves come to this conversation from different experiences and somewhat different perspectives, but with equivalent commitments to the importance of understanding the immigrant experience more fully.

The first author, the daughter of a Trinidadian mother and Guyanese father, has always been interested in the ways in which ethnicity and race do—and do not—intersect. Being a second-generation Caribbean American simultaneously allows for closeness to and distance from the two sides that make up that whole. This bicultural identity adds a nuanced perspective to the consideration of immigrant and American Blacks and; at times, disallows the opportunity to ever feel fully connected with either. It also allows an intimate glimpse at the ways in which social identity can shift across situations and over time.

The second author, who shares neither race nor ethnicity with her coauthor, nonetheless has some historical connection to immigration through the move of one set of grandparents from (the very non-Black region of) Finland to the United States. Although their color made these Finns candidates for upward assimilation, the ethnic isolation of the first generation was profound. A retrospective look at the second generation (i.e., in a comparison of two second-generation brothers) through a contemporary social psychological lens suggests quite different patterns of identification and assimilation, underlining the importance of examining the psychology within demographic ethnic categories.

As we look forward from what we know now to what still remains to be learned, we are impressed with the extent to which the case of Black immigration puts in sharp relief some of the fundamental questions in the field. Work on Black immigrant populations, for example, allows us to separate, at least in part, the distinct influences of race and ethnicity on identity processes. So often conflated in the literature, race and ethnicity are distinguishable concepts, with separate and interactive effects among Blacks (as well as other groups). An increased focus within psychology on ethnicity as a moderator of processes found among Blacks will be an important direction in the measure of the variation among the Black population in the United States. The study of ethnic minority immigrants within the broader framework of cultural psychology can show how ethnic and cultural variation undergirds not only differences in psychological content, but process as well.

We have focused on race and ethnicity in this chapter, attentive to the ways that they play out in the lives of first- and second-generation immigrants from Africa and the Caribbean. This focus should not suggest, however, that we dismiss the more complex cultural context in which immigrants negotiate their lives. Gender, for example, undoubtedly has an influence on the ways in which race and ethnicity play out (Foner, 2002). So too do differences in economic resources and social capital that an immigrant brings to the new environment (Portes & Rumbaut, 2001). Similarly, the place of religion in an analysis of ethnic identity must be investigated, particularly as the number of Black immigrants from Muslim North and West Africa increases (Shryock, 2000).

It will be important to note the impact of rising numbers and increasing familiarity and visibility on the outcomes of first- and second-generation Black immigrants. Although some investigators suggest that the increasing size of an immigrant group leads to more positive views of the group (e.g., Mullen et al., 2001), other research has shown that increases are associated with more negative views (Taylor, 1998). We suspect the issue is more complicated than size alone and must take into account the complexities of interpersonal perceptions and interactions. Furthermore, just as increased numbers may alter the views of those in the host country, increased diversity within the Black population may further challenge definitions of race and ethnicity both within the majority culture and within the Black population itself.

Thus far, social psychology has shown itself to be a cautious gatekeeper, partially recognizing the intrinsic value that the study of Black immigrants offers to the study of race-based group differences while at the same time lacking a full appreciation for the subtleties of the enterprise. A long-standing preference in the field for the study of randomly assigned laboratory groups over existing social demarcations accounts for part of the resistance. A lack of interest or even rejection of data emanating from other methodologies—such as ethnographies—also contributes to the narrowed focus. Thus, although long established within other disciplines such as sociology, history, and anthropology, the study of intraracial group differences is yet to be embraced by psychology. Once we as a field become more open to cultural psychology in general, and the importance of variation within racial groups in particular, we will come closer to a fuller understanding of the varieties of human experience.

ACKNOWLEDGMENT

We are grateful to Bill Cross and to members of the CUNY Graduate Center Identity Research Group for their comments on an earlier version of this chapter.

REFERENCES

Ashmore, R. D., Deaux, K., & McLaughlin-Volpe, T. (2004). An organizing framework for collective identity: Articulation and significance of multidimensionality. *Psychological Bulletin, 130,* 80–114.

Bashi, V. F. (2001). Neither ignorance nor bliss: Race, racism, and the West Indian immigrant experience. In H. R. Cordero-Guzmán, R. C. Smith, & R. Grosfoguel (Eds.), *Migration, transnationalism, and race in a changing New York* (pp. 212–238). Philadelphia, PA: Temple University Press.

Benet-Martínez, V., Leu, J., Lee, F., & Morris, M. W. (2002). Negotiating biculturalism: Cultural frame-switching in biculturals with "oppositional" vs. "compatible" cultural identities. *Journal of Cross-Cultural Psychology, 33,* 492–516.

Biafora, F. A., Jr., Taylor, D. L., Warheit, G. J., Zimmerman, R. S., & Vega, W. A. (1993). Cultural mistrust and racial awareness among ethnically diverse black adolescent boys. *Journal of Black Psychology, 19,* 266–281.

Bobo, L., & Hutchings, V. L. (1996). Perceptions of racial group competition: Extending Blumer's theory of group position to a multiracial social context. *American Sociological Review, 61,* 951–972.

Branscombe, N. R., Ellemers, N., & Spears, R. (1999). The context and content of social identity threat. In N. Ellemers & R. Spears (Eds.), *Social identity: Context, commitment, content* (pp. 35–58). Oxford, England: Blackwell Science.

Butcher, K.F. (1994). Black immigrants in the United States: A comparison with native blacks and other immigrants. *Industrial and Labor Relations Review, 47,* 265–283.

Crocker, J., Luhtanen, R., Blaine, B., & Broadnax, S. (1994). Collective self-esteem and psychological well-being among White, Black, and Asian college students. *Personality and Social Psychology Bulletin, 20,* 503–513.

Crocker, J., Major, B., & Steele, C. M. (1998). Social stigma. In D. T. Gilbert, S. T. Fiske, & G. Lindzey (Eds.), *The handbook of social psychology* (pp. 504–553). McGraw-Hill.

Cross, W. E., Jr., & Strauss, L. (1998). The everyday functions of African American identity. In J. K. Swim & C. Stangor (Eds.), *Prejudice: The target's perspective* (pp. 268–280). San Diego: Academic Press.

Deaux, K. (1996). Social identification. In E. T. Higgins & A. W. Kruglanski (Eds.), *Social psychology: Handbook of basic principles* (pp. 777–798). New York: Guildford.

Deaux, K. (2004). Immigration and the color line. In G. Philogene (Ed.), *Racial identity in context: The legacy of Kenneth B. Clark* (pp. 197–209). Washington, DC: American Psychological Association.

Deaux, K., Gilkes, A., Bikmen, N., Ventuneac, A., Joseph, Y., Payne, Y., & Steele, C. (2005). *Becoming American: Stereotype threat effects in black immigrant groups.* Manuscript under review.

Devine, P. G., & Elliot, A. J. (1995). Are racial stereotypes really fading? The Princeton trilogy revisited. *Personality and Social Psychology Bulletin, 21,* 1139–1150.

Esses, V. M., Dovidio, J. F., Jackson, L. M., & Armstrong, T.L. (2001). The immigration dilemma: The role of perceived group competition, ethnic prejudice, and national identity. *Journal of Social Issues, 57,* 389–412.

Esses, V. M., Jackson, L. M., & Armstrong, T. L. (1998). Intergroup competition and attitudes toward immigrants and immigration: An instrumental model of group conflict [Special issue]. *Journal of Social Issues, 54,* 699–724.

Foner, N. (1998). West Indian identity in the diaspora: Comparative and historical perspectives. *Latin American Perspectives, 25*(3), 173–188.

Foner, N. (2002). Immigrant women and work in New York City, then and now. In P.G. Min (Ed.), *Mass migration to the United States: Classical and contemporary periods* (pp. 231– 252). Walnut Creek, CA: AltaMira Press.

Gibson, M.A. (2001). Immigrant adaptation and patterns of acculturation. *Human Development, 44,* 19–23.

Hao, L., & Bonstead-Bruns, M. (1998). Parent-child differences in educational expectations and the academic achievement of immigrant & native students. *Sociology of Education, 71,* 175–198.

Hintzen, P.C. (2001). *West Indian in the West: Self-representations in an immigrant community.* New York University Press. New York and London.

Jost, J. T., & Banaji, M. B. (1994). The role of stereotyping in system-justification and the production of false consciousness. *British Journal of Social Psychology, Special Issue: Stereotypes: Structure, function and process, 33,* 1–27.

Kalmijn, M. (1996). The socioeconomic assimilation of Caribbean American Blacks. *Social Forces, 74,* 911–930.

Lapinski, J.S., Peltola, P., Shaw, G., & Yang, A. (1997). Poll trends: Immigrants and immigration. *Public Opinion Quarterly, 61,* 356–383.

Levy, S. R., Stroessner, S. J., & Dweck, C. S. (1998). Stereotype formation and endorsement: The role of implicit theories. *Journal of Personality and Social Psychology, 74,* 1421–1436.

Logan, J. R., & Deane, G. (2003). *Black diversity in metropolitan America.* Albany, NY: Lewis Mumford Center for Comparative Urban and Regional Research at the University at Albany.

Maddox, K. B., & Gray, S. A. (2002). Cognitive representations of Black Americans: Reexploring the role of skin tone. *Personality and Social Psychology Bulletin, 28,* 250–259.

Massey, D. S., Charles, C. Z., Lundy, G., & Fischer, M. J. (2002). *The source of the river: The social origins of freshmen at America's selective colleges and universities.* Princeton, NJ: Princeton University Press.

Massey, D. S., & Denton, N. A. (1993). *American apartheid: Segregation and the making of the underclass.* Cambridge, MA: Harvard University Press.

Mendoza-Denton, R., Downey, G., Purdie, V., Davis, A., & Pietrzak, J. (2002). Sensitivity to status-based rejection: Implications for African American students' college experience. *Journal of Personality and Social Psychology, 83,* 896–918.

Mizrahi, K. (2005). *Americans' attitudes toward immigration and immigrants.* Unpublished doctoral dissertation, City University of New York, Graduate Center.

Model, S. (1995). West Indian prosperity: Fact or fiction? *Social Problems, 42,* 535–553.

Mullen, B., Rozell, D., & Johnson, C. (2001). Ethnophaulisms for ethnic immigrant groups: The contributions of group size and familiarity. *European Journal of Social Psychology, 31,* 231–246.

Omi, M., & Winant, H. (1994). *Racial formation in the United States: From the 1960s to the 1990s.* New York: Routledge.

Oyewole, A., & Lucas, J. (2000). *Historical dictionary of Nigeria* (2nd ed.). Lanham, MD and London: Scarecrow Press.

Perry, P. (2002). *Shades of white: White kids and racial identities in high school.* Durham, NC: Duke University Press.

Phelps, R. E., Taylor, J. D., & Gerard, P. A. (2001). Cultural mistrust, ethnic identity, racial identity, and self-esteem among ethnically diverse black university students. *Journal of Counseling and Development, 79,* 209–216.

Phinney, J. S., & Onwughalu, M. (1996). Racial identity and perception of American ideals among African American and African students in the United States. International Journal of *Intercultural Relations, 20,* 127–140.

Plous, S., & Williams, T. (1995). Racial stereotypes from the days of American slavery: A continuing legacy. *Journal of Applied Social Psychology, 25,* 795–817.

Portes, A., & Rumbaut, R. G. (2001). *Legacies: The story of the immigrant second-generation.* Berkeley: University of California Press/ Russell Sage Foundation.

Portes, A., & Zhou, M. (1993). The new second generation: Segmented assimilation and its variants. *Annals of the American Academy of Political and Social Science, 530,* 74–98.

Rimer, S., & Arenson, K. W. (2004, June 24). Top colleges take more blacks, but which ones? *New York Times,* section A, p. 1, col. 1.

Ross, M., Xun, W. Q. E., & Wilson, A. E. (2002). Language and the bicultural self. *Personality and Social Psychology Bulletin, 28,* 1040–1050.

Sánchez, G. J. (1999). Face the nation: Race, immigration, and the rise of nativism in late-twentieth century America. In C. Hirschman, P. Kasinitz, & J. DeWind (Eds.), *The handbook of international migration: The American experience* (pp. 371–382). New York: Russell Sage Foundation.

Shih, J. (2002). "… Yeah, I could hire this one, but I know it's gonna be a problem": How race, nativity and gender affect employers' perceptions of the manageability of job seekers. *Ethnic and Racial Studies, 25,* 99–119.

Shih, M., Pittinsky, T. L., & Ambady, N. (1999). Stereotype susceptibility: Identity salience and shifts in quantitative performance. *Psychological Science, 10,* 80–83.

Shryock, A. (2000). Family resemblances: Kinship and community in Arab Detroit. In N. Abraham & A. Shryock (Eds.), *Arab Detroit: From margin to mainstream* (pp. 573–610). Detroit, MI: Wayne State University Press.

Steele, C. M. (1997). A threat in the air: How stereotypes shape intellectual identity and performance. *American Psychology, 52,* 613–629.

Steele, C. M., & Aronson, J. (1995). Stereotype threat and the intellectual test performance of African Americans. *Journal of Personality and Social Psychology, 69,* 797–811.

Stephan, W. G., Ybarra, O., & Bachman, G. (1999). Prejudice towards immigrants. *Journal of Applied Social Psychology, 29*, 2221–2237.

Stepick, A., Stepick, C. D., Eugene, E., Teed, D., & Labissiere, Y. (2001). In R. G. Rumbaut & A. Portes (Eds.), *Ethnicities: Children of immigrants in America* (pp. 229–266). Berkeley: University of California Press.

Suárez-Orozco, M. M. (2000). Everything you ever wanted to know about assimilation but were afraid to ask. *Daedalus, The end of tolerance: Engaging cultural differences, Fall*, 1– 30.

Suárez-Orozco, C., & Suárez-Orozco, M. M. (2001). *Children of immigration.* Cambridge, MA: Harvard University Press.

Swarns, R. L. (2004, August 29). "African-American" becomes a term for debate. *New York Times*, section 1, p. 1, col. 2.

Taylor, D. M., & Lambert, W. E. (1996). The meaning of multiculturalism in a culturally diverse urban American area. *Journal of Social Psychology, 136*(6), 727–740.

Taylor, M. C. (1998). How white attitudes vary with the racial composition of local populations: Numbers count. *American Sociological Review, 63*, 512–535.

Thomas, T. E. R. (2002). *Perceptions of race and racism among blacks.* Unpublished data.

Thomas, T. E. R. (2003). *Black Americans and black immigrants: The influence of ethnic identification on perceptions or race, prejudice, and individual success in American society.* Unpublished doctoral dissertation, Stanford University.

Tormala, T. T. (2005). *The meaning of blackness: Stereotypes about Black Americans and black immigrants.* Manuscript in preparation.

Tormala, T. T., Steele, C. M., & Davies, P. G. (2006). *Black Americans and Black immigrants: The influence of ethnic identification on expectancies for success and perception of prejudice.* Manuscript in preparation.

U.S. Census. (2000). *2000 Census of Population and Housing.* Washington, DC: U.S. Government Printing Office.

Vickerman, M. (1999). *Crosscurrents: West Indian immigrants and race.* Oxford University Press.

Waters, M. C. (1994) Ethnic and racial identities of second-generation Black immigrants in New York City. *International Migration Review, 28*, 795–820.

Waters, M. C. (1999a). *Black identities: West Indian immigrant dreams and American realities.* Cambridge, MA: Harvard University Press.

Waters, M. C. (1999b). West Indians and African Americans at work: Structural differences and cultural stereotypes. In F. D. Bean & S. Bell-Rose (Eds.), *Immigration and opportunity: Race, ethnicity, and employment in the United States* (pp. 194–227). New York: Russell Sage.

Wheeler, S. C., & Petty, R. E. (2001). The effects of stereotype activation on behavior: A review of possible mechanisms. *Psychological Bulletin, 127*, 797–826.

Zárate, M. A., Garcia, B., Garza, A. A., & Hitlan, R. T. (2003). Cultural threat and perceived realistic group conflict as dual predictors of prejudice. *Journal of Experimental Social Psychology, 40*, 99–105.

9

Cultural Psychology and Marginality: An Explorative Study of Indian Diaspora

Ramaswami Mahalingam
University of Michigan

Cheri Philip
Howard University

Sundari Balan
University of Michigan

Immigrants often experience a sense of alienation, loss, and a feeling of "not belonging" because of their displacement (Alexander, 1996). They have to confront new forms of cultural modes of social participation that increase their self-awareness and sense of identity. Although such experiences are stressful, they also provide opportunities for creating a "new" identity. However, negotiating the social positioning of these "new" identities within existing social hierarchies presents unique challenges. Kim (1999) argues that Asian Americans are marginalized within the "field of racial positions," where Asian Americans are simultaneously valorized as a model minority and denigrated as "outsiders" and "perpetual foreigners." Thus, Asian Americans are "racially triangulated" vis-à-vis Whites and Blacks in this field of racial positions (Kim, 1999, p. 106).

Asian Americans sometimes use the "ancientness" of their culture to further legitimize their "model minority image." Such "imagined" notions of culture assume a "horizontal past" devoid of internal contradictions (Anderson, 1991; Espiritu, 1992; Kurien, 2003; Nagel, 1994; Ong, 1999). Asian Americans carry certain representations of their "home" culture in order to create a positive self identity. Our study addresses the following two broad research questions: (a) How do the "residuals" of Indian culture that Indian immigrants carry in their "head" influence the understanding of their racial positioning in a new social milieu? (b) How do marginalized social experiences and racial triangulation shape Indian Americans' (second-generation) attitudes toward African Americans? Using a theoretical perspective that integrates the cultural psychological research on social marginality and implicit theories of personality, we investigated first- and second-generation Indian Americans' attitudes toward African Americans. Using an adoption paradigm, our study examined Indian immigrants' implicit theories of personality. In addition, we also examined first-generation Indian immigrants' perceptions of race and caste. The rest of the chapter is in four parts. The first part provides a historical background on Indian immigration to the United States. The second part provides a synthesis of theoretical perspectives on cultural conceptions of self among Indians. The third part describes our study of Indian immigrants and Indian Americans. In the last part we discuss the relevance of marginalized experiences to understanding the complex relationship between culture, racial positioning, and the psychology of marginality.

HISTORY OF INDIAN IMMIGRATION

The earliest report of East Indian immigrants in the United States dates back to 1804, when a few Indians settled in Salem and married Black American women (Jensen, 1988). The later wave of Indian immigration to the United States was largely during the early part of the 20th century. Most emigrated from Punjab as migrant workers and worked on farms in California (Leonard, 1992). Because of immigration policies at the time (antimiscegenation laws), Indian immigrants were not allowed to marry American women; nor could they afford to go back to India to get married. Consequently, many of them married Mexican women who worked on the farms, and today a small but thriving Punjabi–Mexican community is still active in California (Leonard, 1992).

The Punjabi Sikhs who came to California were politically active and started a party called the *Gadar Party* (1913–1918), to fight British colonial rule from the United States. Although the party had a high number of Punjabi immigrants, many Leftists of European ancestry also supported the party. Party membership consisted of blue-collar workers, Indian elites, and intellectuals of European ancestry. The party, which produced a newsletter that critiqued both British imperialism and racial discrimination in the United States (Puri, 1994; Sareen, 1994), offered a platform to mobilize expatriate support to fight British imperialism and the racist policies of the American government. Not surprisingly, the party was banned by the U.S. government because of its anti-British activities. The Gadar party members were also opposed to Jim Crow laws of the South (Prashad, 1998, 2000; Puri, 1994), greatly sympathizing with the plight of southern Blacks. Several European immigrants who were active in the labor movement continued to support efforts aimed at fighting racial discrimination against Blacks (Prashad, 2000).

During the 1920s, Indian immigrants fought for their right to gain citizenship; the case of Bhagat Singh Thind illustrates these struggles (Jacobson, 1999). Using government-prescribed criteria for immigrants' eligibility for citizenship, Thind argued that the available "scientific" evidence suggested that Indians could indeed be classified as Caucasians, not only because several Indian languages were of Indo-European origin, but also that the Indians' physical and cultural roots were close to Caucasians. However, the Supreme Court rejected this argument (Jacobson, 1999). The crucial difference between the Gadar Party members and Thind's case illustrates the bimodal relationship between Indian immigrants and Blacks. In the case of the Gadar Party, Indian immigrants strongly identified with Blacks as marginalized proletariats, whereas in the case of Thind, the common identification was with Whites as fellow "Caucasians," not with Blacks. In fact, the prescribed criteria for citizenship stipulated that non-Blacks of Caucasian origin were eligible to become Americans.

Between the 1920s and 1960s Indian immigration slowed greatly because of a ban on Asian immigration. A change in immigration policy occurred during Lyndon B. Johnson's presidency, which allowed many Asian professionals to immigrate (Bacon, 1996; Rangaswamy, 2000). Thousands of engineers and doctors from India came to the United States for better careers and professional opportunities. In fact, estimates within the past 5 years suggest that approximately 35,000 Indian doctors now work in the United States (American Association of Physicians of Indian Origin, 2002). In addition, several leaders in the software industry, such as Bill Gates, have recognized the achievements of Indian professionals in this field. Most of the immigrants working in technology related fields are from the upper caste and higher socioeconomic backgrounds in general. The tradition of community activism seeking social justice and fighting for the rights of minorities is still present among the current, newer wave of immigrants (Abraham, 2000; Khandelwal, 1998). These new immigrants, by and large, are highly successful and fit the label of "model minority." This theme is revisited in the section on race and caste.

CULTURAL PSYCHOLOGY AND IMMIGRANTS

Culture plays a dynamic role in influencing our world views and our concept of personhood, leading to differing conceptions of social ontologies (Shweder & Bourne, 1984). Differing cultural conceptions of personhood exist among East Asian and Western cultures (Nisbett, Peng, Choi, & Norenzayan, 2001). Such conceptions do not merely provide the metaphysical basis for thinking about personhood but also lend a social lens through which the actions, intentions, emotions, and behaviors of self and others are interpreted, shared, communicated, and judged. Such dominant worldviews also mediate the meaning-making process (Roland, 1988). East Asian cultures value an embedded, context-bound notion of self, whereas Western cultures value individuality, autonomy, and an unbounded notion of self (Miller, 1984; Ramanujan, 1988).

Although these are portrayals of culture as a macro system, several researchers have argued that such portrayals of cultural differences underestimate large intracultural variations across caste, race, class, and gender (Mahalingam, 2003). For instance, Gilligan (1982) found that the moral sensibility of American women differs from that of American men. Jones (1999) presented a model of social identity, TRIOS (time, rhythm, improvisation, orality, and spirituality), to characterize the cultural psychology of African Americans. Boykin (1986) presented the concept of a "triple quandary" for African American children, wherein they negotiate around a dominant group-prescribed identity even as they preserve the unique features of their ethnic identity and remain acutely aware of their marginalized status. Landrine (1992) argued that a context-bound, indexical notion of self is more prevalent among various ethnic groups and among women.

These perspectives suggest that culture, social hierarchies, and marginality mediate the differing notions of self. It seems that marginal status may increase our awareness of context. Mahalingam (in press) presents a framework for a psychology of marginality that argues that marginalized status increases one's awareness of context. Social psychologists report that those in power are more likely to essentialize or use category-based information of individuals to judge their actions and behavior (Fiske, 1993). Research on essentialism suggests that individuals from high-status groups are more likely to believe in biological essentialization of group identity, whereas marginalized group members resist such biological essentializations of group differences (Mahalingam, 2003). For example, Mahalingam (1998) found that upper caste Brahmins believe that caste identity is determined at birth, whereas Dalits (former "untouchables") believe that caste identity is not fixed at birth, but instead is transmitted through socialization. In sum, the cultural psychology of marginalized social status could be characterized by a heightened awareness of context, and resistance to ideologies that essentialize group differences and social hierarchies.

RACE, CASTE, AND INDIAN AMERICANS

Several researchers have pointed out that the "model minority myth" positions Indian Americans in opposition to African Americans (Dhingra, 2003; Kim, 1999; Lee, 1994). However, early and current Indian immigrants' participation in community activism (Khandelwal, 1998) indicates that the relationship between their marginalized social experiences, and their attitudes toward African Americans may be complex. Various intersections of social class, generation, group status in the "home" culture, and "residual" aspects of culture play a crucial role in shaping such trajectories. In Indian culture, the caste system regulates the social hierarchy (Parish, 1997), and most of the current wave of Indian immigrants are from the upper castes and are highly educated. Second-generation Indian Americans are also viewed as one of the most successful minorities in the United States (Dhingra, 2003), but they do not share the cultural experience of being part of a caste group. It is pertinent to examine how privileged caste status (such as being a Brahmin), cultural beliefs about personhood, and various intersections of social marginality might influence first- and second-generation Indians' attitudes toward African Americans and to investigate whether first-generation Indian immigrants indeed view caste and race as very similar.

METHOD

Participants

For this study, East Indian immigrant and Indian American graduate and undergraduate students at a large, Midwestern university in the United States were recruited over a one-semester period to participate in a psychology study. The first generation Indian immigrant group consisted of 23 graduate students, and the Indian American group consisted of 27 undergraduate students. Because we did not have a large enough population of first-generation undergraduates or second-generation graduate students to make a comparison within education level, we recruited only first-generation (FG) graduate students and second-generation (SG) undergraduates. Our participants reflected the greater predominance of FG graduate students and SG undergraduates in the university as a whole. The criteria for participation by East Indian immigrants required that primary socialization (birth to 18 years) occurred in India. For Indian Americans, primary socialization (birth to 18 years) occurred in the United States, and participants must also have Indian immigrant parents.

Procedure

Participants were sent an e-mail requesting the participation of East Indian students (immigrants and Indian Americans were given the specific criteria necessary to qualify for the study). Various Indian organizations on campus were also contacted via e-mail and word of mouth. Incentive for participation was in the form of monetary compensation, with graduate students receiving $15 and undergraduates receiving $10. Participants were assured that their participation was voluntary and that their responses would remain confidential and be used only for research purposes.

After respondents completed an informed consent form, they were briefed on the format of the study. They then participated in a think-aloud protocol in which they were instructed to respond to each question orally and to provide the underlying reasoning for each of their responses. They were given some simple, practice mathematical problems so that they could get used to the idea of thinking-aloud before participating in a two-part study. In the first part of the study, think-aloud protocols were collected. In the second part, the participants filled out a questionnaire. On average, they took about 30 minutes to complete the study.

Measures

First, all the students were given a vignette to read about an adoption that depicts the story of a child who after birth is separated from his biological parents and raised by adoptive parents. They were told about certain characteristics of both sets of parents (biological and adoptive) and were asked to make a prediction about the likelihood that the child would inherit or acquire certain traits and characteristics (Gelman & Wellman, 1990; Hirschfeld, 1996). The race of the biological and adoptive parents was manipulated in the vignettes, counterbalancing positive and negative qualities of the biological parents resulting in a 2 (race: White or African American) × 2 (valence: positive and negative) design. Thus, there were in total four different versions of the vignettes. The traits attributed to the parents included intelligence, personality, and biological traits. Each participant was randomly assigned to one of the four vignette conditions.

In addition, participants also completed a questionnaire that included the Modern Racism Scale (McConahay, Hardee, & Batts, 1981; McConahay & Hough, 1976) and Social Dominance Orientation Scale (Sidanious & Pratto, 1998). The Modern Racism Scale consisted of 7 items measuring attitudes toward African Americans. Higher scores corresponded to higher levels of modern racist views. The Social Dominance Orientation (SDO) scale consisted of 16 items. This scale measures attitudes toward social hierarchies. High scores indicate tolerance of social hierarchies. In addition, we asked the Indian immigrant participants to rate their degree of agreement with the statement "Caste and race are similar" on a 1–5 scale (1 *strongly disagree*, 5 *strongly agree*). We also asked them to provide a rationale for their judgment. The responses to the adoption story and the caste–race comparison items were audiotaped.

RESULTS

Quantitative Analyses

The mean scores for various measures are presented in Table 9.1. For the adoption task we calculated the means for all 14 traits. There were

TABLE 9.1
Summary of Mean Values of First and Second Generation

Variables	First Generation	Second Generation
N	23	27
Age	26	27
Gender	Even split between men and women	Even split, 3 cases missing
Modern Racism (MRS)	2.29	3.8
Social Dominance (SDO)	3.14	1.8
Caste status (Brahmin)	48%	33%
Caste/race question	2.5	—
Gene/environmental mean	4.47 (1–7), high = environmental	4.44
Split cases by caste		
Brahmin MRS	2.47	3.80
Non-Brahmin MRS	2.14	3.85
Brahmin SDO	3.51	1.92
Non-Brahmin SDO	2.85	1.71
Adoption Brahmin gene mean	4.5 (1–7), high = environmental	4.47
Non-Brahmin gene mean	4.43	4.42

no differences in the mean scores between first-and second-generation participants. Both groups thought that the environment would play a critical role in shaping the personality of the individual. This finding is consistent with previous research on cultural conceptions of personhood in India (i.e., Indians believe that the environment plays a greater role than heredity in shaping personhood).

However, there were some interesting group differences on modern racism and social dominance orientation mean scores. SG participants scored higher on modern racism than FG Indian immigrants. However, FG immigrants were higher on social dominance than SG immigrants. Regarding the question of whether caste and race were similar, the FG participants felt that caste and race were dissimilar.

Qualitative Analyses

Adoption Task

The audiotapes that were transcribed for analyses showed some similarities as well as some differences between the responses of FG and SG participants. Overall, both groups thought that the environment played a significant role in shaping various personality traits. However, there were qualitative differences in the ways in which they recognized the role of the environment in shaping personality traits.

Examples of FG Participants' Justifications.

It is not exactly enough to have natural ability. I believe that we develop a lot more through sustained effort and the environment as the genetic material.

I would say likely, first of all I think there are two rules—one is genetic background and the environment in which you grow basically, even if you are born intelligent and you are raised dumb, you are going to be dumb some much intelligence you may have acquired—but if you are going to be born dumb but if you are going to be raised smartly, you are going to be smart. I think basically it is the environment in which the child is brought up—it may be inherited but it is also important what you acquire so I think environment plays an important role.

People are responsible and based on their genetic inheritance and as well as depending on the way they are brought up, so both are in equal contribution, which is why I can't really say whether Alex will be responsible because genetically he is supposed to be responsible and if the Smiths are irresponsible, then both will contribute equally.

In general, FG participants believed that genes and the environment would influence each other. They often thought that there was something in the "nature" of the child that was determined by genes. However, this particular trait needed to be activated by the environment or could be shaped by the parents. Environmental factors as well as the role of parents (in this case, the adoptive parents) in shaping personality traits were emphasized by the participants. By contrast, the responses of the SG participants suggested an active role for environment as well personal agency. Unlike FG participants, SG participants talked about the role of personal inclinations or motivations and will in shaping one's personality.

Examples of SG Participants' Justifications.

There is more to it than biological inheritance.

The basis of genetics determining IQ isn't solid.

... a lot of these things are how you are brought up.

... he might not be a quick learner but I think if he's being raised in an environment where education is really stressed, and if he's given opportunities to put his intelligence, whatever studies he is being pushed ...

There's more to it than biological intelligence.

It depends on how you are brought up, the people you are living with, and your environment.

What the parents are really doesn't matter ... it depends on what you as a person are.

Depends on how much he likes music and gets involved in it.

A few SG participants challenged the very notion of a biological basis for intelligence. Their responses suggest that they view personality as more than the interaction between the environment and biology. Rather, personal agency, motivation, and opportunities for personal growth influence the emergence of a personality trait.

Comparison of Caste and Race

Most immigrant participants disagreed with the statement "Caste and race are similar," although several recognized the functional similarities between caste and race and their role in regulating and maintaining social hierarchies.

Race could still be like in some sense be defined as geographical boundaries or something, but caste is totally made by a group of opportunistic people who want to suit their own needs ... both are pretty bad actually for the society.

In India, we have the lower caste and we have the upper caste so they always stay low and we people stay high, and if we come to race we have

Black and White so we are in the same scale ... so it's the inferiority and the superiority is the basic thing between caste and race.

However, several thought that caste was a socially constructed category, and race was an essential category determined by various biological factors.

> I think race has got a bigger scope than the caste, because caste is something which you can easily break up into more different castes but race is something you can't do easily. Caste is a social institution ... you can move from one caste to another, but I think race is more solid and you can't change from one race to another.

> Race is something which is actually got down from your parents with similar genes, and caste is something that is created by the society.

> There is lot of genetic differences between races and I don't think there are so many genetic differences between castes.

> I think race is something like more of your blood group and that it comes by birth, and I believe caste is more all in the mind and the environment.

FG participants essentialized race as something transmitted from parent to offspring, that was fixed at birth, and whose origins could be traced to genetic difference between racial groups.

In summary, several themes emerged from the qualitative analyses. FG participants held an *interactionist* view of genes and environment, believing that genes and environment mutually influence each other in shaping personality traits. They believed in "the power of parents" to transform the lives of the children through their parental effort. SG participants thought that a combination of personal agency and proper environmental conditions would determine the personality traits of individuals. Unlike the FG, a few SG participants even questioned the scientific basis of claims about the genetic basis of IQ and other personality traits. FG immigrants thought that caste and race were dissimilar because the former was socially constructed, whereas the later was biologically determined.

GENERAL DISCUSSION

First-generation participants scored lower on modern racism than second-generation participants. This finding is consistent with several findings on Indian Americans' perceptions of African Americans (Dhingra, 2003). According to Dhingra (2003), class affiliation and suburban upbringing distance Indian Americans from other ethnic minorities. Such formative experiences shape Indian Americans' beliefs about race and ethnicity. Dhingra noted the following:

> The participants had attained the "American Dream," which in turn embedded them further into the nation and, in their opinion, should have de-

fined them as being comparable to middle-and upper-middle-class Whites, instead of as foreigners based on their physical appearance. They also highlighted their educational attainment, use of mainstream institutions like white-collar-occupations, neighborhoods, restaurants, and clubs. [They] saw themselves as "model Americans" as opposed to "model minorities." Participants raised their status as comparable to Whites partly by distancing themselves from African Americans, as immigrants have done at various points in American history. Many consider African Americans as the true "foreigners" for supposedly remaining unassimilated into mainstream norms. (Dhingra, 2003, p. 137)

Kim (1999) argued that by valorizing Asian Americans as a model minority, many conservatives framed affirmative action debates in which Asian Americans were portrayed as "victims" and Blacks as "villains," thereby creating a conflict between Blacks and Asian Americans. Perhaps the social class background and internalization of the model minority myth might have also shaped SG participants' attitudes toward African Americans.

Interestingly, FG participants had higher social dominance orientation scores than SG participants. We wondered whether the social location of the first-generation participants might have played a role. We examined the caste background of the first-generation participants. More than half of our participants were Brahmins, and after splitting group means by caste, we found that the SDO scores of Brahmins were slightly higher than those of non-Brahmins. Perhaps being part of a privileged group influences one's view of social hierarchies (Mahalingam, 2003; Sidanius & Pratto, 1998). Considering the sample size and descriptive nature of this relationship, we think further research with a large sample is needed to examine whether privileged caste origin and SDO affects Indian immigrants' attitudes toward African Americans.

Although both groups believed that nature and nurture both shape personality, there were some subtle differences between FG and SG participants. The qualitative responses of FG participants suggest that they believe in the mutually influential role of genes and environment that shaping various personality traits. They also believe in the power of parents to change the biological makeup of the child. This is consistent with several cultural psychological findings on beliefs about self and personhood in India. The findings confirm that Indians in general believe that personhood is determined by the social context, and parents play an active role in shaping the social context (e.g., Miller, 1984; Shweder & Bourne, 1984; Trawick, 1990).

By contrast, SG participants believe in the will of the individual in changing his or her destiny, which is consistent with the dominant American cultural beliefs about "free will" and personal growth. The marginalized social experience of SG participants sharpened their awareness of context in a way that was consistent with the dominant American cultural beliefs about one's agency to create opportunities for personal growth. However, the FG participants' interactionist view of personality was more in line with Indian cultural construals of personhood. Thus culture, generational status, and privileged social location influence beliefs about personhood as well as attitudes toward African Americans.

Interestingly, FG Indian immigrants' recognition that caste is a socially constructed category did not help them to understand the social constructivist nature of race. Perhaps the relational, multicultural context of race and ethnicity, instead of creating a critical awareness of the social constructivist nature of social categories, might have reinforced essentialist views of race. Such tendencies to essentialize race and ethnicity could become a trope for internalizing and legitimizing group hierarchies (Mahalingam, 2003). Further research is needed to identify specific factors that could foster a greater understanding of the role of social power in the construction and maintenance of social categories such as race and caste among first-generation immigrants.

CULTURE, MARGINALITY, AND IMMIGRATION

We set out to examine how culture and privileged social location shape marginalized social experiences, with a particular focus on how racial positioning shapes attitudes toward African Americans. Mahalingam (in press) argues that an awareness of one's marginalized status increases one's understanding of context and resistance to biological essentialization of person or group differences.

Our analyses suggest that there may be two different kinds of marginality: *discriminating* and *empowering* marginality. *Discriminating marginality* refers to the process by which marginalized group members psychologically distance themselves from other marginalized groups by identifying themselves with the dominant group. *Empowering marginality* refers to the process wherein marginalized group members form coalitions through critical awareness about the commonalities of their marginalized social experience. These two different kinds of marginality affect Indian Americans' attitudes toward Blacks in important ways. Empowering marginality fosters a common identity as marginalized group members, whereas discriminatory marginality transcends marginalized status through forming alliances with the dominant group using either a discourse of shared cultural and biological origins (as in the case of Bhagat Singh Thind) or through shared values, such as beliefs in individualism and meritocracy achieved through greater assimilation and celebration of American cultural norms and ideals.

Our SG participants' discriminatory attitudes toward African Americans could be characterized as discriminating marginality, because they might have internalized their racial positioning as a "model minority," which sets them apart from African Americans (Dhingra, 2003; Kim, 1999). First-generation Indian immigrants had an empowering sense of marginality because they did not endorse discriminatory views of African Americans and perhaps sensed some commonalities among their marginalized social experiences.

First- and second-generation Indians are not monolithic groups, and hence our characterization of these two groups should not be viewed as stereotypical. For instance, although there are several historical examples of Indian immigrants fighting against racism, we also have cases of second-generation Indian Americans who hold a discriminatory view by distancing themselves from African Americans to claim equal or superior status to Whites. According to Prashad (2000),

> Desis [Indians] seek out an "authentic culture" for complex reasons, among them the desire not to be seen as fundamentally inferior to those who see themselves as "white" and superior. To be on a par with, at least not beneath these people, desis, like other subordinated peoples, revel in those among them who succeed in white terms. There is a *sotto voce* knowledge among nonwhites of their various forms of greatness. Parents instruct their children to recognize all kinds of people valued by Europe. (p. 157)

Conversely, we also have evidence of active Indian American organizations on various college campuses fighting against racism by establishing strong coalitions among various ethnic minority groups (see Shankar & Srikanth, 1988). We need more research to identify the critical role of cultural beliefs about social groups and privileged social location in shaping how Indian Americans make sense of their marginalized social identities and how they negotiate, resist, and transcend the racial triangulation of their ethnic identities.

LIMITATIONS

As previously mentioned, FG participants were graduate students, and SG students were undergraduates, both drawn from a convenience sample. A more diverse group of first- and second-generation Indian Americans from a different social location (grocery store clerks, etc.) might yield different results. Considering the small sample size, we need to interpret our quantitative findings cautiously and suggest that more large-scale quantitative studies are needed to understand the complex layers of Indian immigrants' attitudes toward race.

CONCLUSIONS

Although we recognize that the FG participants were less prejudiced than SG participants in their attitudes toward African Americans, personal ideologies and identity politics play a role in shaping FG and SG Indians' attitudes toward African Americans. For instance, an Indian American who is immersed in radical labor politics might also strongly identify with the marginalized status of African Americans and be more sympathetic to the systemic nature of racism. By contrast, another Indian American might strongly identify with Whites and be a proponent of meritocracy (e.g., Dinesh D'Souza). Any immigrant group will consist of a variety of individuals, who may exemplify the empowering as well as discriminating aspects of the immigrant psychology of race. The critical task is to find out how various cultural, social, and psychological factors intersect with aspects of gender and social class to either promote or hinder successful positive interminority relationships.

When we started this project, we were mindful of various intersections of our racialized minority identities. Ram is a first-generation immigrant who emigrated from India to "become" South Asian before recognizing that when someone calls you "Gandhi," it is not necessarily a compliment. Cheri is a second-generation Indian American who because of her ethnically ambiguous appearance as well as her Christian upbringing frequently experienced not being treated as an "authentic Indian." Her Indian ethnic identity is often contested in a predominantly Hinduvized Indian American community (Kurien, 2003). Sundari, a first-generation immigrant from India, already had a migrant experience because her parents migrated from South India to Mumbai. She has often revisited various intersections of her marginality (caste, gender, class, and ethnicity). Since the event of 9/11, we have all been more frequently selected for "random" baggage security checks in airports. We have often talked about the ways in which we negotiate, contest, and make sense of the racialization of our ethnic identities, which are profoundly impacted by the various intersections of our social identities.

ACKNOWLEDGMENTS

Funding for this research was provided by a small grant from Spencer Foundation and a faculty grant from OVPR, University of Michigan, to the first author. We thank Thomas Pettigrew for his insightful comments on an earlier draft of this chapter.

REFERENCES

Abraham, M. (2000). *Speaking the unspeakable: Marital violence among South Asian immigrants in the United States.* New Brunswick, NJ: Rutgers University Press.
Alexander, M. (1996). *The shock of arrival: Reflections on postcolonial experience.* Boston: South End Press.
American Association of Physicians of Indian Origin. (2002). Retrieved February 10, 2003, from http://www. aapiusa.net/membership.htm
Anderson, B. (1991). *Imagined communities.* New York: Verso.
Bacon, J. (1996). *Life lines: Community, family and assimilation among Asian Indian immigrants.* New York: Oxford University Press.

Boykin, A. W. (1986). The triple quandary and the schooling of Afro-American children. In U. Neisser (Ed.), *The school achievement of minority children* (pp. 57–92). Hillsdale, NJ: Lawrence Erlbaum Associates.

Dhingra, P. H. (2003). Being American between Black and White: Second-generation Asian American professionals' racial identities. *Journal of Asian American Studies, 6*(2), 117–147.

Espiritu, Y. (1992). *Asian American pan-ethnicity: Bridging institutions and identities.* Philadelphia: Temple University Press.

Fiske, S. T. (1993). Controlling other people: The impact of power on stereotyping *American Psychologist, 48*(6), 621–628.

Gelman, S. A., & Wellman, H. (1990). Insides and essences: Early understandings of the non-obvious. *Cognition, 38,* 213–244.

Gilligan, C. (1982). *In a different voice: Women's conception of self and morality.* Cambridge, MA: Harvard University Press.

Hirschfeld, L. A. (1996). *Race in the making.* Cambridge, MA: MIT Press.

Jacobson, M. (1999). *Whiteness of a different color.* New York: Columbia University Press.

Jensen, J. (1988). *Passage from India: Asian Indian immigrants in North America.* New Haven, CT: Yale University Press.

Jones, J. M. (1999). Toward a cultural psychology of African Americans. In W. J. Lonner (Ed.), *Merging past, present, and future in cross-cultural psychology: Selected papers from the Fourteenth International Congress of the International Association for Cross-Cultural Psychology* (pp. 52–62). Lisse, the Netherlands: Swets & Zeitlinger.

Khandelwal, M. (1998). Reflections on diversity and inclusion: South Asians and Asian American studies. In L. R. Hirabayashi (Ed.), *Teaching Asian America: Diversity and the problem of community* (pp. 111–122). New York: Rowman & Littlefield.

Kim, C. J. (1999). The racial triangulation of Asian Americans. *Politics and Society, 27*(1), 105–138.

Kurien, P. (2003). To be or not to be South Asian: Contemporary Indian American politics. *Journal of Asian American Studies, 6*(3), 261–288.

Landrine, H. (1992). Clinical implications of cultural differences: The referential vs indexical self. *Clinical Psychology Review, 12,* 401–415.

Lee, S. J. (1994). Behind the model-minority stereotype: Voices of high- and low-achieving Asian American students. *Anthropology & Education Quarterly, 25*(4), 413–429.

Leonard, K. (1992). *Making ethnic choices: California's Punjabi Mexicans.* Philadelphia: Temple University.

Mahalingam, R. (1998). *Essentialism, power and theories of caste: A developmental study.* Dissertation Abstracts International, 60(2-B) (UMI No. AAM9919309).

Mahalingam, R. (2003). Essentialism, culture and power: Rethinking social class. *Journal of Social Issues, 59*(4), 733–749.

Mahalingam, R. (in press). Culture, essentialism and psychology of marginality: A developmental perspective. In A. Fuligini (Ed), *Social identity and academic achievement.* New York: Russell Sage.

McConahay, J. B., Hardee, B. B. & Batts, V. (1981). Has racism declined? It depends who is asking and what is asked. *Journal of Conflict Resolution, 25*(4), 563–579.

McConahay, J. B., & Hough, J. C., Jr. (1976). Symbolic racism. *Journal of Conflict Resolution, 32*, 23–45.

Miller, J. (1984). Culture and the development of everyday social explanation. *Journal of Personality and Social Psychology, 46*(5), 961–978.

Nagel, J. (1994). Construction ethnicity: Creating and recreating ethnic identity and culture. *Social Problems, 41*(1), 152–176.

Nisbett, R. E., Peng, K., Choi, I., & Norenzayan, A. (2001). Culture and systems of thought: Holistic versus analytic cognition. *Psychological Review, 108*(2), 291–310.

Ong, A. (1999). Cultural citizenship as subject making: Immigrants negotiate racial and cultural boundaries in the United States. In R. D. Torres, L. F. Miron, & J. X. Inda (Eds.), *Race, ethnicity and citizenship: A reader* (pp. 262–294). Oxford: Blackwell.

Parish, S. M. (1997). *Hierarchy and its discontents: Culture and the politics of consciousness in caste society.* Delhi, India: Oxford University Press.

Prashad, V. (1998). Crafting solidarities. In L. D. Shankar & R. Srikanth (Eds.), *A part yet apart: South Asians in Asian America* (pp. 105–126). Philadelphia: Temple University Press.

Prashad, V. (2000). *The karma of brown folk.* Minneapolis: University of Minnesota Press.

Puri, H. K. (1994). *Gadar movement: Ideology, organization and strategy.* Amristar, India: Guru Nanak Dev University.

Ramanujan, A. K. (1988). Is there an Indian way of thinking? In M. Marriott (Ed.), *India through Hindu categories* (pp. 41–58). New Delhi: Sage.

Rangaswamy, P. (2000). *Namaste America.: Indian immigrants in an American Metropolis.* University Park, PA: Pennsylvania State University Press.

Sareen, T. R. (1994). *Select documents on the Gadar party.* New Delhi: Mounto Publications.

Roland, A. (1988). *In search of self in India and Japan: Toward a cross-cultural psychology.* Philadelphia: Temple University Press.

Shankar, L., & Srikanth, R. (1988). *A part yet apart: South Asians in Asian America.* Philadelphia: Temple University Press.

Shweder, R., & Bourne, E. J. (1984). Does the concept of person vary? In R. Shweder & R. A. Levine (Eds.), *Cultural theory: Essays on mind, self and emotion* (pp. 158–199). New York: Cambridge University Press.

Sidanious, J., & Pratto, F. (1998). *Social dominance: An intergroup theory of social hierarchy and oppression.* New York: Cambridge University Press.

Trawick, M. (1990). *Notes on love in a Tamil family.* Berkeley: University of California Press.

Part III

Immigration, Self, Gender, and Narratives

10

Racing Transatlantic Passages: James Baldwin's African "America" and Immigrant Studies

Magdalena J. Zaborowska
University of Michigan

They face each other, the Negro and the African, over a gulf of three hundred years .... This alienation causes the [American] Negro to recognize that he is a hybrid. Not a physical hybrid merely: in every aspect of his living he betrays the memory of the auction block and the impact of the happy ending. In white Americans he finds reflected—repeated, as it were, in a higher key—his tensions, his terrors, his tenderness. Dimly and for the first time, there begins to fall into perspective the nature of the roles they have played in the lives and history of each other .... Therefore he cannot deny them, nor can they ever be divorced. (James Baldwin, "Encounter on the Seine: Black Meets Brown," 1985, p. 39)

To do your first works over means to reexamine everything. Go back to where you started, as far back as you can, examine all of it, travel your road again and tell the truth about it. Sing or shout or testify or keep to yourself: but *know whence you came*. (James Baldwin, "The Price of the Ticket," 1985, p. xix)

James Baldwin's call to "know whence you came" urges all Americans to examine their origins, histories, peoples, and places they have sprung from, no matter their skin color. This invocation comes from and echoes throughout "The Price of the Ticket," the late essay that serves as an introduction to Baldwin's last collection of prose, *The Price of the Ticket: Collected Non-Fiction, 1948–1985* (PT; 1985). Weaving together Baldwin's signature autobiographical perspective with

169

astute remarks on the state of the American nation in the late 20th-century world, "The Price" discusses the fallout of racial unrest during the writer's lifetime. However, Baldwin articulated the link between American—or white—and African American—or black—destiny 35 years earlier, in an essay that had first appeared as "The Negro in Paris" (1950), and later became "Encounter on the Seine: Black Meets Brown." In this piece, he brings together Africans, African Americans, Europeans, and white Americans in a sweeping move across continents and centuries of transatlantic history. The "Encounter on the Seine" thus provides the description of our complex national origins—that hybrid "whence"—that Baldwin asks all Americans to look for in "The Price of the Ticket."

These two important essays mark the points of departure and arrival, as they bracket Baldwin's thinking on race across historic, national, and cultural borders. They also rely on vibrant metaphors of journey, passage, and healing through storytelling and ancestral ties. In their focus on movement, travel, and transatlantic locations, "Encounter" and "The Price" bookend a compelling career of an African American writer, whose own diverse transatlantic crossings made him into a passionate, complex, and often conflicted type of traveler. In these pages, I shall refer to him as an "other" kind of immigrant.[1] As I demonstrate throughout this chapter, Baldwin not only embraced but also articulated his literal and literary passages as representative of the rich contexts of transatlantic and transnational Americanness. His works signal the little-known African American perspective on literary representations of immigration and migration, on the one hand, and on the ways in which race and the African Middle Passage have been used to construct the black-and-white dichotomy at the core of Americanness. I am therefore proposing that we take a closer look at Baldwin's work through the interdisciplinary lens of immigrant studies, and, conversely, that we also reassess our approaches to immigration *through* his work.

Given his overall profound, lifelong project of redefining the social and narrative spaces of American identity, Baldwin is an important figure to consider in this context for several reasons. First, despite many scholarly claims that it is predominantly so,[2] Baldwin's complex vision of American identity is only superficially a white-on-black story, or story about race told in binary terms of black and white confrontation. In the introduction to his second collection of essays, *Nobody Knows My Name* (NKMN; 1961), he stresses that his larger

---

[1]Baldwin resisted terms such as "émigré" or "expatriate," pointing at their racialized and elitist connotations. While in Turkey, he began naming himself a kind of exile; he talks about himself as a "transatlantic commuter" in several essays and interviews. See, for example, "James Baldwin Breaks His Silence," interview in the Turkish journal, *Cep Dergisi*, reprinted in *Conversations with James Baldwin*, p. 60.

[2]See also Dwight McBride's very helpful review of earlier scholarship on Baldwin and his astute critique of its shortcomings in the introduction to *James Baldwin Now*.

purpose is to embrace self-knowledge and face and accept other as a writer whose "subject is himself and the world and, for whom it requires every ounce of stamina he can summon to look on himself and the world as they are" (Baldwin, *Essays*, p. 136). Second, and more important, he links his personal quest toward this goal to a similar quest that must be undertaken by the whole nation: "the question of color ... operates to hide the graver questions of the self .... One can only face in others what one can face in oneself" (NKMN, p. 12). Third, as he always, and vehemently, resisted classification, labeling, and stereotyping, Baldwin's works demonstrate that identity as a concept *and* identity of the artist/writer in question should be approached as complex, dynamic, and multidimensional.

Baldwin's views developed, evolved, and changed throughout his career, at the same time as his basic commitment to fight for racial equality and all Americans' civil rights remained constant. This evolution has not been adequately recognized in the Baldwin scholarship,[3] which has tended to classify him in narrow and separatist ways as an either "Black writer" or a "gay writer," and to see his career as sharply divided between the period of artistic ascent that culminated with the publication of *The Fire Next Time* in 1963 and the period of waning creativity that followed.[4] Except for David Roediger (1997), no one has paid attention to the many immigrant characters and themes in his works, perhaps due to the fact that such a focus does not fit either set of categories of critical concentration on this writer.

In my readings of Baldwin's contribution to discourses on immigration, I employ literary and cultural studies approaches, and contend that Baldwin's works explore, elaborate on, and push further the genre identified by William Boelhower as "immigrant narrative."[5] For my purposes, *immigrant narrative* refers to a broad array of texts by-about-and-for immigrants that employs some of the shared formal and thematic elements. In terms of form, it often utilizes first person or autobiographic narrator, journalistic and epistolary writing, glossaries, notes and references, letters or statements of validation and introduction by native-born patrons, and mixing of English with other languages or stylized immigrant speech. In terms of its thematic focus, immigrant narrative follows a clear trajectory of departure–crossing–arrival; important moments include receiving

---

[3]There is very interesting new work emerging on this writer that I cannot do justice to in this chapter. I do so, however, in my new book on Baldwin, *Erotics of Exile*. See especially Scott, McBride, Miller, Ross, Wallace, and Henderson.

[4]There are too many titles confirming this to list in one note. Among the better known are the collections: edited by Standley and Burt, *Critical Essays on James Baldwin* and by Harold Bloom, *James Baldwin*; see also Horace Porter, *Stealing the Fire*, Clarence E. Hardy III, *James Baldwin's God: Sex, Hope, and Crisis in Black Holiness Culture*; Eldridge Cleaver's infamous *Soul on Ice* is an extreme example of a hostile critique.

[5]Boelhower (1981) defines the genre in formalist terms, referring to the specifics of theme, construction, and reader expectation, as conveying "a pluricultural reality in which for the first time the immigrant appears in American fiction as historical protagonist" (p. 3).

news from America, preparing for a journey, crossing of borders, passing over a body of water, and witnessing first sights of the new land on arrival (glimpses of the Statue of Liberty, etc.). Other, less frequent, themes include accounts of acculturation and culture shock, coping with the language barrier, clashes with the dominant culture, changing gender roles, and nostalgia for home. In light of this definition, Baldwin's contribution concerns his engagement of some of the formal and thematic aspects of the genre, and, most important, juxtaposing, in often risky ways, European immigrant and African American perspectives on national identity. I show that in so doing, Baldwin both enriches our understanding of literary representations of immigrant experience and casts in new light our approaches to race, nationhood, and cultural identity.

In the following three parts of this chapter, I first briefly introduce Baldwin's life and works and his focus on European immigration. I then situate my discussion of Baldwin vis-à-vis the recent insights on race in the interdisciplinary immigration studies, some of which his works have clearly anticipated. In the third part, I discuss the ways in which Baldwin's select works bring together elements of (white) European immigrant narrative and African Middle Passage in his explorations of 20th-century Americanness. Baldwin's underappreciated contribution to discourses on immigration, migration, and literary genres used to represent them demonstrates a powerful intertwining of stories of transatlantic passage and their reliance on what Toni Morrison terms the ever-present "Africanist persona" in American literature and culture (Morrison, 1992, pp. 38–39).

INTRODUCTION: LEAVING HOME[6]

My journey, or my flight, had not been *to* Paris, but simply *away* from America. (Baldwin, *No Name in the Street*, 1972, p. 469)[7]

---

[6]A very brief biographic note for those readers who are not familiar with Baldwin's early life: He was born into a lower-class, religious family of displaced Black Southerners in Harlem in 1924. He was an illegitimate child, whose mother remarried an older preacher when James was 2 years old; the Baldwins had eight more children, whom young James helped to raise. His writing talent was quickly discovered and nurtured by his teachers; he published poems and essays, and edited a literary magazine in high school. Torn between his success as a teenage preacher and his desire to write, he gave up the church and, after his father's death, worked menial jobs to support his family and writing. Even though he never obtained a college degree, he amassed tremendous erudition through voracious reading and mentorship of teachers, editors, and friends, and especially the African American painter Beauford Delaney. In his twenties, Baldwin lived in Greenwich Village, where he waited tables while writing as much as he could. After his close friend committed suicide, Baldwin decided that he had to flee his country or he would likely meet a similar end. His experience of the northern brand of racism was compounded by the homophobic hatred he experienced among both Blacks and Whites.

[7]PT, p. 469.

After he left New York for Paris in 1948 as an aspiring young black writer on a Saxton Fellowship, Baldwin was constantly on the move. Interestingly, he never thought of his trip as "going *to* Paris," but rather as, emphatically, *leaving* the City. In that sense, his statement sounds more like that of an immigrant than an expatriate; his was a symbolically inverted passage along the route once taken by the "huddled masses" described in Emma Lazarus' famous poem "The New Colossus" (1888; see Lazarus & Schappes, 1947). Baldwin was also trying to escape from the danger and fury he felt in his white supremacist and homophobic homeland, and was searching for places where he could work without distraction. In his later years, this search would be for havens where he could write in peace and flee the demands and pressures of his fame and public life. The trajectories of Baldwin's multiple journeys crisscross neighborhoods, cities, the country, and reach over and across the Atlantic Ocean. First, Baldwin moved from Harlem to the Bronx, then to Greenwich Village in New York City. Second, as a young writer he fled from the United States to France, and other European countries; he was back in 1957, after nearly a decade, but never to settle down for good. He admits that he returned from Europe to visit the American South and participate in the Civil Rights Movement; this time, his trajectories ran between the North and the South, and then the East and West in the United States. Then, he traveled to Turkey, several African countries, South America, and the Soviet Union. He spent nearly a decade as a semiresident in Istanbul in the 1960s. From 1970 on, he would retire more and more often to the only semipermanent home he knew in the seemingly unlikely locale of the medieval village of Saint-Paul-de-Vence in the south of France. He resided there for nearly 16 years, until his death in 1987, while maintaining his "transatlantic commuter" schedule as long as his health allowed it.

This authorial mobility provides a constant autothematic and narrative thread in Baldwin's works, and its impact on his career has been acknowledged, critiqued, and examined by many scholars. Baldwin's friend, assistant, and biographer, David Leeming (1994), remarks that the flight to Paris was the writer's "desperate attempt to 'cheat the destruction' which he feared would be his fate in New York" (p. 56), whereas his attachment to, for example, Istanbul as a writing haven was motivated by the fact that "he was 'left alone' and could work better there" (p. 263). James Darsey's (1999) study of the writer in a transatlantic context refers to Baldwin's "themes of escape or flight in [his] life and works" and characterizes him as a writer who "simultaneously desires and resists placement" (pp. 195, 201).[8] In *From Harlem to Paris* (1991) Michel Fabre stresses Baldwin's indebtedness to France as a

---

[8] I argue with Darcey's conclusion. It may not be possible to classify Baldwin as simply a feminist, especially given the definition of the term during the second wave of feminism, when his works flourished. As I contend in my forthcoming book, though, his approach to gender as an unstable category deserves careful interrogation.

country about which he famously said that it "'saved my life by allowing me to find out who I am,'" no matter that he remained only "an honorary citizen of the country he had never wanted to call home" (p. 213). Engin Cezzar, Baldwin's close friend in Turkey, stresses that, " from the get-go, it was impossible for a person who's so colorful, full of life, dynamic, and beautiful like Jimmy to stay in one place. It would have stagnated him and he knew this, instinctively."[9]

In the essay "The New Lost Generation" (1961), Baldwin calls attention to his compulsion to travel and change cultural scenery. He sees his immigrant itch of sorts as necessary for creativity and open-mindedness required of a writer, that is, as providing invaluable experience and perspective. Baldwin stresses that every artist must become oneself first, if he or she is ever to gain a "key to the experience of others" (PT, p. 313). Much in the vein of the group of American expatriate writers to whom his title clearly refers—Hemingway, Scott Fitzgerald, Stein, and others—"The New Lost Generation" also emphasizes the necessity of exploring the American connection to Europe. At the same time, Baldwin sharply divorces himself from the modernism of those white writers. He refuses to embrace the term *expatriate* as a black artist with much more complex ties to the Atlantic world. He also puts in question the mythologized ties[10] between the Old and New Worlds by suggesting that, much like for immigrants, for writers, too, an uncomplicated return home is not possible:

> What Europe still gives an American—or gave us [artists]—is the sanction, if one can accept it, to become oneself. No artist can survive without this acceptance. But rare indeed is the American artist who achieved this without first becoming a wanderer, and then, upon his return to his own country, the loneliest and most blackly distrusted of men. (p. 313)

This fragment stresses the complex and troubled links between the American and European cultural identities, and especially those between *African* America and Europe. On the other hand, it gives Baldwin's project of seeking one's identity outside of one's country a clearly temporal, narrative, and racialized dimension that echoes the well-known genre of immigrant narrative.[11]

To Baldwin, the process of gaining transnational experience is a mixed blessing, a journey of ebb and flow, a story of departures, crossings, and arrivals, whose individual and artistic benefits in the larger world are counterbalanced by alienation and "black distrust"

---

[9]Interview with the author, Istanbul, Turkey, 23 May 2001.

[10]I am aware that there are subtle implications of artistic elitism in Baldwin's approach.

[11]I realize that the quotation, taken out of context, may seem to imply a Euro-centric vantage point. It is clear throughout the text, however, and in his later works, that Baldwin was far from embracing such a position.

one faces upon one's return home. To the extent that self-knowledge gained in this process unlocks the enigma of the "other," and thus enables artistic expression and insight *into* the human subject, it also locks one *out* of the seemingly homogenous, familiar everydayness of one's home country. The loneliness and feeling of being "most blackly distrusted" thus hint at a certain link between this state of immigrant isolation and a kind of "racialized segregation," if you will, that an artist experiences once he or she has unlocked a window into the minds of other people.

Baldwin emphasizes further the racialized dimension of this message in the same section of his text. He dismantles the received dichotomy of the Old-versus-New World through a triangulation of perspectives among Africans, black and white Americans, and Europeans. He also draws a paradoxical analogy between the European and African American experience of interaction with American Whites:

> Europeans refer to Americans as children in the same way that American Negroes refer to them as children, and for the same reason: they mean that Americans have so little experience—experience referring not to *what* happens, but to *who*—that they have no key to the experience of others. Our current relations with the world forcibly suggest that there is more than a little truth to this. (PT, p. 313)

In this intriguing inversion of hierarchies, white Americans are denied access to adulthood, or full-fledged mature self. They seem to be victims of the racialized processes of immigrant acculturation that gave them their new national identity in the first place. That Europeans—who reside in the *Old* World, after all—would see them as juvenile is not as surprising, especially given Henry James's, D. H. Lawrence's, and other European writers' diatribes on the mythical youth of the *New* World.[12] Such an approach also resonates in the context of how nativeborns have usually treated newcomers, who are stereotyped as backward, "green," and childlike. Their foreign dress and manner, accent, poor language skills, helplessness, and unfamiliarity with the new country make first-generation immigrants into perpetual juveniles.

To push this reading even further, in Baldwin's triangular relationship among African Americans, Europeans, and white Americans, the holder of the most power—or the white resident of the superpower—is the least mature and developed subject. Baldwin thus inverts the traditional hierarchies again, by making the literal and literary outsiders—African Americans and Europeans—possess insights that "native-born" Americans cannot access. Under the more experienced gaze of the European and the African (American), the American seems to be a kid playing games well beyond his or her ken. In effect, we are implicitly encouraged to look at him or her as a kind of immigrant

---

[12]See H. James, D. H. Lawrence, J. Baudrillard, to name just a few.

"greenhorn." Baldwin's essay, then, floats the immigrant predicament between American Blacks and Whites, and thus thrusts them together in the larger narrative of national origins, suggesting too, that this narrative has transatlantic implications.

In his other writings, however, Baldwin inserts diverse minority groups into this picture and thus breaks the artificial binary of the white–black balance: Native Americans, Puerto Ricans, West Indians, Asians, Mexicans, and others.[13] In "Notes on the House of Bondage" (1980), he rages against the "TV screen which celebrates, night after night and year after year and decade after decade the slaughter of the Native American" (PT, p. 673). He describes the American white native-born, against whom Asian and Jewish immigrants had to measure themselves in the late 19th and early 20th centuries, by pointing at the ways in which the invention of the "American innocence … unassailable, fixed forever" came hand in hand with—if not as a result of—the legitimating of violence against people of color: "For it was not a crime to kill a black or a yellow or a red man … [it was] a duty … it was not a crime to rape a black red or yellow woman—it was sport" (PT, p. 672). In *The Fire Next Time* (FNT; 1963), he places the American imperialist and racist project in the context of European colonialisms in Asia and Africa, as well as linking the birth of fascism and its triumph in the German Third Reich to cross-breeding of global White supremacy and Christian ideology (FNT, pp. 72–75).

Baldwin's later writing shows even more explicitly that games of power based in racism have dangerous consequences for all involved. As Homi Bhabha states, "Nations … like narratives, lose their origins in the myths of time and only fully realize their horizons in the mind's eye." Baldwin reveals his awareness of the fallacy of the American myth of origins and calls its perpetrators on it. Under the facade of national myth and tradition, "nationhood implies violence … of [the] state" (p. 112) and "signifies power at the same time as it enacts prohibitions and commands bodies," as Henri Lefebvre claims (pp. 142–143).[14] By implying the interrelation between and among Europeans, white Americans, and African Americans, then, Baldwin demonstrates, what we have been discussing only recently in comparative ethnic studies, that is, a profoundly transational dimension of Americanness. He shows that the price of becoming an American in the actual spaces of the New World is becoming "white" in the mythic spaces of the national narrative, whose implementation is sanctioned by the power and violence of the racist state.

To Baldwin, state power seems carved in stone, just as does whiteness, its byproduct. The "City" he fled to Paris is also a metaphor for

---

[13]See for example, "Notes on the House of Bondage," "Here Be Dragons," *The Fire Next Time, If Beale Street Could Talk, Blues for Mister Charlie, Tell Me How Long the Train's Been Gone, Just Above My Head*. I will discuss others in the course of the essay.

[14]Lefebvre's *The Production of Space* stresses the spatial underpinning of this paradigm, a dimension of which I am much aware and explore in my larger study of Baldwin.

the nation state that echoes the vision of John Winthrop's "city upon a hill" and that erects for its citizens what he terms in an evocative metaphor the "house of bondage" that imprisons all Americans. This symbolic structure has accomplished:

> For what we will call the classic white American ... the destruction of his moral sense, except in relation to whites .... [And] it also destroyed his sense of reality and, therefore, his sense of white people had to be as compulsively one-dimensional as his vision of blacks. The result is that white Americans have been one another's jailers for generations, and the attempt at individual maturity is the loneliest and rarest of the American endeavors (PT, pp. 672–673).[15]

In thus illustrating the racial strife underlying Americanness, Baldwin gives a new twist to W. E. B. Du Bois's notion of "double consciousness," the notion that has been much quoted in descriptions of the African American condition ever since the publication of Du Bois's landmark work, *The Souls of Black Folk* (1903). In Baldwin's version, as in Du Bois's, the central "problem" of the 20th century is the "color line," and, like Du Bois, Baldwin chooses inventive narrative forms to study and theorize this problem. Where they differ, however, is in Baldwin's insistence that the effects of racism be studied in detail as much in the case of its victims as the perpetrators. Baldwin traces the "color line" in the stories of passage into the New World, triangulates among Africa, Europe, and North America, and makes himself an integral part of these stories as a migrant artist of color.[16]

More than half a century ago, as a Black writer who was successful and thus able to live and write in widely different places on several continents—from Harlem, to Paris, to Istanbul, to France, Switzerland, and Turkey among others—Baldwin was, of course, in a peculiarly compelling and privileged position to comment on migratory and immigrant makeup of American identity. In his well-known and much quoted essay, "The Discovery of What It Means to Be an American" (1959), he explains his journey from the New World to the Old—an inverted immigrant passage—as one that, by making him into a writer, had also made him embrace and wrestle with the mixed blessings of his national identity. While working on his first novel, *Go Tell It on the Mountain* (1953), immersed in the icy whiteness of a Swiss mountain village, Baldwin is "the stranger" amid Western culture, one whose

---

[15]Another part of the text nearby is worth a closer look: "It is terror that informs the American political and social scene—the terror of leaving the *house of bondage*. It isn't a terror of seeing *black* people leave the house of bondage, for white people think that they *know* that this cannot *really* happen ... No, white people had a much better time in the house of bondage than we did, and God bless their souls, they're going to miss it—all that adulation, adoration, ease, with nothing to do but fornicate, kill Indians, breed slaves, and make money" (PT, pp. 672–673).

[16]I deliberately oversimplify this discussion, as it lies well outside of the scope of this paper.

only help line to his roots is a music record—Bessie Smith signing the blues against the backdrop of the towering Alps:

> I had never listened to Bessie Smith in America (in the same way, that, for years, I would not touch watermelon), but in Europe she helped to reconcile me to being a "nigger." I do not think that I could have made this reconciliation here. Once I was able to accept my role—as distinguished, I must say, from my "place"—in the extraordinary drama which is America, I was released from the illusion that I hated America." (*Essays*, p. 138).

This release from hatred of his country opens up the world to Baldwin's narrator. Although he is keenly aware of his African ancestry, he also acknowledges and reconciles to the idea of his hybridity as the "bastard of the West."[17] His re-appropriation and deconstruction of his role as a "nigger"—the brutal legacy of his birthright compressed in one word—has to be negotiated not only in his home country, but also throughout the west. It enables Baldwin to become a witness and prophet who embraces his vocation of the word passionately. "I want to be an honest man and a good writer," he states in "Autobiographical Notes" that open his first collection of essays, *Notes of a Native Son* (1955), which was conceived and written between the United States and Western Europe.

Baldwin's authorial self-fulfillment and complicated love-and-hate affair with his country become his evolving subjects once he has been able to assess "America" from a distance. He stresses in "Autobiographical Notes": "I love America more than any other country in the world, and, exactly for this reason, I insist on the right to criticize her perpetually" (p. 6). His paradoxical patriotism—or a specific brand of "African Americanism"—arises from a deep commitment to dissent, and a desire to improve his country by critiquing the place and people where and with whom he was thrust by accidents of geography and genetics (p. 9). In this sense, it can be said that Baldwin's American "drama" described in the passages from "Autobiographical Notes" and "The Discovery of What It Means to Be an American" gains a dimension of an immigrant passion play. Baldwin seems to echo Anzia Yezierska's working-class Polish-Jewish immigrant heroine, who, having become disillusioned with the American Dream, asks: "But from America where can you go?" (Yezierska, 1991, p. 119). For immigrants there are no other countries to flee to from the Promised Land. For Blacks, there are no other tools but the master's to dismantle the house of bondage; there is no other shelter and country one could claim as one's own. As Baldwin finds out on a trip there, Africa as a homeland is a myth, and the South is the only true "old country" for American Blacks (PT, p. 183).

---

[17]"Autobiographical Notes," *Notes of a Native Son* (1984), p. 6.

In light of this discovery, the only place where racial reconciliation is possible is precisely at home, in "America," which must be transformed and claimed by Blacks. For Baldwin, this means coming to terms with this national identity while away from home, for home cannot be escaped. In "The Discovery" he stresses that upon his arrival in Paris, "I proved, to my astonishment to be as American as any Texas G.I." When he encountered his white compatriots there, away from the "fury of the color problem" at home, "it turned out to make very little difference that the origins of white Americans were European and mine were African—they were no more at home in Europe than I was" (PT, p. 172). But the most astonishing discovery is that, although it is possible to find a momentary haven—and havens are "high-priced" and corroborate delusions that it is possible to escape from oneself—what one really learns in the course of an inverted immigrant journey back to the Old World is that "there are no untroubled countries in this fearfully troubled world; that if he has been preparing himself for anything in Europe, he has been preparing himself—for America" (PT, p. 175).

The kinesthetic character of Baldwin's writing—its focus on literal and metaphorical passages, journeys, and migrations—prompts me to argue that Baldwin's "America" is a story-as-passage, a floating narrative, as it were, a work/vessel in progress traversing the Atlantic back and forth along various historic trajectories. Like Baldwin's own travels and the many stories of transatlantic crossings that he refers to in his writings, his vessel of works triangulates among Africa, Europe, and problematic "America." In search for the self—and "America"—which echoes profoundly such immigrant classics as Carlos Bulosan's *America Is in the Heart* (1943) or Mary Antin's *The Promised Land* (1912), it brings together disparate narrative traditions—uneasy and contentious as they may be. These traditions and stories have been triangulating across the Atlantic, among continents where Baldwin claims his hybrid ancestry, that is, where he maps his ambivalent place as the "American Negro." But it is precisely by weaving the unlikely threads of his complex history and geographic belonging, as much as writing his stories as a new 20th-century black American immigrant, that Baldwin envisages and constructs new, postbinary notions of identity and thus spaces for new Americanness.[18] To him, we all end up in the same boat as quasi-immigrants, once we have recognized and claimed our own complex roots and routes, and acknowledged and embraced our differences.[19] Writing about the meaning of diaspora, Kenneth W. Warren likens it to "a de-

---

[18]Darsey's discussion of Baldwin as an artist in Nietzschean sense of a singular intelligence upon which the west depends is relevant here (p. 202). I disagree, however, that Baldwin ends up a victim of his own racial paradigm.

[19]This could be expanded into a larger discussion in the context of James Clifford's *Routes: Travel and Translation in the Late Twentieth Century*. Cambridge, MA: Harvard University Press, 1997. See especially "Traveling Cultures," pp. 17–46.

sire to speak these contradictions in a simple voice" (Warren, 1993, p. 405). Baldwin's "embrace of a radical identity" (Warren, p. 404) leads to precisely such an articulation.

Baldwin's insights may not be big news in American Studies these days, but, given their early articulation in the 1950s and 1960s, they put his works squarely on the map of landmark studies of 20th-century racialized American identity. In the next section, I would like to pause for a moment in my readings of Baldwin, and suggest that we not only read his contribution through recent scholarship on immigration and race, but that we also interrogate that scholarship through his insights. This is to say that Baldwin's essays and fiction have anticipated by several decades an important discourse that has just made its entry into the study of American immigrations. Thus, he deserves a careful rereading as a theorist of American identity, much in the same vein as, for example, does Franz Fanon, as recently argued by Homi Bhabha (pp. x–xi).[20]

INTERACTION:
UNEASY CROSSINGS, IMPOSSIBLE DIALOGUES

Recent publications in the fields of American and immigration studies have begun paying a lot of attention to race, and the ways in which various historicized Americanization processes have relied on exclusionary politics of identity. Unlike the classic, so to speak, approaches to immigration initiated by historians Marcus Lee Hansen and Oscar Handlin, whose celebrated study of lower-class European newcomers, *The Uprooted* (1951) became a field-defining work, these new works show the instability and often destructive outcomes of the myth of America as a "Promised Land." They problematize and deconstruct the idealized model of passage from poverty to prosperity, from oppression to freedom, and from the Old World hierarchies of descent to the New World liberating individualism of consent.[21] The brief review of these works that I offer here aims to contextualize my reading of Baldwin as a theorist of American identity. Although a thorough discussion of all major works in this field is well beyond the scope of this project, I highlight the perspectives of several scholars, whose work has been especially helpful to my thinking through Baldwin's revolutionary articulation of the importance of race to narratives scripting American national identity as a literal and literary immigrant passage.

Much like Baldwin's "The Price" and "Encounter" essays, Lisa Lowe's *Immigrant Acts* (1996) stresses that in the production of nationalist discourse, "immigration has been historically a *locus* of

---

[20]In fact, bringing together Fanon as a theorist of colonialism and postcolonial movements with Baldwin would make for a very interesting, dialogic rereading of both writers in a transatlantic context.

[21]See Sollors (1986), especially pp. 3–39.

racialization and a primary site for the policing of political, cultural, and economic membership in the U.S. nation-state." Lowe stresses that, as we enter the 21st century, "We are [now] witnessing a 're-racialization' of immigrants that constitutes 'the immigrant' as the most highly targeted object of a U.S. nationalist agenda" (p. 174). Her terms, such as *locus* and *site*, emphasize the play between movement and rootedness/uprooting that are characteristic of immigrant accounts. At the same time they call attention to the power that the state has over newcomers and their relative passivity as objects/bodies placed under its control. Baldwin's works indicate that Blacks in this culture have been constructed in eerily similar ways by some of the state's institutions.[22] As the black jazz musician Rufus Scott learns in Baldwin's third novel, *Another Country* (1962), no matter what he does, he will be pursued by the racist notions Whites hold of him, on the one hand, and by his own rage and self-destructive reaction to and internalization of these notions, on the other. Rufus's life ends in suicide, as he sees no way out of this predicament. Baldwin shows how Rufus's many white friends, including his best buddy, the Irish American integrated immigrant Vivaldo, end up paradoxically and tragically redeemed by this death and thus seem to replicate the national story of whiteness arising from the destruction of its other, or blackness. But even that story is much more complex, as not all European immigrants were "white on arrival" (see Guglielmo, 2003).

As historian Paul Spickard stresses,[23] the so-called Ellis Island model of immigration studies that followed in the wake of Oscar Handlin's "immigrants as American history" in *The Uprooted* (1951) has reduced complex and multivalent histories to a one-directional story of upward mobility and whitening of diverse ethnic groups. Even today, for dark-skinned immigrants from Southeast Asia, the Caribbean, and other parts of the world, immigrating and becoming American necessarily involve a conflict with the prevalent black-on-white classification of the population here. While pondering differences between social constructions of race in the Caribbean and the imperatives of national identification in the United States, Mary C. Waters discusses the paradox facing dark-skinned West Indians: "The pervasive inequalities in American life ... often mean that becoming black American or Mexican American leads to a less bright future than remaining an immigrant" (Waters, 1999, p. 332). Considering the ways

---

[22]At the same time, and post-9/11, the link between the "nationalist agenda" and the "re-racialization" of immigrants and that curious oxymoron, "resident aliens," is especially chilling. Given the fact that American public discourse and corporate media elide the discussions of domestic injustice and racism, their accounts of military and legal actions against foreign national undesirables, suspected terrorists, and citizens of U.S.-occupied countries shift the "problem" to the outside of the United States.

[23]I am referring to Spickard's forthcoming book *Almost All Aliens: Immigration, Race, and Colonialism in American History and Identity* (Routledge). See also, "What's Critical About White Studies," in Spickard (2004).

in which South Asian Americans, or "desis," "are pledged and sometimes, in an act of bad faith, pledge ourselves, as a weapon against
black folk," Vijay Prashad discusses a "racist contract" in *The Karma
of Brown Folk* (2000) as an outcome of a "search of some accommodation in a racist polity" (pp. viii, xi). In a similar vein, in his recent *American Studies in a Moment of Danger*, labor historian George Lipsitz
stresses the importance of immigrants of color to the reification of old
and invention of new "racial enmities and antagonisms, which in turn
promotes new variants of racism" (p. 12). Lipsitz sees these processes
to be especially present in large urban centers like Miami, Los Angeles,
New York, or Boston, which have become the "second largest" cities
with Caribbean, Asian, or Latin American populations after Kingston,
San Juan Laos, Seoul, or Mexico City.[24]

Clearly echoing Baldwin's references to whiteness and blackness as
always at play in narratives of immigrant passage and arrival, Mathew
Fry Jacobson (1998) studies the historic origins of European newcomer "whiteness." Jacobson claims, "Race is not tangential to the history of European immigration to the United States but absolutely
central" (p. 42). This point has found support in many other scholars,
including Prashad (2000) and Waters (1999, p. 328); others discuss
the "in-between," or "not-yet-white" status of certain immigrant groups
in a historic perspective (Roediger, *Colored White*, 2002). Louis
Mendoza and S. Shankar, editors of a recent collection, *Crossing into
America: The New Literature of Immigration*, emphasize that, given
that the most recent immigrants[25] have been predominantly arriving
from Asia and Latin America, "Race is an altogether more complicated
and important an issue in the new literature of immigration" (p. xxi).
That race has been in fact such an issue from the very beginning of the
most populous wave of European immigration to this country,[26] no
matter that these immigrants have quickly become white, is confirmed
in James R. Barrett and David Roediger's study that traces the initial
"in-between" racial status of the late 19th- and early 20th-century East
European laborers (Roediger & Barrett, 2002, pp. 138–168). Historian David Roediger's essay "The First Word in Whiteness: Early Twentieth-Century European Experiences" brings together African
American intellectuals and artists with what, at the time, were considered the "inferior" stocks of southern and eastern Europeans, or "new
immigrants" to show the formation of white immigrant identity

---

[24]On racialization, see Omi and Winant (1994).

[25]Sometimes immigrants are referred to as ethnics; some scholars resist the concept
of race and thus refuse to engage it (e.g., Sollors, 1986); others look for nuanced ways to
trace its workings in a historic perspective (e.g., Roediger, 2002).

[26]Handlin may have been aware of the racist dimensions of the discussions on immigration in early 20th century, even though his pioneering work on the "new immigrants"
came decades before these newomers were seen as having shaped, and been shaped by,
Americanization as "whitening." See epigraphs introducing the sections in *Immigration
as a Factor* (Handlin, 1959), and especially p. 192.

(Roediger, 1997, pp. 354–357). Similarly, in *Colored White* (2002), Roediger argues for a careful reading of the changing racial codes, and emphasizes the immigrant entry into whiteness as a process rather than an overnight transformation in the "nation in which 'becoming white' and 'becoming American' were intertwined at every turn" (Roediger 2002, p. 141).

In their studies of labor movements and unionization, both Roediger and Lipsitz stress links between (de-)racialization and economic success for light-skinned European immigrants to the United States.[27] Lipsitz argues, too, that such ties have global implications. Today, the borders of nations are no longer obstacles for international corporations, but rather assets that can be used to pitch locations against each other in the never-ending competition for cheap offshore labor sources (Lipsitz, 2001, pp. 3–30). Such an approach seems to imply again, much in the way Baldwin's works did decades earlier, that immigration does not have to follow the traditional route of departure–crossing–arrival. The workers migrating to manufacturing sites and plants in their own countries embark on a journey of sorts, too, one that leads into the new worlds of corporate exploitative America that has dispensed with traditional borders. Amy Kaplan's remark that the notion of "borderlands" (see Anzaldúa, 1987) first deployed by Chicana/-no studies helps us to "link the study of ethnicity and immigration inextricably to the study of international relations and empire" (1993, 16–17) is tremendously important in this context. No less important is Kaplan's recent acknowledgment in her American Studies Association presidential address (2003) that we should regard immigration as a "multi-directional movement."[28]

Walter Benn Michaels's exploration of the history of legislation aimed at curbing immigration via quota systems in *Our America: Nativism, Modernism, and Pluralism* (1995) helps to explain some of the reasons for Baldwin's flight to Europe. Michaels explores carefully orchestrated efforts to fuse racism, nativism, modernism, and heterosexist family politics in the literature and legal discourses of the time. That the Immigration Acts of 1921 and 1924 had large impact on the construction of America as a racialized state is even more interesting, given our new knowledge of how gender and sexuality were intertwined in that scheme (Michaels, 1995, pp. 8, 11, 13). In her study of African American migrant narrative, *"Who Set You Flowin?": The African-American Migration Narrative* (1995), the literary critic Farah Jasmine Griffin focuses on such intertwinings of gender, sexuality, and race in the context of the stories capturing black migration from the rural South to the urban North. Unlike Baldwin, Griffin's readings set up the genre as specifically black, even

---

[27]See Lipsitz, *Possessive Investment* (1998) and *American Studies*, and Roediger, *Wages* (1999).

[28]See Kaplan, "Violent Belongings" (2004), *The Anarchy of Empire*, and ed., *Cultures of US Imperialism*.

as she gestures at many features of it that might be seen as shared among other groups comprising American literary traditions (pp. 3–10). Baldwin's novel *If Beale Street Could Talk* (1974) is a good example of a text that locates African American stories of passage in relationship with others, such as Mexican, South American, and European accounts, even if its main focus is on Blacks.

Historian Mae M. Ngai's recent *Impossible Subjects: Illegal Aliens and the Making of Modern America* (2004) is an important study of how race and exclusionary constructs of national identity that obtained, among others, for African Americans, also worked for Asian immigrants. She stresses the importance of the "iconic [Asian] immigrant [who] serves exceptionalist political culture" (p. 5), and articulates an important spatial dimension in her discussions of immigration policies that work by: "drawing lines of inclusion and exclusion that articulate a desired composition—imagined if not necessarily realized—of the nation" (p. 5). In that sense, Ngai's claim that restrictive immigration contributed to the multiplicity of factors that would be complicit in "produc[ing] new categories of racial difference" (p. 7) clearly echoes Baldwin's argument from "The Price of the Ticket."

In light of these recent scholarly arguments, it is clear that Baldwin's lifelong project of seeking and explaining roots of the white–black fissure at the heart of American character foreshadows discussions on historic specificity of racism and its changing role in the design of national identity. Like Ngai, scholars such as Thomas Guglielmo, Eithne Luibhéid, and Toby Rose[29] argue for approaching the immigrant character as always racialized, not to mention gendered and sexualized; like Baldwin, they see immigration and race as central to Americanness. In "The New Lost Generation," Baldwin stresses, "Voyagers discover that the world can never be larger *than* the person that is in the world; but it is impossible to foresee this, it is impossible to be warned" (PT, p. 310). Every immigrant experience is unique and totally subjective, although usually ends up relayed through common genres.

My goal in this brief review of scholarship has not been as much to examine in detail—for such studies abound, as we have seen—but rather to relate the historic processes of representation of immigrant and especially European racialization in the New World to James Baldwin's articulations of national identity. Such an approach is compelled by my focus in the next section on Baldwin's various texts that utilize elements of immigrant narrative and the rhetoric of the Middle Passage. In terms of their formal structure, virtually all of Baldwin's works rely on imageries and experience of departure, passage, crossing, arrival, transition, displacement, diaspora, ghettoization, removal, and erasure. Baldwin helps us to see that, apart from historic sources and data, we must also study in depth the

---

[29]E.g., see Guglielmo, Luibhéid, and Rose.

diverse narrative productions that have resulted from voluntary and forced crossings of the Atlantic Ocean by Europeans and Africans. In this culture, these two groups have been historically overvisible, while also being reduced—if not erased—to the extremes of the color spectrum—black and white. "Blacks" and "Whites" have practically disappeared behind racist stereotypes in dichotomy-loving American cultural imagination, myths of national origins, and ethnic clichés. Baldwin's works show us how, together with many other peoples, they found themselves embroiled in the ambivalent project of building the American "city on a hill."

PASSAGES AND ARRIVALS:
LOST AND FOUND IN THE NEW WORLD

Clearly echoing James Baldwin's ideas in her well-known study of canonical American literature, *Playing in the Dark; Whiteness and the Literary Imagination* (1992), Toni Morrison remarks that "cultural identities are formed and informed by a nation's literature" and that "it is no accident and no mistake that immigrant populations (and much immigrant literature) understood their 'Americanness' as an opposition to the resident black population" (p. 47). Morrison's argument resonates very clearly for many immigrant narratives that map individual and collective trajectories of passage from the Old World of Europe to the New World of North America. The majority of these texts that have been celebrated in American popular imagination—Mary Antin's *The Promised Land* (1912), for example—do not include any mention of the fact that the same Atlantic Ocean that European immigrants crossed in steerage had carried thousands of slave ships and harbored the horrors of the Middle Passage. Clearly, many immigrant writers were either refusing or unable to see the racial strife all around the country that received them, at the same time as they were being constructed according to exclusionary notions of newcomer and native-born identity themselves.

Although Baldwin's works clearly anticipate Morrison's argument in *Playing in the Dark*, they also, as we have seen, foreground some of the more recent discussions on racialization of light-skinned immigrants based on their national origins.[30] For example, in *Another Country* (1962), Baldwin portrays a second-generation Polish American, Richard Silensky, who grew up ashamed to speak Polish and, having escaped his own ethnic ghetto by means of literary success, asserts himself in opposition to black Americans. After years of starving as a highbrow writer, Silensky learns the laws of American dream and makes his literary coup with a mystery novel that becomes a popular bestseller and candidate for a Hollywood hit. His story echoes

---

[30]See especially the work of Jacobson (1998), but also Brodkin's *How Jews Became White Folks*, Guglielmo, Roediger, Lipsitz, and Zaborowska (1995).

the traditional male immigrant narrative of economic success—or all-American rags-to-riches progress.[31] Through it, Balwin also hints, much like such prominent early-20th-century immigrant authors as Abraham Cahan or Anzia Yezierska, at the pressures and contingencies of newcomer cultural identity and authorship in the 20th century United States.

Obviously, many European-American immigrant texts, willingly or unwittingly, naively or slyly, corroborated the project of the "construction of the American as a new white man" (p. 39), as Morrison (1992) stresses. It is important to remember, however, that those texts were not seen, at least until relatively recently, as part of national literature (or as deserving to be called literature at all).[32] That is, they were ghettoized as much as other ethnic and racialized literary traditions, at the same time as they were placed somewhat higher in the epidermally determined, so to speak, hierarchy of these traditions. Their writers were usually bound by the codes and expectations of the dominant culture in terms of content, language, style, and genre; their success and marketability were subject to the perceptions and tastes of those in charge of the business of publishing and marketing. For example, the works by East European Jews, such as the ones by the aforementioned authors Yezierska, Antin, and Cahan, evidence much attention to the expectations of editors and readers, who had a very specific kind of a Jewish newcomer in mind.[33]

This mediation of immigrant texts in early- to mid-20th-century United States was in and of itself a form of literary passage and process of acculturation through the publishing market. Most important, it often took place in ways eerily similar to those that had obtained for African American writers and artists in this country. Ever since the 18th-century poet and African slave Phillis Wheatley had her abilities and intelligence examined by a disbelieving panel of white male judges, marginalized and minority writers have had to face racialized notions of talent and ability.[34] The irony of this paradoxical similarity in the treatment of passages and stories produced by displaced peoples, some of whom would and did become white Americans with time, and those "others" who were branded by constructions of race and excluded from the definition of a citizen and national was not lost on James Baldwin. Baldwin's literary and literal "inverted immigrant journeys"—his experience of migration and works documenting it—re-vision (African) American identity in the second half of the 20th century by finding both points of contention and spaces for uneasy dialogue between white and black stories of displacement in the New World.

---

[31] See my discussion of this gendered model in *How We Found* (Zaborowska, 1995).

[32] See the works of Zaborowska, Lowe, Friedman, Dearborn, and Sollors, among others.

[33] For scholarship that pioneers inclusion of immigrant texts in American national literature, see Dearborn, Zaborowska (1995), Sollors, Lowe, Rose, and Mendoza at al.

[34] See Levernier (1991), O'Neale (1986), Scheick (1984), and Robinson (1965).

Baldwin's own multiple crossings of the Atlantic and his references to immigrants, (im)migration, and language-, identity-, and culture-altering passages function in his novels, essays, and interviews side by side with the rhetoric of the Middle Passage. In the short story "This Morning, This Evening, So Soon" (1960), he mixes up racialized identities, trajectories, and locations to show their constructed character and instability. The story's protagonist is a nameless African American artist in the Old World of Paris, who faces a return to the United States as an international star. He envisages his journey back home as an ironic reenactment of a white immigrant passage to the New World. While on a boat arriving in the New York Harbor, Baldwin's protagonist observes his fellow passengers as they are enjoying a Hollywood-like replay of a clichéd immigrant landing:

> I watched ... [New York] come closer and I listened to the people around me, to their excitement and their pleasure. There was no doubt that it was real. I watched their shining faces and wondered if I were mad. For a moment I longed, with all my heart, to be able to feel whatever they were feeling, if only to know what such a feeling was like. As the boat moved slowly into the harbor, they were being moved into safety. It was only I who was being floated into danger. I turned my head, looking for Europe, but all that stretched behind me was the sky, thick with gulls .... A big, sandy-haired man held his daughter on his shoulders, showing her the Statue of Liberty. (p. 162)[35]

Baldwin upsets here both black and white narrative models' reliance on one-way passages and movements of bodies and stories to pose an alternative, multidirectional, and dynamic story of American nation-and-literature-building across the Atlantic. This excerpt in particular and the whole story in general also foreshadow the preoccupation with immigration and immigrant narrative in the much later Baldwin essay "The Price of the Ticket." For the nameless narrator-protagonist in "This Morning," his sense of danger clashes with the vision of the Whites' happy homecoming. They enjoy it like a theme park ride, complete with the view of the Statue of Liberty and streaming American flags. Although Baldwin places his African American, quite literally, in the "same boat" with the Whites, he emphasizes his isolation from them and his invisibility in their eyes.

As we learn from the rest of the story, the protagonist's feelings of alienation and danger are compounded by the fact that he has been living in France for years, has a (white) Swedish wife and a "mixed-race" son. As he is returning to his place of origins, he fears he may be judged, and even persecuted, for his multiple transgressions against white supremacy. Moreover, his own and his family's safety depend, too, on his being able to "play the Negro," as it were, that is, behave in ways that would not antagonize his white compatriots and the state,

---

[35]See "This Morning, This Evening, So Soon," in *Going to Meet the Man.*

and especially the police. We can see Baldwin preparing ground here for another critical perspective with much currency, that is, Paul Gilroy's (1993) famous "intercultural and transnational formation" of the Black Atlantic, in which identities are instable and mutable, "always unfinished, always being remade" (ix).[36]

Baldwin's creative and subtle appropriation of, or rather innovative improvisation on the (white European) immigrant narrative patterns and imagery and his often unorthodox and ambivalent cross-breeding of this model with the rhetoric of the African Diaspora informs several other of his prominent works.[37] Among them are essays—"'On Being White' and Other Lies," "White Man's Guilt"[38]—and, to a certain extent, even such seemingly "white" novels of his as *Giovanni's Room* (1956) and *Another Country* (1962). Most interesting, in the latter two, Baldwin uses references to immigrant narrative to tell stories of characters burdened by the legacy of the transatlantic slavery on both sides of the color line, as is the case with David in *Giovanni's Room* and Rufus and Vivaldo in *Another Country*, and several protagonists of the short stories collected in *Going to Meet the Man* (1965).[39]

Let us return to *Another Country* (AC; 1962), which has not been sufficiently recognized for its astute examination of the legacy of European immigration, the Middle Passage, *and* intranational migrations. The ending of this rich novel offers a clear reenactment of yet another immigrant arrival cast in a troubling context. Incidentally, this scene was written when Baldwin resided in his semi-immigrant, semiexilic location in Turkey (Leeming,1994, p. 153). It features Yves, a young proletarian Frenchman, who is arriving in the United States by plane to reunite with his older American lover. The lover, Eric, is a white Southerner who escaped his home and landowning legacy to the North, thus following in the footsteps of African Americans who migrated there during Reconstruction. Eric is an actor who has spent a long time in France, where he met and fell in love with Yves. Upon his arrival and soon to be reunited with Eric, Yves is consumed with what is clearly an immigrant anxiety—Will they let me in? Am I good enough? Will they like me?—rather than joy. As the passengers he has chatted with during the flight slip off the "faces they had worn when

---

[36]My book on Baldwin, *Erotics of Exile*, explores manifold and troubling connections between the rhetoric of the Middle Passage, Black Atlantic, and that of Europe-to-"America" immigrant story in Baldwin's life-long project of redefining the social and narrative spaces of American identity.

[37]Like Baldwin, I am fully aware that my focusing on these two underlying narratives somewhat mariginalizes the prior story of European colonization of the continent and Native American genocide. This is not the intention of this study; again, I am exercising the necessary narrowing of my scope.

[38]See also Roediger on this issue and these essays, *Critical White Studies*, p. 356.

[39]See also Irish American Parnell in *Blues for Mister Charlie*, and the nameless female Italian shopkeeper and Mexican café owners and Puerto Ricans in *If Beale Street Could Talk*; *Just Above My Head* includes episodic encounters with West Indians in New York City.

hanging ... in the middle of the air ... for the faces which they wore on earth" (p. 433), Yves feels "helplessly French: and he had never felt French before" (p. 434). While the retreating American passengers seem to convey to him that he is an outsider in their midst—"they did not know who he was" (p. 434)—"It flashed through him that of course he had a test to pass; he had not yet entered the country; perhaps he would not pass the test" (AC, p. 434).

In order to understand the racialized underpinnings of Yves's dilemma, let us leap two decades into the future, returning to Baldwin's essay that we began with, "The Price of the Ticket" (1985). Its conclusion historicizes Yves's experience in *Another Country*, on the one hand, and supports Baldwin's claims about Americanness as an immigrant/racialized construct, on the other. As if answering J. Hector St. John de Crèvecoeur's famous historic interrogation in our century of migrations—"What is an American, that new man?"—Baldwin describes the moment of immigrant arrival as a passage into ready-made whiteness:

> They come through Ellis Island, where *Giorgio* becomes *Joe*, *Pappavasiliu* becomes *Palmer*, *Evangelos* becomes *Evans*, *Goldsmith* becomes *Smith* or *Gold*, and *Avakian* becomes *King*. So, with a painless change of name, and in the twinkling of an eye, one becomes a white American. (PT, p. xix)

Baldwin focuses here on the most clichéd part of the story that concerns passage through and renaming at the immigration station located on Ellis Island in the New York Harbor. This quotation, then, provides the historic and metaphoric context for Yves' arrival, but also echoes Baldwin's description of the land of the free as the house of bondage. Whiteness, he suggests, is a prison. As a newcomer, Yves will learn this only after his passage into America. And if her lets himself become white, he will be forever imprisoned by his race, no matter its privileged position in social hierarchy.

Ellis Island that Baldwin refers to is the palatial building of the immigration station, which has been featured in thousands of photographs and since the early 1990s has housed a museum of immigration. It became an important architectural symbol for European newcomers and a vital image in the iconography of mythic national origins, eclipsing, for example, Angel Island on the West Coast, which received the majority of Asian immigrants. Ellis Island thus has stood for the "gateway to America" in the popular imagination, literature, and visual culture. As such, it erases other arrivals and entry points, and especially the painful and traumatic "other" American passage—that of the African slaves. The majority of Africans in bondage were brought to North America through the port of Charleston, South Carolina; some were stationed on the islands off the southeastern coast. Yet there are no monuments or nationally sanctioned spaces of contemplation in these locations that would come close to Ellis Island.[40]

The glorious immigrant story cherished at the site of the Ellis Island museum today and eulogized in documentaries and publications ends with the triumphant passage into and throwing open the "door to America."[41] The aftermath of the entry is virtually unimportant. It becomes a subject of documentation and study for social workers, schools, governmental commissions, and artists and journalists, from Jacob Riis to the Dillingham Commission. Baldwin ventures into that realm of postpassage to analyze its unglamorous results, and to place them in the context of the transatlantic crossing forced on his enslaved African ancestors:

> Later, in the midnight hour, the missing identity aches. One can neither access nor overcome the storm of the middle passage. One is mysteriously shipwrecked forever, in the Great New World. (PT, p. xix)

The somewhat oblique, implied references to the African and European "middle passage" seem to blend together in the space of just three brief sentences. Baldwin suggests that the freshly minted white Americans find themselves not enriched by a new identity, but rather stripped of the only identity they had ever known upon their arrival—or "shipwreck"—in the "Great New World." Such an approach puts in question the utopia of immigrant progress by negating the mythic story's happy ending.[42] Baldwin does so by suggesting the often tragic realities of European postpassage. Moreover, by bringing this narrative tradition together with the one of African enslavement and Middle Passage, he poses both of them as equally important and painfully interwoven in the larger narrative fabric of national origins. Baldwin's move can be read as ironic, or virtually sacrilegious, in its violation of national myth and of the separate—if not ghettoized—narrative models that in American literary history segregate the "white" and "black" traditions.

Nevertheless, by linking the two disparate narratives of passage and arrival in "The Price of the Ticket," Baldwin obliterates their exclusionary, competitive, as it were, positioning vis-à-vis each other on the opposite ends of the American spectrum of color. He stresses as a point of connection between the two stories the shared loss of self and home, as well as the fact that both groups end caught up, albeit with dramatically different outcomes, in the racial machinery of Americanization:

---

[40]I am aware of the existence of the Avery Museum in Charleston, which is impressive, but not of the caliber I have in mind here.

[41]See the videocassette production of "Island of Hope, Island of Tears," at the Ellis Island Museum.

[42]Here I echo my chapter on Anzia Yezierska and her happy endings in *How We Found America* (1995).

The Irish middle passage, for but one example, was as foul as my own, and as dishonorable on the part of those responsible for it. But the Irish became white when they got here and began rising in the world, whereas I became black and began sinking. (PT, p. xx)

Baldwin not only braids together here the stories of the Irish and African crossings that "made the American people," as Oscar Handlin might put it, but goes on to proclaim that there were comparable causes and costs of the journey for the European newcomers and the black Americans as they encountered the New World. Especially, the shared moment of loss and confrontation with the new alien land is what has been lost; in fact, Baldwin implies this may be the part of the story that *had to* be obliterated, to produce the antagonistic black–white relationship that secured the racial hierarchy at the core of the nation.

In Baldwin's accounting of the economy of race within the constructions of national identity, the shared journey ends up with very different, color-coded outcomes:

The price that white American paid for his ticket was to become white—: and, in the main, nothing more than that, or, as he was to insist, nothing less. This incredibly limited not to say dimwitted ambition has choked many a human being to death here: and this, I contend, is because the white American has never accepted the real reasons for his journey. I know very well that my ancestors had no desire to come to this place: but neither did the ancestors of the people who became white and who require of my captivity a song. They require of me a song less to celebrate my captivity than to justify their own. (PT, p. xx)

In thus revealing the flip side of whiteness as a mask covering up loss and denial of one's past and ancestry, Baldwin fulfills the task of being "a good writer," with which he entrusted himself as a freshly anointed immigrant author in Paris. By showing that, like the African, the Irish immigrant suffered a loss of name in the New World, Baldwin comments on a somewhat structurally similar process of passage, at the same time as he stresses the dramatically different consequences for both subjects upon arrival. It can be said, then, that he is using this risky juxtaposition to create a space for dialogue between the two incompatible narratives of passage into the American house of bondage. Although not free from awkwardness and risk, this maneuver enables him to chip at the "myth of America to which we [all] cling so desperately" (p. 173).

CONCLUSION: AGAINST ESSENTIALISM/SEPARATISM

As I have shown, Baldwin discusses European immigrant crossings and their entanglement with the complex history of African presence in the New World in the essays and fiction that pioneer discussions on constructions of national identity. His works and life story offer profound and provocative theorizations of Americanness as transnational and multiracial, and signal important points of connection, and contention, between the rhetoric of the Middle Passage and (white) European immigrant crossing years before they have begun to be articulated in academic discussions.

Baldwin's explicit goal is not to separate peoples and cultures; his general project brings them all together in a much more comprehensive transatlantic perspective.[43] In "Encounter on the Seine," his autobiographical African American visitor in Paris deliberates the complexities of his status, while encountering his white and black compatriots, on the one hand, and French colonial Africans, on the other: "Perhaps it now occurs to him that in his need to establish himself in relation to his past he is most American, that this depthless alienation from oneself and one's people is, in sum, the American experience" (PT, p. 39). This discovery is not a confirmation of some universal, essential American character, but rather an acknowledgment of a shared heritage of departures, passages, and arrivals—in short, of uprootedness, flux, and constant change as marks of national belonging beyond, *because*, and independently of race. As Baldwin says in the introduction to *Nobody Knows My Name*: "In America, the color of my skin had stood between myself and me; in Europe, that barrier was down. Nothing is more desirable than to be released from an affliction, but nothing is more frightening than to be divested of a crutch" (Essays, p. 135).[44]

While thus boldly displacing the model white American male traveler in Europe popularized by Henry James's or Mark Twain's works, Baldwin insists on the material consequences of social and cultural constructions of race for all Americans and peoples. For example, this lesson hits home to a similar degree for white David of *Giovanni's Room* and black Arthur in *Just above My Head* when they confront love affairs with European men. Although their bodies seem able to do so through sexual encounters, at least momentarily, the identities of these characters cannot escape the American social forces of racism, homophobia, and heterosexism. By signaling the presence of sexuality in negotiations of national and immigrant identity, Baldwin thus gestures towards another aspect of immigrant studies that is in urgent need of exploration.

In Baldwin, the story of the nation is neither black nor white, but shines with the full spectrum of multihued humanity that is in constant motion, migrating, changing places and identities. Given the

---

[43]Although arguably more justified, if not expected for identity politics' sake, to focus on *his* people's plight, Baldwin occasionally falls pray to the white–black dichotomy that he is setting out to dismantle.

[44]See, Introduction, Baldwin (1961), *Nobody Knows*.

many Native peoples that had been living in North America before any immigrants came here, this story cannot be written without them, as Baldwin acknowledges in several essays.[45] Far from signaling facile similarities or unproblematic reconciliations, his works stress the challenge and pain that Americanness entails for those who have inherited its many immigrant narratives. As David, the white American protagonist of *Giovanni's Room* (GR; 1956) defines himself: "My ancestors conquered a continent, pushing across death-laden plains, until they came to an ocean which faced away from Europe into a darker past" (GR, p. 3). Like many other Baldwin characters, David learns that he is a part of a much larger story than he would like to acknowledge. In his literary manifesto, "As Much Truth as One Can Bear," (1962) Baldwin states what seems to be a very apt way of closing this essay on difficult and necessary readings of immigrant stories *beyond* and *for* race: "Not everything that is faced can be changed; but nothing can be changed until it is faced" (p. 38).[46]

REFERENCES

Antin, M. (1912). *The promised land, by Mary Antin; with illustrations from photographs*. Boston, New York: Houghton Mifflin.

Anzaldúa, G. (1987). *Borderlands/La Frontera: The New Mestiza*. San Francisco: Aunt Lute Books.

Baldwin, J. (1955). *Notes of a native son* (Reprinted 1984). Boston: Beacon Press.

Baldwin, J. (1956). *Giovanni's room*. New York: Dial.

Baldwin, J. (1961). *Nobody knows my name: More notes of a native son*. New York: Dial.

Baldwin, J. (1961). The discovery of what it means to be an American. In *Nobody knows my name: More notes of a native son*. New York: Dial.

Baldwin, J. (1962). *Another country*. New York: Dial.

Baldwin, J. (1962). As much truth as one can bear. *The New York Times*, BR 11, 38.

Baldwin, J. (1963). *The fire next time*. New York: Dial.

Baldwin, J. (1964). *Blues for Mister Charlie*. New York: Dial.

Baldwin, J. (1972). *No name in the street*. New York: Dial.

Baldwin, J. (1974). *If Beale Street could talk*. New York: Dial.

Baldwin, J. (1985). The new lost generation. In *The price of the ticket: Collected nonfiction, 1948–1985* (pp. 305–313). New York: St. Martin's/Marek.

Baldwin, J. (1988). Introduction: Nobody knows my name. *James Baldwin: Collected essays* (pp. 135–136). New York: The Library of America.

Baldwin, J. (1993). This morning, this evening, so soon. In *Going to Meet the Man* (pp. 143–194). New York: Vintage. (Originally published 1960)

Baldwin, J. (1998). *James Baldwin: Collected essays*. New York: The Library of America.

---

[45]E.g., "Here Be Dragons," "Notes on the House of Bondage."
[46]Baldwin, "As Much Truth" (1962).

Bhabha, H. (2004). Foreword: Framing Fanon (R. Philcox, Trans.). In *The wretched of the earth* (pp. vii–xli). New York: Grove Press.

Boelhower, W. (1981). The immigrant novel as genre. *MELUS, 8*(1), 3–13.

Bloom, H. (Ed.). (1986). *James Baldwin.* New York: Chelsea House Publishers.

Brodkin, K. *How Jews became white folks and what that says about race in America.* New Brunswick, NJ: Rutgers University Press.

Bulosan, C. (1943). *America is in the heart, A personal history.* New York: Harcourt Brace.

Cleaver, E. (1967). *Soul on ice.* New York: McGraw-Hill.

Clifford, J. (1997). *Routes: Travel and translation in the late twentieth century.* Cambridge, MA: Harvard University Press.

Darsey, J. (1999). Baldwin's cosmopolitan loneliness. In D. A. McBride (Ed.), *James Baldwin now* (pp. 187–207). New York: New York University Press.

Dearborn, M. V. (1986). *Pocahontas's daughters: Gender and ethnicity in American culture.* New York: Oxford University Press.

Delgado, R., & Stefancic, J. (Eds.). (1997). *Critical White studies: Looking behind the mirror.* Philadelphia: Temple University Press.

Du Bois, W. E. B. (1903). *The souls of Black folk; Essays and sketches.* Chicago: A. C. McClurg.

Fabre, M. (1991). *From Harlem to Paris: Black American writers in France, 1840–1980.* Urbana: University of Illinois Press.

Gilroy, P. (1993). *The Black Atlantic: Modernity and double consciousness.* Cambridge, MA: Harvard University Press.

Gilroy, P. (2000). *Against race: Imagining political culture beyond the color line.* Cambridge, MA: Belknap Press of Harvard University Press.

Griffin, F. J. (1995). *"Who set you flowin?": The African-American migration narrative.* New York : Oxford University Press.

Guglielmo, T. A. (2003). *White on arrival: Italians, race, color, and power in Chicago, 1890–1945.* New York : Oxford University Press.

Handlin, O. (1951). *The uprooted: The epic story of the great migrations that made the American people.* New York: Grosset & Dunlap.

Handlin, O. (1959). *Immigration as a factor in American history.* Englewood Cliffs, NJ: Prentice-Hall.

Handlin, O. (1973). *The uprooted: The epic story of the great migrations that made the American people.* Boston: Little Brown.

Hardy III, C. E. (2003). *James Baldwin's God: Sex, hope, and crisis in Black holiness culture.* Knoxville: University of Tennessee Press.

Henderson, M. G. (2000). James Baldwin: Expatriation, homosexual panic, and man's estate. *Callaloo: A Journal of African-American and African Arts and Letters, 23*(1, Winter), 313–327.

Jacobson, M. F. (1998). *Whiteness of a different color: European immigrants and the alchemy of race.* Cambridge, MA: Harvard University Press.

Kaplan, A. (2004). Violent belongings and the question of empire today. *American Quarterly, 56*(1), 1–18.

Kaplan, A., & Pease, D. E. (Eds.). (1993). *Cultures of United States imperialism.* Durham, NC: Duke University Press.

Lazarus, E., & Schappes, M. U. (Ed.). (1947). *Emma Lazarus: Selections from her poetry and prose.* New York: Book League Jewish People's Fraternal Order of the International Workers Order.

Leeming, D. (1994). *James Baldwin: A biography.* New York: Henry Holt and Co.

Lefebvre, H. (2000). *The production of space* (D. Nicholson-Smith, Trans.). Oxford, UK & Cambridge, MA: Blackwell.

Levernier, J. A. (1991). Phyllis Wheatley and the New England clergy. *Early American Literature, 26*(1), 21–38.

Lipsitz, G. (1998). *The possessive investment in Whiteness: How White people profit from identity politics.* Philadelphia: Temple University Press.

Lipsitz, G. (2001). *American studies in a moment of danger.* Minneapolis: University of Minnesota Press.

Lowe, L. (1996). *Immigrant acts: On Asian American cultural politics.* Durham, NC: Duke University Press.

Luibhéid, E. (2002). *Entry denied: Controlling sexuality at the border.* Minneapolis: University of Minnesota Press, 2002.

McBride, D. A. (Ed.). (1999). *James Baldwin now.* New York: New York University Press.

Mendoza, L., & Shankar, S. (Eds.). (2003). *Crossing into America: The new literature of immigration.* New York: The New Press.

Michaels, W. B. (1995). *Our America: Nativism, modernism, and pluralism.* Durham, NC: Duke University Press.

Miller, D. Q. (Ed.). (2000). *Re-Viewing James Baldwin: Things not seen.* Philadelphia: Temple University Press.

Morrison, T. (1992). *Playing in the dark: Whiteness and the literary imagination.* Cambridge, MA: Harvard University Press.

Ngai, M. M. (2004). *Impossible subjects: Illegal aliens and the making of modern America.* Princeton, NJ: Princeton University Press.

O'Neale, S. (1986). A slave's subtle war: Phyllis Wheatley's use of Biblical myth and symbol. *Early American Literature, 21*(2), 144–165.

Omi, M., & Winant, H. (1994). *Racial formation in the United States: From the 1960s to the 1990s.* New York: Routledge.

Pease, D. E., & Wiegman, R. (Eds.). (2002). *The futures of American studies.* Durham, NC: Duke University Press.

Porter, H. A. (1989). *Stealing the fire: The art and protest of James Baldwin.* Middletown, CT: Wesleyan University Press.

Prashad, V. (2000). *The karma of brown folk.* Minneapolis: University of Minnesota Press.

Robinson, W. H. (1965). Phyllis Wheatley: Colonial quandary. *College Language Association Journal, 9,* 25–38.

Rodriguez, R. (2002). *Brown: The last discovery of America.* New York: Viking.

Roediger, D. R. (1997). First word in Whiteness: Early twentieth-century European experiences. In R. Delgado & J. Stefancic (Eds.), *Critical White studies: Looking behind the mirror* (pp. 354–356). Philadelphia: Temple University Press.

Roediger, D. R. (Ed.). (1998). *Black on White: Black writers on what it means to be White.* New York: Schocken Books.

Roediger, D. R. (1999). *The wages of whiteness: Race and the making of the American working class.* New York: Verso.

Roediger, D. R. (2002). *Colored White: Transcending the racial past.* Berkeley: University of California Press.

Roediger, D. R., & Barrett, J. (2002). In between peoples: Race, nationality, and the 'new-immigrant' working class. In D. R. Roediger & J. Barrett, *Colored White: Transcending the racial past* (pp. 138–168). Berkeley: University of California Press.

Rose, T., & Payant, K. B. (Eds.). (1999). *The immigrant experience in North American literature: Carving out a niche*. Westport, CT: Greenwood Press.

Ross, M. B. (1999). White fantasies of desire: Baldwin and the racial identities of sexuality. In D. A. McBride (Ed.), *James Baldwin Now*. New York: New York University Press.

Scheick, W. J. (1984). Phyllis Wheatley and Oliver Goldsmith: A fugitive satire. *Early American Literature, 19*(1), 82–84

Scott, L. O. (2002). *James Baldwin's later fiction: Witness to the journey*. East Lansing: Michigan State University Press.

Sollors, W. (1986). *Beyond ethnicity: Consent and descent in American culture*. New York: Oxford University Press.

Spickard, P. (2004). What's critical about White studies. In Daniel G. Reginald & Paul R. Spickard (Eds.), *Racial thinking in the United States: Uncompleted independence* (pp. 248–274). New York: University of Notre Dame Press.

Standley, F. L., & Burt, N. V. (Eds.). (1988). *Critical essays on James Baldwin*. Boston: G. K. Hall.

Standley, F. L., & Pratt, L. H. (Eds.). (1989). *Conversations with James Baldwin*. Jackson: University Press of Mississippi.

Wallace, M. (1999). "I am not entirely what I look like": Richard Wright, James Baldwin, and the hegemony of vision; or, Jimmy's FBEye blues. In D. A. McBride (Ed.), *James Baldwin Now*. New York: New York University Press.

Warren, K. W. (1993). Appeals for (mis)recognition: Theorizing the diaspora. In A. Kaplan & D. E. Pease (Eds.), *Cultures of United States imperialism*. Durham, NC: Duke University Press.

Waters, M. C. (1999). *Black identities: West Indian immigrant dreams and American realities*. Cambridge, MA: Russell Sage Foundation, Harvard University Press.

Yezierska, A. (1991). *How I found America: Collected stories of Anzia Yezierska*. New York: Persea Books.

Zaborowska, M. J. (1995). *How we found America: Reading gender through East European immigrant narratives*. Chapel Hill: University of North Carolina Press.

11

Model Minority
and Marital Violence:
South Asian Immigrants
in the United States

Margaret Abraham
Hofstra University

The United States is a country built on immigration. Much of the new immigration is the outcome of immigration laws closely connected to concepts of citizenship, family unity, and the economic value of labor. In the United States, people of color have historically experienced institutionalized cultural and economic racism. Often due to issues such as noncitizen status, gender, ethnicity, and race, immigrant women of color experience some of the worst hardship. Drawing from my research in the 1990s on marital violence among South Asian Immigrants in the United States and my ongoing involvement in addressing domestic violence in South Asian communities, I discuss: (a) the importance of ethnicity gender, class, and citizenship status in understanding self and community, (b) the profile of South Asian immigrants in the United States from the 1960s through the 1990s, (c) the construction of the model minority image and its impact on the self and community, (d) immigrant women's experiences of marital violence, and (e) the role of South Asian women's organizations redefining notions of self and community by addressing marital violence.[1] I conclude with a brief discussion of my entrée into research on marital violence among South Asian immigrants, the challenges and value of engaging in action research, and one potential for future research.

ETHNICITY, GENDER, CLASS AND LEGAL STATUS IN DEFINING SELF AND COMMUNITY

Notions of self and community are not absolute and vary in communities based on internally defined and externally imposed factors. Ethnicity, gender, class, race, and citizenship are all important aspects of the construction of self and community for South Asian immigrants in the United States.

Ethnicity is frequently the first explicit marker of differentiation that the dominant group and other groups' use, especially when there are specific physical features that "stand out" and can be used as an easy source of distinction in the construction of the *ethnicized other*. For South Asians there is a certain degree of "cultural discrimination" that Sonia Shah (1994) defines "as "a peculiar blend of cultural and sexist oppression based on our clothes, our foods, our values and our commitments" (p. 182).

Gender too plays a critical role in defining self and community. Women of color have to deal not only with sexism in their day-to-day lives but also with systems of racial and ethnic stratification that label and control the minority group as a whole (Healey, 1995, p. 26). As women, South Asian immigrant women (unlike immigrant men) have to cope with gender boundaries that define them as subordinate based on the patriarchal norms and values of both the immigrant and mainstream cultures. As an ethnic minority, South Asian immigrant women (unlike women from the dominant culture) have to cope with semipermeable boundaries that allow them, as subordinate group members, to partially internalize the norms and values of the dominant culture while being simultaneously excluded by the dominant group from total membership in that culture. Focusing on gender alone excludes cultural distinctions in gender relations and ignores the impact of majority/minority ethnic group distinctions. As Harding (1991) points out, within the United States, a racially ordered society, there are no gendered relations that stand-alone but only those that are constructed by and between races (p. 171). Here, I would add ethnicity and class.

Class distinctions within the South Asian communities also impact on notion of self and community. Class interests and relationship lead

[1] I would like acknowledge the valuable contribution of the women and organizations who participated in this study. This chapter is partially drawn from previously published work written by the author in *Speaking the Unspeakable: Marital Violence among South Asian Immigrants in the United States*, Rutgers University Press, 2000, and the *Indian Journal of Gender Studies Gender Studies*, 1998.

to varying constructions of identity and community, depending on the situational contexts. Class distinctions within the South Asian communities frequently lead to tensions based on exploitative work relations between employers and employees. Often immigrant women are worst situated due to their gender, race, and noncitizen status (Hossfeld, 1994). They are frequently perceived as desperate for work at any wage, particularly if they are known to be undocumented workers, have language barriers, or need an income to sustain themselves or their family. Although gender role stereotypes oppress women under patriarchy, ethnic minority women, especially recent immigrant women, experience multiple subordination based on their courses of action, strategies, distinctiveness of culture, and structural arrangements.

SOCIOHISTORICAL PROFILE OF SOUTH ASIAN IMMIGRANTS IN THE UNITED STATES

Defining self and community entails a quick sociohistorical profile of the South Asian community in the United States. One of the earliest groups among South Asians in the United States was that of the Sikhs from Punjab, who migrated to the West Coast of the United States in the early 20th century as farmers and to work on the railroads. However, it was the 1965 Immigration Act (Hart–Cellar Act) that really set the stage for the growth of the South Asian community in the United States.

Prior to the mid-1980s, the South Asian community was comprised primarily of professionally qualified individuals, culturally bound to their homeland and families in South Asia, but seeking the opportunities for professional growth and economic success that they felt were lacking then in their own home countries. Investing in the image of the successful, hard-working, family-oriented immigrant and in an attempt at upward group mobility, South Asian immigrants who came to the United States in the 1960s and 1970s were viewed by mainstream Americans and viewed themselves as a "model minority"—a minority that was a model community based on its emphasis on strong family ties, high education, and economic success.

The 1980s and 1990s were marked by "chain migration," whereby South Asian immigrants who had become U.S. citizens sponsored their relatives, who in turn sponsored other relatives to migrate to the United States. This chain migration brought about considerable variation within the community along dimensions such as education, occupation, class, and gender experiences. Ethnic homogeneity was replaced with a much more visible class- and region-based heterogeneity by the late 1980s. The image of highly educated professionals was gradually replaced by more heterogeneous visible images of South Asian that included motel owners and workers, gas station attendants, newspaper stand vendors, and taxi drivers.

Despite this heterogeneity of the South Asian population, community leaders continued to represent the community as a monolithic whole. Members of the community worried about their community image. Often as a reaction to the dominant American society's racism and cultural imperialism, they avoided critically looking at themselves or their community. They became so invested in portraying the model minority image that they oppressed some segments of the community, and denied the prevalence of any social problem, including violence against women, within their community.

MODEL MINORITY IMAGE
AND ITS IMPACT ON SELF AND COMMUNITY

As stated earlier, the South Asian community was seen by the mainstream and identified itself as a model minority community. This image was based on the notion that South Asians had achieved a fine balance between upholding the cherished values of South Asian culture, particularly family solidarity and harmony, while simultaneously adopting the principles of modern American capitalism. Women were the main symbol of cultural continuity and were faced with both external and internal pressures to uphold the culture in specific ways, including adhering to culturally prescribed gender roles. The South Asian women in the United States became responsible not only for family honor but also for the honor of the "model minority community" (Abraham, 1998; Dasgupta, 1998).

Investing in the model minority image resulted in narrowly defined notions of self and community and was problematic in several ways. First, it denied the diversity of individuals and the diversity of groups within the South Asian immigrant community across class, gender, regional, and religious lines. Segments that did not fit the "success mold" were constantly faced with a sense of shame, deficiency, and failure. To avoid this shame, individuals and the community often played the cover-up game.[2] This was done through fun-filled cultural activities and stylized social functions by the community to reinforce the collective identity as one that is predominantly successful—and upholds its cultural values of strong, united, harmonious families.

Second, it placed South Asians in a position where they disassociated themselves from other minorities and were sometimes resented by other racial, ethnic minorities and by certain groups of Whites too. For mainstream American society and its leadership, the use of such an operative label as "model minority" served the vital function of "divide and rule" by creating ethnic contrasts that kept minorities hierarchically apart. Like other model minorities, South Asians too carried

---

[2]Here the term "cover-up game" implies using various strategies, in this case, stylized cultural activities that portray a particular image of the community and help to conceal or obscure the problems within the South Asian community.

their own forms of racist beliefs from the countries from which they emigrated. These beliefs were further exacerbated in a racially ordered society such as the United States. Often it was not only the elite among the South Asian community that held onto the model minority image but also economically exploited classes who felt that perhaps this model minority status, especially in terms of family values, differentiated the South Asian community from economically exploited classes in other ethnic or racial communities.

Third, such terms placed considerable pressure on community impression management, that is, a constant pressure on the community to manipulate the group's collective identity so as to portray its model minority status. This model minority status frequently meant denying or making invisible any issue that was perceived as eroding the model minority image, such as poverty, AIDS, homosexuality, substance abuse, and domestic violence, as none of these fit into the concept of the "model minority." The success stories of some segments of those groups labeled a model minority partially hid the fact that other segments were not prosperous, and experienced poverty and exploitation both within and outside of their community.

Fourth, it led to the persistence of narrowly defined cultural constructs of gender relations. To uphold the notion of good family values and strong family ties, an essential attribute for model minority image was to show how the South Asian immigrant community had carried over and retained the cultural values from South Asia.

Notions of women's status and roles in South Asia have varied by region, class, religion, and ethnicity over time. Cultural and economic roles have been shaped and shifted by economic and structural forces such as colonialism, urbanization, capitalism, and globalization in South Asia (Abraham, 2002). However, the dominant image in the cultural rhetoric has been a relatively monolithic one that defined a woman primarily in terms of her reproductivity and her relationship to the men in her family and community. Rather than a self-defined image, she was subject to patriarchal perceptions of woman as defined in religious and cultural rhetoric. The various social, economic, legal, and religious institutions formed the framework that supported and legitimized the dominance of the men and the subordination of women. Women were viewed as guardians of family honor, and the concept of "shame" was deeply ingrained in the socialization process of women but for the interest of men, the family, and the community.

This narrow cultural construct was extended to the immigrant community in the United States, often in more limiting ways than in South Asia itself. The public image of the South Asian community in the United States was primarily male-defined, with women as the cultural transmitters. Many South Asian men who emigrated to the United States often desired their wives to retain South Asian cultural values often framed in "traditional patriarchal" terms while simultaneously expecting them to "Americanize/modernize" in some areas external to the home. Guided by the cultural doctrine of honor and duty, many South Asian immigrant women experienced external and internal pressures to stay within the parameters that defined them as obedient, self-sacrificing, and content in the private realm.

Notions of self, community, and gender relations were also influenced by religion and religious institutions. For many South Asians, their religious institutions played a central role in defining their community identity. Temples, mosques, and churches became the focus of establishing and perpetuating a link with their historic and cultural roots. Religious institutions were not only places of prayer, but also the arena for the construction and maintenance of values, beliefs, and customs of the immigrant community. These centers of worship partially became the caretakers of tradition in the United States. Moral solidarity of the collective was of vital importance, particularly in maintaining the model minority image. Gendered relations were constructed and perpetuated by the socio-cultural activities of these institutions (Rayaprol, 1997). They played a central role in the reproduction and maintenance of the gender identity of South Asian women in America. South Asian women were seen as the caretakers of cultural continuity in the United States.

Acknowledging the problem of domestic violence within the South Asian family was problematic, as it challenged the very concept of "good family values and strong family ties" or what Linda Gordon (1989) called "the myths of harmony of the normative family," which was an integral part of the model minority image for the South Asian community. Domestic patriarchy was assumed by the mainstream immigrant community and was not an issue for public discussion. Men assumed greater power and control within the home, although women worked outside and were still responsible for the home and child rearing Although South Asian women were economic contributors, they were increasingly constructed in cultural terms within the immigrant home and community. Religious institutions became sites for defining these narrow gender relations and ensuring traditional patriarchy. At the same time, South Asian immigrant women and men were struggling against the ethnic/gender image that frequently placed them as targets for ethnic, class, and race discrimination in American society. The social environment was such that issues such as marital violence lay unaddressed by the mainstream segments of the community because they did not fit into the concept of the "model minority" or the happy harmonious South Asian home.

Inattention to social issues, particularly those related to gender and class, partially set the stage for the emergence in 1980s of South Asian women's organizations (SAWOs) that challenged the model minority image. These organizations began to address domestic violence and other problems faced by women in their community while also fighting structured inequality in discriminatory immigration laws that indirectly contribute to violence against women. They redefined community identity so that it was more reflective of the diversity within the community in terms of gender, class, sexuality, and citizenship status. However, prior to discussing the role of these SAWOS, it is important to understand some of the ways that South Asian immigrant women experienced marital violence.

SOUTH ASIAN IMMIGRANT WOMEN'S EXPERIENCES OF MARITAL VIOLENCE ISOLATION

For South Asian women, especially recent immigrants to the United States, one of the worst and most painful manifestations of marital violence perpetrated against them was the isolation factor. Here, isolation refers to the individual's perception and reality of being emotionally and socially alone, economically confined, and culturally disconnected. It is the "feeling and fact" of not belonging or having a meaningful relationship. The individual experiences a sense of being lonely, abandoned, ignored, and disconnected from both intimate and other social relationships. Many experienced a desire to alleviate the isolation through social interaction with members of their own community. However, this was not always possible as the husband controlled all the activities and contacts that the woman made by locking the door from the outside, monitoring all telephone calls, leaving her at home without any money, or questioning her whereabouts. The friends in the United States were often the husband's friends whose loyalty frequently rested with the abused woman's husband.

Yamuna,[3] a 30-year-old woman, who had just got her divorce and green card and worked as a clerical worker, recounting her extreme sense of isolation when she first arrived in the United States to join her husband, explains:

> I was in his apartment ... I think we hardly went out ... I mean you could feel terribly trapped in that kind of thing. I did not know how to operate the locks and he never taught me ... what he would do is when he would go out, he would lock it from outside .... For some reason I never realized that I could open it from inside ... I thought I was locked in and I was locked in and he never tried to explain to me that I could open it if I wished ... he of course never gave me an extra set of keys ... I could not even open the blinds ... so I had this awfully trapped feeling.

Shahida, a 34-year-old woman who worked as a chemist, described her experience of isolation upon coming to the United States as a dependent spouse. Her husband locked her at home from morning until he returned from work in the evening.

---

[3]Pseudonyms have been used to protect participants' confidentiality. Age and other profile details are based at the time of the interviews were conducted with participants.

He took off a day after I came here. The next day he went ... he shut the door and locked it from outside ... he used to come around 6:30 and eat dinner around 7:30 ... So the whole day I was alone in the house ... I spent my time watching TV ... when I asked about a job, he said that he didn't want me to have any small job, if I got a good job I could do it. When I asked for English classes he said that he did not have the money. He told me if I had money, then I could go and take English classes ... after dinner he would go out ... and come around one at night.

Usha, a 32-year-old insurance agent, explained how her husband and her in-laws together made all attempts to isolate her not only from her workplace but also from her own family in India.

It was an everyday problem, they wouldn't let me go to work, they would close the garage door on me. They would lock all the doors and I couldn't get out of the house. It was real real hard ... right before Thanksgiving ... when I was going to India for my sister's marriage, they would not let me go. I had to call my neighbors to let me go out of the home, otherwise I would have just missed the plane. When I came back the same thing started again.

South Asian culture and the challenges of negotiating the day-to-day life as new immigrants tend to create a sense of dependence for many women on their spouses. Added to this problem are the isolation and dependence stemming from leaving behind most of the support system of the larger family in your home country. Back in their own home country, for South Asian women, a husband's lack of interpersonal interaction might have been compensated by the social ties to her family, her friends, or other members of the community. Members of families and friends may act as a buffer against stress and abuse. Through their relative physical proximity, family members and friends could potentially act as a mechanism of social control on an abusive spouse. Many immigrant men and women found themselves in the United States without any equivalent friends or supportive relatives who could be such buffers.[4] The result was that frequently women who experienced marital violence had no family or friends of their own to turn to in a crisis, and experienced alienation and powerlessness.

PHYSICAL ABUSE

The unhealthy isolation of immigrant families in the United States and the subordination of women by men as an integral part of the cultural construction of the family thus set in place the arena where

---

[4]This aspect cannot be overemphasized because the sexism and cultural prescription in South Asia in general also allow considerable latitude and power to men vis-à-vis women in gender relation, and often a woman's family and friends, although sympathetic to the woman's situation, may suggest that the woman stay with her abusive husband due to various cultural factors.

physical violence could take place. A common way in which violence was perpetrated on South Asian women was through physical abuse. This abuse ranged from pushing, hitting, and punching, to beating with an object or choking. Very often the bruises were on areas that could be hidden from others noticing them, thereby making the crime an invisible one and allowing the cycle of violence to continue. Positioned between a South Asian society which legitimized violence by cultural values that defined women as property and an American society that objectifies women's bodies, South Asian men frequently perceived that it was their male right to control women's bodies through coercion. The silencing of women and their rights in South Asian patriarchal culture made it hard for women who are victims of such abuse to discuss this with others, especially in a foreign culture where their contacts were limited.

Zakhia, a 33-year-old woman with a 6-year-old child, who struggled to make a living doing odd jobs and sometimes sewing in a garment factory, talked about how her husband started battering her after coming to the United States.

> After three months [of coming to the United States] he [husband] started hitting me. And every year it just became worse. He didn't think much of working girls. He thought that they had easy morals. He would accuse me of not working and doing other things with my time. He would beat me at night and during the day I had to go out and work. He would beat me once in a few weeks. I used to have bruises on my body and had to work like that ... I never told them [at work] that my husband was beating me ... He was hitting me very badly, and then he started threatening to take my life.

Usha was physically abused by her husband and by her in-laws too for such things as going to work or for spending any of the money she earned, spending too much on groceries, or cooking too much or too little—in fact, for any thing she did. "All three of them, father-in-law, brother-in-law and him [husband] all teamed up [Mother-in-law had passed away]. They started abusing me physically. They kicked me. My father-in-law came and twisted my arms, and threw me in the family room."

"Three days after I arrived here [United States] he started beating me" said 30-year-old Reena, a clerical worker, of the battering her husband inflicted on her.

> He held my neck and beat me [for asking him what was on his mind] ... when I went to lie down he pushed me off the bed ... I felt very sad and I wanted to die ... When he would come home he started to beat me ... for reasons like not eating, not drinking juice, not cooking or cleaning enough ... he would beat and kick me and when I would start crying he would put the T.V. loud so no one could hear outside. He would squeeze my throat. One day when I got unconscious they all [husband, brother-in-law and his wife] put me in a tub and bathed me and fed me for three days.

Zakhia, Usha, and Reena are just three of the many women who have been similarly battered. No matter whether it was money, cooking, groceries, or not drinking juice, their abusers always found a reason to beat these women, thereby demonstrating their power and control. South Asian men, often themselves oppressed on the basis of their ethnicity and class position in the United States, frequently use gender-derived power to control women's bodies through physical and mental coercion. Hence, a gendered understanding of battering requires us to also look into the intersections of ethnicity, class, and race in the immigrant day-to-day experiences.

SEXUAL ABUSE

Another manifestation of violence is through sexual abuse. Until relatively recently, women's sexuality was rarely publically addressed in South Asian culture. Discussion of sex, especially in front of unmarried women, was rare. The high value placed on an unmarried woman's virginity and emphasis on pleasing the husband for a successful marriage resulted in the objectification of women in sexual relations. Often notions of Western sexuality were superimposed by immigrant husbands on their wives while simultaneously drawing on traditional South Asian values of the rights of a husband to demand sexual gratification from his wife. Narrow and rigid constructions of masculinity and femininity also exacerbated the problem. Male sexual gratification was frequently the realm in which domination and control over women was exercised, especially within the context of marital violence. Zakhia's husband felt it was his right as a husband to sexually control her.

> My husband would bother me at night. He would accuse me of doing immoral things at the job and for being tired at night. He would beat me and then do whatever he wanted to ... he never asked me at all. He did whatever he wanted to do. If I refused then fights would start. He would never apologize. I had to apologize to him ... he used to say, I am married to you, I don't have to ask or apologize for anything.

For some women, the abuse against them was not limited to their husband. Attempts at sexual control frequently got extended to male members of his family. Reena recalls:

> That night my brother-in-law molested me ... [when the husband was away] ... he could not get too far but he told me not to repeat to anyone what had happened. But I repeated and he got angry ... I told my husband ... when he [brother-in-law] came to know and was questioned, he got furious and beat me ... when my husband was at work.

Another form of sexual abuse was by manipulating women's reproductive rights. Zarina, a 62-year-old woman with five children, four of whom were born within the first 5 years, explained how her husband controlled her sexual and reproductive rights.

> Most of the time he would force himself on me ... he did not feel any guilt and would go about his activities like nothing happened ... after my fourth child, my sister's friend suggested I go on the pill ... but my husband was reluctant to buy them. He himself never wanted to use condoms or anything ... and by making me pregnant time and time again, he was trying to bind me down to him.

Similarly, Tara, a 37-year-old secretary, described how her husband controlled her sexual and reproductive rights. In Tara's case, it was not by forcing her to have children, but by forcing her to have abortions, thereby denying her right to have a child and going against her religious beliefs.

> Three times he forced me to go for an abortion, which I was totally against ... he said we can't afford it, we have nobody to watch the baby, things like that ... when I finally got pregnant for the fourth time ... I convinced him somehow to keep the baby ... but a year later he said he can't stand this, he does not want to deal with the responsibilities, it is too much for him, he is too young for all this, he should be enjoying his life. He started going out and having an affair.

Some of these South Asian men also sexually abused their wives by manipulating the "other woman" factor as a means of intimidating and exercising power and control. Here flaunting the sexual other involved the process of insinuating, threatening, or actually having a sexual relationship with another woman, thereby making his wife feel sexually inadequate and alienated from her body. For South Asian immigrant women like Yamuna, sexual abuse took the form of her husband threatening to seek sex elsewhere if she did not succumb to his desires, thereby devaluing her, making her feel inadequate, and forcing her to have sex with him in ways that were against her beliefs and values. In short, frequently men initiated the sexual act, defined the nature of the act, and determined when it was over, with women rarely having any choice in the matter. The sexual act was one in which women were silenced, controlled, and subordinated.

INTIMIDATION

Intimidation was an integral part of the abuse that the South Asian immigrant women I interviewed experienced. It often occurred on a day-to-day basis and often escalated when a woman challenged her abuser. Malti, a 47-year-old systems engineer, was intimidated by her husband using violence on objects and threatening to do the same to her.

All of a sudden he would get angry ... from the simplest things to the biggest thing ... he would come and examine the refrigerator everyday, what I had thrown out and what I had kept. The garbage in the house was inspected before it was thrown out ... he wanted to find faults in something ... whenever he was at home there was constant criticism. I could never be right ... the anger was unpredictable. He would be nice and sweet for a few days, and then all of a sudden something very insignificant would make him angry ... he would not show the violence physically, he would get glasses and break them. He would say, see what I can do to that glass, I can do the same to you. *This* type of intimidation.

Another common way of intimidation was the husband threatening the wife that he would send her back to the home country if she did not abide by his demands. For some South Asian women this was traumatic, as they feared the negative social impact of this on their own families in South Asia. Shahida described this intimidation:

One day I heard him (husband) make plans with [American girlfriend] for going out for dinner. I was in the kitchen, and he was using the bedroom phone. I don't know what got over me but I picked up the other extension. Immediately he came, snatched the phone and put it down. He was very angry and said that [girlfriend] could sue me ... another time he wanted to know why I had gone to the store when he had forbidden me ... he said that if I could not stay the way he wanted me, then I could go back to Pakistan ... he told me to ask my father for the ticket money and said that my father does not want me back.

All the different manifestations of violence just discussed were usually accompanied by verbal abuse. As Seema, a 26-year-old woman who worked as a packer and was physically maimed by her husband when she was 24 explained:

He did not want me to ask him anything. But I had a lot of questions, as I had lots to learn. If I ever asked him anything he would get angry with me because I had asked him and shouted instead of explaining it to me. He never answered my questions and was always angry. He would verbally abuse me and I could not sleep as I was scared of him.

The privatization of the home, language and cultural barriers, and the anonymity of immigrant families were conducive to South Asian women being trapped in an abusive marriage, with their perpetrators remaining unaccountable for their actions (Sakhi Collective, 1992).

ECONOMIC DEPRIVATION

Although marital violence cuts across all socioeconomic segments of the South Asian community, factors such as level of education, lack of employment, or inadequate preparation to enter the work force exacerbate a woman's sense of dependency and financial entrapment within the marriage. One important way an abusive husband economically abused his immigrant wife and made her "nonexistent" to the outside world was by controlling all the finances, giving her absolutely no money, thereby restricting her freedom of movement, holding her accountable for every penny she spends, and excluding her from any bank accounts and any moveable or immovable assets. Although some South Asian women are highly educated and financially independent, cultural limitations combined with gender role conditioning result in women feeling pressured to be financially accountable to their spouses. Tara explained how her husband tried to control her finances.

> I was working for two years before he married me ... he started asking me about the money. Like what do you do, what happened? Then he started asking me to give him an account. I said I can't give you an account for what I did with my money in the last two years. I don't keep the receipts ... he said you are talking back to me, you have no respect for your husband ... that's how it started. I couldn't say anything. If he asks me something I have to give him an answer. If he does not like it, then it's not respecting him ... he would slap me.

Usha said:

> Since I came here, I have been working but my husband took the money ... and then they [husband and in-laws] would give me twenty dollars a week, I had to put my gas and for all my lunches. Things kept getting hard, because when you go out and all, you have to contribute in other things. You have to maintain your attire ... First I started talking that I need some more. Then the father [in-law] started interfering, then the brother [in-law] started interfering more and more. If I go for grocery, why did I spend so much, they would open my groceries and go through everything. How much I spent on it. Whatever I do at home is wrong. If I cook two things, why did I cook two?

When Usha tried to maintain a separate account, she was beaten up by her husband.

> One day I thought that I am not going to close the account [an independent account that she had started and was under pressure to close] ... I need a little bit of financial independence ... so he beat me and said that he was going to call his father and brother and they are all going to beat me.

Shahida explained her abuse through fiscal deprivation when she was not working and was financially dependent on her husband:

> He gave me no money for household expenses ... He used to do all the shopping and spending. he never took me for grocery. He told me not to go, because it wasn't a good neighborhood .... I had no slippers to wear at home, so I asked him for one. He bought me one that was one size bigger. So I was in a state, that I couldn't even go out to buy a pair of slippers ....

During Ramzan, I had kept Roza, but he did not. You know I couldn't eat anything the whole day. He never got fruits or anything for me. It was very hot those days. I had found a bag of coins in a drawer. I didn't know that they were old rare coins. I took a couple and bought orange juice. Later he told his friend that I had stolen his money.

By controlling the finances, men ensured that the women remained within abusive situations due to a perceived, and often real, inability to opt out. Although many of the women had been educated in their home country, they did not have the type of preparation in terms of language skills, qualifications, or job training needed for attaining a job that could provide some sort of financial independence in the United States. For others, their qualifications and training were outdated due to abiding by the culturally prescribed norm of the primary role as wife, mother, and keeper of the home. For many women the loss of self-esteem and confidence, especially in an alien country, deterred them from seeking jobs, or in some cases attaining them. Lastly, the lack of a "green card"[5] for some of these women made obtaining any sort of legal employment a nonviable option.

THE "GREEN CARD" OR IMMIGRATION STATUS FACTOR

An extremely important manifestation of marital violence is in relation to immigration issues and the fear of deportation. Although some Indian women emigrate on an independent status, many come into the United States as spouses of U.S. citizens or lawful permanent residents (LPR). Prior to the passage of the Violence Against Women Act (VAWA) in 1994, this legal dependency often placed the husband in a position of dominance and control over his wife. It placed the legally dependent, abused wife in the dangerous position of remaining with her abuser. Often, women who left an abusive marriage prior to attaining a "green card" were faced with the loss of legal immigration status and risked possible deportation. Today, although have been some legal provisions for abused immigrant women, immigration issues continue to be a problem, particularly for women on an H-4 visa.[6]

---

[5]A green card is a permit given to immigrants by the U.S. Immigration and Naturalization Service (renamed Bureau of Citizenship and Immigration Services) to permanently reside and legally work in the United States.

[6]The spouse and unmarried children (below 21 years of age) of an H1B visa holder are eligible for an H4 visa. A person on an H4 status visa cannot legally work unless and until the person gets a Change of Status from the Immigration and Naturalization Service from an H4 to H1B status. This has specific requirements and is not easy automatic process. An H1B visa is given to bring in professional-level foreign employees to the United States. Through the H1B visa program, U.S. employers are able to hire foreign professionals for a specified period of time. The H1B program allows workers in specialty occupations to work in the United States for a maximum period of 6 years and is subject to certain specifications. The H4 visa puts severe constraints on abused women, as they are economically dependent and also fear deportation if they leave their abusers.

Among some of the women I interviewed, the green card was used as a means of power and control by the abuser and had an impact on women getting out of an abusive relationship. Seema's husband used the green card to exercise power and control.

A he [Seema's husband] is a citizen, my green card came within three months but he never let me collect the mail. I knew that the green card had come but he kept it with him. I had not even seen it. Then he started to say that one day he would murder me ... It was six o' clock in the morning ... he said that I had come only for my green card. He said he knew that I had asked his friend about my green card. He kept on saying that I had married him for the green card and was going to ruin his life ... he went and picked up a pitchfork. The big one made of iron ... he aimed it to poke my eyes ... I had not fully woken up so I could not run away ... I became unconscious ... when I regained conscience, I realized that I was all alone ... I saw myself in the mirror and found that I was bleeding profusely ... one eye was totally damaged.

For Shahida, getting out of an abusive marriage caused delays in her attaining a green card since the green card was contingent on her husband's status. She explained:

I have a green card now but earlier I had some other status. I got it after my marriage, under the condition that I will have my interview after two years when they will make the green card [permanent]. But I separated within seven months of my coming here. So the interview that needed both the husband and wife could not be held. I had to file for my green card separately ... one has to file it and give it for their [Immigration and Naturalization Services] consideration. They decide whether to give it to you or not. I filed it and fortunately won the case.

Yamuna, who left her husband before her green card came through, described how her husband tried to intimidate her at work by telling her roommate the following: "I'm going to tell the police, I'm going to tell the immigration that she's a cheat, she's a liar and everything."

Not having their own families in the United States to turn to for some sort of financial support makes getting a job imperative for abused South Asian women who are dependent on their spouses. The lack of a "green card" was an obstacle for some of these women in finding an alternative, through legal employment, that would facilitate their economic independence from their abuser. The need to protect abused immigrant women's rights led to groups seeking members of Congress to initiate or help pass legislation through the Immigration Act of 1991, the Violence Against Women Act (VAWA) 1994, and VAWA 2000. However, various barriers persist, particularly for those abused South Asian immigrant women with an H4 visa status (Raj & Silverman, 2003).

POLICE, COURTS, AND HEALTH CARE PROVIDERS

The police, courts, and health providers also exacerbate women's experiences of domestic violence through racial, gender, and cultural stereotyping. Immigrant women's abuse was compounded when the police, courts, and the department of health were unresponsive or women feared these institutions colluding with government agencies such as the Immigration and Naturalization Service. Issues such as lack of court language interpreters, ethnic, racial, and class biases, and lack of cultural sensitivity in the institutional response also deterred women from seeking institutional support in ending domestic violence. Sometimes the courts being unaware of marriage customs among the various sections of the South Asian community, such as the lack of legal documentation of marriages, dowry, gift giving, and sexuality, placed abused immigrant women seeking a divorce at a disadvantage due to the lack of understanding of the cultural dynamics on the part of lawyers and judges. Stereotypes, negative attitudes, and apathy by providers of medical care toward abused women also reduced victims' willingness to seek help.

STRATEGIES OF RESISTANCE

A discussion of women's experiences of marital violence is not complete without briefly mentioning the strategies of resistance that abused immigrant women use. Often the image of abused immigrant women in the mainstream American society is that they are docile or passive to the abuse perpetrated against them. This is clearly not the case. Despite the many constraints they face, many abused immigrant women that I interviewed used multiple strategies to reduce or end the violence. These included: (a) *personal strategies* such as talking, promising, hiding, avoiding, passive or aggressive defense, (b) *using informal sources* of help such as family members, neighbors, and friends, and (c) *using formal sources* of help such as police, social service agencies, shelters, and lawyers and the court system (Abraham, 2000). Often abused women felt compelled to stay with their abuser as they had no economic independence and could not easily access public benefits and alternative housing.

STRATEGIES FOR CHANGE AND THE ROLE OF SOUTH ASIAN WOMEN'S ORGANIZATIONS

Although women who have been abused have used various strategies of resistance in their own relationships, a more collective and organized approach to shifting domestic violence from a private problem to a public issue occurred with the emergence of South Asian women's organizations (SAWOs) in the 1980s. At the forefront of addressing the needs of abused South Asian immigrant women, challenging the notion of a model minority, and redefining community were South Asian women's organizations such as Sakhi for South Asian Women in New York, Manavi in New Jersey, Sewaa in Philadelphia, Apna Ghar in Chicago, Sneha in Connecticut, Maitri and Narika in California, and Saheli in Texas. Apna Ghar started the first shelter in Chicago in 1990 to provide services for abused South Asian women. These organizations together created a space for South Asian women to discuss issues that were pertinent to them as women and as South Asians in the United States and provided tangible support and services for South Asian abused women. Intersecting gender and ethnicity by their very existence and in issues they articulated, these organizations protected and empowered South Asian women (Abraham, 1995).

The last decade has seen the emergence of many more South Asian women's organizations that address domestic violence. Individually and together, these organizations have developed strategies to start sensitizing law enforcers and health care providers to the needs of South Asian women by providing handbooks and discussing the issues with mainstream services. At the micro level, these SAWOs have shifted notions of self and community through individual advocacy and victim support groups. These SAWOs assist South Asian victims/survivors of marital violence by providing them with relevant information, suggesting the alternative options available to them, listening to their problems, being a social support, counseling them, empowering them, helping them remove their personal belongings if they decide to leave their home, and frequently taking them through the steps necessary to end the cycle of violence perpetrated against them.[7] SAWOs also provide legal assistance for abused South Asian women whenever possible. They have created support groups where victims/survivors meet other victims/survivors, discuss their problems, support each other, provide solidarity, and help each other in the process of ending the violence perpetrated against them. They help empower women and shift the problem from a private problem to a public issue.

The lack of appropriate educational and occupational skills is a major obstacle for some victims of marital violence in the South Asian community. SAWOs help women who lack the language and communication skills to attain suitable jobs by providing language classes and job training classes, and helping them locate suitable jobs so as to attain self-confidence and economic independence. They develop contacts with job training centers and check their accessibility to South Asian women, initiate language training classes or connect victims with already existing programs, provide assistance in attaining work permits, and assist in writing resumes and locating jobs.

---

[7]Counseling provided by the different South Asian organizations varies from trained counselors to volunteers who are trained to counsel on an informal, nonlegal basis.

At the macro level, these SAWOs attempt to bring about legislative reform and cultural sensitization in law enforcement and medical care systems. Similarly, they help redefine the community by working with media to stop perpetuating a distorted imagery of immigrant minorities, as these images often result in discrimination and violence against these groups. They help address domestic violence and other social issues by looking at the ways by which cultural and structural discrimination leads to policies that limit the ways of ending violence against women. Most importantly, these organizations have played a pivotal role in challenging the existing status quo and in raising community consciousness to end violence against women. These SAWOs and with other community-based organizations have redefined the South Asian community in the United States.

Constructions of self and community are constantly undergoing change. Although my research focused on SAWOs that addressed marital violence, the 1990s in the United States also witnessed mobilization around other important issues, including health, poverty, religious fundamentalism, gay and lesbian rights, and domestic worker's rights in the South Asian community (Khandelwal, 1997, 1998). Today the South Asian population is over 2 million, new South Asian organizations have proliferated, and many more scholars, including a new generation of South Asian students, are writing on issues that impact South Asian immigrant women and men's lives. The coming of age of a second generation of South Asians in the United States has led to addressing diverse concerns growing out of their perceptions and experiences of American and South Asian culture. It also plays into the dynamics of organizations and constructions of self, culture, and community of South Asians in the United States.

POSTSCRIPT: REFLECTIONS ON DOING
COMMUNITY-BASED ACTION RESEARCH

Although my goal has to been to keep the voices of abused women central in this chapter, I was asked to briefly describe my own entrée as a sociologist into this research, describe some of the challenges, and suggest some areas for future research. A decade ago, there was considerable research on domestic violence in the United States, but a serious paucity of material on its prevalence in ethnic minority communities. It was in 1989/1990 that I decided to explore marital violence in the South Asian immigrant community in the United States. Interestingly, in the early stages of this research, I found myself being asked by some South Asian activists whether my work as a sociologist would be accessible to a larger audience than academics. This question, together with discussions with academics, friends, and activists about community identity construction, particularly in the context of violence against women, influenced me to critically reflect on my roles as a sociologist and as a South Asian immigrant woman working in the United States.

Although my entrée in the field of domestic violence was primarily as a researcher whose main goal was to contribute to the discourse on domestic violence, I was surprised to see how this goal became much more concrete than I had initially envisioned. Over the years I have increasingly come to see myself as a sociologist engaged in "action research" (Dobash & Dobash, 1979) committed to bridging the gap between scholarship and activism. I believe that doing research on violence against women involves integrating theoretical and methodological rigor within a sociopolitical context. Theoretically, action research entails a commitment to continuously examine the commonalities and differences that exist among women and men based on the intersection of race, ethnicity, gender, class, and nationality. Methodologically, action research recognizes that issues such as where the research takes place, the types of questions asked, data collection strategies, interpretation, dissemination, and the relationship between researcher and respondent are intrinsically sociopolitical in nature.

Today as a sociologist I can truly say that writing and working in ethnic communities that have been historically marginalized or relegated to the ambiguous "third" position in a traditionally dichotomous society such as the United States has sensitized me to the sociopolitical context within which my research is done and applied. We need to deconstruct stereotypes of our communities and help shift issues pertinent to South Asians from the margins to the center.

Currently there is research on the causal factors and the manifestations of domestic violence among South Asians. However, no serious attention has been given to the justice response to domestic violence in this ethnic population. This is an extremely important area for future research. The justice response can shape, to a large degree, the outcomes of survivors' experiences of domestic violence and constructions of community It is important to explore whether domestic violence victims/survivors in the South Asian community experience the police response and courts in patterned ways. This is particularly important given that the last decade has seen the increasing criminalization of domestic violence. We also need to examine some more long-term viable social alternatives to the criminal justice system in addressing domestic violence. In the years to come, more collaborative, comparative analysis will help us understand and address the global pervasiveness of violence against women. To do this we have to build better bridges between sociologists and activists, both national and transnational, while critically reflecting on and sharing our research.

REFERENCES

Abraham, M. (1995). Ethnicity, gender, and marital violence: South Asian women's organizations in the United States. *Gender & Society, 9*(4), 450–468.

Abraham, M. (1998). Speaking the unspeakable: Marital violence among the South Asian community in the United States. *Indian Journal of Gender Studies, 5*(2), 215–241.

Abraham, M. (2000). *Speaking the unspeakable: Marital violence among South Asian immigrants in the United States.* New Brunswick, NJ: Rutgers University Press.

Abraham, T. (Ed.). (2002). *Women and the politics of violence.* New Delhi, India: Har-Anand.

Dasgupta, S. D. (Ed.). (1998). *A patchwork shawl: Chronicles of South Asian women in America.* New Brunswick, NJ: Rutgers University Press.

Dobash, R. E., & Dobash, R. P. (1979). *Violence against wives.* New York: Free Press.

Gordon, L. (1989). *Heroes of their own lives: The politics and history of family violence.* London: Virago Press.

Harding, S. (1991). *Whose science? Whose knowledge?* Ithaca, NY: Cornell University Press.

Healey, J. F. (1995). *Race, ethnicity, gender, and class: The sociology of group conflict and change.* Thousand Oaks, CA: Pine Forge Press.

Hossfeld, K. J. (1994). Hiring immigrant women: Silicon Valley's "simple formula." In M. B. Zinn & B. T. Dill (Eds.), *Women of color in U.S. society* (pp. 65–93). Philadelphia: Temple University Press.

Khandelwal, M. (1997). Communities organizing in an Asian group: Asian Indians in New York City. *Another Side, 5*(1), 23–32.

Khandelwal, M. (1998). Reflections on diversity and inclusion: South Asians and Asian American studies. In L. R. Hirabayashi (Ed.), *Teaching Asian America: Diversity and the problem of community* (pp. 111–122). New York: Rowman & Littlefield.

Raj, A., & Silverman, J. G. (2003). Immigrant South Asian women at greater risk for injury from intimate partner violence. *American Journal Public Health, 93*(3), 435–437.

Rayaprol, A. (1997). *Negotiating identities: Women in the Indian diaspora.* New Delhi, India: Oxford University Press.

Sakhi Collective. (1992). Break the silence. *Committee on South Asian Women Bulletin, 7,* 117–119.

Shah, S. (1994). Presenting the blue goddess: Toward a national, Pan-Asian feminist agenda. In K. A.-S. Juan (Ed.), *The state of Asian America: Activism and resistance in the 1990s* (pp. 147–158). Boston: South End.

12

Refugees and Gendered Citizenship

Patricia R. Pessar
Yale University

Scholarship on women, gender, and migration has grown tremendously since the 1970s. Within this corpus, only modest attention has been paid to *refugee* women and men (e.g., Giles, Mousa, & Van Esterik, 1996; Indra, 1999); instead, refugees are often collapsed into the more universal category of immigrant. There is need to examine how refugee status with its distinctive course of violence and displacement, public discourses, laws, and practices impact women and men differentially. How violence, abuse of human rights, exile, and repatriation become occasions for displays of, or challenges to, patriarchy needs to be interrogated as well. This chapter treats these important issues, and it does so from the vantage point of gendered citizenship. In doing so, I seek to move the engagement of studies of gender and refugees/immigrants beyond the more familiar contours of home and workplace to additional and related sites such as the body, ethic communities, refugee camps, nation-states, international law, and international organizations. The analytical constructs of female consciousness and feminist consciousness, employed in this work, aid in tracing continuity and change in refugee women's consciousness across time and space.

A gendered approach to citizenship demands a critical engagement with that public–private divide that not only has informed a great deal of traditional political theory but also has buttressed the power of male citizens (Pateman, 1989). Certain feminists have urged the abandonment of the public–private binary altogether. Others have called for new ways to envision their character and articulation (Mouffe, 1992).

217

Adopting this latter stance, Ann Phillips (1993) refused the essentialized and gendered qualities of the distinction between the two domains, rather than the distinction itself. In this spirit, Weona Giles (1999) proposed that for refugees and immigrants the connotations, emotions, and norms of "home" extend well beyond the feminized household to include the ethnic community, refugee camps, and the nation. The imbrications of womanhood within such male-dominated domains as the local community and the nation can be highly disciplining and discriminatory for women. This is especially so for those who are persecuted due to their "transgression" of cultural norms and who are involved in war and refugee displacement.

Although commonalities exist, the experiences of refugee women and men are highly varied, both individually and regionally. Consequently, in the first part of this work I draw examples from several domains and localities to underscore patterns of oppression and discrimination against female refugees and claimants. I then turn in the second section to the specific case of Guatemalan refugees in camps in southern Mexico during the 1980s and early 1990s and in return communities as of the mid-1990s. In light of the gains in political and social rights many of these refugee women managed to attain, I explore the potentials and limits of exile as a site for the development of more expansive and active forms of citizenship for women. I conclude with a more sobering assessment of the difficulties encountered by refugee women when they attempt to repatriate into a highly patriarchal and insular Guatemalan state new identities and practices informed by global human rights and women's rights.

GENDER AND REFUGEE STATUS

Rules of international law are purportedly abstract, objective, and gender-neutral. Feminist jurisprudence, however, has documented the ways in which the structures of international law making and the content of its rules systematically privilege men while ignoring or marginalizing women (Binion, 1995; Charlesworth, 1991). Critics insist that a public/private binary infuses the law, with the outcome being that greater significance and privilege are afforded to public/"male" domains than private/"female" ones. Consequently, many problems of concern to women are conceptually relegated to the private sphere: a locale considered inappropriate for legal regulation (Crowley, 1999). This orientation holds grave consequences for women, especially those who seek recognition as refugees based on gender persecution. As Jacqueline Bhabha (1990) wrote: Norms about quotidian life, the various instances of "private behavior" such as "dress codes, personal relationships, sexual conduct and initiation are most amenable to these arguments because within international law generally and human rights law in particular, they have traditionally been disregarded as relatively trivial and frivolous, in contrast to the classic grounds of persecution" (pp. 4–5).

Within international law, human rights arguments are supposed to trump sovereign states' justifications for oppressive or restrictionist actions, and the international refugee regime is charged with putting this policy into practice. Yet in cases of gender persecution directed at women, this understanding is often sidestepped. Rather, as asylum cases over such matters as female circumcision and forced marriage reveal, culturalist arguments advanced by state officials frequently outweigh calls for individual protection. It is argued that although human beings have a common inviolable dignity, a given society may prescribe certain norms of behavior considered to be consistent with such notions of human dignity (Bhahba, 1996).

It is along this "fault line" between the universal and the culturally particular that many postcolonial nation-states not only seek to affirm their membership among modern nation-states, but also endeavor to differentiate themselves as unique nations. Nationalists tend to locate this uniqueness by gazing "backward" to the "traditional." And it is women who are usually associated with "the traditional" and charged with maintaining these values and life ways. Within this division of labor, men are freed to represent and participate in more "modern" realms like the state (Collier, 1995; Nelson, 2000). Women who transgress the traditional by embracing sentiments, subjectivities, and behaviors associated with more global notions of womanhood, modernity, and citizenship challenge patriarchal imaginings of their particular, modern nation-state and the responsibilities of men and women to defend it. In many countries women have paid dearly for such "transgressions," yet their persecution has rarely been met with the protection of refugee law.[1]

THE PREAMBLE TO FLIGHT
AND THE "REFUGEE-CAMP-AS-HOME"[2]

Today's postindependence wars and social revolutions often involve ethnic conflict and the targeting of ethnic minorities. Although, for the most part, men and boys take up arms and leave home communities, women and young children remain behind to struggle with broad-based impacts (e.g., weakened states, economies, and social institutions) and local ag-

---

[1]Advocates of change adopt the feminist position that "the personal is political" and that patriarchy is a system constituted primarily through power relations not biology. They insist that female claimants who oppose institutional discrimination or who express dissenting views on male social or cultural dominance should be recognized as having been persecuted on the grounds of their political opinions and the threat they represent to gendered hierarchies of power (Crowley, 1999; Macklin, 1995). Certain countries, like Canada, have made significant progress in incorporating gender as a criterion for refugee status.

[2]The term "refugee-camp-as-home" is taken from Giles (1999, p. 90).

gressions. In these wars, women's associations with reproduction and the maintenance of ethnic "tradition" render their bodies highly politicized spaces. For example, in the former Yugoslavia a distinction was drawn between "patriotic" and "disloyal" women. The patriots were women through whom the nation could "rebuild links with 'honorable' histories, religions, and traditions." Those who were stigmatized as disloyal allegedly betrayed the "ethnic-national collective" by initiating or maintaining solidarity across ethnic-national boundaries (Kurac, 1995). It was the members of this latter group who were targeted for violence by those whose identities and social practices as Serbs, Bosnians, Croats, and males were threatened. Today gender-oriented violence has become one of the main weapons of refugee-producing conflicts worldwide (Matlou, 1997). In this process, women's bodies emerge "as both the targets of violence and symbols of a violated nation" (Giles, 1999, p. 89).

Assaults against women do not necessarily stop when they are extended "safe haven." Rather, refugee camps can often become sites of continued violence owing to the ways in which ideologies of gender and home infuse camp life. In her useful construct of "refugee-camp-as-home," Wenona Giles wrote: "One of the inevitable outcomes of the interplay between nationalist fantasies of power and ideologies of home and household is the contradictory construction of refugee camps as both places of refuge from the nationalist and gendered violence of war, as well as sites of gendered violence" (1999, p. 90). This paper builds on Giles's claim that "refugees are a deeply informative site for the analysis of ways that naturalized images of home are mapped onto representations of the state, the nation, and international agencies" (1999, p. 90). For women in refugee camps, home, in multiple manifestations, can be a setting for women's confinement and disenfranchisement. On the other hand, either one or several instances of home can be a location for resistance, struggle, and active citizenship.

Although 80% of the refugee population is women and children, domestic units are usually fashioned by camp administrators to conform to the heterosexual, patriarchal model. Consequently, households that are composed of women and children are, nonetheless, often managed and controlled by refugee men and male camp administrators (Giles, 1999). Reports of violence against women within households and camp environs are common (Martin, 1992; Matlou, 1997). Yet owing to the strength and pervasiveness of patriarchal power, assaults frequently go unreported or unpunished. Here, the experience in refugee households may be so powerfully informed by gendered, normative assumptions of the privatized, patriarchal home that women may refrain from, or be disciplined against, protesting. Equally, administrative practices may afford gendered violence and discrimination little significance (Giles, 1999).

Although over the last few decades there have been significant moves on the part of international humanitarian and aid organizations to inject basic values of gender equity into camp life, implementation has been slow and uneven. The challenge is made all the more difficult by a male-dominated international refugee regime that continues to see patriarchy as "natural" and assigns refugee men to leadership positions (Matlou, 1997). Reporting on camps in Africa, Patrick Matlou (1997) noted: "Far too often, the results are that ration allocations for men and women are different, that men receive more material assistance, and that most jobs in the camps go to men .... When women [protest] and [seek] direct contact with aid agencies, men [threaten] them with violence" (pp. 137, 136). In such an environment, forced cohabitation or prostitution may become survival strategies for vulnerable females (Martin, 1992; Matlou, 1997).

Finally, for many refugees, camps are viewed as safe houses for the maintenance—if not intensification—of values and life ways shattered by war and displacement. This moral/political topography may be difficult for certain women to navigate. Over the course of the 1990s, as patriarchal fundamentalism intensified, Afghani camps in Pakistan represented an especially trying case. There, women were warned that international aid workers and their educational programs would "take Islam away from them [and] make [their lives] dependent on the evil ways of life. In this way they will hand your society over to the hands of strangers ... and place their sexual desires upon you." The admonitions ended with the threat: "You groups of women who do [not obey] will be killed, and no one will be able to prevent this" (Cammack, 1999, pp. 106–107). In a significantly milder variant, Mayan nationalists in Guatemalan refugee camps in Mexico denounced refugee women's organizations as Western feminism, and thus wholly alien to Mayan values of complementarity and interdependence (Billings, 1995). Yet as one female leader later quipped, "When did we last hear of complementarity; maybe many hundreds and hundreds of years ago. I certainly never heard my father speak such words when he was ordering my mother about and beating her" (Maria Guadalupe Fernández, personal communication, 2003).

As the examples just presented highlight, in both theory and practice the public–private divide is profoundly gendered and highly political. Those actors and institutions with the power to decide where the line is drawn, for whom, and in relation to what issues have routinely neglected the rights of women to equal participation and protection. Yet, as the Guatemalan case reveals, the public–private divide is also a shifting political construction. Explorations of this dynamic are essential to our understanding of engendered citizenship.

GUATAMALAN REFUGEES: A COUNTERNARRATIVE

Guatemalan refugees were displaced by a bloody war that raged for more than 35 years until an internationally brokered peace agreement was signed in December 1996.[3] The insurgency was ignited by a grossly inequitable distribution of income and land, a brutal history of ethnic genocide and discrimination, and the elite's unwillingness to entertain peaceful organizing around civil reforms and economic rights. Initially, in the 1960s and 1970s, social activists were targeted for repression, disappearance, and murder. In the early 1980s, when such selective violence proved incapable of stemming popular reformist struggles, and at a time when some were even predicting the imminent victory of the guerrilla forces, the Guatemalan government unleashed its horrific Scorched Earth campaign. It targeted the western highlands and adjacent lowland areas (Carmack, 1988; Falla, 1994). At least 100,000 civilians were killed and more than 400 villages razed. Some 150,000 to 200,000 people, the majority of whom were indigenous, fled to neighboring Mexico (U.S. Committee for Refugees, 1993).

Sometimes traveling in entire community groups, thousands of victims of the Scorched Earth campaign began crossing into Mexico in the early 1980s. Many settled in Chiapas, and it was this group that benefited from the Mexican government's agreement to recognize a subset of the Guatemalans as refugees. This group of 43,000 was permitted to settle in camps in southern Mexico, where individuals and families were assisted by the Mexican government's refugee agency, the Catholic church, the United Nations High Commissioner for Human Rights (UNHCR), and international nongovernmental organizations (NGOs) (Aguilar Zinzer, 1991).

In many instances, refugee families had to rent the lands they lived and worked on from Mexican owners. Wages were needed both to pay this rent and to supplement the food aid received from the Mexican government and UNHCR. In the pursuit of wages, women found themselves at a distinct disadvantage. In Guatemala, women had been able to contribute income as artisans and traders. By contrast, in the early years of exile, women found their access to local markets in rural Mexico severely limited. Similarly, wage work was generally hard to find, and the travel and lodging expenses for a couple and their children often outweighed the extremely low wages women were paid. As a consequence, women tended to be left at home by their wage-earning husbands (Billings, 1995).

Women's self-esteem plummeted as they became increasingly dependent upon male partners. In 1992, a 32-year-old Chuj woman lamented: "When I cry I say to myself, 'What a shame that I am a woman.'

---

[3]The second section of the chapter draws from a previously published work, Pessar (2001).

If I weren't I could walk where I want and with money in my hand." And a 35-year-old Chuj stated: "We have no way to help ourselves. We can't go out and earn anything. We see the men. They can earn and we're dependent on them" (Billings, 1995, p. 174).

THE CREATION OF FEMALE REFUGEE SUBJECTS

If in these early years of exile Guatemalan refugee women found themselves particularly adrift and needy, they were to meet up with representatives of an international refugee regime poised to acknowledge this condition and determined to turn it around dramatically. The women were extremely fortunate because, earlier and worldwide, most female refugees had encountered indifference on the part of local and international personnel charged with administering refugee programs (Martin, 1992). It was only in the 1980s that activists in the international women's movement managed to gain the attention of high-ranking officials of the United Nations and convince them to treat refugee women as persons with special needs and potentials. Consequently, in 1991, some 40 years after the founding of the United Nations High Commission for Human Rights (UNHCR), UN guidelines for the Protection of Refugee Women were finally issued. This achievement followed on the heels of international feminist struggles and accomplishments, such as the proclamation of 1976–1985 as the UN Decade of Women and the 1985 Nairobi meeting in which refugee women first emerged as a special category of migrant (Martin, 1992). As the product of a progressive social movement, refugee *women* were refashioned as active subjects with specific needs, obligations, and rights. According to the 1995 Beijing Platform for Action: "The strength and resilience that women refugees display in the face of displacement is not acknowledged. Women's voices need to be represented in policy-making that affects them, including in processes to prevent conflicts before they result in the need for communities to flee (in Mertus, 1997, p. 125). And, more forcefully, the Women's Commission for Refugee Women and Children asserted: "Rather than seeing refugee women as *victims* who need to be protected, protection must be recognized as a woman's *right* (n.d., p. 4).

The fate of Guatemalan refugee women and men was significantly shaped by the convergence in time between their arrival in Mexico and this new construction of refugee women as rights-bearing subjects who were poised for empowerment as women and as citizens of localities, nations, and the world community. As a UNHCR representative who worked with Guatemalan refugees observed:

Women were singled out to implement small economic projects. Even when these were unsuccessful economically, [they] brought refugee women together. NGOs, UNHCR, and the women's organizations eventually approached their work with refugees with a defined agenda of empowering women as a necessary step to ensuring women's participation in creating durable solutions for themselves, their families, and the community. (Worby, 1998b, p. 6)

FROM FEMALE CONSCIOUSNESS TO FEMINIST CONSCIOUSNESS

It is noteworthy that Guatemalan refugee women quickly moved beyond mere participation in modest income-generating projects to create a feminist organization, Mamá Maquín. The latter boasted some 8,000 members in its heyday. In the words of its leadership: "Our demands should not be reduced to small economic projects, but rather to become ourselves—active subjects, women with a consciousness about gender, ethnicity, and class—in order to participate in social and national projects where we women play an active role, side-by-side with men" (Billings, 1995, p. 261).

The founding of Mamá Maquín and the formulation of its feminist platform reveal a marked change in political consciousness. Many women made a transition from a "female consciousness," which places human nurturing above all other social and political requirements (Kaplan, 1982), and from actions based on "practical interests" (Molyneux, 1985) centered around family survival, to a "feminist" and "strategic consciousness" (Molyneux, 1985). These women concluded that all struggles for equality must be connected to a broader, strategic struggle for women's rights. These were notions of female personhood, citizenship, and struggle that emerged largely in exile. While still in Guatemala, some of the refugee women had participated in progressive organizations such as Catholic Action and the Committee of Campesino Unity (CUC), as well as in various guerrilla movements (Colom, 1998; Hooks, 1993; Sinclair, 1995). Although these entities emphasized equity in ethnic and class relations, they were largely silent on matters of gender oppression and certainly did not see the fostering of feminist consciousness as central to their mission.

Although for many women a feminist consciousness was forged in exile, its roots go back to asymmetrical gendered relations that existed long before. For example, a young refugee woman reported during a workshop on human rights:

Before we left Guatemala, when I was 19 years old, I helped my father work the fields. If we didn't work hard enough he hit us. When this happened we had no right to question him or say anything. At home, the women had no right to speak nor to complain that there was too much work. It was worse in the community where only the men make community decisions. They thought that women were only there to have children and serve them. We had to put up with the drinking and hitting and people saying that women weren't worth the same as men. All of this seemed normal .... Now it's different. We know that we have rights and that in order for these rights to be respected we have to carry out the struggle among all of us. (Billings, 1995, p. 225)

Another woman told a representative of a Canadian-based international development agency:

Some people and agencies mistakenly see our indigenous communal approach, where both women and men participate in many tasks, as a sign that women have a sense of their value in the community. This isn't usually so. Women participate as part of the community but their self-esteem remains low .... They don't realize the value of their own contributions nor their capacity to learn new skills and assume new roles. (Arbour, 1994, p. 10)

As these remarks illustrate, the past was revisited in workshops on human rights, women's rights, and violence. Norms and practices that were previously naturalized were now denounced as forms of patriarchal privilege and violence that were no longer tolerable.

VIOLENCE TO BODIES AND HOMES

The first part of this article reviewed how sexual aggression against women during times of war is intended to demean and subjugate them. This, unfortunately, was the experience of many Guatemalan indigenous women, as well. How women were abused prior to their flight and how exile provided new tools for women to interpret these violations are explored next.

To reiterate, in the 1970s during the initial phase of selective repression and violence in Guatemala, the army and death squads focused on popular leaders who operated in such arenas as community cooperatives, labor unions, and local government. These were sites that rural and indigenous Guatemalans perceived as "public" and "male." Although women, either as activists or as close kin of male victims, suffered greatly during this initial phase, they became far more implicated and terrorized over the course of the government's Scorched Earth campaign. In the early 1980s the state aimed to separate the insurgents brutally from their popular base. In practice, this meant destroying the quotidian infrastructure through such acts as massacring *campesino* families, and/or burning their homes and *milpas* (small farming plots). In these acts of broad-based destruction, the army invaded women's "personal" spaces and denied them their most important role: to maintain *la lucha* (the struggle), that is, what women must do simply to keep their families alive from one day to the next (Ehlers, 1990, p. 46).

The state-instigated intrusion into domestic space dissolved the appearance of a fixed divide between male/public and female/private spheres. This was an incursion steeped in ethnic and gender symbolism and fueled by patriarchal rage. Diane Nelson (2000) described a

"terrible intimacy" between Mayan and ladino (p. 332). The latter's vision of the nation evokes the power asymmetries embedded in the patriarchal nuclear family and imagines the nation as home: the ladino
as father/husband, and the Maya as wife and mother. In the 1980s as
the nation bled along class and ethnic lines, powerful ladinos struck
out violently against their "wayward" and "disloyal wives." During the
attacks indigenous females were frequently raped and murdered.
Other atrocities included ripping the unborn from their mothers' bodies and smashing them against house beams and trees. There were
also incidents of ritual burnings of indigenous women's clothing; wo-
ven articles of dress (*traje*) that symbolized both women and their
ethnic communities (Billings, 1995).

A willingness to imbue these searing experiences with alternative
meanings and purpose is what many refugee women brought to their
participation in human rights and women's rights workshops. The following commentary about the Guatemalan organization of war widows,
CONAVIGUA, applies equally well to their refugee sisters in Mexico:

> Their sense of "knowing," of learning from each other's experience,
> which was in conflict with "the [State's official] truth," was continually
> being reconstituted, especially as patterns of violence against them be-
> gan to emerge. [They queried] "If they say we are mothers who should
> be respected, and yet treat us and our daughters with rape and torture,
> who are these men who sexualize us, soil us, and degrade us?"
> (Schirmer, 1993, p. 63)

In rights workshops the refugee women came to question first "the
truth" and then the claimers of "truth." They also came to challenge
those "cultural" prescriptions that held that the home was female, private space. Some came to question why women's authority in the
household was subordinated to men's and why they routinely blocked
female participation in more formal public venues for decision-making. As one woman explained during a workshop on violence:

> In our country it was the rich who kicked us out and made us leave .... In-
> digenous men violate women's rights, yes, but it's not their fault. The rich
> have put that idea in their heads that women are only good for taking care
> of children. They say that a woman is only a woman when she's in the
> house. But we women have no rights to decide what should be done in
> our homes, and then in our country we women have no rights to decide
> or to participate .... The rich have tried to fool all of us for many years.
> None of us knew our rights so we weren't able to defend ourselves. (Bill-
> ings, 1995, pp. 223–234)

In the spirit of "defending themselves" and claiming rights from a
patriarchal state, the rich, and male family members and neighbors, thousands of Guatemalan refugee women in camps in Mexico
joined women's organizations, such as Mamá Maquín, Madre
Tierra, and Ixmucané.

REFUGEE CAMPS
AND MULTIPLE CONSTRUCTS OF "HOME"

The patriarchal household was one among several manifestations of home present in the camps. Others included camps as reenactments of home communities, and camps as international, global villages. Each alternative had its own gender dynamic. Each also placed specific constraints on, and afforded distinct opportunities for, women's empowerment.

For the most part, domestic units were configured according to the norms of the heterosexual, patriarchal family. Although women were assigned to *la lucha* of ensuring their household's basic subsistence, their duties were significantly lightened by the food aid, technology (e.g., electric corn grinders), and income-generation projects available in the camps. Indeed, women commented that these supports freed up their time and enabled many to participate in women's organizations and to attend workshops. Moreover, given the close physical proximity of households, camp residents were well aware of those men who forbade their female kin from participating in these initiatives. Not infrequently, more receptive senior men would be dispatched to counsel reconsideration. Although certain female refugee leaders and administrative staff endeavored to increase gender parity within domestic units, definite constraints were placed on their actions. Consequently, after a group of women urged that problems of domestic violence within refugee households be publicly aired and redressed, they were rebuked by other women and men who insisted on focusing solely on state-orchestrated violence (Billings, 1995).

Camps also come to represent local communities left behind. For example, individual camps were given the names of indigenous Guatemalan communities, and refugees struggled to maintain Mayan practices that had been outlawed in Guatemala by the occupying army (Billings, 1995). Camp life—like local communities—retained highly masculinized features. Only men held positions as *representes*—leaders who coordinated all facets of camp life and served as community spokespersons. Males also predominated among the camps' *promotores*, overseers of such essential activities as food collection and distribution, medical assistance, and education. Men filled the ranks of the Permanent Commission, the refugee body chosen to negotiate the terms of an organized and collective return to Guatemala. Finally, male *responsables*, guerilla organizers, and spokesmen were highly influential in all camps.

Acting on behalf of the larger guerrilla organization, the *responsables* pressed refugee women to create separate women's organizations. With the Cold War receding and external funding for their cause greatly reduced, guerrilla leaders viewed this new interest in refugee women's projects and organizations as a windfall. Although it is the case that guerrilla leaders had earlier refused to include gender equity within their political platform, the men's actions were not entirely manipulative of women. Rather, the overture by international donors created an opening for certain women within the guerrilla organization to advance their long-frustrated goal to foreground gender among the other forms of oppression to be eradicated. Indeed, some of the earliest members of Mamá Maquín were women who had become disaffected by the movement's failure to address patriarchal privilege and female combatants' special needs (e.g., pregnancy and childcare) (Pessar, 2001).

The third manifestation of home present in the camp setting was a supranational formation akin to the global village. Here, officials of Mexican, intergovernmental, and nongovernmental organizations frequently encouraged Guatemalan refugee women to imagine and fashion modes of belonging and participation that included full membership in local, national, and transnational collectivities, such as those linked to human rights, women's rights, and indigenous rights. Not infrequently, women were introduced to values and expectations about gendered citizenship that contradicted those operating in households and ethnic communities. For example, women were urged to move well beyond the household, yet in doing so, they challenged common beliefs that females who routinely interacted with nonfamilial men (especially at night) were prostitutes or witches (Burgos-Debray, 1984; Pessar, 2001).

In the camp-as-global village, refugee women and men were exposed to a universal language of human and women's rights. For example, women who attended workshops on women's rights were given instructional brochures that contained line drawings that simply, but eloquently, positioned indigenous, Guatemalan women—with their subordinated quotidian lives—alongside official national and international legal documents. One brochure, for example, shows a musing indigenous woman who asks, "What is my reality?" Beneath a picture of men attending a public meeting, she is instructed, "Public positions are almost always held by men, based on the inequality between men and women. This impedes our participation." She counters, "And how could it be?" The question is "answered" by an accompanying drawing of women proclaiming, "We win!" And beneath it is article 7–8 of the UN Convention to Eliminate Discrimination Against Women (CEDAW), which reads, "All countries should take measures such that women participate in political life equally with men" (Billings, 1995, p. 285). In another example, on International Women's Day, pamphlets were distributed in the camps stating, "All of us women have the right to struggle for equality, which is a human right. We take our example from Rigoberta Menchú, who won the Nobel Peace Prize in 1992, who struggles for the indigenous and for human rights" (Billings, 1995, p. 278).

The discursive elements contained in these and scores of other similar texts belong to that globalized genre of meanings that Arjun Appadurai called *ideoscapes*. By this term, he referred to the traveling concatenation of tropes "that are often directly political and frequently have to do with the ideologies of states and the counterideologies of movements explicitly oriented to capturing state power or a piece of it" (Appadurai, 1996, p. 36). The ideoscopes refugee women were exposed to exhorted them to widen their horizons, and to stake claim to "pieces" of local and state power that, unbeknown to them, were already legitimately theirs. As women came to weave new tropes of human rights and women's rights into the *testimonios* (testimonial accounts) they delivered publicly in camp workshops, in encounters with international visitors, and at international conferences, they seemed to confirm Ruth Lister's (1997) claim that "We are today witnessing the emergence of a global civil society, in which women are playing a central role" (p. 18).

Women's participation in global civil society was certainly facilitated by their residence in a supranational formation that operated as a transnational entrepôt. Through the comings and goings of internationals and owing to the presence of modern technology, the refugees experienced a marked quickening in the pace and intensity of movement and communication across space, as well as the geographical stretching out of social relations (Massey, 1994). Such time–space compression did not similarly affect all who lived in or passed through the camps. Nor did all benefit equally from its potentials. Employing the concept of "the power geometry," Doreen Massey (1994) observed: "Different social groups, and different individuals are placed in very distinct ways in relation to these flows and interconnections .... Mobility, and control over mobility, both reflects and reinforces power" (pp. 148, 150).

In the case of Mexican refugee camps, the refugees and the internationals differed greatly in their mobility, in their access to transnational flows of people, ideas, commodities, and services, and in their control over the content and directionality of these flows. Clearly, the internationals held the reins of power—a hard lesson the refugee women would learn when they returned to remote communities in Guatemala, still needing the aid of their international supporters. Refugee women and men also differed with respect to their patterns of mobility and control over flows of information and resources. Female leaders concentrated on travels to and contacts with grass-root supporters in North America and Europe. By contrast, men, as guerrilla fighters and representatives of returnee groups, directed their actions more toward Guatemala and toward formal bodies like the UNHCR, the Guatemalan state, and the guerrilla organization, the Guatemalan National Revolutionary Unity (URNG). This division of labor would have profound impacts later on the lives of returnee women and men as well.

THE SUPRANATIONAL MEETS THE NATIONAL: THE ABANDONMENT OF REFUGEE WOMEN

The limitations for women of supranational forms of citizenship became clear when the refugees entered into formal negotiations regarding their collective return. At this juncture the refugees' key political interlocutors became officials of the Guatemalan state. When crucial matters of gendered citizenship within the context of the nation-state were at issue, both the male refugee leadership and the women's previously stalwart supporter, the UNHCR, failed them miserably.

Despite women's objections, men totally dominated the ranks of the Permanent Commissions, the elected body charged with negotiating, alongside representatives of the Guatemalan and Mexican governments and officials of the UNHCR, the terms of the refugees' collective return (Billings, 1995; Morel, 1998; Worby, 1998a).[4] UNHCR assumed a key role in financing the activities of the Permanent Commissions and, had it so chosen, it might have asserted financial leverage to insist on and facilitate a greater role for women. In an extremely frank admission, Terry Morel, a UNHCR representative who worked closely with the refugee women in Mexico, publicly decried this failure of political will when she wrote:

> Initially UNHCR did not take up the matter of women's participation in the representational structures responsible for the refugees' return. I am daring enough to state that this owed to our institutional difficulty in immediately defending the rights of women within traditional spaces of power. [Although we financed the representatives during their negotiations,] we never questioned the absence of women. This means that we [actually] fortified male leadership at the expense of the women's organizations. (Morel, 1998, p. 16)

An unprecedented feature of the October 8, 1992, Accords was the Guatemalan government's agreement to help refugees recover lands occupied by others, and to obtain lands for all landless adult refugees. Although they had not been present during the negotiations, women militated for joint ownership of these properties. They did so only after

---

[4]There was, apparently, interest early on in having some female representation. This interest waned soon after the first group of women was selected. According to an advisor to the Permanent Commissions, the male commissioners complained that the women could not "manage" the difficult working conditions (e.g., clandestine travel to camps in Mexico and camping with large groups of men), and most were found wanting by their male counterparts owing to an alleged lack of experience and training. This same advisor added that the male commissioners were also extremely reluctant to have the women become privy to the men's "leisure-time" activities! (Paula Worby, e-mail, April 9, 1999).

analyzing the extreme vulnerability of women (and their children) who were abandoned by their partners and often deprived of the families' land and belongings.[5] As Mamá Maquín's leadership opined:

> We realized that women who were married or in common law unions were not taken into account in regards to the right to land, [o]nly men, widows and single mothers …. That is when we decided to fight for the right to be joint owners of the land for our own security and that of our daughters and sons, so that we will not be left out in the street if the man sells the land or abandons his partner. This also means recognizing the economic value of the work that we carry out in the house and in the fields. (cited in Worby, 1999, p. 1)

There were early signs that these demands would not be easily met. With all the controversial concessions the Permanent Commission sought to extract from Guatemalan authorities, the provision to provide women explicit rights to land was hardly an item that the all-male negotiating team was eager to press. Indeed, they only did so at the last moment, to placate an insistent female UNHCR official.

Although this was a victory of sorts, female returnees have faced a host of obstacles in their attempts to have this concession formally institutionalized. First, the majority of male returnees failed to make good on their pledge to support the women's access to land titles. As one man explained to me, when I asked if his wife was officially registered as a co-owner of their land in the Ixcán Grande community of Los Angeles: "Why should she be? My name is there on the title, and I represent her and our children." In fact, it took me several tries before this man even understood the gist of my enquiry. His initial bafflement and subsequent remarks underscore how deeply entwined are notions of Mayan masculinity, patriarchal authority in the household, and control over land in highland peasant communities (Wilson, 1995). The male returnee leadership similarly reneged on its promise to joint ownership: a guarantee that some observers believe was extended in an opportunistic fashion to take advantage of international sympathies for the indigenous Guatemalan women, and to gain international support for the overall return and its provision for land (Worby, 1999).

If returnee men developed social amnesia regarding their agreement to extend women co-ownership of land, so too, did Guatemalan state officials. As a UNHCR official explained to me, "Government authorities and government lawyers have never `understood' the need for this initiative. Consequently, they have thus far refused to design and implement administrative policies and practices to facilitate joint

---

[5]In some Guatemalan communities, family problems, such as male abandonment, may be brought before an elders' council (of men) and/or respected community authorities. Although the man may be instructed to leave the family house and/or land to his children and former wife, such an outcome is by no means assured. Redress through the legal system tends to be time-consuming, expensive, and particularly intimidating for indigenous women, especially if they do not speak Spanish (Worby, 1999).

ownership of land."[6] Although correct, I would suggest that this noncompliance had deeper, more troubling roots.

Although the refugees in Mexico were involved in fashioning gender relations in a somewhat more equitable fashion, many of their counterparts back in army-controlled villages were experiencing a hardening of patriarchal values and norms. Guatemala, a nation at war against guerrilla insurgents, chose the familiar path of equating masculinity with patriotism and national belonging (see Yuval-Davis, 1997). Thus, indigenous males—who before the violence had been largely disparaged and forgotten by the state—were now "rehabilitated" as patriots: that is, as long as they agreed to serve in the army or in the ubiquitous civil patrols. In this capacity, indigenous men were charged with protecting rural communities and the Guatemalan nation against the guerrilla enemies of the state. Even women were drawn into highly masculinized displays of loyalty. For example, in a community in the department of Alta Verapaz, the local representative from the army's civic affairs office ordered all the village's women and children to line up in front of the Guatemalan flag post in the main square. As one observer wrote:

> In what appeared to be a well-rehearsed pantomime, the women, all of them dressed in *traje* (indigenous dress), flung themselves reluctantly forward, feigning combat against a non-existent aggressor, their imaginary rifles poised in empty, outstretched arms. (Americas Watch, 1986, p. 17)

In other communities women were required to obtain passes from the army to travel to local markets and they were transported there in army trucks. In this way, masculine discipline and policing were imposed on a set of practices and public spaces in which women had, until recently, experienced a far greater degree of control and autonomy (Bossen, 1984; Ehlers, 1990). Upon return, refugee women bumped up against the norms and practices of this highly masculinized regime when they requested that government authorities make good on their promises to the organized women.

RETURNEES AND THE GUATEMALAN STATE

For over a decade, then, Guatemalan officials had invested heavily in the production of nationalistic, state-surveilled, rural citizens and localities. In the mid-19990s they confronted thousands of already-suspect Guatemalan nationals[7] returning home along with an entourage of UN officials, international accompaniers, and international donors and NGOs—all eager to build civil society. Indigenous

---

[6]Interview number 37, Guatemala City, July 21, 1999.
[7]For example, the Minister of Defense, Héctor Gramajo, publicly labeled the returnees as "subversives" (Manz, 1988).

women, including Rigoberta Menchú, were showcased. Government officials might well have envisioned the need for a "strong-armed" approach to reimposing the state, along with its highly masculinized practices, on the returnees. Paradoxically, though, in many cases it was the returnees who were the instigators of a closer relationship with the state. This was often the case because—as a consequence of their experiences in exile—both returnee women and men came to view themselves as full Guatemalan citizens and modern subjects who had grown used to the amenities and up-to-date transportation, communication, and social services they had enjoyed in exile.[8] The challenges the returnees faced was to make their rural communities conform to these new subjectivities, and to do so they turned increasingly to the Guatemalan state. They needed government officials to help them litigate land conflicts with "recalcitrant" neighboring (nonreturnee) villages, and to obtain such modern amenities as roads, electricity, and licensed teachers (Stepputat, 1997).

In this modernizing project, the state found a formidable ally in the *male* returnee leadership. This new alliance posed significant problems for returnee women, however. In exile, it will be recalled, women had little success in penetrating male-dominated, local and national power structures. Moreover, their allies were often representatives of the very transnational entities—such as, U.S. solidarity groups—that the state distrusted and sought to marginalize. The problems certain refugee women have experienced are illustrated in the case of the Ixcán Grande Cooperative—home of a large number of the returnees.[9]

RETURNEES TO THE IXCÁN GRANDE COOPERATIVE

The Ixcán Grande Cooperative (IGC), located in the tropical lowlands of northern Quiché, had been one of the most progressive localities in all of Guatemala.[10] The five communities that comprise the IGC were sites of early guerrilla organizing in the 1970s, and of brutal state-orchestrated violence in the 1980s. Many members of the cooperative were murdered, joined the guerrilla, or were forced into exile (Falla, 1994). The cooperative's male leaders were among the earliest and most influential authorities in the Mexican refugee camps, and many

---

[8]Returnees in the community of Chaculá refer to themselves as *gentes formales* (formal people), while their "backward" neighbors are depicted in such unflattering and "premodern" terminology as *animales* and people without reason (*a ellos no llegan razón*) (Stepputat, 1997).

[9]For research on other return communities, see Taylor (1998) and Project Counseling Services (2000).

[10]The Ixcán Grande region was settled in the mid-1960s by peasants from Huehuetenango at the urging of Maryknoll priests. Each family was given approximately 40 acres after a probation period. Ultimately the inhabitants grouped themselves into five savings and credit cooperatives, Mayalán, Xalbal, Pueblo Nuevo, Cuarto Pueblo, and Los Angeles. These five communities are all part of the larger Ixcán Grande Cooperative (IGC).

served as representatives in the Permanent Commissions. It was thus with great dismay that Guatemalan and international supporters watched these male leaders make common cause with "the enemy." For example, with the blessing of government officials and military authorities, male (returnee) leaders have actively pursued a brand of development that involves attracting foreign oil interests and privatizing cooperative lands (Davis, 1998).

In 1997 as part of a move aimed at consolidating power and at removing all challengers, the IGC's male leadership accused the members of Mamá Maquín of being guerrilla sympathizers. In flagrant violation of the provisions for free association in the Peace Accords, the cooperative's leaders declared "illegal" any group like Mamá Maquín that held meetings in the community without their permission. This threat was soon followed by the burning of Mamá Maquín's headquarters in the Ixcán Grande community of Pueblo Nuevo. Reflecting on the refugees' years in exile, Paula Worby (1998b) wrote: "[Once] the women began to take charge of their own organizations and conscious-raising to demand visible and formal roles in decision-making, this may have been perceived by men, consciously or unconsciously, as overstepping the acceptable limits they had prescribed for women's roles" (p. 10). What likely constrained male leaders from retaliating against the "uppity" women back then were, of course, the resources organized women obtained from international donors and the public relations benefits all the refugees accrued in international circles from images of fully participatory refugee women. In the burning of Mamá Maquín's headquarters—a flagrant act of erasure directed at the women's only public space within the community—we find sad evidence that once the refugees had returned home and their male leaders had allied themselves with the state, women's "visibility" was no longer needed nor even tolerated.

Although the men sought to disenfranchise the organized women, the leadership of Mamá Maquín based in Guatemala City had other plans. They still believed in their power within the international "community" and, accordingly, sent urgent faxes addressed to "the Guatemalan government," "the people and governments of the world," "the national and international press," and "the popular movement in general." They hoped that international supporters would—as in the past—support them decisively in their latest struggle. Instead, very little if any effective pressure was brought to bear.[11]

---

[11]It is probably the case that a good deal of the inaction resulted from the fact that Mamá Maquín and its local supporters were involved in a factional conflict within the guerrilla organization (URNG). This left international observers and supporters generally confounded and reluctant to step in. For its part, Mamá Maquín released a communiqué shortly after the destruction of its headquarters in Pueblo Nuevo that stated: "The reason for this aggression against our organization and our right to free association is due to the fact that we do not share some of the political stances held by the [community's cooperative] directorate, [since] these opinions relegate women to second place in social and community participation" (Mamá Maquín, communiqué, June 11, 1997, reproduced in Worby, 1999, p. 13).

Reluctantly, then, in the late 1990s many of the members of Mamá Maquín in the Ixcán Grande communities succumbed to the intimidation of the male leadership and to the urging of their husbands to drop out of the organization completely (Worby, 1998a, p. 9). In the cooperative community of Los Angeles, Mamá Maquín had been entirely replaced by a women's development committee that was controlled by the male leadership (the directorate); as one man explained, the directorate comes up with the ideas for women's projects and "write up the requests, and then we get the women to sign them."[12]

The weakening, if not total abandonment, of Mamá Maquín was not the only political loss these returnee women endured. Contrary to the women's understandings prior to their return, only men and widowed women have been granted titles to communal land. Membership to the communities' official governing board is determined by ownership of these titles. Thus, once again, women with partners have found themselves excluded from full citizenship within their communities. Under such unfavorable circumstances, women have seen their interests trampled upon. In one particularly egregious case, the male directorate exacted a far more severe punishment on a man who had stolen a cow than on another who had raped a female member of the community.[13]

CERTAIN GAINS REMAIN

To end on such a resigned note would be inaccurate and would misrepresent the overall struggle that many refugee women and men remain committed to (Women's Commission for Refugee Women and Children, 2000). If we accept the feminist precept that "the political" resides in all cultural and social relations and domains, then women seem to have made their greatest strides in the micropolitics of the household and kinship spheres—not within community politics, as they had anticipated prior to their return (Mamá Maquín & CIAM, 1994). In Los Angeles and Chaculá (Huehuetenango), the two returnee communities I have studied,[14] several couples pointed with pride to such practices as equity between partners in household budgeting and in reproductive decisions. They also noted the reduced incidence of

---

[12]Interview number 5, Los Angeles, March 15, 1999. Most of the former members of Mamá Maquín have refused to join this group, but its existence has clearly demoralized many of these women.

[13]Interview number 32, Nenton, July 27, 1998.

[14]In Chaculá too, women have not gained joint ownership of their land nor are they members of the male-controlled cooperative. In one particularly disheartening incident, the male cooperative leaders asked the women to form a committee to request food from a foundation. When none of the women present at the meeting volunteered, the head of the cooperative said, "Oh, perhaps the problem is that the men have not given their wives permission to form a committee. Men, raise your hand, if you give your wife permission" (Interview number 3, Chaculá, July 15, 1998). A clear sign of the women's demoralization is that the membership in Chaculá's branch of Mamá Maquín has dropped in 4 years from a high of 200 to a low of 3.

domestic violence against women and their greater spatial mobility. It is striking that the majority of the interviewees in both communities employed a human rights discourse when they described more equitable gender relations in their own homes. Evaristo López Calmo, a 30-year-old Mam resident of Chaculá, reflected:

> In the old days when a couple married the woman became the property of the man. In this way he dominated all the decisions because he was the head of the household. And that's what we were taught from the time we were little; but then the situation changed .... In exile the women learned that they had rights equal to men. There's no difference. Before we never practiced this, women were treated like animals .... Now when I earn money I don't put it in my pocket like my father did. I bring it to the house and my wife and I decide together how to spend it.[15]

And Petrona López García explained:

> It used to be that the woman is a woman and the man is a man. She has to feed him, wash his clothes, care for him; and while he's in bed resting, she's there working until 8 or 9 at night, still giving and giving. But [Mamá Maquín] taught us that the woman has ten fingers and the man has ten fingers .... It's not that the man is worth more or the woman worth more; they're equal. My husband gives me liberty to work in whatever job I choose.[16] Now this seems strange to those who remained in my village and continue to follow the old ways. Even my own mother says to my husband, "Aren't you afraid she will find another man and do bad things because you allow her to go wherever she pleases?"[17]

Although many women and some men in both communities publicly expressed consternation over the women's failure to participate more fully and equally in the community's political and economic affairs, these individuals did hold out hope for the future. They pointed admiringly to their daughters, who have higher education levels compared to other Guatemalan rural girls, and who have often chosen to marry later and/or delay childbearing in order to pursue their educations or careers. In writing about such practices, Worby (1999) concluded: "In this way they are varying the roles

---

[15]Interview number 12, Chaculá, July 20, 1998.

[16]Although this woman positions herself as very much a modern, self-actualized woman, it is significant that she views her *husband* as the one who possessed, and continues to possess, the right to give her freedom and to allow her to work at whatever job she chooses.

[17]Interview number 6, Chaculá, July 18, 1998. It should be noted that there is a vocal minority that disputes such assertions about increased gender parity. It includes a nun who has lived in the community since its founding. She characterized local gender relations as "99.9% sexist, machistic [and] patriarchal," and she backed up this statement with recent examples of domestic violence, abandonment, and bride price (Interview number 3, Chaculá, July 15, 1998).

played by women and subsequently increasing recognition among men as to their different capabilities" (p. 6).

Finally, over the course of the last decade as Guatemalan rural communities have absorbed the shocks of the nation's structural adjustment program and the lack of competitiveness of its traditional agricultural commodities in world markets, many returnee women have had to reassess their thinking about the family and local communities. The women's discourse and practices have modulated, no longer focusing so insistently on patriarchy as a primary source of women's oppression. Instead, they more freely acknowledge that families and local communities are sites of protection from, and resistance to, global capitalism and national forms of class and racial oppression. It is in this spirit that the current leadership of Mamá Maquín has developed a program to educate rural communities about the dangers of globalization and Plan Panama and to enlist women and men collectively to analyze the local and national impacts of these new developments. Although there is a gender component to this educational program (e.g., the current and growing demand for female workers in export-processing industries), it is not foregrounded.

CONCLUSION

Although conspicuously absent from much of the literature on gender and migration, citizenship is a concept that merits far greater attention in future studies of refugees and immigrants. As we take this step, however, we should be mindful that some question the very utility of attempting to engender a construct that has enjoyed such a long history of delegitimating women's sphere of activities by relegating it to "the private" (Phillips, 1993). As the first part of this chapter noted, international law and the refugee regime have often adopted this stance, leaving scores of women disenfranchised and vulnerable.

Theorists who take up the challenge to engender our understanding of citizenship argue that it cannot be reduced simply to relations between individuals and the state (Lister, 1997). Rather, citizenship involves a broad range of social relations among individuals along multiple scales and spaces. The latter range from the imagination and the body to transnational and global ideologies and contexts. Consequently, an engendered and feminist understanding of citizenship must examine the socialization of female children to accept a subordinate status to males within key spheres of power, women's economic dependence within the family, their weak position within the labor market and culture industries, and their reduced representation in local, national, and international politics (Hobson, 1999, p. xix). It must also treat gender relationally—that is, not only between men and women, but also as one of multiple, related axes of difference and power. These others include sexuality, race, ethnicity, religion, legal status, and class. Here, the challenge is to examine and theorize the ways in which these multiple axes operate individually and interactively to condition citizenship rights and practices.

As the second section of this chapter documented, through women's programs promoting job training, income generation, literacy, and rights education, a group of highly motivated refugees and internationals struggled to reverse long-standing patterns of female exclusion and dependency. Remarkably, these bids for citizenship rights and active participation occurred within the context of refugee camps where patriarchal households and male leadership and administrative structures predominated. The presence of supranational organizations willing to assist women to forge more equitable social relations within the multiple arenas in which citizenship is constituted and enacted was key. So, too, was the introduction of such universal ideoscapes as human rights and women's rights. Since their return to Guatemala, refugee women have confronted the reassertion of patriarchal ideologies and practices in their homes, communities, and nation, the withdrawal of many international supporters, and the need to cope with Guatemala's costly concessions to international capital. It has been exceedingly difficult to keep newer visions and practices of female citizenship alive. Many returnee women have substituted a "female consciousness" for their previous feminist one. The former, it will be recalled, is one grounded in nurturing and family survival. The dilemma confronting these returnees, and many other poor women in rural Guatemala, is to defend and hold together their families and communities, while attempting gradually to reform the norms and practices that continue to disenfranchise them.

REFERENCES

Aguilar Zinzer, A. (1991). Repatriation of Guatemalan refugees in Mexico: Conditions and prospects. In M. Larkin, F. C. Cuny, & B. Stein (Eds.), *Repatriation under conflict in Central America* (pp. 57–114). Washington, DC: Georgetown University, Center for Immigration Policy and Refugee Assistance.

Americas Watch Committee. (1986). *Civil patrols in Guatemala.* New York: Americas Watch Committee.

Appadurai, A. (1996). *Modernity at large: Cultural dimensions of globalization.* Minneapolis: University of Minneapolis Press.

Arbour, F. (1994). Voices of women: A new force shaping the Guatemalan return. *Refugee, 13,* 16–17.

Bhabha, J. (1996). Embodied rights: Gendered persecution, state sovereignty, and refugees. *Public Culture, 9,* 3–32.

Billings, D. (1995). *Identities, consciousness, and organizing in exile: Guatemalan refugee women in the camps of Southern Mexico.* PhD dissertation, University of Michigan.

Binion, G. (1995). Human rights: A feminist perspective. *Human Rights Quarterly, 17,* 509–526.

Bossen, L. (1984). *The redivision of labor: Women and economic choice in four Guatemalan communities.* Albany: State University of New York Press.

Burgos-Debray, E. (Ed.). (1984). *I, Rigoberta Menchú: An Indian woman in Guatemala*. London: Verso Editions.

Cammack, D. (1999). Gender relief and politics during the Afghan war. In D. Indra (Ed.), *Engendering forced migration: Theory and practice* (pp. 94–123). Oxford: Berghahn Books.

Carmack, R. (Ed.). (1988). *Harvest of violence: The Mayan Indians and the Guatemalan crisis*. Norman: University of Oklahoma Press.

Charlesworth, H. (1991). Feminist approaches to international law. *American Journal of International Law, 85*, 613–664.

Collier, J. (1995). *From duty to desire*. Princeton, NJ: Princeton University Press.

Colom, Y. (1998). *Mujeres en la alborada: Guerilla y participación feminina en Guatemala, 1973–1978*. Guatemala: Artemis & Edinter.

Crowley, H. (1999). Women and refugee status: Beyond the public/private dichotomy in UK asylum policy. In D. Indra (Ed.), *Engendering forced migration: Theory and practice* (pp. 308–333). Oxford: Berghahn Books.

Davis, A. (1998). "Biting at each other, rolling in the dust": Homegrown counterinsurgency in Ixcán Grande. *NCOORD Newsletter, 7*(3), 4–8.

Ehlers, T. (1990). *Silent looms*. Boulder, CO: Westview Press

Falla, R. (1994). *Massacres in the jungle: Ixcán, Guatemala, 1975–1982*. Boulder, CO: Westview Press.

Giles, W. (1999). Gendered violence in war: Reflections on transnationalists and comparative frameworks in militarized conflict zones. In D. Indra (Ed.), *Engendering forced migration: Theory and practice* (pp. 84–93). Oxford: Berghahn Books.

Giles, W., Mousa, H., & Van Esterik, P. (Eds.). (1996). *Development and diaspora: Gender and the refugee experience*. Ontario: Artemis Enterprises Publication.

Hobson, B. (Ed.). (1999). *Gender and citizenship in transition*. London: MacMillan Press.

Hooks, M. (1993). *Guatemalan women speak*. Washington, DC: EPICA.

Indra, D. (Ed). (1999). *Engendering forced migration: Theory and practice*. Oxford: Berghahn Books.

Kaplan, T. (1982). Female consciousness and collective action: The case of Barcelona, 1910–1918. *Signs, 7*(3), 545–566.

Kurac, M. (1995). Ethnic conflict, rape and feminism: The case of Yugoslavia. *Research on Russia and Eastern Europe, 2*, 247–266.

Lister, R. (1997). Citizenship: Towards a feminist synthesis. *Feminist Review 57*, 28–48.

Macklin, A. (1995). Refugee women and the imperative of categories. *Human Rights Quarterly, 17*, 213–277.

Mamá Maquín & Centro de Investigación y Acción para la Mujer. (1994). *De refugiadas a Retornada*. Comitán, Chiapas, México.

Manz, B. (1988). *Repatriation and reintegration: An arduous process in Guatemala*. Washington, DC: Georgetown University, Center for Immigration Policy and Refugee Assistance.

Martin, S. (1992). *Refugee women*. London: Zed Books.

Massey, D. (1994). *Space, place, and gender*. Minneapolis: University of Minnesota Press.

Matlou, P. (1997). Upsetting the cart: Forced migration and gender issues, the African experience. In D. Indra (Ed.), *Engendering forced migration: Theory and practice* (pp. 128–145). Oxford: Berghahn Books.

Mertus, J. (1997). *Local action global change.* New York: United Nations Development Fund for Women and the Center for Global Leadership.

Mouffe, C. (1992). *Dimensions of radical democracy.* London: Verso.

Molyneux, M. (1985). Mobilization without emancipation? Women's interests, the state and revolution in Nicaragua. *Feminist Studies, 11*(2), 227–254.

Morel, T. (1998). *Mujeres Guatemaltecas refugiadas y retornadas: Su participación en las estructuras comunitarias y los procesos de toma de decisiones.* Guatemala City, Guatemala: UNHCR.

Nelson, D. (2000). Stumped identities: Body image, body politics, and the mujer Maya as prosthetic. *Cultural Anthropology, 16*(3), 314–353.

Pateman, C. (1989). *The disorder of women: Democracy, feminism, and political theory.* Stanford: University of California Press.

Pessar, P. (2001). Women's political consciousness and empowerment in local, national, and transnational contexts: Guatemalan refugees and returnees. *Identities, 7*(4), 461–500.

Phillips, A. (1993). *Democracy and difference.* Cambridge: Polity Press.

Project Counseling Services. (2000). *Guatemalan refugee and returning women: Challenges and lessons learned in camps and during repatriation.* Final report for Promoting Women in Development Program to the International Center for Research on Women, Washington, DC.

Schirmer, J. (1993). The seeking of truth and the gendering of consciousness: The CoMadres of El Salvador and the CONAVIGUA Widows of Guatemala. In S. Radliffe & S. Westwood (Eds.), *"Viva": Women and popular protest in Latin America* (pp. 30–64). New York: Routledge.

Sinclair, M. (Ed.). (1995). *The new politics of survival.* New York: Monthly Review Press.

Stepputat, F. (1997). *Repatriation and everyday forms of state formation in Guatemala.* Unpublished manuscript, files of the author.

Taylor, C. (1998). *Return of Guatemala's refugees: Reweaving the torn.* Philadelphia: Temple University Press.

U.S. Committee for Refugees. (1993). *El retorno: Guatemala's risky repatriation begins.* Washington, DC: USCR.

Wilson, R. (1995). *Mayan resurgence in Guatemala.* Norman: University of Oklahoma Press.

Women's Commission for Refugee Women and Children. (2000). *Recognizing the contributions of refugee women.* New York: Women's Commission for Refugee Women and Children.

Worby, P. (1998a). *Organizing for a change: Guatemalan refugee women assert their right to be co-owners of land allocated to returnee communities.* Paper prepared for the Kigali Inter-Regional Consultation on Women's Land and Property Rights Under Situations of Conflict and Resolution, February 16–19. Kigali, Rwanda.

Worby, P. (1998b). *Return as "Lucha": Organized Guatemalan refugees go home.* Working Paper M&N 02, Yale University, Center for International and Area Studies, New Haven, CT.

Worby, P. (1999). *Guatemalan refugee and returnee women petition for their rights: The fight for joint ownership of community land.* Unpublished manuscript, files of the author.

Yuval-Davis, N. (1997). *Gender and nation.* London: Sage.

13

Gender, Sexuality, Language, and Migration[1]

Oliva M. Espín
San Diego State University

MIGRATION AND GENDER ROLES

As migrants cross borders, they also cross emotional and behavioral boundaries. Becoming a member of a new society stretches the boundaries of what is possible. One's life and roles change. With them, identities change as well. Most immigrants and refugees crossing geographical borders, rarely anticipate the emotional and behavioral boundaries they will confront.

It is my contention, based on both clinical practice and research, that at each step of the migration process, women and men encounter different experiences. Women's roles and sexual behavior may be modified more dramatically and profoundly than men's (Espín, 1987). For both heterosexual and lesbian women, the crossing of borders through migration provides the space and "permission" to cross boundaries and transform their sexuality and gender roles. However, this is usually not a smooth process, even for those women who seem to have acculturated easily to the new society. Women who migrate form "traditional" societies may find that new alternatives open to them in the new country. But the new possibilities that migration opens up are not limited to women from traditional societies. Women who migrate form "modern" societies may also find that alternatives open for them in the new country because of the distance from the fa-

---

[1]Paper presented at Conference on Immigration and Psychology (Panel on Immigration and Gender), University of Michigan, Ann Arbor, MI, April 2003.

miliar environment and/or their families. "New learning opportunities emerge, as host society institutional structures interact with the psychological equipment immigrants bring and create in the host society" (Rogler, 1994, p. 706).

We know that the sexual and gender role behaviors of women serve a larger social function beyond the personal. They are used by enemies and friends alike as "proof" of the morality—or decay—of social groups or nations. In most societies, women's sexual behavior and their conformity to traditional gender roles signifies that family's value system. Thus, in many societies, a daughter who does not conform to "traditional morality" can be seen as "proof" of the lax morals of the family. This is why struggles surrounding acculturation in immigrant and refugee families center frequently on the issues of daughters' sexual behaviors and women's sex roles in general. For parents and young women alike, acculturation and sexuality are closely connected with being sexually promiscuous. Policing women's bodies and sexual behavior becomes for immigrant communities the main means of asserting moral superiority over the host culture. Yet it severely limits the personal expression of immigrant women. Groups that are transforming their way of life through a vast and deep process of acculturation, focus on preserving "tradition" almost exclusively through the gender roles of women. Women's roles become the last "bastion of tradition." Women's bodies become the site for struggles concerning disorienting cultural differences. Gender becomes the site to claim the power denied to immigrant men by racism.

It is important to recognize that some of the rigidity concerning the roles of women that we observe in immigrant communities is an attempt to protect and safeguard what remains of emotional stability; so much of it is lost with migration. It is as if the immigrants' psychological sense of safety and their sense of self depended on a sharp contrast between two sets of cultural values conceived as rigidly different and unchangeable. The preservation of "old versions" of women's roles becomes central to this sharp contrast. For people who experience a deep lack of control over their daily lives, controlling women's sexuality and behavior becomes a symbolic demonstration of orderliness and continuity. It gives them the feeling that not all is lost, not all is changing. Obviously, it is easier for immigrants to maintain control over their private world than over their public lives: work schedules, types of work and schooling, housing, and the structures of daily life are controlled by the customs and demands of the new society. But in the privacy of their homes, they can seek to maintain the sense that they are still in control. This is why frequently women themselves join actively in adhering to "traditions" that, from the point of view of outsiders, appear to curtail their own freedoms and opportunities for self-fulfillment.

Moreover, self-appointed "guardians of morality and tradition" that are ever-present among immigrant communities are deeply concerned with women's roles and sexual behavior. These people include religious or community leaders, older women and men, and even younger people who feel a need to preserve old values at all costs. Because immigrant communities are often besieged with rejection, racism, and scorn, those self-appointed "guardians" have always found fertile ground from which to control women's sexuality in the name of preserving "tradition" (Yuval-Davis, 1992).

Pressures on immigrant women's roles and sexuality also emerge from outside their own culture. The host society also imposes its own burdens and desires through prejudices and racism. Although "returning women to their 'traditional roles' continues to be defined as central to preserving national identity and cultural pride" (Narayan, 1997, p. 20) by some immigrants, those same values and behaviors are perceived by their hosts as a demonstration of immigrants' "backwardness" and need for change.

Yet a third oppressive factor comes from people eager to be "culturally sensitive." Under the guise of respect, some members of the host society may "racialize" and "exoticize" immigrant women, particularly those who come from non-European countries. Many well-intentioned people believe that the "true immigrant" has to be "different" even if she does not want to be. Tragically, they contribute to the oppression of immigrant women in the name of respecting their culture and preserving their values. Deployment of "tradition" and "culture" to justify behavior should never remain unproblematized.

Conversely, much is made about the incidence of male dominance in immigrant cultures by individuals in the host culture. However, it is important to remember that any expression of male dominance among immigrant is nothing but the specific culture's version of the myth of male superiority that exits in most cultures, including mainstream American culture.

Many immigrants of both sexes still subscribe to the traditional ideas of male superiority and its consequent forms of expression, but many reject it outright. Let us remember that there are many immigrant women who are actively involved in the feminist movement and who are unwilling to submit to the authority of male relatives. The stories of many of the heterosexual and lesbian interviewees in my studies of immigrant women illustrate this point. Indeed, the existence of lesbians and feminists among immigrant women challenges the myth of their submissiveness to old values so prevalent in mainstream American culture. In fact, research shows that the pace of acculturation tends to be slower for females than males in all aspects but one: Females of all ages acculturate faster than their male counterparts when it comes to gender roles (Ginorio, 1979). As sociologist Silvia Pedraza (1991) reported:

> While men were eager to return [to the home country], women tended to postpone or avoid return because they realized it would entail their retirement from work and the loss of new-found freedoms .... As a result, a

struggle developed over ... return that revolved around the traditional
definitions of gender and privileges which the migration itself had challenged and which many men sought to retain by returning home. (p. 310)

MIGRATION AND SEXUALITY

Although the experience of women in international migration has
begun to draw attention from researchers, policymakers, and service providers (e.g. Cole, Espín, & Rothblum, 1992; Gabaccia,
1992), sexuality and other intimate experiences of women immigrants are mostly absent from these studies. "By contrast, there exists a well-developed scholarship about how immigration ... has
reproduced racial, ethnic, and class distinctions" (Luibhéid, 2002,
p. xi). Little is known, for example, about the experiences of immigrant women in such "private" realms as sexual identity, sexual behavior, and sexual orientation. Yet, as we know, sexuality is not
private, and this explains why so many cultures and countries try to
control and legislate it. Indeed, as one historian observed, "Sexual
behavior (perhaps more than religion) is the most highly symbolic
activity in any society. To penetrate the symbolic system implicit in
any society's sexual behavior is therefore to some closest to the
heart of its uniqueness" (Trumbach, 1977, p. 24). I believe with
Luibhéid (2002) that sexuality is a central axis through which immigration to the United States has been organized. Perhaps the simplest illustration of this point is the importance placed by
immigration legislation and enforcing authorities on issues of
women's sexuality such as prostitution, lesbianism, and pregnancy—all of which have been used as exclusion criteria for female
immigrants at one point or another. Indeed, "the immigration appa-
ratus has been a major site for the construction and regulation of
immigrant women's sexual identities and activities" (Luibhéid,
2003, p. xxvii).

Immigrant women's sexuality and gender-specific behavior are not
static. The established norms for women's appropriate sexual behavior experience constant transformations in both the home and host
cultures/societies. Immigrant women and girls develop their identity
against the backdrop of these contradictions. I believe we need to
reconceptualize how we view women immigrants by expanding our understanding of what migration entails for women in the realms of sexuality and gender roles. The stories immigrant women tell about how
their migration experiences, gender roles, and sexuality have been influenced by the culture/society they came from and the culture/society
in which they now live, and by the language in which the stories are
told. Listening to those stories sheds light on the impact of migration
on gender role and sexuality

MY STUDIES OF IMMIGRANT WOMEN'S
SEXUALITY AND GENDER ROLES

After several decades of clinical work and research on immigrant and refugee women, a few years ago I completed a study that sought to increase knowledge and understanding of sexuality and gender-related issues among this population. Specifically, I wanted to explore how women's sexuality and gender roles are affected by migration to a new country. Between 1994 and 1996 I collected 35 life narratives of women who migrated over a period of 58 years to the United States from different parts of the world. The women interviewed ranged in age from early 20s to mid 70s, and they were all college educated. These women were chosen on the basis of their ability to articulate their experiences with the research topic, their fluency in English, and their knowledge of their first language.[2] They came from Europe, Canada, Latin America, Asia, the Indian subcontinent, and the Middle East. And, contrary to the stereotypical image of all immigrant women as heterosexual mothers, 30% of the women who volunteered to be interviewed were lesbians. The data consist of life story narratives elicited through the use of open-ended questions in in-depth interviews that focused on different aspects of their experience. Individual interviews (and a few focus groups) were conducted in several cities in the United States (San Diego and San Francisco, CA; Boston; Chicago; Miami; New York; and Seattle, WA). The results of this study combined with those of two previous studies appeared in my book entitled *Women Crossing Boundaries: A Psychology and Immigration and Transformations of Sexuality* (Espín, 1999). The two previous studies focused on adolescent experiences of migration and on mother–daughter separation through migration, respectively. These studies also used life narratives as their source of data. The migration narratives of the interviewees are intertwined with their telling about the development of their sexualities, their relationships, and their identities. Their stories are the product of unique personal and cultural contexts dislocated by migration. The events surrounding migration and its precipitants are central to these women's lives. Thus, their stories are both prototypes and individual tales. Together these narratives challenge common stereotypes about immigrant women. What I present here are some of the main results and conclusions from these studies. In the interviews, choice of language to discuss issues of sexuality emerged as one of the important components of the subjective ex-

---

[2]This may raise the objection that these women are not "typical" immigrants. There is a common misconception that all immigrants are poor, uneducated, and unable to communicate in English. The reality is that immigrants to the United States, particularly after 1965, come from all social classes in their countries of origin and adapt to their new environment in a variety of ways, including becoming successful and well educated.

perience. Given their responses, I found myself focusing particularly on the role of language in shaping and expressing the experiences of immigrant women concerning sexuality, gender roles, and identity.

Narratives of gender and sexuality, like all stories lived and told by people, are influenced by what is culturally acceptable. Acceptable accounts of behavior are regulated by society. Individual desire and societal possibilities both push the limits and constrain the boundaries of the lived story. When societal transformations occur, the lived story and the acceptable accounts of that story are also transformed. Immigration constitutes one of the most powerful transformative processes in a given person's life. Surely, we agree that culture and historical events are powerful forces in human development. What, then, happens to the individual life, sense of self, and life story when the cultural narrative changes abruptly as with migration? Although "the story about life is open to editing and revision" (Polkinghorne, 1988, p. 154), some editing and revision may require more work than others. "Re-writing one's story involves major life changes" (Polkinghorne, 1988, p. 182). What happens when events that are not "personal events" in the usual way "invade" the life story? Events that happen "out there" in the world are not only "social" but also "psychological." These events transform the "plots" provided by the culture and the social context, either because the culture itself is transformed, or because the individual finds herself in a new cultural context that allows a different kind of story. Some classical studies of life history have their source in these cataclysms (e.g., Thomas & Znaniecki, 1918–1920/1927).

Through the collected narratives, I explored how questions of cultural identity and sexual identity are negotiated by immigrant and refugee women. I tried to understand how the stories women immigrants tell about themselves and are both made possible and constrained by social constructions of reality and by the language in which the stories are told. I was particularly interested in the vicissitudes of gender and sexual construction as the transformations created by migration, developed in these women's lives.

Almost all of the interviewees in my studies actively attributed the transformations in their gender roles and sexuality to their migration. Not all of them were fully comfortable with their sexuality or gender roles, but then, sex is not unproblematic for most women. Sex and sexuality can be a source of fear, pain, and embarrassment, and they can also be a source of happiness, pleasure, and fulfillment. In this, the interviewees are no exception. In any case, the transformations in their gender roles and sexuality did not occur independently from other identity transformations, but rather were part of a process characterized by a move toward greater autonomy in all areas of their lives. Because the women interviewed had experienced dramatic transformations in their lives, the evidence for a social construction of sexuality and gender roles provided by their life narratives becomes even more poignant. Listening to these women's stories, the power of this social construction manifests in: (a) their struggle to either maintain or reflect the values of the immigrant communities concerning women's sexuality—meaning both values brought from the home country and values of their identified community that developed during the migration process; (b) the internalized desires of the women themselves, which have originated both in the home and host cultures; and (c) the "uses" both the woman herself and her community make of female sexuality in the process of establishing identities different from the host society, or, conversely, to signal assimilation.

THE SIGNIFICANCE OF LANGUAGE

In the in the course of the interviews, it became evident that language changes were central to the transformation of identity and the expression of sexuality in the interviewees. Indeed, language—the forced learning of the new and the loss of the old linguistic community—is central to the migration experience. In fact, language change is one of the most difficult problems the immigrant faces—and I am not referring to issues of vocabulary, grammar or pronunciation.

Language loss and its concomitant sense of identity loss and transformation are one of the most powerful components of the immigrant experience. In her autobiographical account of migration, *Lost in Translation*, writer Eva Hoffman (1989) vividly described the intensity of this experience for immigrants:

> Linguistic dispossession is ... close to the dispossession of one's self ....
> [There is feeling that] this language is beginning to invent another me ....
> [And] there is, of course, the constraint and the self-consciousness of an
> accent that I hear but cannot control. (p. 121)

Beyond allowing the immigrants to function in the new context, a new language has profound impact on their sense of self and identity, as Hoffman's statements illustrate. The immigrant learns "to live in two languages"; similarly, she learns to live in two social worlds. Learning to "live" in a new language is not merely an instrumental process. It is not a neutral act. It implies becoming immersed in the power relations of the specific culture that speaks the specific language. Paradoxically, learning the language of the host society implies learning one's place in the structures of social inequality. To speak with a foreign accent places one in a less privileged position within those power relations.

> Even supposing that the immigrant is in a country where his [sic] own
> language is spoken (although it can never be the exact same language),
> his speech act will take place at a particular moment of time and in a dis-
> tinctive set of circumstances different from those he has known.
> (Grinberg & Grinberg, 1984, p. 100)

"One of the primary places where issues of national culture and family coherence come together is the question of language" (Bammer, 1994, p. 96). This issue becomes further complicated when different generations within a family have different levels of proficiency in the different languages spoken. While the first language or mother tongue may be taken to mean the native language of the mother, in the case of immigrants or refugees, children may be more fluent in the language of the host culture, which is really their first language, rather than the language their mothers speak best (Bammer, 1994). In other words:

> Language can play a complex role, both binding and dividing family members. For not only do parents and children often end up with different native languages, their different relationships to these languages can have notable social consequences. (Bammer, 1994, p. 100)

Every language is linked to a culture. Every language depends on the concrete context that provides it with its meaning and its boundaries. "Language determines one's knowledge of the world, of others, and of oneself. It provides a basis of support for one's identity" (Grinberg & Grinberg, 1984, p. 109). To some extent, our language and our way of life are one and the same. When parents and children are fluent in different languages, they may, in fact, be guided by different cultural codes.

Language—the parents' lack of fluency in the new language and the children's lack of fluency in the "mother-tongue"—subverts authority in the family. The power of children is increased because they become "cultural brokers," whereas the power of parents is decreased because they depend on their children's assistance to survive in the new world. The inordinate amount of power children may acquire because of their language proficiency can be at the source of conflicts over authority issues. It also magnifies children's conscious or unconscious fears that their parents are now unable to protect them as they used to.

An immigrant's resistance to language learning may be an expression of a desire for self-preservation. Entering the world of a new language may pose a threat for the individual's sense of identity. Individuals who learn the new language at a fast pace may have less of a stake in preserving another identity. This may be why the young learn faster.

Conversely, learning a new language provides the immigrant with the opportunity to "create a new self." This facilitates working through early intrapsychic conflicts, and finding new ways of self-expression that may not have been available in the world of the first language.

> People who learn to use two languages have two symbols for every object. Thus, from an early age they become emancipated from linguistic symbols—from the concreteness, arbitrariness, and "tyranny" of words—developing analytic abilities ... to think in terms more ... independent of the actual word .... By contrast, monolingual may be at a disadvantage. (Portes & Rumbaut, 1996, pp. 200–201)

LANGUAGE AND SEXUALITY IN THE INTERVIEWS

The interviewees' descriptions of their relation to their languages and to English illustrate some of the twists and complications created by the multilingual experience. The first language often remains the language of emotions, even among immigrants who may be fluent in English. The topic of sexuality is an emotional one for most of us. For women, particularly immigrant women, the subject is additionally charged with the many contextual layers within which it develops. Because most of what we know about people's inner feelings comes to us through language, the language chosen to discuss important emotional issues such as sexuality and relationships may determine the accessibility and awareness of emotional content.

Most of the women interviewed resorted to English when describing their sexuality—both during the interview and in other contexts where the topic was discussed. This pattern was present equally for women coming from "traditional" and "modern" societies. However, some respondents preferred their first language in their sexual interactions. They found words in their first language more sexually arousing. As one of them stated, it seemed difficult, if not impossible, to "make love in English."

In some instances, the use of English, rather than the mother tongue, may act as a barrier or resistance in dealing with certain components of the psyche. Conversely, the second language can act to facilitate the emergence and discussion of certain topics. These topics may be taboo in the native language. González-Reigosa (1976) demonstrated that taboo words in the language of origin elicit maximum anxiety. They cause more angst than either taboo words in the second language or indifferent words in the first language. Words that relate to sexuality easily qualify as emotionally charged taboo words. Thus, speaking in a second language may "distance" the immigrant woman from important parts of herself. Yet a second language may provide a vehicle to express the inexpressible in the first language—either because the first language does not have the vocabulary, or because the person censors herself from saying certain taboo things in the first language.

Turkish-Danish scholar Mehmet Necef (1994) contended that the issue is one of clashes in values more than language. If the words learned to discuss sexuality in the first language are "dirty" words, then the native speaker of that language may be at a loss to describe positive experiences. Sometimes a society/culture lacks the language to describe an experience. It may have not developed the vocabulary that would validate that experience. The second language, then, may become helpful as it provides an acceptable vocabulary to talk about these issues. In short, when a good experience has no name in one language, the bilingual person has the option of resorting to the other language. These two issues may be intertwined because—although this is not a linear relationship—the absence and/or presence of terms in any language is often suggestive of cultural values. Cultures that have fairly conservative views of female sexuality and agency frequently make it difficult to speak about these issues (Espín, 1984, 1987; Necef, 1994). If one comes from such a culture, English provides a vehicle for discussing sexual issues that may be too difficult or embarrassing to discuss with either nonexistent or forbidden words in one's first language. Interestingly, some of the interviewees, who came from cultures they defined as "more liberal" than mainstream American culture, still preferred to use English in discussion of sexuality. For example, Marguerite, Hilde, and Ursula, immigrants from Austria, Germany, and Switzerland, respectively, after the completion of interviews conducted in English, stated that although they believed most Americans were very "puritanical" about sexuality and although they had a larger vocabulary in their first language, it was easier for them to talk about these topics in English. Feelings of shame, they reported, would have prevented them from addressing these topics in depth had they used their first language.

Clearly, the interviews revealed how the access to more than one language pushes at the boundaries of what is "sayable" or "tellable." Interviewees stated repeatedly that the second language facilitates ease of communication when the topic discussed is sexuality. Some participants said that they did not know or were unfamiliar with vocabulary about sexuality in their native language. These women had migrated at an earlier age, usually before or during early adolescence. They had developed their knowledge of sex while immersed in English. They used English more consistently in other spheres of life as well and felt more comfortable with it. Therefore, they found it inconceivable to use their first language to talk about adult interactions, including sex and sexuality.

In my therapeutic practice, I observed that the preference for English was particularly significant for bilingual lesbians. They described their life situation and choices most frequently in English. They tended to avoid equivalent words in their native tongue. The description of her relationship to her first language provided by Lorena (one of the interviewees) vividly illustrates this point.

Lorena is a Puerto Rican-born nurse who immigrated to the U.S. mainland at age 30, and has been out as a lesbian for almost 20 years. When Lorena was growing up, she had to confront the realities of women's lives and the idea of marriage. She found it hard to imagine herself a married woman, but had not imagined the possibility of lesbianism. During her college years, Lorena had male friends but never imagined herself as a wife or a mother. Her sex fantasies then, however, were all about men.

A general sense of dissatisfaction with her everyday life in Puerto Rico prompted her emigration to the mainland. Like all Puerto Ricans, she was an American citizen; no major legal preparations were required. She hoped that a change in the environment and autonomy from her family would energize her life. Little did she know what this change would entail. Shortly after her arrival in the United States mainland, Lorena met a long-time lesbian and fell in love with her. A quick transformation occurred. In her words, "It was as if the pieces of the puzzle had now all suddenly fit in place." She has never returned to Puerto Rico since then except for brief visits.

She speaks with some degree of comfort about her sexual orientation, *in the United States and in English.* She is far less comfortable speaking of it in Spanish or in Puerto Rico. She attributes this to the plethora of "dirty words" in Spanish that describe lesbians and also to her family's presence in Puerto Rico.

> I can be out in English but not in Spanish. When the plane lands in Puerto Rico it is as if I "shut down" and do not become lesbian again until I come back to the U.S. It took me forever to say certain words in English. It is still impossible for me to say those words in Spanish. I can now find pride in saying some words in English, but I still feel only shame saying those words in Spanish. I would only use those words when absolutely necessary to talk to Latina lesbians, not on my own .... It is not that I think that English is "liberating" or that people are so "free" in this country. It is just that English is much less charged for me, not only about sexuality but about practically anything emotional.

When I asked about the language she preferred while making love, she said she uses both languages but that English "comes easier" because she discovered her "lesbian self" in English. She is fluently bilingual but believes that some parts of her emotional self are more "in English" while others are more "in Spanish."

She equates her lesbianism to another form of biculturalism: "You are always on the margins. Being gay or lesbian is living in a different subculture. Being a Latina immigrant is like that too." Despite her sense of marginality, she believes her coming out was eased by being in the United States mainland.

Another interesting perspective was provided by Ayla, an immigrant from Turkey. Ayla found that in the United States, "It is imperative to talk about sex and sexuality if you want to make friends." Although Ayla matured sexually in Turkey and could speak in Turkish about sex, she prefers to talk about it in English. Even with her Turkish women friends, it is easier to speak in English about sexuality. Perhaps this is because "one has more practice and less prohibition talking about this in English."

To summarize, many intriguing questions are raised by these data on the uses of language. First, is the immigrant woman's preference for English when discussing sexuality motivated by characteristics of English as a language (i.e., do characteristics of a specific second language offer a vehicle for expression that is unavailable in the first language)? Or does a second language (no matter which one) offer the degree of emotional distance needed to express taboo subjects? If the later were true, then people whose second language is not English would find it easier to discuss sexuality in their second language. Because English was the second or third language for all interviewees (with only one exception), it was impossible to assess this possibility. Second, does the new cultural context—where English is spoken—allow more expression of the women's feelings? To many immigrants, American society seems more sexually permissive behaviorally and verbally than their society of origin. Perhaps the presumed permissiveness of American society encourages and facilitates the expression of these topics in English. This may be true for women who immigrated from traditional societies. Yet it does not explain the preference for English among those women who migrated from more "progressive" societies. A third possibility may be particularly relevant for those who migrated as children or adolescents. Because they "came of age sexually" in English, its expression may become inextricably associated with the language. This scenario would make their preference for English dependent on their learning context, rather than on emotional factors, cultural background, or the characteristics of either language.

LANGUAGE AND INTERCULTURAL MARRIAGES

Many of the women interviewed were in interracial or intercultural relationships or marriages. If, as it appears to be true from the results of my study, people who speak more than one language are able to defend from and withhold the expression of deep emotion by switching between languages, what happens for women in intimate relationships with individuals who do not speak their first languages? Do these women become truly intimate in these relationships? Are these relationships a manifestation of healthy personal transformations or are they a form of escaping intimacy and vulnerability? Is it possible that a deep and significant relationship may develop despite these barriers? Regardless of the deep desires to connect with their partners they may have, are they able to do so? Or are the splits in identity created by language differences an impediment to the success of these relationships? Perhaps, particularly concerning sexuality, nonverbal communication creates the bridge to overcome the language divide. But, in any case, this is an unanswered question in my study.

MIGRATION: LOSS AND GAIN

The loss involved in migration was addressed repeatedly by most of the women interviewed. Simultaneously, they countered forcefully the perception of losses with the argument that the experience of migration had enriched them, given them choices, options, and fluency in a repertoire of languages, modes of thought, and social networks.

The opportunities in work, education, and routines of life provided by the migration had a special significance for these women. Regardless of differences in their countries of birth concerning the roles of women, they all benefited from the liberating effect of being "outsiders" in the host culture of the United States. A quote from Marguerite illustrates this point:

> I'm not sure if it is being in America or just being a distance from my country but I feel I am being affected by this atmosphere that gives me the freedom to experience myself. But I definitely feel that something is changing; the change is in general but also about sexuality. And it is very important for me that it is about sexuality because I felt so oppressed there.

Nevertheless, migration also carries with it the possibility of limiting women's private spheres of influence and their moral authority within traditional cultural contexts. Traditional patriarchal contexts have always provided the opportunity to carve separate—if inferior—spaces for women. The cultural transformations brought about by migration upset these spaces without yet giving women full access to equal power in the public sphere. For immigrant daughters, it may become difficult to invest their mothers with positive images and characteristics when migration has limited the mothers' sphere of influence even further.

MIGRATION AND DEVELOPMENTAL STAGE

Another significant factor present in the experience of the interviewees was the life stage/age at the time of migration. This connection between age and the impact of a life event is almost self-evident. It confirms psychologist Abigail Stewart's (1994) assumption that "one important factor in the attachment of individual meaning to social events is an individual's age, because of the connection between age and stage of psychological development" (p. 231). The women who had migrated as children seemed to have adapted more rapidly and easily. However, children whose lives have been affected by major social historical events may be affected in their broad values and expectations about the world at a deeper psychological level. "Children's experiences of social historical events is, of course, filtered through their experiences in their own families" (Stewart, 1994, p. 232). Because the migration altered the course of their psychological and material lives early in life, interviewees who had migrated at a very early age were less able to image who and what they could have been without the impact of migration.

Most conflicts about gender roles and sexuality were manifested—either presently or in the past—by those who migrated during adolescence. Negotiating gender roles, sexual behavior, and sexual identity in both the home and host cultures becomes one of the major developmental tasks for immigrant adolescents. Thus young women or adolescent girls confront the question of how to "become American" without completely losing their cultural heritage. Conflicts over parental authority often are played out around issues of appropriate sexual behavior: Dating and other behaviors related to sexuality become the focus of conflict between parents and daughters. This is understandable because of the multiple tasks required of young women immigrants. As a young immigrant woman constructs her cultural identity in a new country, she simultaneously develops a sexual identity. The inherent connection between discourses on sexuality and sources of power in a new and different cultural context may result in split identities for young women immigrants. Religious and cultural injunctions may further limit the young woman's decision making.

Young women from "racialized" groups may confront additional conflicts concerning their sexuality and body image. They have to find a balance between the imposed hypersexualization of immigrant women as "exotic" and the "hyperpurity" expected of them by their families and communities. Nevertheless, many young immigrant women successfully negotiate a place for themselves despite these injunctions and limitations and struggle to find their own sexual expression.

Those who migrated after adolescence appear to be less conflicted about their identity. This is due in part to their already somewhat solid identities before undergoing the extra tasks involved in the migration. This is clearly true for lesbian interviewees. Even when "coming out," with its attendant identity changes, had occurred after the migration, the process seemed to have been less disrupting for those who migrated at a later age.

LESBIANS AND MIGRATION

Although lesbians and gay men obviously exist among immigrants, many immigrant communities prefer to believe otherwise. Some posit that homosexuality is just an evil acquired by contagion or through the bad influence of American society. They prefer to believe either that homosexuality is nonexistent in their communities or that it could be eradicated were it not for the bad influence of the host society. Ironically, the propensity to attribute sexual vice to immigrants has a long history in American society and, in fact, Americans frequently blame one or another ethnic group for their supposed propensity to homosexuality. Some of the congressional commissions created to deal with immigration in the past have blamed immigrants for the introduction of homosexual practices into the United States (Luibhéid, 2002).

Difficulties prevail in obtaining adequate statistics on lesbian populations among immigrants—a hardly surprising fact considering that until very recently the mere appearance of homosexual inclinations was considered grounds for exclusion and denial of entry into the country. Most likely, several million lesbians and gay men are among the immigrant population in the United States.

From this and other studies we can surmise that lesbian immigrants face specific emotional and practical difficulties. Disclosure of sexual orientation affects them as individuals and it affects the community. "Coming out" as a lesbian may jeopardize not only family ties but also their much needed contributions to their community. Because most lesbian immigrants are self-supporting and take advantage of employment and educational opportunities in the United States (Espín, 1984), they are frequently involved in services and advocacy for their communities. The fear of being "discovered" and rejected may constitute a serious concern for them. These fears are compounded by the difficulties created by prevalent stereotyped conceptions of womanhood and sexuality in both the home and host cultures, familial and societal rejection of their sexual identities, and legal restrictions on their immigration. Still, the new environment may open possibilities hitherto unavailable in the country of birth, as illustrated by the example of Lorena.

The immigrant lesbian acculturates to the new society as an immigrant as well as to the particular lesbian culture in which she is situated. Thus, immigrant lesbians share experiences with heterosexual women from their particular immigrant community as well as with lesbians in the host culture. They also share some experiences with gay males who are immigrants or refugees. Their political, religious, and social affiliations vary greatly. In different degrees, both the immigrant community and the lesbian community provide them with a sense of identification in the host country.

The typical immigrant's ruminations about "what could have been" are magnified for lesbians by questioning whether they would have the opportunity or the desire to live a lesbian life had they not emigrated. For those who were aware of their sexual orientation before migration, the questions may have to do with what a lesbian life would have been like in their country of birth.

ENDING THOUGHTS

Many of the interviewees described their early sexual experiences and desires—both heterosexual and lesbian—as troubling and fraught with secrecy and ignorance. Many managed to find their own ways and happiness despite their confusion and the struggles and opposition of families.

I have tried in this chapter to convey something of what the process of immigration into another country means for women. My intention was not to create a sense of grand narrative but rather to present a window into the individual life narratives developed by women who have been immersed in the transformations brought about by migration.

My focus has been on psychological aspects of their experience, with a particular emphasis on sexuality and gender roles.

I have spent my professional life working in therapy with immigrant women, doing research or teaching about issues of concern to them. Because I have shared similar life experiences with these women, I have been both glad to serve as their mouthpiece and wary about the dangers of representing them. No matter how similar those experiences, the researcher and the researched (or therapist and client) may have very different ideas about "who we are." And no matter how strong the similarities, vast differences in experience were also present. Differences originate in the dissimilar countries of birth, ages of migration, historical period when the migration took place, circumstances surrounding it, and the ultimate consequences of the process for each individual life. Each one of these women carried into the interview the history of all these events intertwined with her personal history. I also carried my own, which was an important motivation for my studies. Despite the differences among them, several behavioral patterns became clear through the interviews. Most of the women revised their social and gender role expectations as a consequence of their migration. They worked hard at renegotiating gender roles with both the traditions of their home country and the expectations of the host culture. Their experiences illustrate the simultaneous process of acculturation and identity formation. In general, their adaptations appear to be successful despite differences in individual histories and personalities and in their choice of individual paths.

In the studies I have undertaken throughout my career and in these pages I have tried to respond not only to my own interests but also to some important issues raised by the United Nations concerning women immigrants and refugees. The United Nations (UN International Research and Training Institute, 1994; UN Expert Group Meeting, 1995) unequivocally stated in recent documents that

> improving the status of women is increasingly recognized as fundamental to improving the basic human rights of over half the population of the world and also contributing to social economic progress ....Women's migration, both internally within developing countries and internationally across borders ... to developed countries, is inextricably linked to the status of women in society. (1994, p. 1)

This assertion is followed by questions yet unanswered:

> But what do we know about women's migration? ... For example, does migration lead to improvements in the status of women, breaking down patriarchal structures and enhancing women's autonomy or does it lead to perpetuate dependency? (1994, p. 1)

Ultimately, the questions faced by these studies is, who "owns" women's sexuality and women's lives? "Modern" ideas about women's rights and free choices concerning their lives have not entirely replaced more "traditional" ideas about gender obligations and differences in rights. These questions are alive in all societies. Yet they become more poignant and dramatic in the context of traditional groups trying to acculturate in a new context which is itself in transition concerning the role of women. Perhaps participation in these studies and the transformational tales created in these interviews allowed participants to get in touch with their own sexuality and their own erotic power. Hopefully, these studies contributed to awareness and integration of experiences for the participants as they contributed to others' increased understanding of women's experiences of crossing geographical and emotional boundaries.

I have the experience of leaving Cuba, crossing a language and culture to make a new home in a new place. As a lesbian who celebrates her identity, I have the experience of a woman challenged to live a marginalized existence, but I have created a loving community among women and men who share and/or celebrate her experiences. My willingness to disclose personal challenges and joys has made my teaching and scholarly work vibrant. I have always invited psychologists to ask questions that were not considered by most. I would not accept that psychological theory was accurate when it was based only a small percentage of the population. As such, my early work demanded that we understand human development in relation to the experiences of women and particularly the experiences of women of color.

REFERENCES

Bammer, A. (1994). Mother tongues and other strangers: Writing "family" across cultural divides. In A. Bammer (Ed.), *Displacements: Cultural identities in question* (pp. 90–109). Bloomington: Indiana University Press.

Cole, E., Espín, O. M. & Rothblum, E. (Eds.). (1992). *Refugee women and their mental health: Shattered societies, shattered lives.* New York: Haworth.

Espín, O. M. (1984). Cultural and historical influences on sexuality in Hispanic/Latin women. In C. Vance (Ed.), *Pleasure and danger: Exploring female sexuality* (pp.149–164). London, UK: Routledge and Kegan Paul.

Espín, O. M. (1987). Psychological impact of migration on Latinas: Implications for psychotherapeutic practice. *Psychology of Women Quarterly,* 4(11), 489–503.

Espín, O. M. (1999). *Women crossing boundaries: A psychology of immigration and transformations of sexuality.* New York: Routledge.

Gabaccia, D. (Ed.). (1992). *Seeking common ground: Multidisciplinary studies of immigrant women in the United States.* Westport, CT: Praeger.

Ginorio, A. (1979). A comparison of Puerto Ricans in New York with native Puerto Ricans and Caucasian—and Black—Americans on two measures of acculturation: Gender role and racial identification (Doctoral dissertation, Fordham University). *Dissertation Abstracts International, 40,* 983B–984B.

González-Reigosa, F. (1976). The anxiety-arousing effect of taboo words in bilinguals. In C. D. Spielberger & R. Díaz-Guerrero (Eds.), *Cross-cultural anxiety* (pp. 309–326). Washington, DC: Hemisphere.

Grinberg, L., & Grinberg, R. (1984). *Psicoanalisis de la migracion y del exilio.* Madrid: Alianza Editorial. [English translation by N. Festinger. *Psychoanalytic perspectives on migration and exile.* New Haven, CT: Yale University Press, 1989.]

Hoffman, E. (1989). *Lost in translation.* New York: Dutton.

Luibhéid, E. (2002). *Entry denied: Controlling sexuality at the border.* Minneapolis: University of Minnesota Press.

Narayan, U. (1997). *Dislocating cultures: Identities, traditions and Third World feminism.* New York: Routledge.

Necef, M. (1994). The language of intimacy. In L. E. Andersen (Ed.). *Middle East studies in Denmark* (pp.141–158). Odense, Denmark: University of Odense Press.

Pedraza, S. (1991). Women and migration: The social consequences of gender. *Annual Review of Sociology, 17,* 303–325.

Polkinghorne, D. E. (1988). *Narrative knowing and the human sciences.* Albany, NY: State University of New York Press.

Portes, A., & Rumbaut, R. (1996). *Immigrant America: A portrait* (2nd. ed.). Berkeley: University of California Press.

Rogler, L. H. (1994). International migrations: A framework for directing research. *American Psychologist, 49*(8), 701–708.

Stewart, A. J. (1994). The women's movement and women's lives: Linking individual development and social events. In R. Josselson (Ed.), *The narrative study of lives* (Vol.2, pp. 230–250). Thousand Oaks, CA: Sage.

Thomas, W. I., & Znaniecki, F. (1927). *The Polish peasant in Europe and America.* New York: A. Knopf. (Origianl work published 1918–1920)

Trumbach, R. (1977). London's sodomites. *Journal of Social History, 11,* 1–33.

United Nations International Research and Training Institute for the Advancement of Women. (1994). *The migration of women: Methodological issues in the measurement and analysis of internal and international migration.* New York: United Nations.

United Nations Expert Group Meeting on International Migration Policies and the Status of Female Migrants. (1995). *International migration policies and the status of female migrants.* New York: United Nations.

Yuval-Davis, N. (1992). Fundamentalism, multiculturalism and women in Britain. In J. Donald & A. Ratansi (Eds.), *Race, culture, and difference* (pp. 278–291). London: Sage.

14

Cultural Psychology of Gender and Immigration

Ramaswami Mahalingam
University of Michigan

Jana Haritatos
University of California, San Francisco

Cultural psychological research on gender has traditionally focused on documenting sex role beliefs in various cultures (Best & Williams, 1997). However, such approaches often do not adequately address how issues of power and social marginality shape beliefs about gender among immigrants. Additionally, although there have been many qualitative accounts of the impact of immigration on traditional gender roles and the experience of gender among female immigrants to the United States (e.g., Espín, 1999; Hondagneu-Sotelo, 1994), much of the existing psychological literature on gender socialization has often focused on the "universal" nature of sex role development in studies of White middle-class American children, many times failing to account for varieties of contextual and cultural processes (Schaffer, 1996). Cultural psychological research on immigration and gender, as well as more general theoretical models of gender socialization, would benefit greatly from combined approaches to these complex issues; however, very little such work exists. This focus on the process of socialization during and after immigration is a much-needed one, yet again is lacking from the existing literature.

In this chapter we propose a cultural psychology of gender framework to study immigrant women and men, foregrounding the complex relationship between idealized cultural beliefs about gender and the

259

marginalized status of immigrants, and focusing on their impact on immigrants' lives. This approach is important because immigrants face a unique predicament. In a new cultural context, they may feel the need to assert their identities through various modes of cultural practices that authenticate these identities and distinguish them from the "natives." Often they imagine a culture with a "glorious" historical past that provides them a sense of superiority over the "natives." We argue that over time such idealizations of cultural identity become salient and acquire new meanings in the immigrant context with increasing awareness of the power and material differences between new immigrants and the "host" culture.

Gender becomes a major site to anchor such articulation of idealized notions of cultural identities. For example, several gender theorists have pointed out that women are believed to be the "purveyors" of culture. The "purity" and restrained, chaste behavior of women are believed to symbolize the essential characteristics of their kin, family, and group identity (Lindisfarne, 1998). Using Indian immigrants as an example, we explore the role of dominant Indian cultural representations of gender in shaping cultural expectations of women in the immigrant context. Specifically, we focus on the dominant role of gender ideals in the gender socialization of second-generation daughters in the Indian diaspora. In doing so, this chapter is divided into three sections: In the first section, we discuss the salience of idealized gender representations using two examples of idealized womanhood within the cultural narratives of Indian womanhood; in the second section, using a qualitative study, we investigate various aspects of gender socialization of second-generation Indian immigrant women in the United States; and in the final part, we discuss the relevance of these findings for developing a cultural psychological framework for the study of gender and immigration.

REPRESENTATIONS OF GENDER
AND THE IDEAL HINDU WOMEN—"PATIVIRDA"

Hinduism, in general, holds a patriarchal definition of the role of women. Women's roles and duties are defined by Manu, the Hindu lawgiver. According to Manu, women are to be protected by their fathers when they are young, and then by husbands when they are married, and by their sons during their old age. The psychological realities of women thus can be condensed in three stages: First, she is a daughter to her parents, second, she is a wife to her husband, and third, she is a mother to her sons (Kakar, 1978, p. 57). If the husband turns out to be an unworthy person, what can she do? Manu prescribes the code of conduct for women who are in such a state of affairs.

Though destitute of virtue or seeking pleasure elsewhere, or devoid of good qualities, yet a husband must be constantly worshipped as a God by a faithful wife …. By violating her duty towards her husband, a wife is disgraced in this world, [after death] she enters the womb of a jackal, and is tormented by the punishment of her sin. (Manu, cited in Kakar, 1978)

The notion of *"Pativirda"* (one who is devoted to her husband through all her sufferings) is reinforced by various stories and *"Puranas"* or epics. In the great Indian epic *Ramayan*, Sita follows her husband Ram to the forest and is taken away by a demon, Ravana. Later Ram fights Ravanan and kills him. Then he asks Sita to prove her fidelity by asking her to walk through fire, and Agni, the fire god, testifies to her purity. Sita's suffering does not stop here. After coming back to his country, Ram sends pregnant Sita back to the forest because of the gossip among his citizens about Sita's fidelity. Sita gives birth to two sons and raises them in the forest. When the sons are grown up she sends them back to their father. Then Ram invites her back. Again, she is asked to go through the fire. This time Sita cannot bear it any more. She prays to the earth mother to take her. The earth mother takes her back into her womb. The notion of Pativirda is epitomized in Sita, who embodies the suffering and humiliations an ordinary woman/mother goes through in a Hindu society.

A variant of the pan-Indian notion of Pativirda (dedicated wife) is the story of the ideal Tamil woman—*"Pattini"* (a virtuous wife), who is angry and takes the law into her own hands. Kannagi, the dominant female, is a devoted wife, who becomes a protagonist when her husband is executed without trial on the grounds that he had stolen the anklets of the queen. She goes to the king's court and proves her husband's innocence. Then she calls the fire god, and orders him to burn the city except for women, elders, and children. Then she walks for days and waits under a tree. Her husband comes from heaven alive and takes her with him to heaven. Thus Kannagi, a quiet devoted housewife, turns into a protagonist only *after* her husband's death. She burns the city by virtue of her loyalty to her husband. She derives her moral force exclusively from her dedication and virtuosity. The virtue of Pattini, symbolized by Kannagi, illustrates the powerful role of cultural narratives in defining a pan-Indian ideal womanhood.

Cultural narratives such as Sita and Kannagi underscore the power of chaste women (Wadley, 1991). Various popular narratives also valorize women who are devoted, virtuous, self-sacrificing, and patient as the embodiment of the cultural identity. Although an idealized Indian woman's identity is built on the purity of her body, an Indian woman lives outside her body so that the realities of life do not affect her (Lakshmi, 1984). Lakshmi (1984) argued that as a result of such excessive cultural idealization of the female body, Indian women develop a nonconsciousness of their bodies as a way of coping with excessive concerns about the female body. This concern for the female body, along with a cultivated nonconsciousness of the body for women themselves, is a cultural inheritance that has been preserved over the years.

This nonawareness of the body is only one kind of muted consciousness. Motherhood, wifehood, and daughterhood, combining qualities
of sacrifice, suppression, self-denial, and self-control, are also off-
shoots of this one form of muted consciousness. This has made
nonawareness in general an admired female quality. Nonawareness is
also recognized as an asset that has helped in saving the inner world of
the family by retaining traditional family relationships (Lakshmi,
1984, p. 236). Roland (1988) also reported that among Indian women,
there exists a familial "we" self—a self that encompasses the feelings of
inner regard for the individual as well as her family. As a result, any
public behavior (success or failure) not only affects the individual but
also reflects the honor of the family and its members, particularly in
relation to other families in the community (Roland, 1988).

The interesting cultural psychological question is, to what extent do
these cultural ideals affect the psychological well-being of women and
men in India? Mahalingam and Haritatos (under review-a) proposed a
dual-pathway model, arguing that cultural ideals are a source of both
strength and stress because they provide a cultural referent for
self-pride as well as for critical self-evaluation. Using measures of gender ideals, such as chastity (Mahalingam, under review) and masculinity (Mahalingam & Jackson, under review), Mahalingam and
colleagues examined the mental health consequences of idealized notions of gender in Tamilnadu, India. They found that idealized cultural
beliefs about gender, such as chastity and masculinity, although increasing self-esteem, also contributed to shame, leading to depression
for men as well as for women. This finding is consistent with the
dual-pathway model proposed by Mahalingam and Haritatos (under
review-a). In sum, these qualitative and quantitative studies suggest
that idealized gender beliefs play a critical role in women's and men's
lives in India. However, less is known about these important processes
among immigrants. Therefore, it is critical to understand the contextual modalities of how and when these gender ideals become salient
for Indians when they migrate to the United States.

CULTURE, GENDER, AND IMMIGRATION:
AN INTERSECTIONALITY PERSPECTIVE

Stewart and McDermott (2004) proposed an intersectionality perspective for the study of gender. This intersectionality perspective argues
for the need to study gender in relation to race, ethnicity, social class
and sexual orientation. Extending the intersectionality perspective,
Mahalingam and Haritatos (under review-a) proposed an Idealized
Cultural Identities (ICI) model to study gender. According to ICI,
marginalized social groups sense the need to assert a positive
self-identity to negate negative stereotypes in popular dominant representations. They embrace or "imagine" an idealized representation of
their cultural identity whose roots typically are traced to an "ancient"

civilization with a "glorious" past. Marginalized social locations, and in particular the relational context of immigrant identities, play a significant role in accentuating the need to hold on to or articulate newer forms of idealized notions of cultural identities. Several cultural theorists have pointed out that gender becomes a critical site of such articulations of idealized identities (Dasgupta & Dasgupta, 2000; Ortner, 1974). Thus, the intersections of gender, ethnicity, and social class engender the very creation of such idealized representations. Hence idealized cultural identities might play a critical role in gender socialization. Ethnographic reports on gender socialization among immigrant families also suggest that cultural ideals play a central role in various aspects of gender socialization practices, as immigration has been shown to have complex effects on traditional gender roles and the experience of gender among female immigrants to the United States (Espín, 1999; Hondagneu-Sotelo, 1994).

Using a qualitative study of gender socialization among second-generation women, we investigated whether there was cultural continuity in the socialization of gender ideals among Indian immigrants. To do so, our study examined how the process of immigration impacts gender socialization among American-born daughters of first-generation Indian immigrants. Specifically, we explored whether beliefs about the expectations and appropriate life choices for males and females were transmitted through a gender socialization process of differential treatment and differential allocation of resources to sons and daughters in Indian immigrant families.

Indian Immigrants

The Indian diaspora community was cited by the Immigration and Naturalization Service as being one of the fastest growing immigrant groups in the United States as of the mid-1980s. In 1990, there were estimated to be 815,447 Indians living in the United States (Shah, 1994), and by the 2000 census, there were 1,678,765 U.S. residents reporting Asian Indian ethnic backgrounds (Barnes & Benett, 2002). Since we are interested in the role of idealized representations of gender, we were particularly interested in what "residual" aspects of "Indian culture" had been appropriated or reproduced in a new, postmigration context, or whether, and under what conditions, immigrant daughters also retain some agency while changing their behavioral repertoire in response to idealized cultural representations. This study explored the role of family socialization of traditional or nontraditional gender beliefs, and examined the relationship between gender socialization and young women's academic achievement, career options, social behaviors, and dating/marriage expectations. Considering the extreme forms of gender discrimination in India as documented by several demographers (see Hudson & den Boer, 2004, for a review), we also focused on whether there was any "residual" cultural influence in the differential treatment of daughters.

Study Methods

Seven second-generation Indian women were recruited to participate in the study through various Indian American student associations at a large, Midwestern university. The selection criteria were that women must be second-generation Indian college students, they must have at least one brother, and their parents must have emigrated from India. Each Indian American woman participated in an individual structured interview, which investigated her perceptions of treatment of boys and girls in her own family with respect to the following themes: specific behavior modifications, resource allocation (i.e., toys, money, college funds), curfews, dating rules and marriage expectations, career options, and communicative relationships with parents and grandparents. Each interview was conducted by a trained member of the research team and lasted approximately 75 to 90 minutes. After completing the interviews, each woman received $15 for her participation.

Data Analysis

All of the women interviewed for this study were undergraduate students at the university and were between 19 and 21 years old. Most grew up in the Midwest with relatively small nuclear families, typically consisting of both parents, the participant, and one to three brothers. Often the participants' families lived relatively close to the university these women were attending; however, in a few cases, the women had left families living in other states to go study. As is typical in Indian families, most of our college student participants were majoring in either engineering or a medicine-related field. The average yearly family income of our participants was relatively high, ranging from $50,000 to over $125,000, and the most commonly reported income was in the salary range of $100,000–125,000 per year.

For example, Poonam (names have been changed for this chapter) is a 21-year-old biology major at a large, Midwestern university. She has one younger brother, and her parents emigrated to the United States from New Delhi, India. As is typical of many participants, her father came here first as a high school student, and after returning to India for the arranged marriage to Poonam's mother, the couple returned together to the United States and settled in the Midwest. Now her father owns a small electronics business and her mother works as a systems analyst for a technology firm.

Shobha is a 20-year-old business major with two younger brothers, one attending a different university, and the other still in high school. As with Poonam, Shobha's father was already living in the United States when his marriage was arranged in Punjab, after which he returned to the Midwest with Shobha's mother. Now her father owns his own real estate company and her mother is not employed outside the home.

In a final example, Priti is a 20-year-old computer engineering major with one younger brother, and she is slightly unusual in that she traveled out of state to attend college, rather than going to school close to home. Her parents came to the United States from New Delhi, India, after getting married, and after settling in the Midwest her father established a career as a chemist for a pharmaceutical corporation, and her mother owns a small business.

After collecting all of the interview data from these seven women, the interview transcripts were analyzed through quantitative coding and thematic analysis. In general, the responses could be organized into two dominant themes: the "good daughter/woman" ideal and domain-specific differential treatment.

"Good Daughter"

In general, these second-generation Indian daughters have to be *"good daughters."* This refers to the overwhelming theme among all interviews in which the daughters of these immigrant parents described feeling immensely responsible and dedicated to maintaining an image of adherence to family/community rules and traditions. Thus, these daughters describe feeling more responsible than their brothers, and in some cases having more responsibility expected of them by their parents. This was often reflected in the kinds of chores and behaviors performed by daughters, compared with their male siblings. For example, Priti always came home by her curfew, and helped her mother out around the house, worked hard to receive good grades in high school, and went on to attend a competitive university. These types of "good" behaviors were done voluntarily by Priti, rather than having to be coerced or rewarded. However, Priti explained that she knew that her younger brother did not seem to feel as conscientious as she did, and her parents ended up giving him money, privileges, and gifts as rewards for obtaining good grades and for doing chores such as mowing the lawn. For instance, although Priti did well in high school, which ensured that she got in to a competitive university, her parents offered her youngest brother a Honda Ninja motorcycle if he could manage to get a good SAT score and make himself eligible for college. When Priti complained to her parents that this seemed like a double standard, her parents said, "It's different for you and your brother. You didn't need to be motivated, but he did." This pattern is typical of most of the daughters we interviewed, and given that most daughters did not outwardly question why this difference in motivation existed between themselves and their brothers, this seems to be evidence of the extent to which daughters themselves internalized, and behaved according to, this ideal.

The "good daughter" complex could have deeper psychological consequences as well. In the interviews, the daughter is often viewed as the more responsible one of her siblings, and in some cases is even considered more likely to succeed in professional matters than her brothers. However, this seemed to create a sort of "burden of being the best," and many of the daughters we interviewed described spending quite a bit of time and energy living up to these standards, whether it be grades in school or maintaining the image of social obedience and chastity. Very few participants described any type of rebellion against these standards, and most actually very much wanted to live up to their parents' expectations. On the other hand, according to these women, this burden is not present for their brothers, and thus their brothers were described as being more casual about adhering to family expectations and rules.

Often the extent to which our participants themselves endorsed the "good daughter" persona was reflected through their statements concerning feelings of pride in their freedom to pursue high-status careers and to choose their own future mates. At the same time, many of their descriptions of "freedom" were coupled with intense pressure to always do well and succeed in school and careers, along with powerful social restrictions about who and when to marry, how to maintain the image of chastity in the public sphere, and the appropriate method of going out with friends or boys (usually by way of chaperones or constant checking with parents). In the case of one participant, Shobha, both parents and extended family members constantly referred to her as "setting the example." Throughout her interview, Shobha often described having to be a role model for everyone, including her female cousins and other community members, and she was often encouraged in her school work or social behaviors by reminders from her parents that she should not let people down. Even in the case of her father's family business, although Shobha's two younger brothers were pressured to continue in the business, her father expects Shobha to be the one to run it someday because, as she explained, "He thinks I am more responsible, so he expects the most from me ... I guess they think I have the most potential."

Although there is a "good son" archetype in the mythical story of the god Ram, who epitomized the "ideal son" by following his father's orders and going to the forest for 14 years, still, the "good son" ideal is related to the self-interest of the parents. The "good son" ideal highlights the filial obligations of the sons to take care of their parents in their old age. In a sense, the "good son" ideal is indirectly linked to, and controls, the psychological and social production of the "good woman" (i.e., through the good daughter-in-law, who takes care of her in-laws during their old age). This filial duty to the husband's parents is a crucial characteristic expected of the good daughter-in-law, and is examined by the family when selecting a suitable bride. Often as a result, in Indian cultural narratives, the daughter-in-law and mother-in-law conflicts occupy a legendary status (see Kakar, 1978).

In India, typically the wife moves in with her husband's family, and mothers-in-law are the major source of stress in the lives of newly-weds. Thus, selecting a partner for the son traditionally requires a careful weighing of various factors, such as whether the prospective bride will get along well with the parents, on top of compatibility between the bride and bridegroom. Because there are no Social Security benefits in India, how "accommodative" a daughter-in-law would be plays an important role in making decisions about choosing prospective daughters-in-law. Interestingly, even in the United States, where aging parents are not financially dependent on their offspring, we found that Indian immigrant parents hold on to their traditional beliefs about looking at the family history of the prospective brides (i.e., girlfriends of their sons). For example, in the case of Poonam, the reputation of her own mother and grandmother has become a problem in her current dating relationship. This concerns an incident that occurred several years ago but that is still known in the community.

When Poonam was younger, her parents were living with her widowed paternal grandmother and were planning a move to a new city. At the last minute, Poonam's grandmother decided that she couldn't leave the family house, which contained so many memories, and although she had committed to helping Poonam's parents put a down payment on the new house, she was backing out. This lead to an intense fight while Poonam was away at summer camp, and by the time she returned, her grandmother had moved out and gone to live with her father's sister. According to traditional Indian culture, having a mother leave her son's home and move in with her daughter is considered a culturally shameful event and reflects poorly on the entire family. In Poonam's case, apparently her grandmother complained to many community members (including Baljit, the woman whose son would later become Poonam's boyfriend) that she had left because Poonam's mother had given her father an ultimatum: Either he had to leave his mother, or his wife was leaving him. The idea that an Indian daughter-in-law would force such a confrontation between her husband and mother-in-law was shocking and extremely shameful, and this event caused a great deal of gossip in the community. Several years later, when Poonam began dating Baljit's son, Baljit became very upset and worried that Poonam came from a bad family, and that if the relationship got serious, Poonam would similarly "steal" her son from her. After relaying this story during the interview, Poonam revealed that recently, Baljit had called her on the phone and told her to stay away from her son. Although this seems to be an extreme case, it epitomizes the cultural theme of the mother-in-law versus daughter-in-law conflict, and highlights the ways in which expectations and demands are placed on girls not only by their own parents but also by the larger community, even after immigration to the new and distinct cultural context of the United States.

Differential Treatments

A secondary yet highly related theme involved the presence of certain types of domain-specific differential treatment of sons and daughters. Almost all participants reported some types of differential treatment in the realm of dating, marriage, curfews, and other social behaviors. However, this gendered set of rules and expectations did not seem to translate to the academic/career domain. In terms of college, expectations for grades, and careers, daughters were given equal opportunities and resources. At least as much, if not more, was expected of them compared with their brothers. In terms of the comparison between our participants and their brothers, for girls, dating was never explicitly allowed in high school; although this was sometimes the case for their brothers, often the rules had greatly relaxed by the time the male siblings reached dating age.

Concerning marriage, respondents often said that it was important to their parents that their brother marry a similar woman in terms of caste and religion, but this had to do less with him than with the expected role of his future wife. That is, the concern was that because a son didn't seem to always know enough about the culture and language (as compared with daughters, who almost always did), his future wife should be the "protector" and transmitter of cultural knowledge. Parents had other specific restrictions for their daughters' marriage prospects. Most participants described firm age expectations for when a daughter is too old to get married, the best time being between ages 23 and 28 years. In addition, it is important that the daughter be married before her brothers, a traditional belief still upheld in the postmigration context.

Some parents pushed for arranged marriage, but almost all settled for compromise, where they were allowed to introduce young men to their daughters. This concern highlights an issue of who the future spouse should be, and the fact that most daughters said their parents would be upset if matching traits such as race, religion, and caste weren't chosen in a marriage partner. This seemed to fall on a continuum, however, with some choices, such as Caucasian Americans, leading to only temporary disappointment, whereas others, notably Muslims or African Americans, might provoke outrage, lectures/arguments, and even "outcasting" or cutting off all contact. Several participants explained this by saying that basically the family was concerned with their potential mates being "respectable" according to the Punjabi community, and overall, this emphasis on the community's evaluation of the family, the children, their behaviors, and their achievements is another recurrent theme in the interviews. Although participants described this influence reaching all members of the community, it seemed that the burden of upholding community standards fell especially heavy on second-generation daughters, and several women explained that who they dated and married had to set an example for their brothers, cousins, and others in the community.

In terms of other social restrictions, parents were more restrictive when their children were in high school, but this was typically more the case for daughters than for their brothers. Often, our participants described having implicit curfews that meant they should be home by 10 or 11 p.m.; however they often related that their brothers, in many cases younger, typically stayed out until 2 or 3 a.m. and nothing seemed to happen to them. When asked why this difference existed, Shobha said that her parents know that her brothers are "just doing harmless things with friends, but they think I'm doing the wrong things." Despite this, Shobha reported that she can always stay out later if she is accompanied by a trusted male chaperone, such as a brother or a male cousin. This was also very common with our participants, even in cases where the chaperone was a younger brother, and even when parents had explicitly indicated that in other domains, such as school and work, the daughter was viewed as the more responsible one.

IMPLICATIONS FOR CULTURAL PSYCHOLOGY OF GENDER AND IMMIGRATION

We had two main goals for the qualitative study just described: (a) to investigate whether there was any systemic gender discrimination in the ways in which boys and girls were raised in immigrant Indian families, and (b) to examine whether idealized notions of gender did permeate various gender socialization practices among second-generation Indian American women. It is very encouraging to note that based on our interviews, we found that Indian immigrant parents were generally enthusiastic and supportive about their daughters going to school and pursuing a career. In this domain, the immigrant experience seems to have resulted in the better treatment of daughters and an equitable investment in their careers, in comparison to the growing problem of female feticide and neglect in various parts of India. Unlike in India, the daughters and sons growing up in the United States seem to get similar encouragement from their parents to succeed in schools and to pursue high status careers.

At the same time, however, the message in the social domain seems to be entirely different. Idealized gender identities play a pivotal role in shaping various aspects of gender socialization practices of these immigrants. Daughters described experiences full of implicit messages about being a "good daughter." Although this good daughter/woman ideal has roots in Indian culture, that ideal is carried over to the immigrant experience in the United States through control of social lives, community image, and sexuality of daughters. There seems to be some cultural continuity in the ways in which idealized cultural beliefs about gender control immigrant daughters' lives in the United States. More than for the sons, the chastity of these daughters seems to be strongly tied to the sense of family honor and respectability. This is reflected in the recurrent themes among our participants concerning anxiety that behaviors or decisions will bring shame to the family. In fact, the entire family plays a role in maintaining the daughter's purity, and even brothers are expected to chauffeur their sisters so that they do not engage in anything that might bring shame to the family.

Thus, our results suggest that culture works as a "residual" in selective and complicated ways. Indian immigrant parents seem to have disregarded traditional patterns of lower investment in the schooling and careers of daughters in favor of a more American-style emphasis on high achievement and financial independence; at the same time, however, they have retained the "good woman" ideal from Indian culture, and continue to value traditional social/sexual control over daughters even in the new, postmigration context. Further complicating the picture, however, were several instances in the narratives in which the daughters also found creative ways of negotiating the demands of the cultural ideals to exercise their own sense of agency.

In this study, we interviewed only second-generation female students. Given the content of many issues raised in these interviews, a promising future direction would be to follow up the study by also interviewing young men from Punjabi immigrant families. In addition, because several of our participants attend the same university as their brothers, and in some cases even share the same apartment at college, we are very interested in obtaining data from these brothers as well. Interviewing both brothers and sisters from the same families would provide a more full account of the process and the effects of gender socialization within the family.

This study focuses on the process underlying cultural beliefs, and how young women experience the impact of their family's immigration to a new cultural setting. This provides a useful starting point from which to construct a theoretical base for continuing work on gender and immigrants in the United States, as well as a glimpse into how the lives of second-generation immigrant women are shaped by the existence of these dual cultural contexts. For example, the "good daughter" theme seems to create a certain degree of stress among young women to live up to high expectations of both perfect academic/professional achievement and obedient, pious purity in the social/sexual realm. Based on this research, we became interested in examining the possible mental health implications of the strain caused by idealized gender beliefs such as "good daughter," as well as the "good son" ideals, and to investigate how relationships within the family are impacted by these expectations and resulting stress. To do so, we developed a Model Minority Scale (Mahalingam & Haritatos, under review-b) that tapped into various gendered aspects of idealized cultural identities rooted in the myth of Asian Americans as model minorities. The scale contains the following subscales: (a) model minority stereotype, (b) model minority male ideal, (c) model minority female ideal, (d) model minority pride, and (e) model minority pressure. We found that as a cultural ideal, the model minority ideal contributes to pride and pressure in gender-specific ways. Women who endorsed the model minority female ideal also experienced pride and pressure, and pride and pressure negatively and positively contributed to depression, respectively. The findings were consistent with the dual pathways to mental health as delineated in the ICI model.

The converging evidence suggests that social positioning of Asian American women leaves them in a unique predicament. On the one hand, these women hail from a culture that favors sons. There is enormous social pressure on them to be successful and prove themselves against various forms of differential treatment. Being viewed as a "model minority," Asian immigrant women (both first and second generations) also face the burden of "carrying their cultures." In addition, as minority women, they also often have to position their gender identity in opposition to "White" women (Constable, 2003; Espiritu, 2001; Mahalingam & Leu, 2005). Thus Asian American women face a *triple predicament*—they need to confront the gender discrimination within their ethnic group, the gender discrimination as minority women, and the pressure to uphold the "purity" of their culture, which contrasts them with "cultureless White women." Such multiple intersections of marginalized gender experiences affect Asian American women's lives in complex ways. The psychological well-being of these women also seems to depend on how they negotiate the competing demands of these cultural ideals in various aspects of their lives. However, individual difference factors such as optimism and resilience may also shape the various pathways to successfully negotiating the positive and negative consequences of internalizing cultural identities, and these individual characteristics have not been examined in relation to idealized identity constructs. In addition, the developmental changes involved in transmission and internalization of cultural ideals need to be examined to identify various developmental trajectories to successful negotiation of idealized cultural identities.

In summary, we set out to propose a cultural psychology of gender perspective to study immigrants. We proposed, and found support for, the notion that idealized cultural identities play a critical role in the life experiences and psychological well being of Asian immigrant women. However, although researchers from the disciplines of anthropology and sociology have examined the complex relationship between ethnic identity and gender and its impact on men and women's lives, very little cultural psychological work has investigated issues surrounding the role of idealized identities among immigrants. We suggest, then, that cultural psychology needs to adopt an interdisciplinary framework using a variety of methods to investigate how intersections of culture, ethnicity, immigrant generation, and social class influence the production, transmission, and internalization of various cultural ideals, and the complex realities of how intersecting identities have unique effects on the psychological well-being of immigrant women and men. Such a task would enable us to begin the important work of identifying meaningful cultural psychological antecedents to immigrant mental health.

While working on this project, we often talked about our own intersecting social identities. Ram is a first-generation immigrant who comes from a small town in India. He is the first generation in his family who went to college. Prior to immigration, he led a more or less "cultureless" life because he did not need to have a reflective understanding of his "culture." Jana comes from a small Midwestern town in the United States, although her paternal grandfather and great-grandparents immigrated to the United States from Greece. She is also married to a Malaysian Chinese immigrant. By appearance, though, she could pass for a "cultureless White" woman. In formulating this work, we often talked about the axes of privileges (gender and ethnicity) and axes of marginality (ethnicity and gender) of our identities, circumscribed by the various complex relational and situational aspects of our lives. We indeed pursued a line of research that examined many of our assumptions and "learned wisdoms" about gender, culture, and immigration. We were often overwhelmed by the realization that embodiment of social experiences at the intersections of race, class, ethnicity, and gender has complex consequences and by the immensely challenging task of developing a sophisticated understanding of these consequences. We believe, however, that pursuing such a challenge is critical and would greatly vitalize the relevance of cultural psychology for the study of gender and immigration in the new millennium.

REFERENCES

Barnes, J. S., & Bennett, C. E. (2002). *The Asian population: 2000.* Retrieved January 30, 2006 from the U.S. Census Bureau, Department of Commerce News Web site: http://www.census.gov/prod/2002pubs/c2kbr01-16.pdf

Best, D. L., & Williams, J. E. (1997). Sex, gender and culture. In J. W. Berry, M. H. Segall, & C. Kagitcibasi (Eds.), *Handbook of cross-cultural psychology* (Vol. 3, pp. 163–212). Boston: Allyn Bacon.

Constable, N. (2003). *Romance on a global stage.* Berkeley: University of California Press.

Dasgupta, S., & Dasgupta, S. D. (2000). Women in exile: Gender relations in the Asian American community in the United States. In J. Yu-wen Shen & M. Song (Eds.), *Asian American studies: A reader* (pp. 324–337). New Brunswick, NJ: Rutgers University Press.

Espín, O. M. (1999). *Women crossing boundaries: A psychology of immigration and transformations of sexuality.* New York: Routledge.

Espiritu, Y. (2001). "We don't sleep around like White girls do." Family, culture and gender in Filipina American lives. *Signs, 26*(2), 415–440.

Hondagneu-Sotelo, P. (1994). *Gendered transitions.* Berkeley.: University of California Press.

Hudson, V. M., & den Boer, A. M. (2004). *Bare branches: The security implications of Asia's surplus male population.* Cambridge, MA: MIT Press.

Kakar, S. (1978). *The inner world: A psycho-analytic study of childhood and society in India.* New Delhi, India: Oxford University Press.

Lakshmi, C. S. (1984). *Face beind the mask.* Delhi, India: Vikas.

Lindisfarne, N. (1998). Gender, shame, and culture: An anthropological perspective. In P. Gilbert (Ed.), *Shame: Interpersonal behavior, psychopathology, and culture* (pp. 246–260). New York: Oxford University Press.

Mahalingam, R. (under review). *Beliefs about chastity, masculinity and caste identity.*

Mahalingam, R., & Haritatos, J. (under review-a). *Cultural psychology and gender: A cultural ecological intersectionality perspective.*

Mahalingam, R., & Haritatos, J. (under review-b). *Model minority myth: Engendering cultural psychology of Asian immigrants.*

Mahalingam, R., & Jackson, B. (under review). *Idealized gender beliefs, self appraisals and mental health: The Idealized Cultural Identities model.*

Mahalingam, R., & Leu, J. (2005). Culture, essentialism, immigration and representations of gender. *Theory and Psychology, 15*(6), 841–862..

Ortner, S. (1974). Is male to female as nature is to culture? In M. Rosaldo & L. Lamphere (Eds.), *Woman, culture, and society* (pp. 67–88). Stanford, CA: Stanford University Press.

Roland, A. (1988). *In search of self in India and Japan.* Princeton, NJ: Princeton University Press.

Schaffer, H. R. (1996). *Social development.* Malden, MA: Blackwell.

Shah, S. (1994). Presenting the blue goddess: Toward a national, Pan-Asian feminist agenda. In K. A.-S. Juan (Ed.), *The state of Asian America: Activism and resistance in the 1990s* (pp. 147–158). Boston: South End.

Stewart, A. J., & McDermott, C. (2004). Gender in psychology. *Annual Review Psychology, 55,* 519–544.

Wadley, S. (1991). The paradoxical powers of Tamil women. In S. Wadley (Ed.), *The powers of the Tamil women* (pp. 153–167). Syracuse, NY: Syracuse University.

Part IV

Immigration and Family

15

Conceptual and Research Considerations in the Determinants of Child Outcomes Among English-Speaking Caribbean Immigrants in the United States: A Cultural-Ecological Approach

Jaipaul L. Roopnarine
Ambika Krishnakumar
Syracuse University

During the last three decades, there have been sharp increases in population movement from the Caribbean to North America and Europe. In certain cases, the number of people who migrated from Caribbean countries to postindustrialized societies constitutes a significant portion of the sending country's entire population. For example, between 1981 and 2002, approximately 187,600 individuals immigrated from Guyana to the United States, which amounts to roughly a quarter of Guyana's current population of about 750,000 people. As can be gleaned from Fig. 15.1, Cuba, the Dominican Republic, Haiti, Ja-

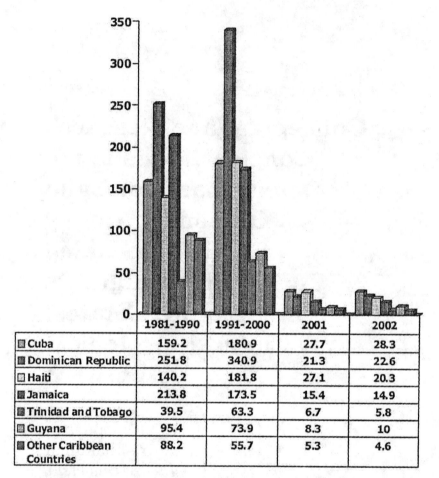

	1981-1990	1991-2000	2001	2002
▣ Cuba	159.2	180.9	27.7	28.3
▣ Dominican Republic	251.8	340.9	21.3	22.6
▢ Haiti	140.2	181.8	27.1	20.3
▣ Jamaica	213.8	173.5	15.4	14.9
▣ Trinidad and Tobago	39.5	63.3	6.7	5.8
▣ Guyana	95.4	73.9	8.3	10
▣ Other Caribbean Countries	88.2	55.7	5.3	4.6

FIG. 15.1.   Immigrants to the United States during 1981–2002 (in thousands). Data from U.S. Department of Homeland Security, 2002 Yearbook of Immigrant Statistics.

maica, and Trinidad and Tobago show similar trends and are also the origins of sizable numbers of immigrants to the United States. A majority of the immigrants tend to be relatively young, below 50 years of age, and have attained only a high school education or below (see Figs. 15.2 and 15.3). Despite their low levels of educational attainment upon arrival, several accounts suggest that Caribbean immigrants have done well economically when compared to other immigrant and ethnic groups in the United States (Kasinitz, 2001; Roopnarine & Shin, 2003). Although demographically they are a sizable group in the United States, very little is known about the social and psychological aspects of the lives of Caribbean immigrants.

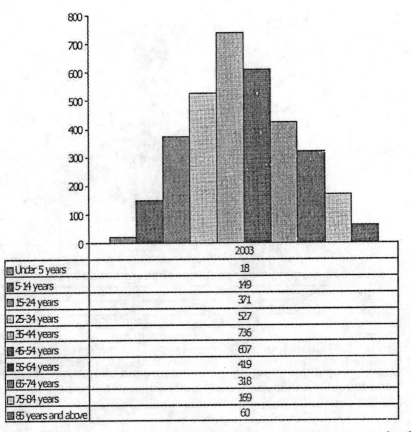

FIG. 15.2. Age groups of foreign-born Caribbean immigrants (naturalized citizens, legal permanent residents, temporary migrants, refugees, and people illegally present in the United States) in 2003. Numbers in thousands. Data from U.S. Census Bureau, Current Population Reports, P20-551.

This chapter has its genesis in attempts to bridge our own experiences as immigrants who have studied and remained in the United States to pursue research and teaching careers and a desire to contribute to a better understanding of key psychological factors that may help to define the experiences and daily lives of immigrants in general, and Caribbean immigrants more specifically. That is, we aim to further unravel the developmental changes that presumably occur in different domains of families' lives as they move from one cultural community to another. On the one hand, we have personally dealt with issues of acculturation, identity confusion, alienation, discrimination, and anti-immigrant sentiments, as well as encountered tremendous opportunities to realize our educational and career goals. On the other hand, as we spend time in immigrant communities, particularly in the

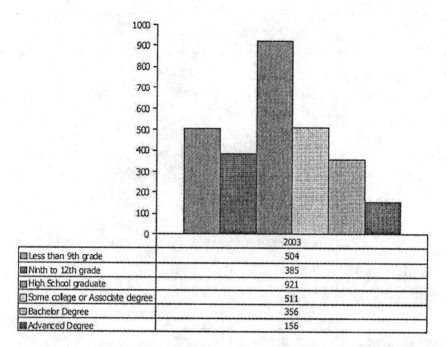

	2003
▦ Less than 9th grade	504
▨ Ninth to 12th grade	385
▩ High School graduate	921
☐ Some college or Associate degree	511
▤ Bachelor Degree	356
▦ Advanced Degree	156

FIG. 15.3. Education level of foreign-born Caribbean immigrants (naturalized citizens, legal permanent residents, temporary migrants, refugees, and people illegally present in the United States) 25 years and older in 2003. Numbers in thousands. Data from U.S. Census Bureau, Current Population Reports, P20-551.

New York City area, we come face to face with the complex mix of achievements and challenges that characterize the experiences of Caribbean immigrants in the United States. Using a cultural-ecological approach, our aim in this chapter is to accomplish two primary objectives: (a) piece together what we know about some of the contextual and familial factors that are central to the mental health and psychological well-being of English-speaking Caribbean immigrants, and (b) discuss conceptual and methodological issues that may enhance our research understanding of their psychological and social functioning.

PSYCHOLOGICAL FUNCTIONING AND THE FAMILY

Obviously it would be difficult to cover the multitude of social and psychological factors that may contribute to the mental health and overall well-being of Caribbean immigrant families in this chapter. Nor is there much empirical data on these domains of family functioning among Caribbean immigrants. Thus, we focus on a few issues that have been identified by others (e.g., Arnold, 1997; Fuligni, 2001, 2003;

Gopaul-McNicol, 1993) and what we deem is of particular relevance to the organization of Caribbean immigrant family life postimmigration: husband–wife/partner relationships, socialization and childrearing practices, separation from and reunification with parents, and ethnic identity. As has been acknowledged by several researchers (e.g., Foner, 2001; Fuligni, 2001, 2003; Phinney. 2003; Roopnarine & Shin, 2003), the immigration process is not static; it involves periods of continuity and discontinuity in family functioning with the eventual goal of striking an adaptive balance between intrapersonal and interpersonal relationships and the quest to meet the social and material needs of the family. Additionally, population movement assumes different patterns (serial, stair-step process, familial, transnational movement, etc.), necessitating diverse adjustment strategies and coping skills (see Berry, 1998; Duany, 1994; Roopnarine, Bynoe, & Singh, 2004). There are continuing disagreements about whether changes that accompany population movements are unidirectional or bidirectional, encompassing a network of interrelated factors and processes (Best-Cummings & Gildner, 2004; Fuligni, 2001, 2003; Roopnarine et al., 2004). Because of the heterogeneity in ethnic and linguistic groups in the English-speaking Caribbean, whenever possible, we refer to familial processes that relate to specific ethnic groups.

HUSBAND–WIFE/PARTNER RELATIONSHIPS

Perhaps one of the most emotionally laden of all human relationships, the marital or couple/partner relationship exerts major influences on family stability, parent–child interactions, and child development outcomes (see Cummings, Goeke-Morey, & Raymond, 2004). Notably, the psychological functioning of each individual, commitment to the couple/partner relationship, economic resources, and gendered ideologies determine pair-bond stability and the degree of efficiency in childrearing (see Belsky, Steinberg, & Draper, 1993; McLoyd, 1998). How these variables affect the nature of the diverse patterns of couple/partner relationships among Caribbean immigrants is a matter of conjecture at this point. Nevertheless, stability and instability in couple/partner relationships are likely to be influenced by challenges to natal traditions, beliefs and practices, and customs about the formation and dynamics of couple/partner relationships.

In the Caribbean, mate-shifting is a prevalent practice among African Caribbean families (see Brown, Newland, Anderson, & Chevannes, 1997; Senior, 1991), whereas more traditional forms of marriage are evident among Indo Caribbean and Chinese Caribbean families (see Roopnarine, 2004; Roopnarine, Bynoe, Singh, & Simon, 2005; Smith, 1996). The relationship patterns for individuals with mixed ethnic ancestry or couples from different ethnic backgrounds are unclear. Generally speaking, it appears that marital/relationship patterns found in the Caribbean may be maintained for

Caribbean immigrants in the United States (Grasmuck & Grosfoguel, 1997; Roopnarine, 1999).

Emerging out of traditional beliefs about husband–wife/partner relationships and roles, gendered ideologies drive the nature and quality of the relationships between African Caribbean and Indo Caribbean immigrant men and women (see Roopnarine, 2004; Roopnarine & Evans, in press). Possibly because of Hindu religious doctrines that reinforce the differential roles of men and women and the socialization of boys and girls in the Caribbean (see Roopnarine & Evans, in press), Indo Caribbean men largely see themselves in a hierarchical position in the couple relationship. In an interview study of Indo Caribbean immigrants residing in the New York City area, men (98% married) overwhelmingly endorsed the position that they are the heads of their households, the main breadwinner, and that women were largely responsible for caring for children, even in cases where the woman was better educated and earned more than the man (Roopnarine, 1999). Likewise, in a large-scale survey of African Caribbean immigrants in the northeastern United States, there was evidence that men subscribed to the double standard in male–female relationships (sexual exclusivity, loyalty, obedience) that is ingrained in Caribbean societies (Millette, 1998). At the same time, both Indo Caribbean and African Caribbean women in the United States were more in sync with the values and norms of the host society, which emphasized the equal rights of individuals in relationships, and they were dismayed at their husband's/partner's perceptions of women in and out of couple relationships (Millette, 1998; Roopnarine, 1999). Undoubtedly, traditional views about male domination and gender roles vary among Caribbean immigrants and are modulated by social location and educational attainment. Lack of synchrony in gender role expectations in Caribbean couples can have implications for the physical and mental health of family members.

Taking into consideration the dearth of data on the internal dynamics of couple/partner relationships in Caribbean families, we offer some speculations as to how the couple relationship can affect the mental health and personal well-being of Caribbean immigrants. Our suggestions are located in work conducted in other cultures and on practices within couple relationships in families in the Caribbean. Among African Caribbean couples/partners, mate-shifting has been known to cause jealousy and gender mistrust (see Brody, 1981; Flinn, 1992; Wedenoja, 1989). However, a deeper problem for Caribbean immigrant couples/partners is that temporary relationships with multiple partners and high-risk sexual behaviors may contribute to the spread of HIV/AIDS. Heterosexual contact is the predominant mode of transmission of HIV/AIDS among women, and Black women make up the largest group infected (DHHS, 2000). People of Caribbean ancestry constitute one of the largest HIV/AIDS-infected immigrant groups in New York City (see Spooner, Daniel, & Mahoney, 2004, for a discussion of HIV/AIDS and Caribbean immigrants).

The dominant role presumed by men may be in opposition to women's increasing need to express their individuality and sense of equality in their new cultural community. Because they are in direct contrast to cultural beliefs about women's roles in the Caribbean, expressions of independence and individuality on the part of women may lead to spousal/partner conflicts and psychological tensions (see Herman, 2004). Arguably, this may be more pronounced for Indo Caribbean than for African Caribbean immigrant women, who historically have had little latitude to express their sexuality, individual rights, and need for equality in the marriage pre-immigration. Domestic violence, partner abuse, and rates of community violence are serious concerns among Caribbean families (see Haniff, 1998; Prasad, 1999; Soyibo & Lee, 2000), and immigrant women may be less inclined to report domestic abuse because of legal status or lack of community resources (see Spooner et al., 2004). Instability in the husband–wife/partner relationship (Wilson & Brooks-Gunn, 2001), distrust, jealousy, fear of abandonment (Holden & Barker, 2004), and patriarchal attitudes toward women (misogynistic attitudes) that entail having power and dominance over them (Graham-Berman & Brescoll, 2000) have all been linked to domestic violence. The impact of marital/couple tensions and conflicts and domestic violence on the mental health and well-being of women and men (e.g., Cummings et al., 2004; Holden & Barker, 2004) and children (e.g., Davies & Cummings, 1994) has been well documented across cultural groups in the United States. There is no reason to believe that the negative consequences of domestic violence and family conflicts may not generalize to Caribbean immigrant families.

PATTERNS OF SOCIALIZATION AND CHILDREARING

Recent reviews (Roopnarine et al., 2005; Roopnarine & Evans, in press) of patterns of socialization and childrearing beliefs and practices among English-speaking Caribbean families highlight three salient features: a prevalence of an autocratic parenting style, punitive methods of childrearing, and unrealistic developmental expectations of young children. These issues and their effects on the development and well-being of young children are examined next.

Parenting Styles

In the Caribbean, low-income mothers and fathers are more apt to use an authoritarian parenting style (see Leo-Rhynie, 1997). This method of childrearing is devoid of two-way verbal exchanges (Meeks-Gardner, Grantham-McGregor, Himes, & Chang, 1999) and emotional closeness (see Leo-Rhynie, 1997). By comparison, an authoritative parenting style, characterized by more democratic principles in childrearing, is more prevalent among middle and upper socioeconomic status families (Payne & Furnham, 1992; Ramkissoon, 2001). The limited database on parenting styles among Caribbean immigrant families in the United States permits few, if any, conclusive statements about modes of childrearing. DeYoung and Zigler (1994) found that Indo Guyanese parents in Newark, New Jersey, reported using a more authoritarian style in parenting that was more controlling and less nurturant than Caucasian families did. By contrast, our own work on academic socialization among a diverse group of families in the New York City area indicated that mothers and fathers preferred an authoritative over a permissive or authoritarian style of parenting (Roopnarine, Krishnakumar, Metindogan, & Evans, 2005).

Although some research shows differential outcomes of parenting styles based on ethnicity (see Leung, Lau, & Lam, 1998; Steinberg, Dornbusch, & Brown, 1992), we found that among Caribbean immigrants an authoritarian parenting style suppresses academic growth in the area of language development and that the authoritative style supports the growth of social skills that are expected of Caribbean children (e.g., obedience, compliance) (Roopnarine, Krishnakumar, Metindogan, & Evans, 2005). Basically, this finding is in accord with the assumption that an authoritative parenting style fosters cognitive and social competence in children (see Baumrind, 1967). Are Caribbean immigrant families changing their internal working models about parenting styles as they confront other methods of childrearing in their new cultural communities? Or could it be that previous research confounded parenting styles, social class, and ethnicity? Answers to these questions may partially lie in parents' opinions about and the use of physical punishment during everyday socialization.

HARSH DISCIPLINARY PRACTICES

That Caribbean adults use physical punishment regularly in the home and school contexts has been demonstrated in several studies (Anderson & Payne, 1994; Arnold, 1982; Rohner, Kean, & Cournoyer, 1991). Further, the negative consequences of harsh discipline on children's psychosocial functioning are detailed in a recent meta-analysis of studies on physical punishment (Gershoff, 2002), and the connection between domestic violence and physical/harsh discipline in childrearing has been borne out in research investigations (see Holden & Barker, 2004). Do Caribbean immigrant parents change their beliefs about physical punishment when they live in a society that discourages it?

Returning to our study on academic socialization among Caribbean immigrants, we asked parents about the use of physical punishment in disciplining children. Most parents endorsed the use of physical punishment and reported employing it in dealing with children's misbehaviors and social transgressions (Roopnarine, 1999). Similarly, Indo Guyanese immigrants had higher rates of scolding and physical punishment than Caucasian families did (DeYoung &

Zigler, 1994). These beliefs and practices tend to suggest that a key tenet of socialization practices in the Caribbean remains with immigrants as they confront more democratic principles in childrearing in their new communities. Inflexible and harsh parenting practices in Caribbean immigrant families may cause children to rebel or become disobedient, which, in turn, may lead to abandonment of children or children running away from home. Despair and depression are not unusual among Caribbean immigrant mothers who find out that harsh discipline may result in childhood difficulties (see Arnold, 1997; Rambally, 1995).

DEVELOPMENTAL EXPECTATIONS

Anthropological and sociological studies suggest that English-speaking Caribbean parents have unrealistic expectations of children (see Leo-Rhynie, 1997) and that they rank obedience and compliance as the "most desired" characteristics of children (Durbrow, 1999; Wilson, Wilson, & Berkeley-Caines, 2003). They also stress academic training early in children's lives and seem less impressed with the importance accorded play in early childhood development (see Grantham-McGregor, Landman, & Desai, 1983). Do these ethnotheories about childhood development and schooling become modified as Caribbean immigrant parents become immersed in life in the United States? How do they influence the early schooling of children of Caribbean immigrants?

Once again, we refer to our on data on English-speaking Caribbean immigrants (Roopnarine, Krishnakumar, Metindogan, & Evans, 2005) who, at the time of data collection, had resided on average about 13 years in the United States. A few key themes emerged regarding parental beliefs about childhood development: With few exceptions, mothers and fathers from different socioeconomic backgrounds indicated that it was appropriate to require preschool-aged children to do homework; the role of play as an important factor in childhood social and cognitive development received some support among parents; and the psychological role of parents in influencing children's well-being was rarely mentioned.

Belief theorists (see Siegel & McGilliCiuddy-DeLisi, 2002; Super & Harkness, 1997) argue that parental ideas about childhood care and development have direct and indirect outcomes for school achievement and behavior. Such beleifs also influence the structuring of everyday settings and experiences for children (Super & Harkness, 1997). In view of these claims, how do Caribbean immigrant parents engage themselves in the early schooling process? Congruent with their beliefs, both mothers and fathers were quite involved in selecting and enrolling their children in private schools that emphasize strong discipline and early academic training, and they spent on average 8.21 and 7.83 hours each week in educational activities with children, respectively (Roopnarine et al., 2005). Does this amount to "hothousing" or pressuring children to achieve early in life, placing them at risk for difficulties later in their school careers? Caribbean immigrant parents see the early emphasis on strong academic training as necessary during a "sensitive period"—the preschool years—when children are in a position to learn the academic and social skills necessary for school success. This view is in direct contrast to the position espoused by the National Association for the Education of Young Children (NAEYC) (Bredekamp & Copple, 1997) and raises questions about so-called "expert knowledge" concerning what is developmentally appropriate for different immigrant groups (see LeVine, 2004). So far, studies show that children's early academic group performance on standardized tests is at or above average (Roopnarine, Krishnakumar, Metindogan, & Evans, 2005) and may be a reflection of parents' rigorous early investment in children's academic training. Less is known about behavioral difficulties such as bed-wetting, teeth-grinding, and the like that may result from early academic pressures.

SEPARATION AND REUNIFICATION

As noted earlier, different migratory patterns place divergent adjustments and coping demands on families. Although a good number of Caribbean families migrate as a unit, others engage in a serial migration process where individual members migrate without family members to a postindustrialized country directly or in a stair-step manner to a neighboring country with better economic opportunities first, before migrating to a postindustrialized country. This phenomenon is experienced worldwide as increasing numbers of parents leave children behind in search of economic opportunities in other countries (e.g., Bangladeshis, East Indians, and Egyptians who work in the oil-rich nations of the middle-east). Arnold (1997) and Suarez-Orozco and Todorova (2001) estimated that Caribbean immigrant families from different linguistic backgrounds who migrate in a serial pattern are separated from family members on average a little over 5 years. Of interest here are the difficulties in familial processes associated with separation and reunion inherent in serial and stair-step migration patterns.

A highly reputable body of work indicates that the consistent, reliable, and predictable pattern of relationship with a primary caregiver is important for the development of parent–child attachment bonds and subsequent relationships with other individuals (see Ainsworth & Bowlby, 1991). In other words, the history of care a child receives predicts patterns of social adjustment and maladjustment with diverse individuals, and this is true across a number of cultural groups (see Grossman, Grossman, & Keppler, 2005). Although child-shifting is a common practice in the Caribbean (see Crawford-Brown, 1997), the number of times children are shifted and the nature of the social contacts they have with mothers are correlated with behavioral difficulties among adolescents (Russell-Brown, Norville, & Griffith, 1997). But child-shifting occurs for different reasons (e.g., when parents enter a new romantic relationship, migration, economic reasons, fosterage) and in some cases may involve normative transition from one family member to the next with only minor difficulties. The problem with serial migration is that children enter into a protracted cycle of separation and reunion from different attachment figures without full knowledge of when they will sever ties with substitute caregivers and join their biological caregivers again. In the intervening years, children are expected to plod ahead, maintaining strong bonds to parents while developing affective and social ties to new caregivers.

Major concerns about migratory patterns that leave children behind with the explicit assumption that they will be reunited with parents at a later date are: the quality of contacts parents have with children after separation, the affective relationships children develop with new caregivers, and the ability of parents to integrate children into their families upon reunification. No consensus has been reached on the frequency or quality of contacts Caribbean immigrant parents have with children who are left behind. Similarly, the emerging relationships children have with their new caregivers have not been the focus of systematic investigations despite their far-reaching significance for children's mental health, physical health, and well-being. A panel convened in Barbados in the summer of 2003 concluded that parents had increasing contacts with children via a process termed "transnational parenting" (Salandy, 2003). Clearly, contacts with children were insufficient as children continued to mourn silently for their parent(s) (Crawford-Brown, 1999). At the moment, these "barrel children," as they are pejoratively termed, elude the interests of social scientists.

In terms of reunification, Arnold's (1997; Robertson, 1975) research revealed that some Caribbean immigrant parents in England encountered difficulties in integrating children into their families because of rigid parenting styles, cultural conflicts, disappointment with parents' own economic and social standing, and parents' psychological functioning (see also Baptiste, Hardy, & Lewis, 1997). On occasion the "reconnection process" took a turn for the worse once parents became more cognizant of the transitional difficulties. When children became distraught, withdrawn, and resentful, the frustration that began to set in caused some parents to withdraw affection from children; others experienced depression (Arnold, 1997; Cheetham, 1972). Entering new relationships that produce offspring, a practice that is not uncommon among Caribbean immigrants, can also compound transitional difficulties for the entire family.

ETHNIC IDENTITY

Because they are immigrants of color, ethnic identity defines and shapes major components of the lives of Caribbean immigrants and their children. It affects the quality of education children receive, access to health and mental health services, types of employment and business opportunities, and where people live (see Bayne-Smith, Graham, Mason, & Drossman, 2004; Campbell & McLean, 2002; Francis, 1993; Roopnarine et al., 2004; Vickerman, 2001). Just as children do, adult Caribbean immigrants face the dilemma of negotiating cultural identities. African Caribbean immigrants see themselves as distinct from other ethnic groups of color in the United States. Yet they have to grapple with what being designated "Black" means, because it has traditionally referred to African Americans who have experienced oppression over several centuries. African Caribbean families are aware of the costs of being "Black" in American society (see Waters, 1999) and must contend with the issue of where and how minority status intersects with their ethnicity. Indo Caribbean immigrants too must decide whether to identify as East Indians, even though Indians from India often display a supercilious attitude toward them in America. Prior to migration, their ethnic identity may not have been an issue for either group.

Admittedly, adults have firmer beliefs about their ethnic identity and are in a better position to understand the values and experiences that shaped and continue to shape those beliefs than children do. A challenge for children is to effectively combine or alternate between the values and beliefs of at least two different cultural communities (Phinney, 2003; Phinney & Devich-Navarro, 1997). In the process of developing themselves, young children of immigrants and immigrant children have to negotiate their way through beliefs about childhood, identity, and childrearing from the parental culture and those present in their new environment. To complicate matters further, they may be called on to serve as cultural brokers for adults. Needless to say, this can heighten the challenges associated with developing a cultural identity.

It is our hunch that ethnic identity is far more complex than simply negotiating two cultural traditions. Given the multicultural complexion of our democracy, it may be that we are at an interesting crossroad where children in general are beginning to blend different cultural elements to fuse an understanding of who they are. This is quite evident in our conversations with Indo Caribbean immigrant youth in New York City, where they proclaim that they "borrow" distinct styles of behavior from Hispanic and African American youth. Adding complexity to the process of developing an identity is the fact that Caribbean immigrant parents and children live transnational lives—moving freely between the Caribbean and North America. In other words, they accept both cultural communities as central to their existence, and, therefore may attenuate potential stress or confusion associated with the primacy of one set of cultural values over the other.

CARIBBEAN IMMIGRANTS IN THE UNITED STATES: SETTING PRIORITIES IN RESEARCH UNDERSTANDING

Lumping Caribbean immigrants as a single group in research investigations would essentially disregard the heterogeneity that exists by country of origin (e.g., Jamaica, Trinidad and Tobago, Guyana) and ethnicity (e.g., Afro-Caribbean, Indo-Caribbean, Chinese-Caribbean etc.). Family researchers and developmentalists (e.g., Gopaul-McNichol, 1993; Roopnarine et al., 2004; Roopnarine, Bynoe, Singh, & Simon, 2005) who study Caribbean immigrant families support the premise that the nature, beliefs, and meanings that specific cultures attribute to child development are indeed unique and are primarily a reflection of a culture's traditions and ethos suggesting an emic approach to research conceptualizations. Cross-cultural scholars (see Greenfield, 1997, for a review of cultural and cross-cultural frameworks) have opined that several characteristics of childhood development are universal, fundamental to human existence, and shared among different cultures, essentially transcending the uniqueness of race, culture, and geographic location, supporting an etic approach. In this segment of the chapter, we propose that studies on Caribbean immigrant families should reflect a blend of both these approaches. Although cultural and ecological differences exist in ways in which researchers have interpreted the nature of family life across and within various Caribbean immigrant families, we suggest that much is to be learned from a combination of the specificity of family life within Caribbean immigrant groups and the elements of Caribbean immigrant family life that are generalizable across other immigrant families.

Many of the challenges linked to acculturation and ethnic identity may be common across immigrant groups, but some, such as school failure and nonmarital childbearing, are somewhat higher for Caribbean immigrant families compared to other immigrant groups (e.g., Asian immigrants). Parenting outside of marriage should be understood alongside the strengths and protective factors unique to Caribbean immigrant families that enable their successful adjustment (e.g., extended kin networks) and those that they share with other immigrant groups (e.g., hard work). Much of the current scholarship on Caribbean immigrant families has been shaped by descriptive accounts of family life and has not been informed by systematic analytic frameworks. Beyond the qualitative accounts of family life that explore the adaptation of Caribbean American families and children, future investigations call for contextually and culturally sensitive approaches with rigorous quantitative model testing that enables researchers to investigate both pathways of influence and conditionalizing effects (see Fig. 15.4). Accordingly, we present suggestions for future research in this

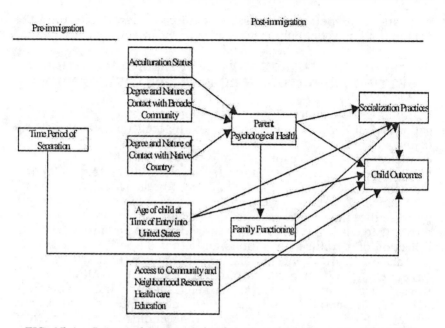

FIG. 15.4.   Proposed conceptual cultural-ecological model on factors impacting child outcomes in Caribbean immigrant families.

area, and draw on examples from current findings on Caribbean families to substantiate our points.

A common limitation in studies of immigrant families is how the term *acculturation* has been understood. Researchers have traditionally used the length of stay in the United States as a measure of "Americanization" and have associated longer duration of residence in the United States with socioeconomic gains and the adoption of values and norms that resemble American society (see Rumbaut, 1997, and Zhou, 1997, for discussions of the assimilationist view). However, in several investigations with Caribbean immigrant families (e.g., Roopnarine, Krishnakumar, Metindogan, & Evans, 2005), the length of stay in the United States is considered a poor measure of acculturation and is weakly associated with various family and child outcome measures. The conceptualization of the term *acculturation* is currently not captured by the *operationalization* of the construct, which should move beyond either "length of stay" or "fluency in speaking English" to include multiple markers of successful adaptation (e.g., job security, economic mobility etc.). Furthermore, greater attention needs to be paid to what is meant by the term *American culture*. American society is far too complex to be considered wholistic. Rather, it represents a macrocosm of values and traditions from the various ethnic and immigrant groups in this country. An operationalization of acculturation that captures these complexities will most likely be found to be a strong predictor of family life, socialization practices, and child outcomes.

Tied to acculturation are the preimmigration histories of families. Indeed, the cultural histories of various Caribbean groups are different (indentured labor or enslaved persons or voluntary immigration) and may be instrumental in shaping current family life and individual development (Gopaul-McNicol, 1993). Some good examples include separation of adults and children during migration, parenting practices, emphasis on early educational training, beliefs about parental involvement with schools, spousal/partner relationships, and gendered ideologies. These factors represent a blend of African and Indian traditions and customs and cultural, social, political, religious, and educational practices imposed by European colonizers. As immigrant life proceeds in the new culture, it is likely that aspects of family functioning may undergo significant transformations. The extent of the transformations in various aspects of family life could be determined by the degree and nature of contact with the host society and its institutions, the degree to which families have contacts with their countries of origin, their preimmigration experiences, and cultural, religious, and racial norms. Therefore, studies of acculturation of Caribbean immigrants should incorporate the cultural norms and social patterns of behaviors in the countries of origin, the nature and degree of change from their native culture, and the concept of what it means to be "American." At minimum, this would require a partialing of developmental changes inherent in life course transitions from changes that may be attributed to the immigration process itself (see Fuligni, 2003; Phinney, 2003).

As mentioned earlier, there is a need for researchers to incorporate contextually and culturally sensitive frameworks when investigating issues of child and family development in Caribbean families. Toward this end, researchers have continually weighed the theoretical stance of cross-cultural generalizations involving issues of conceptualization, operationalization, and propositions against the need for unique theoretical frameworks and measurement strategies within specific cultures. When focusing on generalizability across Caribbean groups and between Caribbean and other immigrant groups, the examination of cultural generality should be understood within the framework of measurement equivalence. Cross-cultural studies on socialization have been critiqued for bringing in Western philosophies and applying them to other cultures without examining their applicability in other cultural contexts. Thus, several theoretical and methodological issues should be taken into consideration when implementing investigations of cross-cultural generalizability. Four aspects of measurement equivalence should be addressed.

1. First, *conceptual equivalence* proposes that the definition and meaning of the various aspects of socialization should be understood within the frame of the specific culture. Definitions for socialization, for example, cannot be assumed to be similar across the Caribbean. African Caribbean parenting behaviors may have different meanings than those of Indo Caribbean socialization behaviors.

2. Next, *operational equivalence* proposes that children in different cultures respond to the same item similarly. Hence, instruments or observational methods should be similar in content (e.g., meaning of terms) and have similar response scales. It is here that the major weaknesses of cross-cultural research are most evident. Questionnaires are applied with translations to other cultures without assessment of their validity and reliability in different cultures. Back-translations of instruments will not suffice. Using appropriate cultural phrases, words, speech patterns, and meanings should be incorporated within measurement of constructs. Literacy levels of families, cultural mores and practices, place of administration (which may vary within the culture; e.g., in many Caribbean families children may be the primary responsibility of women and interviews or questionnaires may need to take place at the respondent's home), and methods used (interview, questionnaire, observation) are integral to assuring operational equivalence.

3. *Scalar specificity* refers to item equivalence across cultures. Conceptual and operational equivalence do not assure equivalence at the item level. Similarity in the factor structure and strength of loadings ensure item equivalence. Affirmation of equivalence at the item level allows for meaningful interpretation of similarities or differences of the construct at the scale level.

4. Finally, *functional specificity* is a measure of similar correlates of the constructs across cultures (correlations among aspects of socialization and development). Even though similarity in the nature and strength of relationships may imply a universal pattern, the meaning of relationships should be interpreted from the perspective of the cultural lens that is applied (Krishnakumar, Buhler, & Barber, 2004; Van de Vijver & Leung, 1997).

SUMMARY

We have speculated a good deal about some familial processes that may aid or conspire against attempts made by English-speaking Caribbean immigrants to adjust to life in a new cultural community. Undoubtedly, there are other facets of immigrant family life that may cause stress and conflict. For example, factors such as meaningful employment and underemployment, racism, crime and drug use, anti-immigrant sentiments, parental involvement in issues of children's schooling, and social isolation can be quite stressful for families. However, as we have pointed out elsewhere (Roopnarine et al., 2004), English-speaking Caribbean immigrants of the last two decades are very familiar with life in the United States, they do not have to face linguistic barriers, and they place a strong emphasis on educational achievement. As a result, they are better prepared to cope with life in the United States. Yet the inequality in husband–wife/partner relationships, beliefs about women's roles, and parenting beliefs and practices present the greatest challenges to the mental heath and well-being of Caribbean immigrant families. It is hoped that the proposed model for studying the mental health and well-being of families and the short discussion of cultural equivalence in measurement will scientifically advance our understanding of the psychological lives of Caribbean immigrant families.

REFERENCES

Ainsworth, M., & Bowlby, J. (1991). An ethological approach to personality development. *American Psychologist, 46*, 333–341.

Anderson, S., & Payne, M. (1994). Corporal punishment in elementary education: Views of Barbadian school children. *Child Abuse and Neglect, 18*, 377–386.

Arnold, E. (1982). The use of corporal punishment in childrearing in the West Indies. *Child Abuse and Neglect, 6*, 141–145.

Arnold, E. (1997). Issues in re-unification of migrant West Indian children in the United Kingdom. In J. L. Roopnarine & J. Brown (Eds.), *Caribbean families: Diversity among ethnic groups* (pp. 243–258) Norwood, NJ: Ablex.

Baptiste, D. A., Hardy, K. V., & Lewis, L. (1997). Clinical practice with Caribbean immigrant families in the United States: The intersection of emigration, immigration, culture, and race. In J. L. Roopnarine & J. Brown (Eds.), *Caribbean families: Diversity among ethnic groups* (pp. 275–303) Norwood, NJ: Ablex.

Baumrind, D. (1967). Child care practices anteceding three patterns of preschool behavior. Genetic Psychology Monographs, 75, 43–88.

Bayne-Smith, M., Graham, Y. J., Mason, M. A., & Drossman, M. (2004). Disparities in infant mortality rates among immigrant Caribbean groups in New York City. *Journal of Immigrant and Refugee Services, 2*, 29–48.

Belsky, J., Steinberg, L., & Draper, P. (1991). Childhood experience, interpersonal development, and reproductive strategy: An evolutionary theory of socialization. *Child Development, 62*, 647–670.

Berry, J. W. (1998). Acculturation and health: Theory and research. In S. S. Kazarian & D. R. Evans (Eds.), *Cultural clinical psychology: Theory, research, and practice* (pp. 39–57). New York: Oxford University Press.

Best-Cummings, C., & Gildner, M. A. (2004). Caribbean women's migratory journey: An exploration of their decision making process. *Journal of Immigrant and Refugee Services, 2*, 83–101.

Bredekamp, S., & Copple, C. (1997). (Eds.). *Developmentally appropriate practice in early childhood programs* (rev. ed.). Washington, DC: NAEYC.

Brody, E. B. (1981). *Sex, contraception, and motherhood in Jamaica*. Cambridge, MA: Harvard University Press.

Brown, J., Newland, A., Anderson, P., & Chevannes, B. (1997). In J. L. Roopnarine & J. Brown (Eds.), *Caribbean families: Diversity among ethnic groups* (pp. 85–113). Norwood, NJ: Ablex.

Campbell, C., & McLean, C. (2002). Ethnic identities, social capital and health inequalities: Factors shaping African-Caribbean participation in local community networks in the UK. *Social Science & Medicine, 55,* 643–657.

Cheetham, J. (1972). *Social work with immigrants*. London: Routledge & Keegan Paul.

Crawford-Brown, C. (1997). The impact of parent-child socialization on the development of conduct disorder in Jamaican male adolescents. In J. L. Roopnarine & J. Brown (Eds.), *Caribbean families: Diversity among ethnic groups* (pp. 205–222). Norwood, NJ: Ablex.

Crawford-Brown, C. (1999). *Who will survive our children? The plight of the Jamaican child in the 1990s*. Kingston, Jamaica: Canoe Press, University of the West Indies.

Cummings, E. M., Goeke-Morey, M. C., & Raymond, J. (2004). Fathers in family context: Effects of marital quality and marital conflict. In M. E. Lamb (Ed.), *The role of the father in child development* (4th ed., pp. 196–221). New York: Wiley & Sons.

Davies, P. T., & Cummings, E. M. (1994). Marital conflict and child adjustment: An emotional security hypothesis. *Psychological Bulletin, 116,* 387–411.

Department of Health and Human Services. (2000). *HIV/AIDS Surveillance Report. U.S HIV and AIDS cases reported through December 2000, 13 (1)*. Atlanta, GA: Center for Disease Control.

DeYoung, Y., & Zigler, E. F. (1994). Machismo in two cultures: Relation to punitive child-rearing practices. *American Journal of Orthopsychiatry, 64,* 386–395.

Duany, J. (1994). Beyond the safety valve: Recent trends in Caribbean migration. *Social and Economic Studies, 43,* 95–122.

Durbrow, E. H. (1999). Cultural processes in child competence: How rural Caribbean parents evaluate their children. In A. S. Masten (Ed.), *Cultural processes in child development: The Minnesota symposia on child psychology* (Vol. 29, pp. 97–121). Mahwah, NJ: Lawrence Erlbaum Associates.

Flinn, M. (1992). Paternal care in a Caribbean village. In B. Hewlett (Ed.), *Father–child relations: Cultural and biosocial contexts* (pp. 57–84). New York: Aldine de Gruyter.

Foner, N. (Ed.). (2001). *Islands in the city: West Indian migration to New York*. Berkeley: University of California Press.

Francis, E. (1993). Psychiatric racism and social police: Black people and the psychiatric services. In W. James & C. Harris (Eds.), *Inside Babylon* (pp. 179–205). London: Verso.

Fuligni, A. (2001). A comparative longitudinal approach to acculturation among children from immigrant families. *Harvard Educational Review, 71,* 566–578.

Fuligni, A. J. (2003). The adaptation of children from immigrant families. *International Society for the Study of Behavioral Development Newsletter, 44,* 9–11.

Gershoff, E. T. (2002). Corporal punishment by parents and associated child behaviors and experiences: A meta-analytic and theoretical review. *Psychological Bulletin, 128,* 539–579.

Gopaul-McNicol, S. (1993). *Working with West Indian families.* New York: Guilford Press.

Graham-Berman, S. A., & Brescoll, V. (2000). Gender, power, and violence: Assessing the family stereotypes of the children of batterers. *Journal of Family Psychology, 14,* 600–612.

Grantham-McGregor, S., Landman, J., & Desai, P. (1983). Child rearing in poor urban Jamaica. *Child: Care, Health and Development, 9,* 57–71.

Grasmuck, S., & Grosfoguel, R. (1997). Geopolitics, economic niches, and gendered social capital among recent Caribbean immigrants in New York City. *Sociological Perspectives, 40,* 339–363.

Greenfield, P. M. (1997). Culture as process: Empirical methods for cultural psychology. In J. W. Berry, Y. H. Poortinga, & J. Pandey (Eds.), *Handbook of cross-cultural psychology. Vol 1: Theory and method* (pp. 301–346). Needham Heights, MA: Allyn & Bacon.

Grossman, K. E., Grossman, K., & Keppler, A. (2005). Universal and culturally specific aspects of human behavior: The case of attachment. In W. Friedlmeier, P. Chakkrath, & B. Schwarz (Eds.), *Culture and human development: The importance of cross-cultural research to the social sciences.* London: Psychology Press.

Haniff, N. Z. (1998). Male violence against men and women in the Caribbean: The case of Jamaica. *Journal of Comparative Family Studies, 29,* 361–369.

Herman, K. A. (2004). Developing a model intervention to prevent abuse in relationships among Caribbean and Caribbean-American youth by partnering with schools. *Journal of Immigrant and Refugee Services, 2,* 103–116.

Holden, G. W., & Barker, T. (2004). Fathers in violent homes. In M. E. Lamb (Ed.), *The role of the father in child development* (4th ed., pp. 417–445). New York: Wiley & Sons

Kasinitz, P. (2001). Invisible no more: In N. Foner (Ed.), *Islands in the city: West Indian migration to New York* (pp. 257–275). Berkeley: University of California Press.

Krishnakumar, A., Buehler, C., & Barber, B. (2004). Cross-ethnic equivalence of socialization measures in European American and African American families. *Journal of Marriage and the Family, 66,* 808–820.

Leung, K., Lau, S., & Lam, W. (1998). Parenting styles and academic achievement: A cross-cultural study. *Merrill-Palmer Quarterly, 44,* 152–172.

Leo-Rhynie, E. (1997). Class, race, and gender issues in child rearing in the Caribbean. In J. L. Roopnarine & J. Brown (Eds.), *Caribbean families: Diversity among ethnic groups* (pp. 25–55). Norwood, NJ: Ablex.

LeVine, R. (2004). Challenging expert knowledge: Findings from and African study of infant care and development. In U. Gielen & J. L. Roopnarine (Eds.), *Childhood and adolescence in cross-cultural perspective* (pp. 149–165). Westport, CT: Praeger.

McLoyd, V. C. (1998). Socioeconomic disadvantage and child development. *American Psychologist, 53,* 185–204.

Meeks-Gardner, J., Grantham-McGregor, S. M., Himes, J., & Chang, S. (1999). Behavior of stunted and nonstunded Jamaican children. *Journal of Child Psychology and Psychiatry, 40,* 819–827.

Millette, R. (1998). West Indian families in the United States. In R. Taylor (Ed.), *Minority families in the United States: A multicultural perspective* (2nd ed., pp. 46–59). Upper Saddle River, NJ: Prentice Hall.

Payne, M. A., & Furnham, A. (1992). Parental self-reports of child rearing practices in the Caribbean. *Journal of Black Psychology, 18,* 19–36.

Phinney, J. S. (2003). Commentary: What is development about immigration. *International Society for the Study of Behavioral Development Newsletter, 44,* 14–15.

Phinney, J. S., & Devich-Navarro, M. (1997). Variations in bicultural identification among African American and Mexican American adolescents. *Journal of Research on Adolescence, 7,* 3–32.

Prasad, B. S. (1999). Marital violence within East Indian households in Guyana: A cultural explanation. In R. Kanhai (Ed.), *Matokor: The politics of identity for Indo-Caribbean women* (pp. 40–61). St. Augustine, Trinidad: School of Continuing Education, University of the West Indies.

Rambally, R. T. (1995). The overrepresentation of Black youth in the Quebec social service system. *Canadian Social Work Review, 12,* 85–97.

Rumbaut, R. G. (1997). Assimilation and its discontents: Between rhetoric and reality. *International Migration Review, 31,* 923–960.

Ramkissoon, M. W. (2001). *The psychology of fathering in the Caribbean: An investigation of the physical and psychological presence of the Jamaican father.* Unpublished doctoral dissertation, University of West Indies, Mona, Jamaica.

Robertson, E. E. (1975). *Out of sight—Not out of mind. A study of West Indian mothers living in England, separated for long periods from their children, leaving them behind when migrating and subsequently reuniting.* Unpublished master's thesis, Sussex University, Sussex, England.

Rohner, R. P., Kean, K, J., & Cournoyer, D. E. (1991). Effects of corporal punishment, perceived caretaker warmth, and cultural beliefs on the psychological adjustment of children in St. Kitts, West Indies. *Journal of Marriage and the Family, 53,* 681–693.

Roopnarine, J. L. (1999). *Father involvement and parental styles in Caribbean immigrant families.* Paper presented at the American Educational Research Association conference, Montreal, Canada, April.

Roopnarine, J. L. (2004). African American and African Caribbean fathers: Levels, quality, and meaning of involvement. In M. E. Lamb (Ed.), *The role of the father in child development* (pp. 58–97). New York: Wiley & Sons.

Roopnarine, J. L. & Brown, J. (Eds.). (1997). *Caribbean families: Diversity among ethnic groups.* Norwood, NJ: Ablex.

Roopnarine, J. L., Bynoe, P. F., Singh, R., & Simon, R. (2004). Factors tied to the schooling of children of English-speaking Caribbean immigrants in the United States. In U. P. Gielen & J. Roopnarine (Eds.), *Childhood and adolescence: Cross-cultural perspectives and applications* (pp. 319–349). Westport, CT: Praeger.

Roopnarine, J. L., Bynoe, P. F., Singh, R., & Simon, R. (2005). Caribbean families in English-speaking countries: A rather complex mosaic. In J. L. Roopnarine & U. P. Gielen (Eds.), *Families in global perspective* (pp. 311–329). Boston: Allyn & Bacon.

Roopnarine, J. L., & Evans, M. E. (in press). Family structural organization, mother–child and father–child relationships and psychological outcomes in English-speaking African Caribbean and Indo Caribbean families. In M. Sutherland (Ed.), *Psychology of development in the Caribbean*. Kingston, Jamaica: Ian Randle.

Roopnarine, J. L., Krishnakumar, A., Metindogan, A., & Evans, M. (2005). *Links between parenting styles, parent–child academic interaction, parent–school interaction, and early academic skills and social behaviors in young children of English-speaking Caribbean immigrants*. Manuscript submitted for publication.

Roopnarine, J. L., & Shin, M. (2003). Caribbean immigrants from English-speaking countries: Sociohistorical forces, migratory patterns, and psychological issues in family functioning. In L. L. Adler & U. P. Gielen (Eds.), *Migration, immigration, and emigration in international perspectives* (pp. 123–142). Westport, CT: Praeger.

Russell-Brown, P., Norville, B., & Griffith, C. (1997). Child shifting: A survival strategy for teenage mothers. In J. L. Roopnarine & J. Brown (Eds.), *Caribbean families: Diversity among ethnic groups* (pp. 223–242). Norwood, NJ: Ablex.

Salandy, A. (Convener). (2003, July). *Symposium on "Barrel Children."* Caribbean Association of Social Work, Bridgetown, Barbados.

Senior, O. (1991). *Working miracles: Women's lives in the English-speaking Caribbean*. Institute for Social and Economic Research (ISER), University of the West Indies, Barbados. London: James Curry, and Bloomington: Indiana University Press.

Sigel, I., & McGillicuddy-DeLisi, A. (2002). Parental beliefs are cognitions: The dynamic belief systems model. In M. H. Bornstein (Ed.), *Handbook on parenting* (Vol. 3, 2nd ed., pp. 485–508). Mahwah, NJ: Lawrence Erlbaum Associates.

Smith, R. T. (1996). *The matrifocal family: Power, pluralism, and politics*. London: Routledge.

Soyibo, K., & Lee, M. G. (2000). Domestic and school violence among high school students in Jamaica. *West Indian Medical Journal, 49*, 232–236.

Spooner, M., Daniel, C. A., & Mahoney, A. M. (2004). Confronting the reality: An overview of the impact of HIV/AIDS on the Caribbean community. *Journal of Immigrant and Refugee Services, 2*, 49–67.

Steinberg, L., Dornbusch, S. M., & Brown, B. B. (1992). Ethnic differences in adolescent achievement: An ecological perspective. *American Psychologist, 47*, 723–729.

Suarez-Orozco, C., & Todorova, I. (2002, June). *The transnationalization of families: Immigrant separations and reunifications*. Paper presented to the American Family Therapy Academy, Miami, FL.

Super, C., & Harkness, S. (1997). The cultural structuring of child development. In J. Berry, P. Dasen, & T. Saraswathi (Eds.), *Handbook of cross-cultural psychology. Vol. 2: Basic processes and human development* (pp. 1–39). Needham, MA: Allyn & Bacon.

Van De Vijver, F. & Leung, K. (1997). Methods and data analysis of comparative research. In J. W. Berry, Poortinga, Y. P., & J. Pandey (Eds.), *Handbook of cross-cultural psychology* (Vol. 1, 2nd ed., pp. 257–300). Boston: Allyn & Bacon.

Vickerman, M. (2001). Jamaicans: Balancing race and ethnicity. In N. Foner (Ed.), *New immigrants in New York* (pp. 201–228). New York: Columbia University Press.

Waters, M. (1999). *Black identities: West Indian immigrant dreams and American realities*. Cambridge, MA: Harvard University Press.

Wedenoja, W. (1989). Mothering and the practice of "Balm" in Jamaica. In C. S. McClain (Ed.), *Women as healers* (pp. 76–97). New Brunswick, NJ: Rutgers University Press.

Wilson, L. C., Wilson, C. M., & Berkeley-Caines, L. (2003). Age, gender and socioeconomic differences in parental socialization preferences in Guyana. *Journal of Comparative Family Studies, 34,* 213–227.

Wilson, M., & Brooks-Gunn, J. (2001). Health status and behaviors of unwed fathers. *Children and Youth Services Review, 23,* 377–401.

Zhou, M. (1997). Segmented assimilation: Issues, controversies, and recent research on the second generation. *International Migration Review, 31,* 975–1008.

16

On the Development of Identity: Perspectives From Immigrant Families

Karen Kisiel Dion

University of Toronto at Scarborough

Negotiating and understanding different aspects of one's identity is a central feature of development during adolescence and early adulthood. Major psychological theories concerning the development of identity assume a model of optimal or mature development that is itself culturally constructed. Understanding the dynamics of identity development in the children of immigrants—the role of the family, intergenerational consensus and conflict, the distinctive contribution of gender—reveals the nature of these cultural constructions. It is therefore important to consider not only how theories of identity development can be applied to understanding the challenges faced by the children of immigrants, but also how the experiences of immigrant families can advance existing theories.

IDENTITY DEVELOPMENT IN ADOLESCENCE AND EARLY ADULTHOOD

Psychological Theories and Concepts

As part of his theory of life-span development, Erikson (1968) described establishing a sense of identity as a central feature of (although not limited to) adolescence. Central to his view was the idea of a "moratorium", enabling the adolescent to consolidate different facets of identity, with "identity confusion" resulting when attempts at integration

299

did not succeed. Marcia (1980, p. 159) defined identity as "an internal, self-constructed, dynamic organization of drives, abilities, beliefs and individual history," which facilitated psychological differentiation from others. A sense of emerging identity, characterized by "a flexible unity," should in turn make an individual less likely to rely on others' views and expectations for self-definition.

Marcia (1980) proposed four different "identity statuses," with the optimal being "identity achievement," involving a period of personal reflection and consideration of alternatives, then making commitments based on individual choices. The other identity statuses were "diffusion" (unable to make commitments), "foreclosed" (making commitments but based on parental/family influence, rather than personal choice), and "moratorium" (transitional phase trying to decide on and resolve commitments). In this phase of the life span, key issues for consideration concerned occupational choices and issues concerning ideology/worldviews (such as religious beliefs; political beliefs).

More recently, it was suggested by Arnett (2000) that in societies or segments within a given society where individuals can postpone assuming adult role responsibilities, identity exploration extends beyond adolescence well into the twenties. He argued that this "emerging adulthood" (ages 18–25 years) is a distinct developmental phase from either adolescence or early adulthood. Of relevance here, a defining feature of this period concerns exploring different facets of personal identity in different domains. Thus, "trying out" different relationships, educational and work possibilities, and travel and volunteer opportunities contributes to identity development. These experiences contribute to a sense of "self-sufficiency" (Arnett, 2000). Among adolescents in the United States in the late 1990s, surveys indicated that personal qualities such as "accepting responsibility for oneself" and "making independent decisions" were regarded as the defining criteria for adulthood, rather than role transitions such as completing one's education or getting a job (Arnett, 1997).

As is evident from the points just described, psychological accounts of identity development in adolescence and "emerging " adulthood have stressed the importance of personal reflection and choice, considering alternatives, and constructing a sense of identity based on one's preferences and experiences.

Identity Development and Family Relationships

What impact do family relationships have on identity development in adolescence and early adulthood? The views just described imply that the optimal role for parents is to tolerate, encourage, and facilitate various initiatives on the part of their son or daughter (see, e.g., the case study cited by Erikson, 1968, pp. 130–131). Identity search involves questioning earlier worldviews and values, many of which have been acquired in the family. Concepts such as "identity foreclosure" indicate acceptance of others' views without questioning (Marcia, 1980). As the label suggests, this approach is not regarded as the ideal developmental outcome. Arnett (2000) pointed out that by age 18 years, many young adult daughters and sons have left their parents' home for college or work opportunities. Leaving home to live elsewhere means that much of their identity-related exploration is likely to be undertaken apart from their family of origin. However, in the United States, not all young adults leave home, and those who do leave may eventually return. Arnett (2000) cited findings from the United States that physical proximity to parents was negatively related to various indicators of the parent–child relationship. Perhaps one reason for these results is that coresidence with one's adult children is inconsistent with the belief by parents and children concerning the latter's expected self-sufficiency by early adulthood.

CULTURE AND FAMILY: IMPLICATIONS FOR IDENTITY DEVELOPMENT

Identity Issues

Among adolescent and young adult children of immigrants, the process of identity exploration involves not only aspects of personal development (relationships; work choices; examining values), but also culture-related contrasts pertaining to these choices. Given these contrasts, constructing a sense of cultural identity is an important facet of identity development in adolescence and early adulthood for immigrant youth. Both a sense of personal efficacy (self-sufficiency) and cultural identity contribute to bicultural competence (LaFromboise, Coleman, & Gerton, 1993). For LaFromboise and her colleagues (1993), the development of bicultural competence was facilitated by "a strong sense of oneself in relation to others" but hindered if a person was "enmeshed in his or her social context" (p. 402, footnote 2).

Based on Marcia's concept of identity statuses, Phinney (1989) proposed a four-stage progression of ethnic identity development among adolescents from ethnocultural minority groups: not examining issues pertaining to ethnicity (diffused); commitment without personal exploration (foreclosed); exploring the meaning of ethnicity for oneself (moratorium); and clarity about and commitment to one's ethnicity after personal reflection and exploration (identity achievement). Applications of this framework have mostly focused on ethnic minority adolescents in the United States. For example, among high school students (U.S.-born), Phinney (1989) found support for three identity statuses among 10th graders who were from three groups (Asian American, Hispanic, and Black): diffusion/foreclosure (the majority response in each group), moratorium, and achieved. Based on a small follow-up sample, Phinney and Chavira (1992) found preliminary support for development towards achieved identity status between the ages of 16 and 19 years among adolescents from three ethnic groups (Asian American, Black, and Hispanic). More recently, Phinney and her colleagues examined the relation between ethnic identity and different aspects of psychological well-being among immigrant youth in several societies (see Phinney, Horenczyk, Liebkind, & Vedder, 2001).

Tse (1999), using a qualitative approach, analyzed first-person narratives of 39 Asian Americans to examine ethnic identity. In their accounts of this process, she noted descriptions of "ethnic emergence," which included self-awareness of minority status followed by attempting to learn about different facets of ethnic heritage and eventually, for many, arriving at "ethnic identity incorporation," resulting in identification with Asian Americans. The preceding examples suggest that for adolescents and young adults from ethnocultural minority groups, a distinctive feature of identity development concerns its cultural grounding—that is, the extent to which issues pertaining to ethnicity are explored and examined.

For those who are the children of immigrants, issues of ego development emerge in the context of a sense of cultural identity. Arredondo (1984) studied identity development among young adults from 13 different cultural backgrounds who immigrated to the United States in their early to mid adolescence (ages 14–17 years). She looked at both ego identity and the contribution of cultural values in the development of self-definition. A second testing after a 5-year period on a subsample of the group indicated higher levels of ego identity using a measure based on Erikson's stages. Using journal entries kept by participants and interviews with them, she also noted several themes related to identity development. These included creating a sense of being part of and belonging in a new cultural context, the importance of "primary group/cultural values" and their impact of educational and career plans, and, more specifically, the importance of family relationships in helping them to make various choices. Families were discussed as a source of support and strength in this process.

At the same time, these young adults were aware of the complexities of identity negotiation, given competing demands learned in their family's society of origin and subsequent experiences in the United States. The comments of a young woman reflected this awareness: "It's like being born again. You have to find out who you are while getting messages from two sides, saying this is how you were raised, and this is how you should be" (Arredondo, 1984, p. 984).

For adolescents and young adults from immigrant families, identity negotiation can be particularly complex, both for those who immigrated with their parents and especially for the second-generation children of immigrants. They not only must deal with aspects of personal development shared by all adolescents and young adults (relationships, work choices, examining values) but also often confront culture-related differences concerning these choices. Seeking to create a sense of identity through personal choices surrounding relationships, occupation, and worldviews/values sometimes may conflict with parental and other family expectations. Moreover, if conflict occurs, it may not be simply over a specific choice or preference (which occupation; what area of study; the suitability of a romantic partner) but also with the assumption that these choices should be made independently by the young adult daughter or son.

Family Dynamics and the Development of Identity

In many societies, the primary goal of socialization is not the development of an individual who by adolescence or early adulthood is becoming psychologically autonomous from her or his family of origin (LeVine, 1990). Rather, it is assumed that family members will continue to be involved in and influence each other's lives and choices. The goal of childrearing is to foster interconnectedness and interdependence among family members (Shweder & Bourne, 1984). Hence young adults from immigrant families residing in societies such as the United States and Canada encounter differences not only in specific cultural practices but more fundamentally, different culture-related belief systems concerning optimal human development.

To illustrate with one example, the expectation that a young adult should be free to pursue her or his individual development and desires in close relationships beyond the family without undue parental interference ultimately encourages the young adult's personal autonomy from his or her family of origin. The view of "emerging adulthood" discussed by Arnett (2000) illustrates this point. The choice of a partner is implicitly focused on issues related to personal identity as the young adult asks "Given the kind of person I am, what kind of person do I wish to have as a partner through life?" (Arnett, 2000, p. 473). This emphasis on individual autonomy and personal identity search in the context of intimate relationships not only reflects culture-related belief systems but also may have some paradoxical outcomes for the quality of relationships (see Dion & Dion, 1991, 1993, for further discussion of this issue). In contrast, alternative culture-related belief systems about the nature of adolescence and early adulthood advocate a different view, one stressing continuing high levels of parental and family involvement. From this perspective, "letting go" and encouraging one's young adult children to "strike out on their own" are not necessarily the guiding metaphor for childrearing.

One important motivation for immigrating to another society is the goal of providing educational and occupational opportunities for one's children. Thus the fact of having immigrated itself can contribute to family dynamics, with parents expecting to have greater influence over children's decisions and plans given the disruption and uprooting of their own lives, particularly if immigration was undertaken mainly for economic reasons and family advancement. The parents may expect their children not only to succeed but also to succeed in a specific domain of achievement. Moreover, factors related to immigration, such as the economic survival and well-being of the family, may mean that an adolescent's occupational choices are regarded as a family rather than an individual matter.

Illustrating this point, Markowitz (1994) interviewed women of Soviet Jewish parents who came to the United States when the respondents were in preadolescence to mid-adolescence. These women commented that schooling and job decisions were strongly influenced by their parents' wishes, in part because of the parents' own personal sacrifices. The saying "After all I've done for you" gains extra impact under these circumstances. As one woman said who became a computer scientist rather than a musician, "My parents depended on me, and on my sister, too, to get good, high-paying jobs, to have better lives than they did" (p. 156). Markowitz characterized these families as having "high expectations and blurred ego boundaries" (p. 158)—qualities that were sources of both strength and stress for these immigrant families.

Parents who are immigrants often also want their children to adhere to their view of culture-related values and behavior. Evidence from several sources suggests that one factor contributing to parents' behavior is perceived threat to what they regard as core values. The greater the perceived discrepancy between these values and those in the receiving society, the greater the parental restrictiveness which may occur. This point was illustrated in one of Das Gupta's (1997, p. 579) interviews with a young Indian woman living in New York whose family had previously lived in two other countries. She commented that her mother's behavior toward her children had become much more restrictive upon arrival in the United States because of perceived threat to values from the family's society of origin. By contrast, when the family lived in two other societies, its members had participated more fully, including learning the local language.

An additional complexity for adolescent and adult children from immigrant families is that what is considered to be prototypic family life in the receiving society may differ from their lived experience in their own family. Images of family life appearing in various media and observed in others' families function as an "interpretive structure" or frame of reference influencing the assessment and appraisal of one's own family (Pyke, 2000). In her interviews with young adults whose parents were either Korean or Vietnamese immigrants, Pyke (2000) found that the grown children negatively assessed some aspects of family life (perceived emotional distance from their parents, greater parental control) when they compared it to the emotional expressiveness and egalitarianism depicted in American media (e.g., fictitious families depicted on television). At the same time, however, their ideas about the "Normal American Family" also were a negative reference point when assessing other features of their own family life. For example, these young adults were strongly committed to cultural ideals of eventual filial care for their aging parents and regarded their commitment as a point of positive contrast with what they regarded as the neglect of older family members in American (United States) society.

Moreover, societal-level factors, such as policies toward the immigrants in immigrant-receiving societies, provide a context that supports or hinders in varying degrees immigrant parents' transmission of systems of beliefs and values. For example, since the early 1970s, Canada's official policy has espoused multiculturalism (Berry, 1984 ; Esses & Gardner, 1996) , and there is public support for this policy (Berry & Kalin, 1995). Key components include respect for heritage cultures and intergroup tolerance and respect for different groups within Canada. Thus there is explicit societal support for what many immigrant parents are trying to do at the level of the family—that is, foster respect for their own family's cultural heritage. Georgas and his colleagues (Georgas, Berry, Shaw, Christakopoulou, & Mylonas, 1996) predicted and found greater endorsement of traditional Greek family values among Greek immigrants in Canada compared to Greek immigrants in two European societies (the Netherlands and Germany). This difference occurred for both first- and second-generation immigrants. One interpretation for this difference is the difference in societal-level responses to retention of heritage cultural values in immigrant families.

Another factor that may facilitate the likelihood that parents continue to affect the daily lives and choices of their children is continuing coresidence, which may occur even when children are of university and work age. Although many U.S. adolescents and young adults leave their parents' home by age 18 years as noted earlier, not all do so. Among Canadian students, although some do leave home for postsecondary schooling, a substantial number of undergraduates attend a university in their home city or nearby. For example, as part of a survey of entering students conducted at the University of Toronto (UTSC campus) in 1993, students were asked about their expected place of residence while in university. Most (80.1%) expected to live with parents or other relatives.

Many of the core values immigrant parents from diverse ethnocultural groups wish to foster in their children pertain to personal relationships, especially views of marriage and family relationships, and intergenerational conflict is especially likely to occur in this domain (K. K. Dion & K. L. Dion, 1996). Within Chinese immigrant families, there are several aspects of family-related values that may be associated with parent–child conflict (see K. L. Dion & K. K. Dion, 1996). For example, Fong (1973) commented on the importance of filial piety and parental authority in Chinese families. Sung (1985) noted conflict concerning the perceived formality of their family relationships, as well as parental restrictiveness, expressed by Chinese immigrant children and adolescents.

Various studies have found evidence of immigrant Indian and Pakistani parents' concern over dating and marriage practices in the society to which they had immigrated (e.g., Vaidyanathan & Naidoo, 1991; Wakil, Siddique, & Wakil, 1981). Unsupervised association between young women and young men was one of the greatest sources of parental stress (e.g., Kurina & Ghosh, 1983; Naidoo & Davis, 1988). One factor underlying this concern expressed by Indo-Canadian parents was competing belief systems concerning the nature of marriage and family relationships (Filteau,1980).

Kibria (1993) interviewing Vietnamese Americans found mothers expressing concern over the potential weakening of family bonds and interdependence as a result of immigration. Worry over loss of their authority over their children was mentioned as the greatest disadvantage of living in the United States. The issue of parental control is also salient to adolescents from immigrant families. Rosenthal and Feldman (1990) studied first- and second-generation immigrant adolescents (ages 15–18 years) in Australia and the United States. These adolescents regarded their families as exercising greater control and having greater expectations for achievement when compared to either nonimmigrant adolescents (Chinese teenagers living in Hong Kong) or two other comparison groups of White, native-born adolescents from Australia and the United States.

GENDER, FAMILY RELATIONSHIPS, AND NEGOTIATING IDENTITY

Gender and Parent–Child Interaction

Gender provides an important framework for understanding personal relationships (Dion & Dion, 2001b), including family expectations and interactions among members of immigrant families (Dion & Dion, 2001a). Research conducted in Canada and in the United States indicates that in immigrant families from various ethnocultural groups, parents are more likely to monitor and control the behavior of their daughters compared to their sons (e.g., Ghosh, 1984; Pettys & Balgopal, 1998). Culture-related differences exist in core values such as the criteria for choosing a spouse, the expected involvement of the families of origin in this decision, and obligations of adult children to parents and other relatives. The desire to protect these values is one factor that underlies gendered socialization practices, such as the greater monitoring and control over daughters' compared to sons' activities. Daughters more than sons often are expected to embody cultural ideals of behavior from their parents' society of origin. In particular, daughters born in the receiving society (second generation) may encounter pressures from parents and other family members. Even when their daughters' educational and occupational goals are supported, parents may also expect them to adhere to norms of family behavior from the parents' society of origin (e.g., Naidoo,1984).

Moreover, parents' gender-related expectations about their children's behavior are based on norms that were prevalent in their society of origin at the time of emmigration, which can add to tension between parents and young adult daughters (Ghosh, 1984). Due to societal changes, the parents' beliefs and behavior may be inconsistent with some contemporary practices in the parents' society of origin (Pettys & Balgopal, 1998). Das Gupta (1997) noted that first-generation Indo-American immigrant parents may regard themselves as preserving important aspects of their culture even in the face of change in their society of origin. Thus, parents and adolescent children may differ on what the meaning of "tradition" is, with the result that "tradition becomes an embattled category" (p. 580).

At the same time, not all aspects of culture-related values and practices are "embattled." Gender-related expectations about women's important role in the context of family traditions is not only a source of conflict but also—often simultaneously—a source of pride and respect. Ambivalence over some aspects of family functioning does not necessarily imply rejection of all parental values among adolescents and young adults from immigrant families. For example, Kibria (1993), interviewing Vietnamese Americans from immigrant families, commented that a greater dislike of hierarchical family relationships coexisted with a positive view of other aspects of family relationships, such as cohesion and cooperation, among young adults who were the children of immigrants.

Gender and Ethnocultural Identity

What are the implications for young adults' sense of ethnocultural identity in view of the complex pattern of gendered family expectations and behavior? How does gender contribute to the construction of ethnocultural identity? In collaboration with Ken Dion as part of our program of research on the social psychology of immigration, I examined this question in an ethnically diverse group of young women and men (Canadian university students) from immigrant families where both parents were born outside Canada (Dion & Dion, 2004). To place this research in context, within Canada, Toronto has the largest immigrant population, with nearly 44% of the population born outside Canada as of the 2001 census (Statistics Canada, 2003). Moreover, as an urban area, Toronto has one of the largest proportions of immigrants in the world (Statistics Canada, 2003). This demographic trend is evident not only in downtown Toronto but also in the suburban areas of the city, where this research was conducted.

The participants for this research were young adults (university students) who reported that both parents had immigrated to Canada. Both first-generation and second-generation women and men took part. The first-generation participants had arrived in Canada, on average, when they were just over 12 years old. Most (93%) reported that both parents were from the same ethnocultural background. Of this group, the majority of our participants' parents were from diverse Asian ethnocultural backgrounds, in particular, Chinese, as well as Indian, Pakistani, Sri Lankan, Filipino, Korean, Laotian, and Vietnamese. There were also students whose parents were from several Caribbean (West Indian) backgrounds, as well as several Eastern and Western European groups. Finally, a few students were from several different African or Middle Eastern groups. Almost all students were either Canadian citizens or landed immigrants.

We asked these young adults to respond to several measures assessing different aspects of identity, including ethnocultural identity (Phinney, 1992). Phinney (1992) developed this measure in the context of studying ethnic identity among adolescents from minority ethnic groups in the United States. It is also of relevance for examining ethnic identity among immigrant youth from different societies (Phinney et al., 2001). Ethnocultural identity (ethnic identity) refers to the component of self reflecting both knowledge and evaluation of one's membership in one more more ethnocultural groups (Tajfel, 1981). This construct has several different components/facets: including self-identification (i.e., labeling oneself as a member of one or more groups); a sense of belonging/attachment to one's group(s); and resolving identity issues (identity achievement), as well as behavioral involvement in group-related practices and traditions (Phinney, 1992).

Most participants' response to the open-ended question about self-description pertaining to ethnicity referred to specific ethnic groups (e.g., Vietnamese; Somalian; Italian) rather than pan-ethnic categories (such as Asian). In other words, self-categorization was differentiated rather than reflecting broader labels. It is of interest to note that Portes and Rumbaut (2001) found in their longitudinal research on the children of immigrants in the United States that during the 3- to 4-year interval between testing, the proportion of adolescents choosing to describe themselves in terms of national or ethnic origin had increased so that it was just over a third of the sample at the time of the second testing when students were completing high school. There was also a sizable increase in the proportion choosing a pan-ethnic label, in contrast to the participants in our study.

We expected that gender and immigrant generation would jointly contribute to ethnocultural identity, and we proposed alternative hypotheses about the nature of this interaction. It could be argued that tensions resulting from some aspects of family interactions might contribute to a psychological distancing from their ethnocultural background on the part of second-generation women compared to their male peers from immigrant families. There is some evidence of gender differences in the endorsement of gender-role ideology in the United States (e.g., Dasgupta, 1998) and in Canada (Tang & Dion, 1999), with women from different ethnocultural groups endorsing less traditional views than men. Lee and Cochran (1988) reported that young women from immigrant families in Canada experienced stresses between striving for personal freedom and their family-related obligations and responsibilities. Given these pressures, women might be more prone than men to be more conflicted about their sense of cultural identity, resulting in less interest in and commitment to that aspect of self.

On the other hand, gender-related family expectations and behavior, even when associated with tension and conflict, may heighten the psychological salience of ethnocultural identity for women compared to their male peers. This analysis is consistent with dialectical views of human development (e.g., Riegel, 1976) in which conflicting perspectives are viewed as having the potential to instigate greater reflection and ultimately, psychological growth. Illustrating this point, Das Gupta described an interview with a young woman in the United States whose parents were immigrants from India. They wanted her to become a physician, a goal that was not her preference. She chose instead to specialize in South Asian studies, which was "her way of cherishing and learning more about her Indian heritage which, she felt, was interpreted too narrowly by her community" (Das Gupta, 1997, p. 585). In this instance, one approach to dealing with conflicting expectations was to move toward—not away from—cultural identity and to redefine its meaning.

Consistent with this second view, we found support for what might be labeled an affirmation hypothesis. Among young adults who were the second-generation children of immigrants, gender differences occurred pertaining to identity exploration (seeking to learn more about and understand one's ethnicity) and on reported behavioral commitment. Women indicated greater involvement in both components compared to men. Among this second immigrant generation group, there were, however, no gender differences in the sense of pride and attachment to their ethnocultural background. Both women and men indicated high positive regard for their group membership, nor did they differ in evaluating its importance. Similarly, in Portes and Rumbaut's research (2001) mentioned previously, when examined along with a number of other predictors, gender predicted the stability of ethnic identity (choosing the same ethnic self-categorization on both testing occasions in early and later adolescence) but not its personal importance, as obtained at the time of the second assessment.

In our research, we found gender differences therefore not in the evaluation and attachment to one's ethnocultural group among the second-generation children of immigrants but in the *enactment* of this core attachment. As we noted (Dion & Dion, 2004), the pattern of findings suggested that issues concerning ethnocultural identity may be a more salient developmental task for second-generation young women from immigrant families compared to young men. This gender difference is most likely to occur when parents and adult children perceive a marked divergence between the belief systems and behavioral norms in the society to which the parents immigrated and parents'own culture-related values and behaviors.

This is one research example, but it suggests the value of starting with gender as an important conceptual lens for understanding identity issues among the children of immigrants. In doing so, both gender and culture must be considered together. Often these two constructs have been addressed in separate scholarly traditions, namely psychology of women and gender and cultural psychology. Considering them together can offer insights about the gendered nature of cultural assumptions and the cultural context of gender pertaining to identity development in early adulthood.

In this final section, I have focused on issues confronted by adolescent and young adult daughters compared to sons whose parents are immigrants because gender is differentially associated with roles, duties, and obligations across diverse cultural groups. It is also important to address the nature of the identity-related issues that confront women and men from different immigrant groups and of equal importance, within a specific group, the various ways in which young adults negotiate personal and cultural identity.

CONCLUSIONS

At the start of this chapter, I suggested that theories of identity development can help to understand the challenges faced by immigrant youth. However, the experiences of these young adults and their families also have the potential to deepen understanding the nature of the development of identity in adolescence and early adulthood. Psychological theories concerning the development of identity in adolescence suggest that this is a phase of transition between the values and goals acquired in childhood and an adult's sense of a coherent self based on consideration of a range of alternatives. For some individuals, the societal structure in which they live may allow the active identity explorations may be prolonged into the late twenties, illustrated by the term *emerging adulthood*. This latter quest is highly individualized with different areas of life serving to enhance one's personal development (work choices, educational choices, relationships, travel). In both earlier and recent discussions of identity development, the role of the family is one of developmental facilitation, with the aim of encouraging eventual independence from the family of origin. Parents are there to offer advice, with the hope (but not necessarily the assumption) that this advice will be heeded, and also to offer support both emotional and instrumental. Although individual parents may find this situation more or less satisfying, it is consistent with the view of assisting their children's "growing up."

This view of the parental role is, however, culturally constructed and, as such, is not always shared by parents who immigrate to societies in which this view is prevalent. An alternative view is that parents and other relatives can and should seek to play a much more active role in their adult children's lives as their daughters and sons begin to consider important issues and choices that are identity related—a view not always shared by their adolescent and young adult sons and daughters. In essence, in immigrant families, there may be intergenerational divergence about (a) the basis for constructing one's identity and (b) the criteria for mature adulthood. This greater parental involvement and control is based in part on the concept of a "good parent."

Daughters, in particular, are likely to the focus of greater parental scrutiny compared to the sons. Gender is therefore an important framework for understanding identity formation in adolescence and early adulthood. One important area for continuing research is to examine the gendered nature of identity formation and the manner in which competing expectations are addressed.

An emerging sense of personal identity for adolescents and young adults from immigrant families occurs therefore in a family context in which divergent cultural expectations are often explicit. However, research also indicates that parents and their adult children can and do agree on what they perceive as culture-related family strengths, such as family cohesion. Identity negotiation involves the incorporation of both these aspects of family functioning.

RESEARCH DIRECTIONS

I am fortunate that my university is located in one of the most culturally diverse large urban areas. Within Toronto, there are not only many different ethnocultural communities, but also many individuals have arrived quite recently in Canada. Therefore, many are either first- or second-generation immigrants. Their experience is invaluable for understanding transitions between different cultural contexts and the impact of these transitions at both the individual (e.g., identity) and the group (e.g., family processes) level. Particularly on my campus of the University of Toronto, many students are from immigrant families. Their participation in research can provide insights into important issues such as cultural identities, negotiating family relationships, and the development of identity in early adulthood.

REFERENCES

Arnett, J. J. (1997). Young people's conceptions of the transition to adulthood. *Youth & Society, 29,* 1–23.

Arnett, J. J. (2000). Emerging adulthood: A theory of development from the late teens through the twenties. *American Psychologist, 55,* 469–480.

Arredondo, P. M. (1984). Identity themes for immigrant young adults. *Adolescence, 19,* 977–993.

Berry, J. W. (1984). Multicultural policy in Canada: A social psychological analysis. *Canadian Journal of Behavioural Science, 16,* 353–370.

Berry, J. W., & Kalin, R. (1995). Multicultural and ethnic attitudes in Canada: An overview of the 1991 national survey. *Canadian Journal of Behavioural Science, 27,* 301–320.

Das Gupta, M. (1997). "What is Indian about you?" A gendered, transnational approach to ethnicity. *Gender & Society, 11,* 572–596.

Dasgupta, S. D. (1998). Gender roles and cultural continuity in the Asian Indian immigrant community in the U.S. *Sex Roles, 38,* 953–974.

Dion K. K., & Dion K. L. (1991). Psychological individualism and love. *Journal of Social Behavior and Personality, 6,* 17–33.

Dion, K. K., & Dion, K. L. (1993). Individualistic and collectivistic perspectives on gender and the cultural context of love and intimacy. *Journal of Social Issues, 49,* 53–69.

Dion, K. K., & Dion, K. L. (1996). Cultural perspectives on romantic love. *Personal Relationships, 3,* 5–17.

Dion, K. K., & Dion, K. L. (2001a). Gender and cultural adaptation in immigrant families. *Journal of Social Issues, 57,* 511–521.

Dion, K. K., & Dion, K. L. (2001b). Gender and relationships. In R. K. Unger (Ed.), *Handbook of the psychology of women and gender* (pp. 256–271). New York: Wiley.

Dion, K. K., & Dion, K. L. (2004). Gender, immigrant generation, and ethnocultural identity. *Sex Roles, 50,* 347–355.

Dion, K. L., & Dion, K. K. (1996). Chinese adaptation to foreign cultures. In M. H. Bond (Ed.), *The handbook of Chinese psychology* (pp. 457–478). Hong Kong: Oxford University Press.

Erikson, E. H. (1968). *Identity: Youth and crisis.* New York: Norton.

Esses, V. M., & Gardner, R.C. (1996). Multiculturalism in Canada: Context and current status. *Canadian Journal of Behavioural Science, 28,* 145–152.

Filteau, C. H. (1980). The role of the concept of love in the Hindu family acculturation process. In K. V. Ujimoto & G. Hirabayashi (Eds.), *Visible minorities and multiculturalism: Asians in Canada* (pp. 289–299). Toronto: Butterworths.

Fong, S. L. M. (1973). Assimilation and changing roles of Chinese Americans. *Journal of Social Issues, 29,* 115–127.

Georgas, J., Berry, J.W., Shaw, A., Christakopoulou, S., & Mylonas, K. (1996). Acculturation of Greek family values. *Journal of Cross-cultural Psychology, 27,* 329–338.

Ghosh, R. (1984). South Asian women in Canada: Adaptation. In R. Kanungo (Ed.), *South Asians in the Canadian Mosaic* (pp. 145–155). Montreal, Quebec: Kala Bharati.

Kibria, N. (1993). *Family tightrope: The changing lives of Vietnamese Americans.* Princeton, NJ: Princeton University Press.

Kurian, G., & Ghosh, R. (1983). Child-rearing in transition in Indian immigrant families in Canada. In G. Kurian & R.P. Srivastava (Eds.), *Overseas Indians: A study in adaptation* (pp. 128–138). New York: Advent Books.

LaFromboise, T., Colemen, H. L. K., & Gerton, J. (1993). Psychological impact of biculturalism: Evidence and theory. *Psychological Bulletin, 114,* 395–412.

Lee, C. C., & Cochran, I. R. (1988). Migration problems of Chinese women. *Canadian Journal of Counseling, 22,* 202–211.

LeVine, R. A. (1990). Enculturation: A biosocial perspective on the development of self. In D. Cichetti & M. Beeghly (Eds.), *The self in transition: Infancy to childhood* (pp. 99–117). Chicago: University of Chicago Press.

Marcia, J. E. (1980). Identity in adolescence. In J. Adelson (Ed.), *Handbook of adolescent psychology* (pp. 159–187). New York: Wiley.

Markowitz, F. (1994). Family dynamics and the teenage immigrant: Creating the self through the parents' image. *Adolescence, 29,* 150–161.

Naidoo, J. C. (1984). Women of South Asian and Anglo-Saxon origins in the Canadian context: Self-perceptions, socialization, achievement aspirations. In C. Stark-Adamec (Ed.), *Sex roles: Origins, influences, and implications for women* (pp. 50–69). Montreal, Quebec: Eden Press Womens' Publications.

Naidoo, J. C., & Davis, J. C. (1988). Canadian South Asian Women in transition: A dualistic view of life. *Journal of Comparative Family Studies, 19,* 311–327.

Pettys, G. L., & Balgopal, P.R. (1998). Multigenerational conflicts and new immigrants: An Indo-American experience. *Families in Society: The Journal of Contemporary Human Services, 79,* 410–423.

Phinney, J. S. (1989). Stages of ethnic identity development in minority group adolescents. *Journal of Early Adolescence, 9,* 34–49.

Phinney, J. S. (1992). The multigroup ethnic identity measure: A new scale for use with diverse groups. *Journal of Adolescent Research, 7,* 156–176.

Phinney, J. S., & Chavira, V. (1992). Ethnic identity and self-esteem: An exploratory longitudinal study. *Journal of Adolescence, 15,* 271–281.

Phinney, J. S., Horenczyk, G., Liebkind, K., & Vedder, P. (2001). Ethnic identity, immigration and well-being. *Journal of Social Issues, 57,* 493–510.

Portes, A., & Rumbaut, R. (2001). *Legacies: The story of the immigrant second generation.* New York: Russell Sage.

Pyke, K. (2000). "The Normal American Family" as an interpretive structure of family life among grown children of Korean and Vietnamese immigrants. *Journal of Marriage and the Family, 62,* 240–255.

Riegel, K. F. (1976). The dialectics of human development. *American Psychologist, 31,* 689–700.

Rosenthal, D. A., & Feldman, S.S. (1990). The acculturation of Chinese immigrants: Perceived effects on family functioning of length of residence in two cultural contexts. *Journal of Genetic Psychology, 15,* 495–514.

Shweder, R. A., & Bourne, E. J. (1984). Does the concept of the person vary cross-culturally? In R. A. Shweder & R.A. LeVine (Eds.), *Essays on mind, self and emotion* (pp. 158–199). Cambridge: Cambridge University Press.

Statistics Canada. (2003). *Canada's ethnocultural portrait: The changing mosaic.* Analysis series 96F0030X1E2001008. Retrieved January 31, 2003, from http://www12.statcan.ca/english/census01/prodcts/anaytic/companon/etoimm/content

Sung, B. L. (1985). Bicultural conflicts in Chinese immigrant children. *Journal of Comparative Family Studies, 16,* 255–269.

Tajfel, H. (1981). *Human groups and social categories.* Cambridge, England: Cambridge University Press.

Tang, T. N., & Dion, K. L. (1999). Gender and acculturation in relation to traditionalism: Perceptions of self and parents among Chinese students. *Sex Roles, 41,* 17–29.

Tse, L. (1999). Finding a place to be: Ethnic identity exploration of Asian Americans. *Adolescence, 34,* 121–138.

Wakil, S. P., Siddique, C. M., & Wakil, F.A. (1981). Between two cultures: A study of socialization of children of immigrants. *Journal of Marriage and the Family, 43,* 929–940.

Vaidyanathan, P. & Naidoo, J. (1991). Asian Indians in Western countries: Cultural identity and the arranged marriage. In N. Bleichrodt & P. Drenth (Eds.), *Contemporary issues in cross-cultural psychology* (pp. 37–49). Amsterdam, the Netherlands: Swets & Zeitlinger.

17

Negotiating Culture and Ethnicity: Intergenerational Relations in Chinese Immigrant Families in the United States[1]

Min Zhou

University of California, Los Angeles

In the United States, most children of Chinese immigrant parentage live in two-parent, nuclear families, with a smaller number in extended families and transnational families. In these various immigrant households, the Confucius values of filial piety, education, hard work, and discipline have been modified to serve as normative behavioral standards for socializing the younger generation. Many Chinese immigrant parents claim that they have sacrificed for their children's better future in America. They would expect that their children achieve the highest level of education possible, help move the family up to middle-class status, and, most importantly, take care of the parents when they are old and frail. Deviation from these expectations is considered a shame, or a failure, on the part of the family and is thus sanctioned by the family and even the entire ethnic community.

It is not easy, however, for immigrant families to enforce these cultural values and behavioral standards and guarantee that familial ex-

---

[1]The original version of this chapter was presented at the Conference on Immigrant Psychology: Rethinking Culture, Race, Class & Gender, April 11–12, 2003, University of Michigan, Ann Arbor. I thank Ram Mahalingham for his helpful comments.

pectations are met, because of vulnerabilities associated with parental foreign birth, intense bicultural and intergenerational conflicts, and different paces of acculturation between parents and children. Like all other immigrant children, the children growing up in Chinese immigrant families have simultaneously and constantly encountered two different sociocultural worlds: one—the "old" world—from which they attempt to distance themselves, and the other—the mainstream American society—to which they aspire, and are also pushed, to assimilate. Often, children regard their immigrant parents as *lao-wan-gu* (old stick-in-the-mud or stubborn heads from the old world) and parental ways as feudal, outdated, or old fashioned. The children's consequential rebellion against tradition is constant and intrinsic to their experience of straddling two sociocultural worlds. Parents, on the other hand, view their own parenting ways as the best to ascertain success. But they are constantly worried about their children becoming too Americanized too soon and are horrified by their children's acting up. Moreover, contemporary Chinese immigrants are an extremely diverse group in their socioeconomic backgrounds and settlement patterns. The diverse sociocultural contexts—ethnic enclaves, ethnoburbs,[2] and White middle-class suburbs—in which these families live further constrain parent–child relationships. This chapter examines how immigration and cultural change affect family life in the Chinese immigrant community in the United States. In particular, it explores the paradoxical family process through which children and parents cope with intricate relationships and negotiate priorities in life that benefit both individual family members and the family as a whole.

THE "OLD" VERSUS THE "NEW" SECOND GENERATION

Chinese Americans are by far the oldest and largest Asian-origin group in the United States. They have endured a long history of migration and settlement that dates back to the late 1840s, including some 60 years of legal exclusion. With the lifting of legal barriers against Chinese immigration during World War II and the enactment of a series of liberal immigration legislation since the passage of the Immigration Act of 1965 (also referred to as the Hart–Cellar Act), the Chinese American community has increased more than 10-fold: from 237,292 in 1960, to 1,645,472 in 1990, and to nearly 2.9 million (including some half a million mixed-race persons) in 2000. Much of this extraordinary growth is primarily due to immigration. According to the U.S. Citizenship and Immigration Services (formerly Immigration and Naturalization Service or INS), more than 1.3 million immigrants were admitted to the United States from China, Hong Kong, and Taiwan as permanent residents between 1961 and

---

[2]*Ethnoburb* is a term developed by Wei Li (1997) to refer to suburban ethnic clustering of diverse groups with no single racial ethnic group dominates.

2000 (USINS, 2002).[3] China has been on the list of top ten immigrant-origin countries in the United States since 1980. The U.S. Census also attests to the big part played by immigration. As of 2000, the foreign born accounted for more than two-thirds of the ethnic Chinese population in the United States. The majority of the U.S.-born is still very young, living in immigrant families, and is just beginning to come of age in large numbers. At present, the ethnic Chinese population is primarily made up from the first generation (foreign-born), approximately a quarter belongs to the second generation (U.S.-born of foreign-born parentage), and only a small fraction (about 10%) belongs to the third-plus generation (U.S.-born of U.S.-born parentage).

The "Old" Second Generation

As is well documented in the history of Chinese immigration to the United States, Chinese immigrants initially came to this country from the southern region of China's Guangdong Province (Chan, 1991). Many were young men leaving behind their parents, wives, and children in rural villages in search of a sojourner's dream—to make money and then return home with "gold and glory" (Zhou, 1992). They helped develop the American West and built the most difficult part of the transcontinental railroad west of the Rockies, but ended up being targets of nativism and racism when their work was no longer needed (Saxton, 1971). Poor economic conditions in the late 1870s exacerbated anti-Chinese agitation, leading to the passage of the Chinese Exclusion Act in 1882, which lasted until 1943. Consequently, immigrant Chinese built Chinatowns and reorganized their sojourning lives within these socially isolated enclaves on the West Coast, such as in San Francisco and Los Angeles, and in other major urban centers to which many had fled, such as New York and Chicago. Within Chinatown, levels of coethnic interaction and solidarity were high, almost entirely through working in Chinese-owned businesses and socializing in various family or kinship associations, hometown or district associations, and tongs or merchants' associations.

During the exclusion era, there were few women, families, and children living in Chinatowns, known as bachelors' societies. The sex ratio was nearly 27 males per female in 1890, and dropped to 9 males per female in 1910. Although the sex ratio gradually evened out over time, males still outnumbered females by more than 2:1 in the 1940s. The shortage of women combined with the "paper son" phenomenon and other illegal entry of young men stifled the formation of "normal" families and the natural reproduction of the ethnic population. Because of restricted immigration, the size of the second generation was small but had become increasingly visible among the aging bachelors since the

---

[3]The number was 792,529 between 1961 and 1990, and 528,893 between 1991 and 2000.

early 1930s. In 1900, less than 9% of the ethnic Chinese population was U.S.-born; because of low immigration, the U.S.-born share increased steadily to over half between 1940 and 1970. The children born in the United States prior to World War II were mostly born in the late 1920s and the 1930s and were still very young at the outbreak of the war. As of 1930, the proportion of US-born went up to 41%. Like other racial minority children, the children of Chinese immigrants were not permitted to attend public schools with White children, and as they grew up, few were able to find jobs in the mainstream economy commensurate with their levels of education.

During and after World War II, more Chinese women than men were admitted to the United States, most of them as war brides, but the annual quota of immigrant visas for the Chinese was only 105 after the lifting of the Chinese Exclusion Act. In the 1950s, hundreds of refugees and their families fled Communist China to come to the United States, and despite low immigration, the arrival of Chinese refugee families contributed to the increased proportion of U.S.-born children, which went up to 61% in 1960. Between 1940 and 1970, the U.S.-born outnumbered the foreign-born in the Chinese American community. This "old" second generation was disproportionately young; almost all of them had immigrant parents, and the majority grew up in Chinatown.

The "New" Second Generation

After World War II, the ethnic Chinese community in the United States grew steadily as the old second generation reached adulthood and had shifted to a more settled community comprising a U.S.-born majority by 1960. However, contemporary Chinese immigration brought about an unprecedented transformation. As impacted by the Immigration Act of 1965, which abolished the national origins quota system and gave priority to family unification and to the importation of skilled labor, the Chinese American community rapidly transformed from a bachelors' society to an immigrant-dominant family community. The 10-fold growth of the Chinese American population from 1960 to 2000 is not merely a matter of numbers but rather a significant turning point for community development and identity formation. What characterizes this social transformation is the tremendous within-group diversity in terms of place of origin, socioeconomic background, patterns of geographic settlement, and modes of social mobility.

Compared to earlier Chinese immigrants, contemporary Chinese immigrants have arrived not only from mainland China but also from the greater Chinese diaspora—Hong Kong, Taiwan, Vietnam, Cambodia, Malaysia, and the Americas. In Los Angeles, for example, 23% of Chinese American population was born in the United States, 27% in mainland China, 20% in Taiwan, 8% in Hong Kong, and 22% from other countries around the world as of 1990. Diverse origins entail diverse cultural patterns. Linguistically, for example, Chinese immigrants come from a much wider variety of dialect groups than in the past. Although all Chinese share a single ancestral written language (varied only in traditional and simplified versions of characters), they speak numerous regional dialects—Cantonese, Mandarin, Minnan, Hakka, Chaozhou, and Shanghai—that are not easily understood even among Chinese immigrants.

Contemporary Chinese immigrants have also come from diverse socioeconomic backgrounds. Some arrived in the United States with little money, minimum education, few job skills, and from rural areas like their counterparts of the past, which forced them to take low-wage jobs and settle in deteriorating urban neighborhoods. Others came with considerable family savings, education, and skills far above the levels of average Americans. Nationwide, for example, levels of educational attainment among foreign-born Chinese were significantly higher than those of the general U.S. population. In 2000, 65% of foreign-born Chinese aged 25 to 39 years had attained at least 4 years of college education, compared to 30% of U.S.-born non-Hispanic Whites.

Contemporary Chinese immigrants have also shown diverse patterns of settlement, which are characterized by concentration as well as dispersion. Geographical concentration, to some extent, follows a historical pattern: Chinese Americans have continued to concentrate in the West and in urban areas. One state, California, accounts for nearly 40% of all Chinese Americans (1.1 million). New York accounts for 16%, second only to California, and Hawaii, 6%. However, other states that historically received few Chinese immigrants have now witnessed phenomenal growth, such as Texas, New Jersey, Massachusetts, Illinois, Washington, Florida, Maryland, and Pennsylvania. Among large cities (with populations over 100,000), New York City (365,000), San Francisco (161,000), Los Angeles (74,000), Honolulu (69,000), and San Jose (58,000) have the largest numbers of Chinese Americans. Small suburban cities in Los Angeles and the San Francisco Bay Area have also seen extraordinarily high proportions of Chinese Americans in the general population. Traditional urban enclaves, such as Chinatowns in San Francisco, New York, Los Angeles, Chicago, and Boston, have continued to exist and receive new immigrants, but they no longer serve as primary centers of initial settlement, as many new immigrants, especially the affluent and highly skilled, bypass inner cities to settle into suburbs immediately after arrival. Currently, only 2% the Chinese in Los Angeles, 8% of the Chinese in San Francisco, and 14% of the Chinese in New York live in old Chinatowns. The majority of the Chinese American population is spreading out in outer areas or suburbs in traditional gateway cities as well as in new urban centers of Asian settlement across the country, and half of all Chinese Americans live in suburbs. New ethnoburbs—multiethnic, immigrant-dominant suburban municipalities—have appeared since the 1980s, showing a completely new pattern of immigrant settlement

(Li, 1997). The 2000 Census records 11 suburban cities in the United States in which Chinese Americans make up more than 20% of the city's population.

These demographic changes in the Chinese American community have created multiple contexts under which the new second generation (the U.S.-born or U.S.-raised children of contemporary immigrants) is coming of age. Three main neighborhood contexts are particularly important analytically: (a) traditional ethnic enclaves, such as inner-city Chinatowns, (b) ethnoburbs, and (c) White middle-class suburbs. The challenges confronting new Chinese immigrant families are constrained by the interaction between unique family dynamics and immediate contextual factors. How these challenges affect family relations is what I now turn to discuss.

NEW CHALLENGES CONFRONTING THE CHINESE IMMIGRANT FAMILY

During the era of legal exclusion, most of the Chinese immigrants were isolated in inner-city ethnic enclaves, which were characterized as bachelors' societies. Many Chinatown "bachelor" workers were actually married but left their wives, children, and parents behind in their villages in China. Of the few "normal" families that existed in the bachelors' society, many were families of merchants or of workers who were able to claim to be partners of the merchants for immigration purpose. In old Chinatowns, individuals and families were well connected to the ethnic community, highly dependent on it for social, economic, and emotional support, while also subject to its control. Chinatown children grew up in a unique extended family environment, surrounded by and under the watchful eyes of many "grandpas" and "uncles" who were not related by blood but related by an intricate system of family kin or parental friendship associations. Their behavior and that of their parents were closely monitored by a closely knit ethnic community. They were either "good" kids—loyal, guai (obedient), and you-chu-xi (promising)—or "bad" kids—disrespectful, bai-jia-zi (family failure), and mei-chu-xi (good-for-nothing). They grew up speaking fluent Chinese, mostly in local dialects, going to Chinese schools, working in Chinese-owned businesses in Chinatown, and interacting intimately with other Chinese in the ethnic enclave. Many wished to become like other American children but faced resistance from the larger society as well as from their own families. The larger society looked down on the Chinese and set barriers to keep them apart, such as segregation in schools and workplaces. The Chinese families tied their children to Chinatown and its ethnic institutions, with Chinese school being the most important one, to shield them from being harmed by overt discrimination. Consequently, despite much adolescent rebellion and intense generational conflicts within the family, the children often found themselves going full circle back to ethnic networks without much room to act up and eventually becoming nobody but Chinese.

Unlike members of the old second generation, who were legally excluded from participating in the American mainstream and who simply did not have the freedom to choose whom they wanted to be, the new second generation lived in a more open and more accepting society even though their growing-up experiences were constrained by diverse family socioeconomic backgrounds and immediate neighborhood contexts. Those who reside in inner-city Chinatowns are generally from recently arrived, low-income families. Like the old second generation, they speak Chinese fluently, interact primarily with people in a Chinese-speaking environment, and participate in various cultural and social institutions of the ethnic community. However, they no longer live in a hostile environment that socially and legally excludes the Chinese. Even though they may still go to schools with mostly immigrant Chinese and other minority children in their neighborhoods, they have more opportunities to interact with non-coethnic children, move around in society, and choose what they want to do in life. But because of the structural constraints associated with disadvantaged class status, Chinatown children would face greater risks of being trapped in permanent poverty and downward assimilation than their middle-class peers (Portes & Zhou, 1993).

Those who reside in multiethnic ethnoburbs are mostly from upper- and middle-income families mixed with some low-income families. They generally go to suburban public schools that are better and have more resources than inner-city schools, although those schools are also likely to be dominated by coethnic and other minority children. They also have easy access to a wide range of ethnic institutions quite different from those in old Chinatown, such as after-school tutoring (*buxiban*), academic enrichment centers, and sports and music programs offered by Chinese-owned private businesses. They too speak Chinese fluently, interact with other Chinese, and are associated with things "Chinese," including food, music, and customs. But they also interact with people of diverse racial/ethnic backgrounds.

The children of Chinese immigrants who reside in suburban White middle-class neighborhoods tend to have parents who have achieved high levels of education, occupation, income, and English proficiency and who are fluent bicultural, transnational, cosmopolitan, and highly assimilated. These children attend schools with predominantly White students and have few primary contacts with coethnic peers. Many grow up speaking only English at home and have friends who are mostly Whites.

Overall, the new second generation grows up in a more open society than the old generation. These children are free of most of the legal barriers to educational and occupational attainments that blocked the mobility of the old second generation. They also tend to live in "normal" family neighborhoods and have more sources of social support beyond the ethnic community. And they have much more opportunities to "find themselves," "be themselves," and "become American" and have more leverage to rebel if they choose to. For example, they have to power to report to authorities, call 911, or even threaten to throw their parents in jail when they feel being "abused" at home, because social institutions and the legal system in the large society provide such support. And should they decide to run away from home, they would have more options to get by. Ironically, immigrant parents in a more open society often find it harder than in the isolated enclave to raise children according to their ways, because of the more intense bicultural conflicts between the parents' social world and the mainstream society.

Like all other immigrants, contemporary Chinese immigrants confront some of most profound challenges when they move to America. The first challenge is the drastic change in the sociocultural context surrounding the family. In their respective homelands—mainland China, Taiwan, Hong Kong—Chinese families are often extended in nature, with grandparent(s) and other relatives either in the home or in close contact. Upon arriving in the United States, these close family, kin, and friendship ties and the associated support and control mechanisms are disrupted. In the past, individual migrants and their families came from the same rural villages in sending countries and arrived in a transplanted village in the United States, so the broken ties could be easily rebuilt in Chinatowns that resembled those left behind in villages in the homeland. Today, however, immigrants are from diverse origins; even if they are from the same region and share the same local dialect, they are unlikely to belong to the same social circle and are just as likely to be strangers as they were to move from one place to another in their own homelands. The unfamiliar sociocultural environment, combined with the lack of American cultural literacy, English language proficiency, and education and job skills for some, adds to the difficulty in initial settlement. When immigrant families arrive first in ethnic enclaves or ethnoburbs, they may be able to reconnect to or rebuild ethnic networks, but these new ethnic networks tend to be composed of coethnic "strangers" rather than close kin and friends and tend to be more instrumental than emotionally intimate and homey. As I have just mentioned, the majority of contemporary Chinese immigrant families disperse into White middle-class suburbs. Such geographic dispersion further detaches new immigrants from the existing ethnic community and makes it more difficult for them to rebuild social networks based on common origins and a common cultural heritage. Although affluent Chinese immigrant families may not need ethnic networks and ethnic resources as much as their working-class counterparts, many find them comforting, convenient, and at times instrumental for enforcing certain traditional Chinese values to which they hold firm, but they are physically far away from the ethnic community.

The second challenge is the significant change in family relations in the immigrant family. The majority of the children live in families with both parents working full-time and some at several jobs on different shifts. Because of disadvantages associated with immigrant status, many Chinese immigrant men experience downward mobility and have difficulty in getting jobs that secure their role as main breadwinners. Women have to work outside the home, and many contribute equally, if not more, to the family while continuously taking the principal responsibility for childrearing, which has subtly changed the spousal relations. That women work outside the home often creates difficulty in the family. Without the help of grandparents, relatives, and other close friends, many young children become latch-key children, staying home alone after school hours, which is in violation of government regulations. Changes in parent–child relations are also noteworthy, particularly in families where the parents have low levels of education and job skills and speak little or no English. Often these parents have to depend on their children as translators and brokers between home and the outside world, which severely curtails parental authority.

The third challenge is the generation gap that is exacerbated by a cultural gap between the immigrant family and the larger society. This gap is particularly discernible in the discrepancy in goal orientation and the means of achieving goals between immigrant parents and their U.S.-born or -raised children. Because of immigrant selectivity, most adult immigrants and the parent generation are busy working, focusing first on putting food on the table and then moving themselves or their families up in society. They structure their lives primarily around three goals, as a Chinese immigrant put it: "To live in your own house, to be your own boss, and to send your children to the Ivy League." They too try to acculturate or assimilate into American society but only in ways that facilitate the attainment of these goals. The children, in contrast, want more. They aspire to be American like everyone else, in the words of a U.S.-born high school student from Los Angeles' Chinatown, "looking cool, going to the ball games, eating hamburgers and French fries, taking family vacations, having fun … feeling free to do whatever you like rather than what your parents tell you to."

This cultural gap sets the parents and children apart, often dampens the already strained parent–child relations. Often children regard their immigrant parents as *lao-wan-gu* and parental ways as outdated and old-fashioned, and they consciously rebel against parental traditions. The parents, aside from juggling work and household responsibilities that devour most of their waking hours, are worried that their children have too much freedom, too little respect for authority, and too many unfavorable stimuli in school, on the street, and on the television screen at home, and are horrified by their children's acting up. However, they experience difficulty in communicating with their Americanized children and in mediating between their expectation and their children's own needs, which further intensifies intergenerational conflicts. To make matters worse, the parents' customary ways of exercising authority or disciplining children, which were considered normative and acceptable in the old world, have suddenly become obsolete and even illegal, further eroding parental power in parent–child relations.

It should be noted that the cultural gap also affects the relations between foreign-born adolescents and their U.S. born or -raised coethnic peers. Immigrant youth, those who arrived in the United States as teenagers, had spent the majority of their formative years in a different culture, were schooled in a different language, had established peer groups, and were immersed in a different youth culture than that in the United States. In their homeland, they played a leading role in defining what was *in*, what was cool, and what was trendy, and many were average students in their schools. However, once in the United States, they suddenly find themselves standing out the wrong way, becoming the objects of mockery and ridicule and being referred to derogatively as FOBs (fresh-off-the-boat) by their U.S.-born or raised coethnic peers (Chiang-Hom, 2004; Pyke & Dang, 2003). They also experience hardship in school. Because of the language cultural difficulties, many newly arrived adolescents are unable to express themselves and are thus misunderstood by the teacher and fellow students; they are frequent teased, mocked, or harassed by other students because of their different look, accent, and dress; and they fear to bring these problems up at the dinner table for fear that their parents will get upset or blame them. When their problems are unaddressed by schools or by parents, the youth become discouraged, and the discouragement is sometimes followed by losing interest, plunging grades, and eventually dropping out of school and joining gangs. These problems are summed up in a community organizer's remark: "It is sometimes easier to be a gangster. These kids were generally considered 'losers' by their teachers, parents, and peers in school. In school or at home, they feel uncomfortable, isolated, and rejected, which fosters a sense of hopelessness and powerlessness and a yearning for recognition. In the streets, they feel free from all the normative pressures. It is out there that they feel free to be themselves and to do things wherever and whenever they want, giving them a sort of identity and a sense of power."

These challenges are real and serious with a far-reaching impact on the well-being of immigrant parents and children as they both strive to get ahead and get accepted in American society. Next, I explore some of the most intense points of intergenerational conflicts and the ways in which parents and children come to appreciate and reconcile differences.

STRADDLING TWO SOCIOCULTURAL WORLDS: CONFLICTS AND RECONCILIATION

Today second-generation Chinese Americans are still very young and are just beginning to come of age in significant numbers.[4] The 2000 Current Population Survey indicates that 44% of the U.S.-born Chinese are between ages 0 and 17 years and another 10% between ages 18 and 24.[5] Differing from their foreign-born parents, children of immigrant parentage lack meaningful connections to the sociocultural world from which their parents came. Thus, they are unlikely to consider a foreign country as a point of reference, and are much more likely to evaluate themselves or to be evaluated by others by the standards of their country of birth or the one in which they are raised (Gans, 1992; Portes & Zhou, 1993; Zhou, 1997). However, because of their immigrant parentage, the children have constantly found themselves straddle two sociocultural worlds—Chinese versus American—which is at the core of head-on intergenerational conflicts within the Chinese immigrant family.

In the Chinese cultural context, filial piety dictates parent–child relationships (Sung, 1987). But this norm is often expected more of the children than of both parents and children reciprocally. That is, the child's filial responsibility is the debt of life owed to parents and the children are expected to suppress their own self-interests to satisfy parental needs, regardless of whether parental needs are appropriate or rational (Dion & Dion, 1996; Yeh & Bedford, 2003). Relative to filial piety is the notion of unconditional obedience, or submission, to authority—the parent, the elder, and the superior. The parent is the authority in the home, as is the teacher in the school. The parent, often the father, is not supposed to show too much affection, to play with children, or to treat children as equals. The parental stone-faced authoritative image often inhibits children from questioning, much less challenging, their parents. Furthermore, in the traditional Chinese family, there is little room for individualism. Every member is tied to one another, and every act of individual members is considered an honor or a shame to the whole family. Thus, Chinese parents are expected to bring up their children in ways that honor the family.

Asymmetric filial piety, unconditional submission to authority, and face-saving override other familial values in the traditional Chinese family. Even though changes have occurred through modernization,

---

[4]Estimated from the Current Population Survey (CPS) data, 1998–2000. See Logan et al. (2001).

[5]Compared to 8% between 0 and 17 years and 8% between 18 and 24 years in the first generation.

these traditional influences are still quite substantial after families migrate to a new social environment. In the American context, such absolute familial practices are frowned on, and children and parents are expected to be independent individuals on equal terms. So parent–child conflicts in the immigrant Chinese family are not just intergenerational but cultural.

SENSITIVE PRESSURE POINTS

The immigrant Chinese family is often referred to by the children as a "pressure cooker," where intense intergenerational conflicts accumulate and sometimes boil to the point of explosion. There are some sensitive pressure points in the immigrant Chinese family—the issues of education, work ethic, consumption behavior, and dating, among others, which can stir up potentially intense conflicts (Sung, 1987).

Education is perhaps most important for the immigrant Chinese family when it come to raising children. Chinese parents, who were raised in Confucian tradition, tend to be particularly demanding and unyielding on their children's educational achievement. Although education is generally considered a primary means to upward social mobility in all American families, it is emphasized in some unique ways in the immigrant Chinese family. First and foremost, the children's success in school is very much tied to face-saving for the family (Sung, 1987; Zhou, 1997). Thus, parents consistently remind their children that achievement is a duty and an obligation to the family rather than to an individual goal and that if they fail, they will bring shame to the family. So children are under tremendous pressure to succeed. Parents are also pressured to ensure children's success, because bragging is common among relatives, friends, and coethnic coworkers.

Immigrant parents also take a pragmatic stance on education. They believe that education is not only the most effective means to success in society but also the *only* means. The parents are keenly aware of their own limitations as immigrants and the larger structural constraints, such as limited family wealth even among middle-income immigrants, lack of access to social networks connecting to the mainstream economy and various social and political institutions, and entry barriers to certain occupations because of racial stereotyping and discrimination. Their own experience tells them that a good education in certain fields would be a safe bet for their children to get good jobs in the future. These fields include science, math, engineering, and medicine, as well as business and law to a lesser extent. So in practice, the parents are concerned more about their children's academic coursework, grades, and majors in their preferred fields than about the children's well-rounded learning experience and extracurricular activities. They would discourage their children's interests in pursuing history, literature, music, dance, sports, or anything that they consider unlikely to lead to good-paying, stable jobs. Instead, they pressure their children to get involved in these academic fields and extracurricular activities only to the extent that such involvement would enhance the children's chance of getting into an Ivy League college. The children often get frustrated by the fact that their parents choose the type of education for them and make decisions for their future, even although they share the same value of education with their parents.

Another sensitive point issue is the work ethic. Immigrant Chinese parents believe that hard work, rather than natural ability or innate intelligence, is the key to educational success. Regardless of socioeconomic backgrounds, they tend to think (also tend to make their children believe) that their children can all get A's in their tests in school if they just work hard. If the children get a grade lower than what the parents expect, they will be scolded as not working hard enough. The parents also believe that by working twice as hard, one can overcome structural disadvantages associated with immigrant and/or racial minority statuses. Although they are very concerned about their children's learning, they are interested mostly in their children's report cards and will not be satisfied with any grades other than an "A." And they tend to ignore the fact that not everybody learns English, catches up with school work, and established productive relationship with teachers and fellow students at an equal rate. Many do not participate in the parent–teacher associations at their children's schools, considering these an "interference" with school in educating their children (but they do get actively involved in Chinese schools). As a result, the children often find themselves working at least twice as hard as their American peers and simultaneously feeling that their parents never think that they work hard enough.

A third sensitive issue is related to the value of thrift. Immigrant Chinese parents emphasize savings as a means of effectively deploying available family resources. They often bluntly reject material possessions and conspicuous consumption on the part of children and perceive spending money on name-brand clothes, luxurious accessories, and fashionable hairstyles as a sign of corruption, which they often term as becoming "too American" (the code word for "bad"; Sung, 1987). However, these parents seldom hesitate to spend on whatever they consider good for their children, such as books, computer software, after-school programs, Chinese lessons, private tutors, and other educational-oriented activities. They do not just do it in the best interest of their children but are also driven by the mentality of "turning sons into dragons (and daughters into phoenixes)."

The fourth sensitive issue is dating, especially dating at an early age. Chinese parents consider dating in high school not only a wasteful academic distraction but also an unhealthy, promiscuous behavior, especially for girls (Dion & Dion, 2001). But parents' attitudes toward dating in high school grow more ambivalent over time. It is interracial dating, rather than early dating in general, that "freaks them out." The parents' overconcern about girls is more out of practical consideration about the potential risks of unwanted pregnancy than out of moral consideration about having sex.

The different views on these issues between parents and children have become the sources of intense parent–child conflicts as the children rapidly acculturate into American ways. For both parents and children, there is often a bitter feeling about being so far apart from each other. Working-class Chinese immigrant parents living or working in ethnic enclaves or ethnoburbs are usually demanding and unbending when it comes to their children's education and behavioral standards, but they do not have the time, the patience, the cultural sensitivity, and the financial and human capital resources to be more compromising, and their reference group is usually made up of other Chinese immigrant parents with whom they maintain frequent contacts. Middle-class Chinese parents living in White middle-class suburbs are demanding too and expect high performance of their children, but because of their higher socioeconomic status and higher level of acculturation, they consciously try to be more like other American parents while adhering to what they believe is good for their children. Although most are unyielding to the cultural expectations, some middle-class parents develop a sense of guilt for not being model American parents and thus become more easygoing and less strict with their children. For example, when a child refuses to do schoolwork on weekends as the father demands, talking back with "nobody works on weekends," a middle-class father living in the suburb would shrug with a smile and do nothing much but let his child run off with his friends, because he himself doesn't have to work on weekends. But the working-class father would get mad and make the child feel guilty about his own sacrifice, because he has to work on weekends to support the family.

ETHNIC NETWORKS AND ETHNIC INSTITUTIONS AS MEDIATING GROUNDS

Tremendous parental pressures for conformity and achievement in the Chinese immigrant family can lead to intense intergenerational conflict, rebellious behavior, withdrawal from school, and alienation from the networks that are supposed to help. Alienated children fall easy preys to street gangs. Even those children who do well in school and hope to make their parents happy and proud are at risk of being rebellious. A high school student said, "But that [doing well to make parents happy] never happens. My mother is never satisfied no matter what you do and how well you do it." This remark echoes a frustration felt by many other Chinatown youths, who voiced how much they wish not to be compared with other children and how much they wish to rebel.

Intense bicultural conflicts, coupled with the American popular culture that glorifies self-indulgence and youth rebellion, severely circumvent the role of the family in socializing children in the expected direction. Paradoxically, however, many Chinese immigrant children, regardless of socioeconomic backgrounds, seem to have lived up to their parents' expectations. Most remarkable is in the area of education, where Chinese immigrant children outperform other Americans, including non-Hispanic Whites, by significantly large margins. They have scored exceptionally high in standardized tests, have been overrepresented in the nation's prestigious and Ivy League schools, and have disproportionately made the top lists of many national or regional academic contests. They have appeared repeatedly in the top-10 award winners' list of the Westinghouse Science Talent Search, now renamed as the Intel Science Talent Search, one of the country's most prestigious high school academic contests. In 1991, 4 of the top 10 winners were Chinese Americans; all of these were either foreign-born or U.S.-born of foreign-born parentage. Their level of educational achievement is far above that of the immigrant generation, which is also already much higher than the national average. For example, at the University of California, Los Angeles, where I teach, the proportion of Chinese Americans in the entering class in the past few years has reached 18%, higher than the proportions of Blacks and Latinos combined.

Is the extraordinary educational achievement of Chinese Americans a result of the parental pressure for success and enforcement of Confucian values? There is no simple answer. A more appropriate question is: How is it possible for the Chinese immigrant family, plagued with potential and real intergenerational conflicts, to exercise parental authority and enforce the Confucian value of education? As I have just discussed, the home is usually where conflict erupts and boils up to a point that neither parents nor children have any room to breathe. Why would the children end up doing what their parents expect them to do? Based on my research in the Chinese immigrant community, I highlight two of the less obvious but most sensible lessons—the formation of an ethnic institutional environment and multiple ethnic involvements.

In Chinatowns, there have developed an ethnic enclave economy and a range of ethnic social and cultural institutions to support the daily needs of Chinese immigrants. As the community shifts from a bachelors' society to a family-based community, traditional ethnic institutions also shift their functions to serve families and children, ranging from weekend Chinese schools to a much wider variety of educational and recreational enterprises, such as daily afterschool classes that match formal school curricula, English enhancement classes, exam cram schools, college prep schools, music/dance/sports studios, and so on. These children-oriented enterprises, both nonprofit and private, have also developed in Chinese ethnoburbs.

The Chinese language school is particularly illustrative. In New York City, the Chinatown Chinese Language School (*Zhongwen xuexiao*), run by the Chinese Consolidated Benevolent Association (CCBA), is perhaps the largest children- and youth-oriented organization in the nation's Chinatowns.[6] The school annually (not including summer) enrolls about 4,000 Chinese children, from preschool to 12th grade, in its 137 Chinese language classes and over 10 specialty classes (e.g., band, choir, piano, cello, violin, T'ai chi, ikebana, dancing, and Chinese painting). The Chinese language classes run from 3:00 to 6:30 p.m. daily, after regular school hours. Students usually spend one hour on regular school homework and two hours on Chinese language or other selected specialties. The school also has English classes for immigrant youths and adult immigrant workers (Zhou, 1997; Zhou & Li, 2003).

As Chinese immigrants became residentially dispersed, Chinese language schools likewise have begun to spring up in suburbs. As of the mid-1990s, there were approximately 635 Chinese language schools in the United States (189 in California), enrolling nearly 83,000 students (Chao, 1996). The Chinese language school experience is a definitive ethnic affirming experience for most Chinese immigrant children. In response to the question "What makes you Chinese?" many Chinese students agree that "going to Chinese school" defines what is Chinese. In Chinese language school, Chinese immigrant children come to understand their own problems with their parents as common in all Chinese families and that their parents are simply acting like all other Chinese parents. They come to terms with the fact that growing up in Chinese families is different. As Sung (1987, p. 126) observed:

> For Chinese immigrant children who live in New York's Chinatown or in satellite Chinatowns, these [bi-cultural] conflicts are moderated to a large degree because there are other Chinese children around to mitigate the dilemmas that they encounter. When they are among their own, the Chinese ways are better known and better accepted. The Chinese customs and traditions are not denigrated to the degree that they would be if the immigrant child were the only one to face the conflict on his or her own.

Ethnic institutions not only provide a site where Chinese children meet other coethnic peers, but also allow the children to develop their own strategies to cope, some of which may be disapproving. For example, when it comes to dating, a girl can tell her parent that she is going out with so-and-so from the Chinese school whom her parent knows, but runs off with her White sweetheart to a movie or to the shopping mall. And the parent would confirm it with the reference from the Chi-

---

[6]The Chinese Consolidated Benevolent Association (CCBA) is a quasi-government in Chinatown. It used to be an apex group representing some 60 different family and district associations, guilds, tongs, the Chamber of Commerce, and the Nationalist Party, and has remained the most influential ethnic organization in the Chinese immigrant community.

nese school, whom the girl has already warned in advance. Chinese parents usually trust their children's friends from Chinese schools because they also know the parents of these Chinese school friends.

Chinese language schools have become an ethnic community for Chinese immigrants, especially those who do not live in Chinatown or Chinese ethnoburbs. Most of the suburban Chinese language schools are registered as nonprofit organizations that require much parental volunteer support.[7] When children enroll in Chinese schools, their parents automatically become members of the school's administrative body, and volunteer their time to serve as principal and/or administrative officials (Chao, 1996; Wang, 1996). As a result, suburban Chinese schools function as ethnic social organizations where adults (parents) come to socialize. A Chinese parent likens the suburban Chinese school to a church, and said in an interview at a Chinese school:

> We are non-religious and don't go to church. So coming to Chinese school weekly is like going to church for us. While our children are in class, we parents don't just go home because we live quite far away, we hang out here and participate in a variety of things that we organize for ourselves, including dancing, fitness exercise, seminars on the stock market, family financial management, children's college prep. I kind of look forward to going to the Chinese school on Saturdays because there is the only time we can socialize with our own people in our native language. I know some of our older kids don't like it that much. When they complain, I simply tell them, "this is not a matter of choice, you must go."

In these ethnic settings, parents meet with other parents who share similar concerns and problems and work out strategies to deal with them.

In summary, ethnic institutions are vital in positively affecting the younger generation. Instrumentally, these institutions provide a safe, healthy, and stimulating environment where youngsters, especially the ones whose parents are at work, can go after school. The Chinese schools and various after-school programs not only ensure the time spent on homework or on other constructive activities, but also help to keep children off the streets and to reduce the anxieties and worries of working parents. More important, these ethnic institutions offer some space where children can express and share their feelings. A Chinese school teacher said, "It is very important to allow youths to express themselves in their own terms without parental pressures. Chinese parents usually have very high expectations of their children. When children find it difficult to meet these expectations and do not have an outlet for their frustration and anxiety, they tend to become alienated and lost on streets."

---

[7]For-profit Chinese language schools are often found in Chinatowns or ethnoburbs, including many kindergartens and child care centers for young children, and offering various tutorial programs for secondary school students (Wang, 1996).

Ethnic institutions also serve as a bridge between a seemingly closed immigrant community and the mainstream society (Zhou & Li, 2003). Immigrant parents and the children who live in ethnic enclaves or ethnoburbs are relatively isolated, and their daily exposure to the larger American society is limited. Many parents, usually too busy working, tend to expect their children to do well in school and to have successful careers in the future, but are unable to give specific directions to their children's educational and career plans, leaving a gap between high expectations and realistically feasible means of meeting these expectations. Ethnic institutions fill this gap to help young people to become more aware of their choices and potentials and to help them find realistic means of moving up socioeconomically into mainstream society instead of being stuck in Chinatown. After-school programs, tutor services, and test preparation programs are readily available in the enclave, making school after school possible and an accepted norm. An educator said, "When you think of how much time these Chinese kids put in their studies after regular school, you won't be surprised why they succeed in such a high rate."

Furthermore, ethnic institutions function as cultural centers, where Chinese traditional values and a sense of ethnic identity are nurtured. Students participating in the after-school programs, especially the U.S.-born and -reared, often speak English to one another in their Chinese classes, and they actually learn a limited number of Chinese words each day. However, they are exposed to something that is quite different from what they learn in school and are able to relate to Chinese "stuff" without being teased about it. They also listen to stories and sing songs in Chinese, and these reveal different aspects of Chinese history and culture. Children and youths learn to write in Chinese such phrases as "I am Chinese" and "My ancestral country is in China," and to recite classical Chinese poems and Confucius sayings about family values, behavioral and moral guidelines, and the importance of schooling. A Chinese school principal made it clear: "These kids are here because their parents sent them. They are usually not very motivated in learning Chinese per se, and we do not push them too hard. Language teaching is only part of our mission. An essential part of our mission is to enlighten these kids about their own cultural heritage, so that they show respect for their parents and feel proud of being Chinese." Like other ethnic businesses, ethnic educational enterprises also attract suburban middle-class Chinese immigrants to return to Chinatown or ethnoburbs regularly, even though some may do so less frequently than others.

With the development of a wide range of ethnic economies and ethnic sociocultural institutions, Chinese immigrants, despite differences in origin, socioeconomic backgrounds, and geographic dispersion, have many opportunities to interact with one another as they participate in the ethnic community in multiple ways. Working, shopping, and socializing in the ethnic community tie immigrants to a closely knit system of ethnic social relations. Social networks, embedded in the broader Chinese immigrant community, function to reinforce common norms and standards and exercise control over those who are connected to it. Involvement in different type of ethnic institutions also helps children alleviate parental pressure. In many respects, the ethnic community and the tangible and intangible resources it provides have proven effective. Pressures and conflicts in a well-integrated ethnic community can serve to fulfill familial and community expectations. Children are motivated to learn and do well in school because they believe that education is their only way to get out of their parents' status and out of their parents' control. This motivation, while arising from parental pressure and being reinforced through their participation in the ethnic community, often leads to desirable outcomes. A community youth program organizer summed up in these words: "Well, tremendous pressures create problems for sure. However, you've got to realize that we are not living in an ideal environment. Without these pressures, you would probably see as much adolescent rebellion in the family, but a much *larger* [emphasis in tone] proportions of kids failing. Our goal is to get these kids out into college, and for that, we have been very successful."

CONCLUDING REMARKS

In America, many Chinese immigrant families expect their children to attain the highest levels of educational achievement possible and rely on them to move families up to middle-class status as a way to repay parental sacrifices and to honor the family name. Deviation from these normative expectations is considered shameful or "losing face" for the family. This study shows that it is not easy for immigrant families to enforce these cultural values and behavioral standards and to guarantee that familial expectations are met because of structural vulnerabilities associated with disadvantaged immigrant status and intense bicultural conflicts. In this situation, both parents and children have to constantly negotiate culture and ethnicity, make compromises, and resolve conflicts in order to navigate the "right" way into mainstream American society. However, this undertaking is by no means a family-only matter, but requires the involvement of broader networks of social support. In the case of contemporary immigrants, a well-organized, resourceful ethnic community that gears itself toward social mobility into mainstream American society plays a crucial role in providing not only tangible resources, in the form of ethnic educational institutions and children-oriented programs, but also intangible ethnic networking, serving as effective mechanisms of social control and sanctioning.

As a sociologist of immigration and race and ethnicity, I believe that cultural values and behavioral patterns seemingly unique to an ethnic group are not intrinsic to that group, but that they emerge from constant interactions with structural circumstances, including favorable (or unfavorable) contexts of reception of the immigrant group from the host society and the group's own orientation toward the host society and its ability to muster moral and instrumental supports. Thus, examining the immigrant family through the perspective of cultural psychology is helpful insofar as it pays close attention to various structural factors mediating the role of the family in affecting educational achievement. I thus reiterate that the processes leading to desirable outcomes are highly contingent on context, or on unique ethnic social environments.

It is evident from various quantitative data sources that young Chinese Americans are extremely driven to do well in school and are disproportionately represented at the nation's best universities, and that being Chinese has a significantly positive effect on educational achievement. However, what comes next has often gone unnoticed. On a personal note, as an immigrant mother who has raised a 1.5-generation child in America and as a professor at a university attended by a high concentration of Asian American students (making up nearly 40% of UCLA's undergraduate student body), the subject matter I have explored here holds personal significance for me. Although Chinese immigrant parents have been overwhelmingly preoccupied with their children gaining admission to prestigious colleges, many of them have overlooked the costs that come with success. My random observations at home and on campus, coinciding with my qualitative fieldwork, indicate that once these children get into their families' desired colleges, they are more or less on their own just like everyone else. Without the clear guidance and all the family and community supports to which they have gotten so accustomed, some of them feel lost and even suffer from emotional breakdown. This underscores the importance of shifting focus on the mental health and intellectual growth of the individual—how the children fare all on their own in a highly competitive academic environment that is simultaneously ultraliberal, and how they survive and thrive in this new environment. In this respect, the perspective of cultural psychology is beneficial.

AUTHOR BIOGRAPHY

Min Zhou, PhD, is a professor of sociology and the inaugural chair of the Department of Asian American Studies at the University of California, Los Angeles. Her main areas of research are immigration and immigrant adaptation, immigrant youths, Asian Americans, ethnic and racial relations, ethnic entrepreneurship and enclave economies, and the community and urban sociology. She is the author of *Chinatown: The Socioeconomic Potential of an Urban Enclave* (Temple University Press, 1992), coauthor of *Growing up American: How Vietnamese Children Adapt to Life in the United States* (Russell Sage Foundation Press, 1998), coeditor of *Contemporary Asian America* (New York

University Press, 2000), and coeditor of *Asian American Youth: Culture, Identity, and Ethnicity* (Routledge, 2004). Her web site is http://www.sscnet.ucla.edu/soc/faculty/zhou/

REFERENCES

Chan, S. (1991). *Asian Americans: An interpretive history.* New York: Twayne.

Chao, T. H. (1996). Overview. In X. Wang (Ed.), *A view from within: A case study of Chinese heritage community language schools in the United States* (pp. 7–13). Washington, DC: National Foreign Language Center.

Chiang-Hom, C. (2004). Transnational cultural practices of Chinese immigrant youth and parachute kids. In J. Lee & M. Zhou (Eds.), *Asian American youth: Culture, identity, and ethnicity* (pp. 143–158). New York: Routledge.

Dion, K. K., & Dion, K. L. (2001). Gender and cultural adaptation in immigrant families. *Journal of Social Issues, 57,* 511–521.

Dion, K. L., & Dion, K. K. (1996). Chinese adaptation to foreign cultures. In M. H. Bond (Ed.), *The handbook of Chinese psychology* (pp. 457–478). Hong Kong: Oxford University Press.

Gans, H. J. (1992). Second-generation decline: Scenarios for the economic and ethnic futures of the post-1965 American immigrants. *Ethnic and Racial Studies, 15*(2), 173–192.

Li, W. (1997). *Spatial transformation of an urban ethnic community from Chinatown to Chinese ethnoburb in Los Angeles.* PhD dissertation, Department of Geography, University of Southern California.

Logan, J. R., Stowell, J., & Vesselinov, E. (2001). *From many shores: Asians in Census 2000.* A report by the Lewis Mumford Center for Comparative Urban and Regional Research, State University of New York at Albany, viewed on October 6, 2001, at http://mumford1.dyndns.org/cen2000/report.html

Portes, A., & Zhou, M. (1993). The new second generation: Segmented assimilation and its variants. *Annals of the American Academy of Political and Social Science, 530,* 74–96.

Pyke, K., & Dang, T. (2003). "FOB" and "Whitewashed": Identity and internalized racism among second generation Asian Americans. *Qualitative Sociology, 26,* 147–172.

Saxton, A. (1971). *The indispensable enemy: Labor and the anti-Chinese movement in California.* Berkeley: University of California Press.

Sung, B. L. (1987). *The adjustment experience of Chinese immigrant children in New York City.* New York: Center for Migration Studies.

U.S. Immigration and Naturalization Service. (2002). *Statistical yearbook of the immigration and naturalization service, 2002.* Washington, DC: U.S. Government Printing Office.

Wang, X. (Ed.). (1996). *A view from within: A case study of Chinese heritage community language schools in the United States.* Washington, DC: National Foreign Language Center.

Yeh, K., & Bedford, O. (2003). *Filial piety and parent-child conflict.* Paper presented at the International Conference on "Intergenerational Relations in Families' Life Course," cosponsored by the Institute of Sociology, Academie

Sinica, Taiwan and the Committee on Family Research, International Sociological Association, March 12–14, Taipei.

Zhou, M. (1992). *Chinatown: The socioeconomic potential of an urban enclave.* Philadelphia, PA: Temple University Press.

Zhou, M. (1997). Social capital in Chinatown: The role of community-based organizations and families in the adaptation of the younger generation. In L. Weis & M. S. Seller (Eds.), *Beyond Black and White: New voices, new faces in the United States schools* (pp. 181–206). Albany, NY: State University of New York Press.

Zhou, M., & Li, X. (2003, Winter). Ethnic language schools and the development of supplementary education in the immigrant Chinese community in the United States. *New Directions for Youth Development: Understanding the Social Worlds of Immigrant Youth,* pp. 57–73.

18

Acculturation or Negotiation? What Japanese Academic Migrants Teach Us About Family Processes and Gendered Experiences of Cultural Adaptation

Izumi Sakamoto
University of Toronto

In the era of transnationalization, experiences of dealing with an unfamiliar culture are no longer limited to a small segment of society (Rodriguez, 1999). In fact, "unbounded transnational flows" of people (Lederman, 1998, p. 428) resulted in an estimated 175 million individuals living outside of their home countries (United Nations, 2002).

Besides immigrants and refugees whose aim often is to immigrate permanently to another country, there are international migrants whose stay in another country may be temporary. Manual laborers, migrant farm workers, multinational corporation employees, high-tech engineers, and their families could all be migrants experiencing movement across national boundaries. Scholars and students who pursue their academic training and opportunities in another country are another example of such transnational migrants. These migrants are what I call "academic migrants." Arguably the transnational move of academic migrants toward North America is necessitated by the increasingly Anglo- and U.S.-centric international academic environment (Swales, 1997). These populations include temporary workers, students, and scholars from other countries. In fact, approximately 655,000 "foreign" students/scholars were present in U.S. higher education institutions in the academic year of 2004–2005. Many of these academic migrants bring their families along, and contribute over $13 billion annual to the U.S. economy (Institute of International Education [IIE], 2005). Even though the increase has slowed down after 9/11, there are still triple the number of international students/scholars studying in the United States compared to that of 20 years ago (IIE, 2005). However, the experiences of these migrants are not fully accounted for in the existing psychological literature.

The study I present in this chapter is part of a larger project examining the flexibility of cultural socialization of the self, and the processes of cultural adaptation of these academic migrants and their spouses as they moved from Japan to the United States, two cultures that are arguably very different from each other (Markus & Kitayama, 1991). Japanese academic migrants constitute a significant population, as, in the last 10 years, Japan has consistently ranked within the top five countries of origin for international students enrolled in the U.S. higher education institutions (IIE, 2005). Further, the field of cultural psychology has studied Japanese selves more than any other national/cultural group (Fiske, Kitayama, Markus, & Nisbett, 1998). Thus, the context of the current research can be established without difficulties. The research questions asked were: If the view of self always requires a cultural context, as argued in cultural psychology literature (e.g., Fiske et al., 1998; Markus & Kitayama, 1991; Shweder & Bourne, 1984), how flexible is the cultural socialization of self? Second, what are the change processes of cultural socialization of the self? This chapter focuses specifically on how family and gender roles affect the change/negotiation processes of cultural self and cultural practices.

PSYCHOLOGICAL STUDIES
OF CULTURAL SELF AND ACCULTURATION

In the past decade, cultural psychology has offered numerous findings highlighting that an individual's mind and behavior are largely influenced by the contexts that he or she is in, which may vary dramatically from culture to culture (e.g., Fiske et al., 1998; Markus & Kitayama, 1991; Miller, 1997; Nisbett, Peng, Choi, & Norenzayan, 2001). For example, Markus and Kitayama (1991) described the differences between the interdependent and independent construals of self, specifically, East Asian views of the self versus European American views of the self. European American self-construals are characterized as being somewhat more autonomous or independent of context, whereas East Asian self-construals are described as more communal, interdependent, or embedded in social relationships. Although the former model of the self has a distinct boundary around the individual self to differentiate oneself from others, the latter incorporates close others into self as a culturally normative way of being a person. These cultural construals of self have been shown to affect people's cognitions, affect, and behaviors.

In addition to the outcome and process of culture, Markus, Mullally, and Kitayama (1997) also focused on the practices of culture, conceptualized as "selfways." *Selfways* are defined as ways in which being a person in the world is understood in the sociocultural context, including key cultural ideas and values such as how to be a "good," "appropriate," or "moral" person as well as cultural practices and identities. Although not used as frequently as the construct, "cultural construal of self," selfways has much potential in offering a more comprehensive view of the cultural influence on the self. Considerable research has been published in this area since Markus and Kitayama's 1991 article, highlighting the differences between Anglo North Americans and East Asians (Japanese, Chinese, Koreans; e.g., Fiske et al., 1998; Heine & Lehman, 1997; Heine, Lehman, Markus, & Kitayama, 1999; Nisbett et al., 2001). However, the selfways of people who are exposed to more than one distinct culture have not been explored. In learning the routines of a new culture, what happens to the "old" and "new" cultural selfways? To what extent can people actually learn new thought styles and new selfways?

Another body of literature that can possibly complement the *culture and the self* literature is acculturation. Acculturation literature and related areas (e.g., biculturalism, intercultural communication) have always been concerned with people who move between different cultures (Berry, 1990, 1997; Berry, Kim, Power, Young, & Bujaki, 1989; Cushner & Brislin, 1997; Frable, 1997; Hong, Morris, Chiu, & Benet-Martinez, 2000; LaFromboise, Coleman, & Gerton, 1993; Phinney & Devich-Navaroo, 1997). John Berry's model of acculturation attitudes is a representative of the orthogonal model of acculturation (Ryder, Alden, & Paulhus, 2000) and has been influential in the field (Berry, 1997; Berry et al., 1989). In his model, an acculturation attitude is determined by the extent to which an individual is willing to retain an old culture and to adopt a new one, which results in four types of acculturation attitudes, namely, *integration* (accept old culture; accept new culture), *assimilation* (reject old culture; accept new culture), *separation* (accept old culture; reject new culture), and *marginalization* (reject old culture; reject new culture). Although Berry and others studying acculturation from psychological perspectives have done much important groundwork in this area of research, relatively little is known about the ongoing everyday processes constructing their surrounding cultures, and the responses invoked by the negotiation process of "old" and "new" cultures. Moreover, often, psychological acculturation literature has lacked a view from the immigrants themselves, looking from the margin to the center (an exception would be Espín, 1999).

Furthermore, although the issues of gender, gender roles, and family in regards to migration have gained much attention in other areas of the social sciences, such as immigration studies, women's studies and sociology (Espiritu, 1999; Hondagneu-Sotelo, 1999; Man, 2004; Lim, 1997; Pessar, 1999; Valenzuela, 1999), psychological research on acculturation and (im)migration often lacks the focus on how gender and other power differentials affect cultural adaptation processes. Psychologists K. K. Dion and K. L. Dion (2001) called for a focus on the importance gender plays in the cultural adaptation of immigrant families.

Theories of biculturalism (e.g., LaFromboise et al., 1993; Hong et al., 2000; Phinney, 1990), when compared to acculturation literatures (e.g., Berry, 1997), are more sensitive to a person's interaction with the immediate environment and its impact on the resultant cultural mix internalized by the person. These theories, however, still do not address how different forms of power differentials may affect the process of becoming bicultural or being primed to act in one culture over another. For example, family dynamics and gender roles, as well as relative social power, would have to do with how freely one can go back and forth between the two cultural spaces.

Hermans and Kempen (1998) criticized current psychological studies of culture and identity for not accounting for the complexities and hybridization of cultures in an increasingly heterogeneous global system. Instead, they suggested alternative approaches that focus on "the contact zones of cultures," "the complexities of self and identity," and "the experience of uncertainty" (p. 1111–1112). These issues are central to the research reported here.

Acculturation literature that focuses on the change process of the marginal and the *culture and the self* literature that mainly celebrates the difference of the other have not yet had a significant cross-fertilizing encounter. However, there does seem to be a potential for creating a new field of research, given similar areas of interests but different perspectives. Further, both of the literatures will be largely enhanced by the focus on the gender and power differentials. To fill the empirical and theoretical gap, the study presented in this chapter investigated the negotiation processes and everyday practices of cultural adaptation of Japanese academic migrant families from a sociocultural self perspective (Sakamoto, 2001). Part of the findings relevant to the family is presented in this chapter.

METHOD

As part of a larger study examining the flexibility of selfways over different cultural contexts and the processes of such change as experienced by individuals, a grounded-theory study using in-depth interviews was conducted with Japanese academic migrants and their spouses in a Midwestern college town.

Informants

This study included 18 Japanese individuals (9 women and 9 men; mean age early 30s) who moved from Japan to the United States as adults. I interviewed some of them more than once, leading to a total of 26 in-depth interviews. Theoretical sampling[1] processes (Strauss & Corbin, 1998) guided the definition of the current sample. The criteria for informants, in addition to being adult migrants from Japan, included being born and raised by Japanese-ethnic parents in Japan, being in the mid-20s or older at the time of the interview, not having lived abroad longer than a couple of months, and having had some socially recognizable "adult" roles in Japan before coming to the United States (e.g., businesspeople, engineers, journalists, "housewives", mothers, and junior academics). Different sampling methods were used to seek a diverse sample of Japanese academic migrant families, using snowball and deviant sampling methods (Patton, 1990, p. 182). These informants were all voluntary participants and signed an informed consent form.

All the informants initially came to the United States for the purpose of study/research of their own or their spouses. The informants were all associated with a local, large state university, known to attract many international students and scholars, and their affiliation included graduate students, postdoctoral fellows, visiting scholars, and their spouses. All but four informants planned to return to Japan after 1 to 7 years in the United States. One female informant, a graduate of the university, was a professional working for a U.S. accounting firm. Fourteen of them were married to persons of the opposite sex, and came with their spouses to the United States, whereas one was divorced and the rest (three) were single. Single individuals were also interviewed for comparison purposes. Eleven informants were parents. Seven out of nine female informants initially came to the United States due to their husbands' study or research, and three of them later became master's level students themselves.

Data Collection: In-Depth Interviews

In-depth interviews were conducted in Japanese by the investigator. Attempts were made to conduct repeated interviews, with at least several months between interviews, to investigate changes over time, and to explore the validity of the emerging hypothesis about their experiences. Six informants were interviewed two or three times longitudinally. If the informants had spouses, attempts were made to interview

---

[1]Theoretical sampling is defined as "sampling on the basis of concepts that have proven theoretical relevance to the evolving theory" (Strauss & Corbin, 1990, p. 176). In theoretical sampling, "successive cases are chosen on the basis of the likelihood that they will advance the development of findings" (Gilgun, 1994, pp. 117–118).

both of them, which were partially successful. Two couples preferred speaking to me together, instead of individually, at least initially. For some other couples, the husbands were too busy or not accessible (out of the country). In one case the husband was reluctant for me to interview his wife, so I did not interview her. However, when husbands and wives were both interviewed, I was able to interview them both separately and together most of the time.

The interview lasted for approximately 2 to 2½ hours, with two exceptionally long interviews lasting up to 6 hours at the informants' requests. The general domains of the interviews included "life in the U.S. in general," "differences between the U.S. and Japan, or Americans and Japanese," "change in self," and "family and cultural adaptation." Sample questions regarding the family consisted of the following: How is your family (here or in Japan)? Has your relationship to your family members changed since you came to the U.S.? If so, how? How have your family members adjusted to the U.S.? How has your family members' adaptation affected your own adaptation to the U.S.? How do you share family chores with your spouse [for those with spouses/partners only]?

Data Analysis

For analysis, I used the techniques and methods suggested by grounded theory[2] (Charmaz, 2000; Glaser & Strauss, 1967; Strauss & Corbin, 1998), where the process of data collection and data analysis is conducted simultaneously to allow explanations of the phenomena to emerge from the data. First, I conducted open coding in Japanese and my Japanese research assistant also coded the data independently. These two sets of codes were then compared with each other's set of codes, validated or modified, and later synthesized. Updated codes were applied again to the data for further coding. Through axial and thematic coding processes (Strauss & Corbin, 1998), the core categories were developed. These categories were again applied to the data, which meant that the process of data analysis became more deductive. Finally, the boundaries and definitions of the categories were further examined, which was followed by organizing them into a coherent structure of the *Model of Cultural Negotiation* (discussed in the Discussion section).

---

[2]Strauss and Corbin (1990) explained a grounded theory as follows:

A grounded theory is one that is inductively derived from the study of the phenomenon it represents. That is, it is discovered, developed, and provisionally verified through systematic data collection and analysis of data pertaining to that phenomenon. Therefore, data collection, analysis, and theory stand in reciprocal relationship with each other. One does not begin with a theory, then prove it. Rather, one begins with an area of study and what is relevant to that area is allowed to emerge. (p. 23)

To increase the trustworthiness of the findings (Drisko, 1997; Lincoln & Guba, 1985), member check was conducted toward the end of the research process. Member check is the process by which the researcher returns to the informants or the community, shares the analysis, and receives feedback (validation) from them (Lincoln & Guba, 1985). In addition, prolonged engagement (Drisko, 1997) through repeated interviews was addressed. Further, during the research process the researcher wrote reflexive journals to raise her critical consciousness (Sakamoto & Pitner, 2005) regarding her relationship to the topic and the study participants.

FINDINGS

Although the experiences of these 18 Japanese academic migrants and their spouses were far from homogeneous with respect to family and gender roles, there were common themes that cut across the group. The study participants discussed how they liked certain aspects of American culture and did not like certain other aspects. Similarly, they openly discussed things that they came to dislike about Japan, while missing some other aspects of Japanese culture. Many wanted to be more "assertive" ("American" cultural traits, as discussed by my informants) while questioning at the same time "overly confident" attitudes of fellow American students.

These processes of encountering and dealing with cultures as they perceived them were affected by the presence of family and gender roles. The next section begins by discussing how gender roles manifested themselves in the cultural adaptation processes of women migrants, how family affected individual cultural adaptation process in general, and how individual's immigration goals influenced the rest of the family. This sets the stage for later exploration of cultural adaptation and negotiation processes of academic migrants and their spouses. Through the process of integrating these themes that emerged through the data analysis, I developed a *Model of Cultural Negotiation*. A more detailed description of the Model of Cultural Negotiation is in the Discussion section.

Encountering Cultures, Negotiating Gender Roles

"Just a Housewife"

Spouses of academic migrants often found themselves acquiring a new role upon migration: becoming a full-time "housewife" in the U.S. middle-class, academic context. Some of these spouses worked full-time in Japan. Some others got married just before their migration. Some others were proud, competent housewives in Japan, but they found that the word *housewife* in the predominantly academic community seemed to take a different meaning than *shufu* in Japanese contexts with which they were familiar.

The following episode was shared by one woman (G) who came to the United States with her husband, who was in the PhD program in a social science discipline:

> At a party, a professor asked if I was a student. I couldn't answer in English well at the time, then my husband goes, "she is just a housewife." The professor said, "That's not nice" on my behalf. But, really, I couldn't speak English or drive a car either. It was very miserable. People would just move away from me at parties when I said "I study English." They thought there was nothing to talk about .... Riding a university bus, I could tell who were students and who were housewives. Housewives looked uncomfortable and small. I felt small and hated myself.

Until she came to the United States, she did not necessarily imagine housewives as "uncomfortable and small." Initially G became "obsessed with" becoming a perfect Japanese housewife, for example, by immaculately cleaning the house all the time and hosting a number of elaborate dinner parties at home. However, she was not satisfied with her role as a "housewife," and perhaps felt depressed about her role. After a long 5 years, she learned English, learned how to drive (which afforded her more independence from her husband), was finally able to enter a graduate program, and even obtained a merit-based scholarship, each of which was a step away from being "just a housewife" with limited English proficiency. Looking back, she realized that when she was "just a housewife," she always felt self-conscious about her behavior and had decreased self-esteem: A "housewife" is "like a child" (in another female informant's word), and in G's account, is nameless and statusless. If the housewives do not speak English well, then their status is even lower. In G's case, she felt constrained and frustrated by a newly acquired gender role as a "housewife," which ultimately motivated her to set and attain her own immigration goals.

Performing Okusan *in a Local Japanese Community*

Like G, many spouses of international students/scholars expressed the "misery" of feeling like "nobody" in a university town, for being "just a housewife." On the one hand, my informants reported frustrating experiences of being devalued as "housewives" in an academic environment; on the other hand, they also referred to forces that compelled other women to stay within the "housewife" role within small Japanese communities. The following anecdote is by X, a single female visiting scholar in her late 30s who was in the United States for 1 year. X told me the experience she had at a farewell party for her, attended by several male visiting scholars and their spouses. Some of the spouses used the word *okusan* (which means wife, but with a domestic connotation to it) as a primary identifier of themselves:

> So there were about 8 people at the party, including myself. It was a gathering where I knew everybody but some people did not know each other. So somebody suggested that we first introduce ourselves .... Then when it was a turn for the first *okusan* [wife], she goes "Oh, ah, well, I just accompanied my husband, yes," and that was it .... Ha! [sarcastic laughs] ... So I thought, "Okay" but couldn't help but say, "Well, even if you are a couple, you are still separate individuals, so please do the self-introduction .... (laughs) Then the older visiting scholar went, "Ahh, Ms. X is *radical*, well, but it is her farewell party, so please do the self-introduction" and tried to mediate .... Then next, another *okusan* goes, "Thank you for taking care of my husband. I am S-san's *okusan*." Arghhhh! I was appalled, naturally.

X continued to share with me that there were other occasions in which these Japanese women only acted as "wives," and not as "individuals" with characters. These wives' behaviors could be seen as appropriate in conservative Japanese business settings, considering that X was a colleague of their husbands'. Although some of these women might have felt comfortable behaving just as "wives," it is also likely that such situations could be stressful for some other women if they felt pressured to perform well as *okusan*, limiting the expression of their individuality. Regardless of how these women felt about their own behaviors, it made it very difficult for X to get to know them. Even though they were women of similar ages to X, they did not come out of the roles as "wives," leaving little room for X to be close to them. In turn, X's status as a single female professional was highlighted even more on other occasions, such as being in the classroom with these male Japanese visiting scholars or interacting with other academic colleagues. For X, this was a bitter reminder of the constraint she felt in Japanese society as a professional woman, the constraint that she had conveniently forgotten about while in the United States. By encountering a rather exaggerated version of Japanese gender roles in a small Japanese academic migrant community, X became weary about her anticipated return to Japan.

Effect of Family on Individual Cultural Adaptation: Family-Based (Couple-Based) Cultural Adaptation

The informants expressed different patterns of family/couple dynamics in cultural adaptation; however, one thing that was common throughout was that the family/couple was one of the key factors that shaped the individual cultural adaptation. Here, by "family" or "couple," I mean the dynamics within the family or the couple in dealing with the new cultural environment, as well as the mere presence of partners and children.

For the academic migrant families in my study, adaptation to a new culture often took place in a family unit (or a couple unit), as each family member (or each spouse) took on different roles to accomplish cultural adaptation as a whole family unit. I call this mechanism *family-based (couple-based) cultural adaptation.* This became a working hypothesis as I interviewed more people in a later phase of the in-depth interviews and consulted the existing literature. Because I interviewed only adults for this particular study, *couple-based cultural adaptation* is probably a more accurate term to describe what is observed in the interviews. However, as evidenced in studies on language brokering (see below), family as a whole as a basis of cultural adaptation has a theoretical possibility. Therefore, in this chapter, I use the term *family-based (couple-based) cultural adaptation.*

Although not termed in that way, the idea of family members helping each other's cultural adaptation is not new. For example, the idea of language brokering (cultural brokering) is often reported in Latino families and some Asian families, in which parents have limited commands of English and their children help the parents carry out daily routines (Espín, 1999; Morales & Hanson, 2005; Tse, 1995; Valenzuela, 1999). However, in our study, cultural adaptation in relation to the family is examined through the lens of cultural negotiation, in which cultural adaptation tasks as well as gendered power relationships within the couple are negotiated.

Couple Role Sharing

Couples often divided cultural adaptation tasks along gender lines, and negotiated with the host culture as a family unit rather than on an individual basis. Thus, the cultural adaptation experiences were also gendered. One exception that my informants talked about is the external relations such as returning merchandise and making claims to businesses, which some of the husbands took on. Initially, husbands seemed to have been exposed to many areas of living in the United States in general (thus, cultural adaptation); however, as time passed by their focus seemed to have returned mainly to their work and study, a pattern many wives mentioned was the same when they were in Japan. In the long run, therefore, husbands' contexts of cultural adaptation might be more focused on the work domain (thus more predictable) than their wives'. On the contrary, wives' domains of adaptation were often locally contexualized (thus more learning was required), which were not necessarily restricted in one narrow area (e.g., housekeeping, children's schools, neighbors, applying for graduate schools for themselves). Thus the husbands' public sphere of work seemed to be more universally defined than the wives' mainly private sphere of work, causing different difficulties in cultural adaptation tasks (for further references on gender role in general, please refer to, e.g., Kimmel, 2000; Paludi, 1998).

Social Life

T, a visiting scholar who spent 2 years in the United States, told me how his social life was expanded after his wife had joined him in the United States:

> I had three months before my wife and daughter came over. But since they came, things are going very smoothly. My wife is a very social type, so since she came my social life has been expanded.

In other words, T's wife filled in the gap in his life and facilitated his cultural adaptation to the United States.

The case of S was a bit different from the other cases due to his family composition, but in his case, too, another family member facilitated his social life and adaptation in the social domain. S, a recent divorcé, was a researcher in an engineering field, who came to the United States with his 8-year-old son. Without having a wife to facilitate the process, S himself seemed to take on a lot of the social role. Interestingly, however, the presence of his son seemed have made it easier for him to be social. For example, he would invite other Japanese parents who had children his son's age, and developed friendships with these parents. Or he would invite Japanese acquaintances to join him when he and his child went out for a picnic, or attended sports games. S admitted to me that having fun with his son was his way of reducing stress from his work. It seemed to me that as much as he enjoyed spending time with his son, the son's presence was crucial for him to maintain his balance of work and fun and that the son provided much reassurance to him in a way. The son stayed up as late as S did, and ate as much as S did. During the interview, S would often turn to his son and seek assurance, asking "Isn't it like that?" and "Wasn't it how it went?" to which his son would nod or say something to him in reply. To me, the son seemed to have been playing the role of S's partner, sharing and validating S's experiences in the private domain and helping him to feel grounded. Thus, S's son in a way seemed have been playing a major role in S's social life and adaptation to a local Japanese community as well as to the larger American society.

Improved Family Relationships

After initial conflict, which occurred in almost all of the couples, the couples often built closer relationships with each other during their stay in the United States. Their relationships with the children, especially the father's relationship to the children, often improved as well. For many, this was partly due to the fact that the husbands now had more time in the United States, away from companies or work relationships in Japan: no social drinking after work, no social golf, more family meals, and less work over the weekend or at night. For some, it was because the husband, although busy with schoolwork, felt guilty for making his wife accompany him, so he tried to compensate for this by doing more chores around the house. Many informants expressed that because there was now nobody else to rely on or talk to, their marital and family relationships had improved. In the process of attaining better relationships, some people seemed to rediscover the wonderful qualities of their spouses, and improved their relationships. In the R couple's case, they were on the verge of divorce right before they came to the United States, but were able to restore their marriage after several months in the United States.

The meaning of family often became more important, especially for the husbands. In the R family's case, the husband (RH) confessed that he used to see the family as a burden to his work, but he came to appreciate his family more and enjoy spending time with them since they moved to the United States. This, in turn, removed feelings of guilt that the wife (RW) had, and they now talk to each other more often. RW also used to feel resentful toward her husband for not helping with the chores enough while in Japan. For example, she established a system between the two that whoever changed a diaper would receive money for each diaper, which led her to make the equivalent of $600 to $700 when the third child was a baby. However, like RH, the meaning of the family also changed for her. She used to be tormented between the two contradicting ideas: "It's cruel [pitiful; *kodomo ga kawaisou*] for children if the mother works outside of the house" versus "Career should not be interrupted." However, she felt less obliged to stay with the children and was more spontaneously willing to do so after spending time in the United States:

> I feel that our children won't be happy [if I stay very busy with work]. I want to give a little more of my space, a little more warmth to the children. I used to feel that myself, our children, and my husband exist in an inorganic [or mechanic] way [*mukishitsu*], but now I feel that there is a lot more that I can give to them.

It seems that the improved family relationship as a whole made her re-evaluate her own life goals. At the same time, a loss of socially recognizable roles for RW might have also played a role in her change, for, in Japan, she was a health care professional working side by side with her husband. One caveat of the R family stories is that neither RW nor RH was sure whether these changes would last once they returned to Japan. Although RH was curious about his own future changes, RW said she was "scared" of RH's return to his previous state of being an uncooperative, distressed, accusatory, and workaholic husband who would see the family as a burden.

Cultural Adaptation Goals Negotiated Within the Family

Cultural adaptation goals were often negotiated within the family. In the E family's case, it was very important for the husband (EH), a visiting scholar in a bio-medical field, to return to Japan as an internationally recognized researcher. To achieve this immigration goal, EH wanted to carry on his job at least with the same intensity as when he was in Japan. This had an impact on his wife (EW), as EH wanted her to be as independent as possible so that he could devote himself to work. At first EW was not able to drive and did not know how to carry out small tasks needed for housekeeping and parenting (e.g., what to buy for groceries, how to find a good babysitter), which made her "feel like a child." EH pressured her to learn to drive so that she wouldn't have to depend on him to carry out daily routines. EH shared with me that for the first couple of months, every weekend, the entire family of four would get into their small car so that EW could practice driving. EH resented that he had to take time away from his work to do this, but at the same time saw it as a necessary step toward the family's successful resettlement. When EW was able to drive and the older child started day care, she was able to reclaim her role as a competent mother and wife, which, in turn, made her feel more comfortable and competent living in the United States. Driving allowed her to make her own friends through outside activities, and to be able to do errands on her own with the younger child. Another immigration goal that both EH and EW shared was to raise their children in Japanese culture so that they could reintegrate successfully when they returned to Japan. Cooking Japanese meals, speaking proper Japanese at home, playing with other Japanese children, and watching the videotapes of Japanese TV programs that their parents sent them were important in realizing this goal.

In T's case, his immigration goals were "taking a break from" his busy Japanese life and having fun with his family. He enjoyed very much how his wife's presence made his life more social and eventful in the new country. However, his wife's immigration goal was more than taking a break from her own job. She wished to take advantage of the opportunity to pursue her own education. Eventually, T's wife, with their child, relocated to another part of the United States to enroll in a graduate program, leaving T alone in the Midwest. Without the "social" domain of his family unit, T, a rather quiet person, felt lonely and, in his word, his "days became dark." He later decided to push himself to become more social through creating an "alter ego," which he enacted in evening English classes that he took every day of the week. He believed (and I concurred) that his classmates and teachers only knew him as a social and articulate person, an accomplishment of which he was proud. In sum, when his and his wife's immigration goals did not harmonize well, T, after some struggle, had to let go of his initial immigration goal and shift it to self-improvement.

For the Q family, the husband's (QH) immigration goal was to finish a 2-year master's program in 12 months, which meant much pressure and hard work. Initially, he resented that he had to help out his wife (QW) in carrying out initial resettlement tasks in the United States:

It's not just me, but it's a common story. When I talk to other husbands [who are academic migrants in the US], there were those complaints [by husbands], complaints about their wives. In sum, unless the husbands have to take care of the important parts [of the tasks] nothing will happen, and that is *komaru* [bothering, annoying, or hard to deal with].

QW, in turn, did not appreciate her husband's initial attitude; after all, it was not her decision to come to the United States. Nevertheless, QW decided to take advantage of the opportunity of living in the United States. She picked up English quickly and was willing to get involved in the community life. When she became more comfortable in getting around by herself with the child, she started to enjoy her life in the United States, which, in turn, led her husband (QH) to feel less stress from studying because he could think "at least one of us is having fun." He also enjoyed the parties and activities that QW arranged.

Sometimes the dynamics within the family played out differently. The wife of a PhD student in natural science, NW resigned from a career-track job in a large manufacturing company in Japan that she had held for 5 years, and joined her husband a few months after he came to the United States. The women on "career-track jobs" (*sogoshoku*) are still a small elite minority in the Japanese women's work force. Although the system had been in place for more than 10 years when NW was working, these jobs were usually under very high pressure, because the women had to deal with both sexism in the work place and high job demands. NW's husband is a progressive person compared to many Japanese men and supported his wife's career; thus, the situation that NW was faced with was rather atypical for spouses of academic migrants:

I like this situation [of being in the U.S. and not working], and I feel I don't want to work any more [laughs]. I really don't have any social pressure any more, but the pressure from my husband with whom I am living, is *very* high .... He doesn't like his wife to be staying home.

In NW's case, the husband, who wished his wife continued success in her career, wanted NW to pursue something other than "sitting around in the house" like "other wives." He might also have felt guilty about the fact that she gave up a hard-to-get position as a woman that she had successfully held in Japan.

Although I did not observe or interview children, OW, a wife of an engineering student sent by his company, shared her observation with me about children's adaptation in relation to their parents:

I think whether the children can speak English or not is related to whether or not the parents are using English actively ... no matter how much English you want the children to study, if the parents cannot use it, the children cannot speak either.

Of course, if the child is in school or day care, the story might be different. Whether the parents speak English or not, the child would still pick up English from the peers and teachers. However, the willingness of the parents to speak/learn English and their openness to people different from their own would still have an impact on their children. I was impressed by the following story that OW told me about a Japanese girl, 4 or 5 years old, who was playing in the sandbox in the courtyard of one of the townhouses. When another girl of similar age with blond hair approached the sand box, this Japanese girl started to cry, saying "I am scared of *gaijin* [foreigner]." OW told me that the girl's mother was also scared of *gaijin* (i.e., Americans), although it was several months after they had come to the United States when this incident happened. OW thought that because the mother is so afraid of Americans, the child is afraid of them as well, an example that illustrates how the state of cultural adaptation of the parents may affect the children's cultural adaptation.

Family-Based (Couple-Based) Cultural Adaptation: Summary

These and previous examples of family members affecting each other's cultural adaptation process highlight the importance of the family context for understanding the cultural adaptation of individuals who come to the United States with their families. Two themes of cultural adaptation that affect and are affected by the existence of the family emerged from this work. The in-depth interview data presented here suggest that family-based (couple-based) cultural adaptation entails two major components:

1. Cultural adaptation task sharing: Family members (often couples in the current sample) may share tasks of cultural adaptation so that *as a unit* they complete the necessary tasks more successfully than one individual trying to do everything alone. The task sharing involves dividing and distributing tasks mostly along gender lines in the family so that the unit can achieve its immigration goals. For example, external negotiations are tasks for the husbands, social relations are for the wives, and matters regarding housekeeping and childrearing tend to be for the wives.

2. Negotiation of immigration goals and processes: Family members closely affect each other's state, goals, and process of cultural adaptation. This process is also influenced by who has the power within the family; the powerful person might have a greater capacity to affect others' cultural adaptation. For example, a visiting scholar husband like EH or RH, having an immigration goal of being a successful academic both in Japan and in the United States, would want to acculturate to the U.S. cultural context as well as keeping close ties to the Japanese local community and the academic community back home. This, in turn, affects how the other family members deal with U.S. and Japanese cultural contexts.

Both cultural adaptation task sharing and negotiation of the cultural adaptation process are often accompanied by stress. Very commonly, the informants with families expressed intense stress associated with family relations in the initial period of their stay. These incidents were coded as "family conflict," which was one of the most frequently used codes in this study (e.g., the family burden discussed by QH earlier).

DISCUSSION

The Model of Cultural Negotiation

Through the process of data analysis and integration of emergent themes, I developed the *Model of Cultural Negotiation* (Sakamoto, 2001; see Fig. 18.1). I define the process of cultural negotiation as the way in which individuals encounter, understand, construct, reconstruct, negotiate, and reevaluate the multiple cultural contexts of their everyday lives. The Model of Cultural Negotiation has six states, which

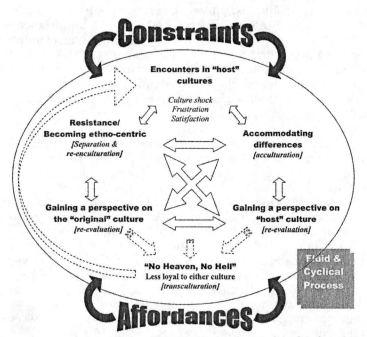

FIG. 18.1.   A Model of Cultural Negotiation. The Model of Cultural Negotiation is a loose stage model. Constraints (inhibitors) and affordances (facilitators) affect all states of cultural negotiation. Examples of the constraints include social regulatory powers, such as the presence of the parents, workplace, and some examples of the affordances include social power and a sense of agency. The presence of the family and family dynamics could be both affordances and constraints of an individual's cultural negotiation processes.

are not mutually exclusive. It is likely that an individual experiences several states at the same time, depending on the context and/or depending on the domains of interaction (e.g., communication with American friends, communication with superordinates). One state is not necessarily superior to the other. Negative repercussions for not moving through different states also depend on each individual or family and their cultural adaptation goals.

The first state of the model is *encounters in "host" cultures*. These encounters may be with people or nonhumans, such as institutions and media, and lead newcomers to construct their own interpretation of "the host culture." This state consists of making sense out of what they observe. These observations and interpretations may be colored by prearrival stereotypic beliefs. The next is the state of *accommodating the differences (acculturation)*. My informants had different strategies to accommodate the differences that they observed, especially in the areas of communication styles (e.g., assertiveness, direct communication style) and interpersonal relationships. For example, some husbands pressured their wives to be more assertive so that the wives could act more independently and could be integrated more into the "American" society. Some wives felt that their husbands had gone overboard by becoming too aggressive in dealing with local "Americans," including their supervisors. This state of accommodating the differences could be followed by, or progress simultaneously with, the state of *resistance/becoming ethnocentric*. Some thought Japanese ways were "better" in communication styles, styles of service delivery, and other domains such as food. One of the families had believed that once they moved to "America," they, too, had to eat bread everyday, so they did (*accommodating the differences*). After a few weeks, they became so tired of "American" food that they switched completely to an all-Japanese diet (*becoming ethnocentric*).

These first three states (*encounters in host cultures, accommodating the differences, resistance/becoming ethnocentric*) may recycle or progress simultaneously at any time, as migrants have more encounters in the host cultures and understand different cultural norms and selfways. Through this process, they may gradually gain perspectives on their culture of origin (Japanese culture; *reevaluation of the "original" culture*), as well as on American culture (*reevaluation of the "host" culture*). My informants reevaluated what was healthy and unhealthy for them about Japanese selfways, and wanted to discard some of its features (sense of agency). Further, several informants talked about sexism and racism in Japan. Once they stepped outside of the familiar environment, they could see more clearly the forces that were oppressive to women and ethnic minorities. On the other hand, they may revise what they thought was "American" and deconstruct some of their stereotypic beliefs. For example, the family that kept eating Japanese food realized later on that even if they had been in Japan they would not eat typical "Japanese food" every single day. Similarly, they observed that "Americans," too, eat dishes that originate in many different cultures. They switched again, to this time to a more eclectic diet, such as Italian pasta dishes, Mexican beans, and Chinese noodles. Accordingly, the behaviors or thoughts that they accommodated earlier on may be affected as well. Through this process of reevaluation of the two cultures that they constructed and reconstructed, they may approach the state of *transculturation* ("No heaven, no hell" in the R couple's words)— where they feel less committed to or constrained by either culture, although they still firmly identify themselves as Japanese.

Through uneven states (statuses) of cultural negotiation in different domains of interaction (e.g., communication with work colleagues, friendship, tasks related to family), some individuals and families were moving toward the transculturation state, where they still had a firm sense of Japanese cultural identity, but did not feel entirely committed to either Japanese or American cultures. This state of transculturation is still a temporary *state*, and not necessarily a permanent stage achieved, as in a stage model such as W. E. Cross's (1995) or a racial identity development model such as Helms's (People of Color Racial Identity Models; 1995). As one encounters a new cultural situation, the process of cultural negotiation will resume.

Furthermore, various social regulatory forces as moderating factors affected one's movement between the states, and the progression through them. These social regulatory powers may include family, gender roles, the presence of in-laws, and social status. Moreover, cultural practices could inhibit the kinds of changes that one would like to make to one's cultural selfways. For example, some female study participants shared how they were trying very hard to discard the "mutual apology norm,"[3] but has been very difficult to do so because of the cultural habit that they have developed over the years.

The informants in my sample, most of whom had initial plans to stay in the United States for 2 to 6 years, might have felt a stronger sense of agency and fluidity than permanent U.S. residents of Japanese origin, because they would be less likely to have experienced glass ceiling effects or other serious consequences arising from being a visible minority in U.S. society. In addition, the fact that they were socialized in Japan, where the idea of "fitting in" is encouraged as a social value, might facilitate their willingness to accommodate and fit into their surroundings. Thus, being Japanese might, in turn, facilitate them to be adaptive and even transcultural, as conceptualized by

---

[3]A Japanese cultural norm described by a few female informants in my sample. I coined the term, *mutual apology norm*. It is a norm in which a woman would often apologize first, rather automatically, even when she knows that she was not at fault, only because that would make the situation smoother and allow the other to apologize more easily. Some of my informants discussed it with frustration because their American counterparts did not often reciprocate these women's habitual apologies, leaving these women in awkward positions.

Markus and Kityama (1991) and other studies on Japanese sense of self (Lebra, 1992; Lebra & Lebra, 1986; Rosenberger, 1992). Gender roles did seem to affect the cultural negotiation process; the women who came to the United States as spouses reported different sets of cultural adaptation difficulties than the men did. The differences in their gender roles created different challenges for adaptation. Because women in the academic migrant families were disproportionately accompanying spouses,[4] rather than academic migrants themselves, it is not clear whether gender itself or gender roles were operating here.

How do Gender Roles and Family Affect the Cultural Negotiation Processes?

For the academic migrant families in my sample, the family and relations within it deeply affected individual cultural negotiation processes. Gender roles seemed to play a central part in the influence of family on cultural adaptation. Different members of the families participated in and shared the tasks of cultural adaptation, whereas migrants without families must try to attend to all the domains of cultural adaptation or neglect some that they cannot cover.

Within the family, the gendered division of labor that it had in Japan was often thought to be transportable to the new cultural environment. In addition, the roles of the wives, who were often without child care or a work permit, were often centered around the areas that were traditionally thought to be women's roles. Because the majority of the wives had held paid jobs in Japan, this change in status (working women vs. being a "housewife") often meant that gender roles became even more pronounced than when they were in Japan. This could cause problems when the women had difficulties carrying out tasks associated with these "women's roles."

In most of the households, the wives were expected to carry out all the tasks that were considered to be in the "private" sphere of work (domestic work, childrearing), as opposed to the husbands' tasks, which tended to focus on the "public" sphere of work (outside work, school, research). The "private" sphere of work was complicated when the larger social environment changed drastically; often wives initially

---

[4]Although there are no comprehensive data that shows the total number of Japanese academic migrants and their families staying in the United States, the current available data indicate that women make up the overwhelming majority of the accompanying family members to Japanese students and researchers in the United States. However, this does not mean that most Japanese international students and scholars in the United States are men. The number of women who stay in the United States over 3 months for the purpose of study and research has more than doubled in the past 10 years, representing over 46% of the total Japanese students and researchers registered with the local Japanese consulates in 1999 (the Japanese Ministry of Foreign Affairs data, reported in Ono & Piper, 2004, p. 106).

needed help from their husbands to complete the tasks (e.g., driving to the grocery store to buy groceries, needing help making appointments for clinics), thus requiring the husbands to cross spheres. The husbands commonly felt frustrated and resentful about needing to offer "extra help" to perform tasks that were "supposed to be" performed by the wives. This sphere crossing, in turn, made wives often feel guilty and made them "feel like a child."

However, after the initial settling-down process, the wives commonly gained more competence and confidence in taking charge of the private sphere of work, which allowed the husbands to concentrate on the narrow domain of work and the cultural adaptation tasks for that domain. On the other hand, as many of the wives continued to be responsible for the private sphere of work, they necessarily had a more wide-ranging exposure to the American society at large. This was because in order to accomplish the private sphere of work, these wives had to deal with people who were outside of the university world (e.g., children's school teachers, neighbors who are Americans or from other countries, maintenance people). Thus, the husbands' work tended to be more "universal" across cultures, focusing on their area of specialty, whereas the wives' work tended to become more "local" and diverse after the initial resettlement period. Given this diversity of exposure, at least some of the wives experienced much difficulty with language, and understanding the meaning and context of the communication, compared to the men, whose primary language context was more narrowly focused on their academics. Further, this was a difference that neither the husbands nor wives seemed to understand fully, so that when the wives were not functioning completely successfully in their private sphere of work, the husbands were often frustrated and the wives guilty.

Gender roles also had positive effects for the cultural adaptation of the family when, after the initial settlement stress, wives took on more a social role within the family, thus expanding the social life of their husbands as well. At the same time, wives who were quiet and/or were not confident in English seemed to have expressed this expectation as challenging.

All aspects of cultural negotiation and adaptation were affected by the goals of cultural adaptation that the individuals and the family/couple had. Often, the powerful member of the family set the tone for the rest of the family, sometimes "dragging them along" in the direction he had chosen. This was especially the pattern for husbands with high career aspirations. They often saw success in the U.S. research environment as central to their success as a researcher, and wanted to adopt "American ways" they thought were crucial to being successful. They expected the rest of the family (especially wives) to support this endeavor and often indirectly or directly pressured the family to accommodate their cultural adaptation goals. This often meant that the husbands wanted the family to move along toward the direction of cultural adaptation that the husbands were moving toward. Thus, the states of cultural negotiation of the individual members of the family were deeply affected by the powerful member of the family—often the husbands. On the other hand, when the husbands had a lower level of cultural adaptation goals (e.g., "just get by for two years," "enjoy life in the U.S."), there was less pressure for the family to act as a cohesive unit in adapting to a new cultural context, thus relaxing the regulatory power within the family to acculturate.

The idea that these Japanese people construct a representation of Americanness—a social constructionist view—emerged as an important aspect of the study presented here. Japanese academic migrants and their families were constantly engaging in interpretation and meaning-making in the new cultural context. However, the understanding of the new culture was not necessarily translated into the behavioral or affective domains of cultural adaptation, and vice versa. The individuals and couples expressed a sense of agency in the adaptation processes, whereas the processes were affected by the cultural adaptation goals negotiated within the family/couples, and by many other inhibitors and facilitators. To highlight the fluid, complex, and nonlinear nature of cultural accommodation, I have proposed a Model of Cultural Negotiation (see Fig. 18.1). The impacts of gender roles and power differentials on the cultural negotiation processes were discussed as facilitators and inhibitors of cultural negotiation processes.

Next Steps

Currently, I am conducting a research project with an additional sample of Japanese academic migrants (both longitudinal and cross-sectional) to further validate the Model of Cultural Negotiation. Preliminary results with this more diversified sample show that the Model of Cultural Negotiation does apply to other groups of Japanese academic migrants. In addition, I am conducting a series of studies examining the processes and strategies of cultural negotiation for Chinese immigrants in Toronto. This project examines the applicability and limitations of the Model of Cultural Negotiation to another professional immigrant population. Arguably, the flexibility of cultural negotiation for Japanese migrants was accommodated by the relative affluent economic status and political stability of their home country. In this second wave of studies, I have chosen skilled immigrants from Mainland China, because they have similar educational and class backgrounds as well as cultural traits to Japanese professional migrants (Fiske, et al., 1998), but also there are differences in the political and economic situations in their home countries. The results from the Chinese project confirm the gendered experiences of cultural negotiation processes that were revealed in the earlier Japanese sample (Sakamoto & Zhou, 2005). At the same time, income security emerges as a critical issue that fundamentally influences the cultural negotiation process, which is different from the Japanese sample (Sakamoto & Zhou, 2004). The second phase of the Chinese project focuses on refining the Model of Cultural Negotiation for the Chinese skilled immigrant population.

CONCLUSION

A grounded theory study with Japanese academic migrants and their spouses explored the processes, status, and structure of cultural negotiation, focusing on gender role and family. The study highlighted the complex and fluid processes of cultural adaptation that these Japanese individuals and families negotiated in their North American cultural contexts; in particular, the moderating factors—affordances and constraints—of such cultural negotiation processes were examined. Academic migrants expressed a sense of agency in the processes of negotiating multiple cultural contexts (e.g., transculturation), which was variously affected by occupational status, social power, gender roles, and family relations. The concept of family-based cultural adaptation emerged, leading to a new integrative model depicting the nonlinear, fluid, and uneven nature of cultural negotiation and transculturation, that is, the Model of Cultural Negotiation.

Culture is more complex than has often been described in psychology, and individuals may have more flexibility and adaptability in unfamiliar cultures than has been traditionally assumed in psychology literatures. Although psychology often fails to go beyond the notion of culture and the self as has traditionally been conceptualized in the social sciences, there is a dire need to reflect the multicultural, multifaceted reality of the interdependence of culture and the self, and the potential for change processes in cultural selfways as called for by cultural psychologists (Hermans & Kempen, 1998; Miller, 2002; Shweder & Bourne, 1984).

The study presented in this chapter aims to conceptualize culture and the self from family, gender role, and power-differential perspectives. The proposed Model of Cultural Negotiation affords a more sophisticated understanding of the properties and processes of culture than traditional models, and makes room for the malleability of cultural selfways and the intersectionality of multiple identities.

AUTOBIOGRAPHICAL NOTES TOWARD THE FUTURE OF CULTURAL PSYCHOLOGY OF IMMIGRATION

My professional and academic interests in working with immigrants primarily arose from my personal experiences. I first came from Japan in 1993 as a Fulbright scholar to pursue graduate studies in Michigan. Besides being a gender minority as a woman, I was not used to being seen as so "different" all the time due to my language, culture, and physical appearance. This was a truly new experience for someone who grew up in the seemingly homogeneous environment of middle-class Japan. As a PhD student in social psychology and social work at the University of Michigan, I struggled to find a niche in which my experiences and cultural perspectives were valued, or even recognized as valid. I felt as if North American racial politics reserved the term *racism* to mean oppression against African Americans, and found it difficult to find a space to talk about my experience of being a foreign Asian woman with an accent in a predominantly White society. I eventually came to represent myself and others in similar situations (international students/scholars and their families) through campus-based activism, advocacy, and a community-based participatory action project. From these experiences, my scholarly and professional work started to focus more on culture, identities, and various forms of oppression, including gender, race/ethnicity, and foreignness (e.g., Gutiérrez, Sakamoto & Morson, 2003; Pitner & Sakamoto, 2005; Sakamoto, 2001, 2003; Sakamoto & Pitner, 2005).

Joining the Culture and Cognition Program in Michigan helped my intellectual growth as a cultural psychologist. First, it was such an invigorating experience to be able to talk about "my culture" before a captive audience. People wanted to know more about "the Japanese culture" to contrast to "the American culture." Then I faced the challenge of balancing my agenda of inserting my voice while not self-exoticizing or overly generalizing "the Japanese culture." Of course, there are various power differentials within Japan or any other country. How much of those power differentials can we represent in cultural psychology? How generalizable is my "indigenous knowledge"? These are some of the questions that must be raised in cultural psychology.

Another challenge I see in cultural psychology is that although psychologists and anthropologists have come together to form an interdisciplinary field, the barriers still remain in methodology and epistemology. Furthermore, those who truly cross the methodological and epistemological boundaries of these distinct disciplines face challenges in getting their work published in "mainstream" journals, which limits the publication from reaching a wider audience. For example, rarely can one publish a qualitative psychological study from a constructivist or critical perspective in a mainstream psychology journal. In my own experience, my dissertation had both a controlled lab experiment and an inductive, constructivist qualitative study. Bridging the epistemological gaps underlying these two distinct methodologies was truly a challenge for me in forming one cohesive body of work.

In summary, I see the future direction for the study of cultural psychology of immigrants in the following:

1. Recognizing the limitations of postpositivism and exploring different methodologies and epistemologies to create new

knowledges (for epistemologies, please refer to Guba & Lincoln, 1998): Different approaches may raise and answer new, important questions. For example, how can cultural psychology draw from community-based participatory research projects with immigrants that could highlight indigenous knowledges?

2. Reflecting the transnational reality and recognizing multiple identities: We need to reflect the idea that culture can be a flexible, changeable system that at the same time constrains individuals and the collective. As Hermans and Kempen (1998) argued, cultural psychologists need to tolerate the ambiguity and uncertainty that emerge when cultures shift and come in contact with one another. This also calls for not only looking at central tendencies within a culture using inferential statistics but also using a variety of methodologies to reflect the diversity within a culture and its shifting nature.

3. Integrating more fully gender, sexual orientation, class, and various other power differentials: Psychology is often criticized for being apolitical. Cultural inquiry in psychology is also guilty of offering sweeping heuristics equating a culture with a nation/state or an ethnic group (Miller, 1997). We can learn much from anthropology and sociology as we incorporate the impact of power differentials and diversity within a "culture."

4. Engaging in critical interrogation of "culture": Many anthropologists in the last decades criticized the utility and integrity of the notion of "culture" (e.g., Abu-Lughod, 1991; Brightman, 1995). I am not quite sure yet whether or not cultural psychologists, too, can "forget culture" (Brightman, 1995, p. 509) completely. Nevertheless, we need to recognize the fact that the notions of "culture" and "cultural differences" have had problematic histories and, even in the present day, are often used to create and reinforce hierarchies (Abu-Lughod, 1991). In that regard, it is crucial to examine who is naming the "culture" in question and who is practicing it. As long as culture is a publically available concept, which I expect it will be for at least some time, I believe cultural psychologists have an important role to play in identifying, questioning, and interrogating culture in a critical manner.

REFERENCES

Abu-Lughod, L. (1991). Writing against culture. In R. Fox (Ed.), *Recapturing anthropology: Working in the present* (pp. 137–162). Santa Fe: School of American Research Press.

Berry, J. W. (1990). Psychology of acculturation. *Nebraska Symposium on Motivation 1989, 37*, 201–224.

Berry, J. W. (1997). Immigration, acculturation, and adaptation. *Applied Psychology: An International Review, 46*(1), 5–68.

Berry, J. W., Kim, U., Power, S., Young, M., & Bujaki, M. (1989). Acculturation attitudes in plural societies. *Applied Psychology: An International Review, 38*(2), 185–206.

Brightman, R. (1995). Forget culture: Replacement, transcendence, relexification. *Cultural Anthropology, 10*(4), 509–546.

Charmaz, K. (2000). Grounded theory: Objectivist and constructivist methods. In N. K. Denzin & Y. S. Lincoln (Eds.), *Handbook of qualitative research* (2nd ed., pp. 509–535). Thousand Oaks, CA: Sage.

Cross, W. E., Jr. (1995). The psychology of Nigrescence: Revisiting the Cross Model. In J. G. Ponterotto, J. M. Casas, L. A. Suzuki, & C. M. Alexander (Eds.), *Handbook of multicultural counseling* (pp. 93–122). Thousand Oaks, CA: Sage.

Cushner, K., & Brislin, R. W. (Eds.). (1997). *Improving intercultural interactions: Models for cross-cultural training programs, volume 2.* Thousand Oaks, CA: Sage.

Dion, K. D., & Dion, K. L. (2001). Gender and cultural adaptation in immigrant families. *Journal of Social Issues, 57*(3), 511–521.

Drisko, J. W. (1997). Strengthening qualitative studies and reports; Standards to promote academic integrity. *Journal of Social Work Education, 33,* 185–197.

Espín, O. M. (1999). *Women crossing boundaries: A psychology of immigration and transformations of sexuality.* New York: Routledge.

Espiritu, Y. L. (1999). Gender and labor in Asian immigrant families. *American Behavioral Scientist, 42*(49), 628–647.

Fiske, A. P., Kitayama, S., Markus, H. R., & Nisbett, R. E. (1998). The cultural matrix of social psychology. In D. T. Gilbert, S. Fiske, & G. Lindzey (Eds.), *Handbook of social psychology* (Vol. 2, 4th ed., pp. 915–981). New York: McGraw-Hill.

Frable, D. E. S. (1997). Gender, racial, ethnic, sexual, and class identities. *Annual Review of Psychology, 48,* 139–162.

Gilgun, J. F. (1994). Hand into glove: The grounded theory approach and social work practice research. In E. Sherman & W. Reid (Eds.), *Qualitative research in social work* (pp. 115–125). New York: Columbia University Press.

Glaser, B. G., & Strauss, A. L. (1967). *The discovery of grounded theory: Strategies for qualitative research.* New York: Aldine de Guyter.

Guba, E. G., & Lincoln, Y. S. (1998). Competing paradigms in qualitative research. In N. K. Denzin & Y. S. Lincoln (Eds.), *The landscape of qualitative research* (pp. 195–220). Thousand Oaks, CA: Sage.

Gutiérrez, L. M., Sakamoto, I., & Morson, T. (2003). Using groups for action and research: Asian mothers support group. In J. Lindsay, D. Turcotte, & E. Hopmeyer (Eds.), *Crossing boundaries and developing alliances through group work* (pp. 133–146). Binghamton, NY: Haworth Press.

Heine, S. J., & Lehman, D. R. (1997). The cultural construction of self-enhancement: An examination of group-serving biases. *Journal of Personality & Social Psychology, 72*(6), 1268–1283

Heine, S. J., Lehman, D. R., Markus, H. R., & Kitayama, S. (1999). Is there a universal need for positive self-regard? *Psychological Review, 106*(4), 766–794.

Helms, J. E. (1995). An update of Helms''s White and People of Color Racial Identity Models. In J. G. Ponterotto, J. M. Casas, L. A. Suzuki, & C. M. Alexander (Eds.), *Handbook of multicultural counseling* (pp. 181–198). Thousand Oaks, CA: Sage.

Hermans, H. J. M., & Kempen, H. J. G. (1998). Moving cultures: The perilous problems of cultural dichotomies in a globalization society. *American Psychologist, 53*(10), 1111–1120.

Hondagneu-Sotelo, P. (1999). Introduction: Gender and contemporary U.S. immigration. *American Behavioral Scientist, 42*(4), 565–576.

Hong, Y.-Y., Morris, M. W., Chiu, C.-Y., & Benet-Martinez, V. (2000). Multicultural minds: A dynamic constructivist approach to culture and cognition. *American Psychologist, 55*(7), 709–720.

Institute of International Education. (2005). *Open Doors 2005* [web page]. Retrieved December 8, 2005, from http://opendoors.iienetwork.org

Kimmel, M. S. (2000). *The gendered society.* New York: Oxford University Press.

LaFromboise, T., Coleman, H. L. K., & Gerton, J. (1993). Psychological impact of biculturalism: Evidence and theory. *Psychological Bulletin, 114*(3), 395–412.

Lebra, T. S. (1992). Self in Japanese culture. In N. R. Rosenberger (Ed.), *Japanese sense of self* (pp. 105–120). Cambridge, UK: Cambridge University Press.

Lebra, T. S., & Lebra, W.P. (1986). *Japanese culture and behavior: Selected readings.* Honolulu: University of Hawaii Press.

Lederman, R. (1998). Globalization and the future of culture areas: Melanesianist anthropology in transition. *Annual Review of Anthropology, 27,* 427–449.

Licoln, Y., & Guba, E. (1985). *Naturalistic inquiry.* Newbury Park, CA: Sage..

Lim, I.-S. (1997). Korean immigrant women's challenge to gender inequality at home: The interplay of economic resources, gender and family. *Gender and Society, 11,* 31–51.

Man, G. (2004). Gender, work and migration: Deskilling Chinese immigrant women in Canada. *Women's Stuides International Forum, 27,* 135–148.

Markus, H. R., & Kitayama, S. (1991). Culture and the self: Implications for cognition, emotion, and motivation. *Psychological Review 98*(2), 224–253.

Markus, H. R., Mullally, P., & Kitayama, S. (1997). Selways: Diversity in modes of cultural participation. In U. Neisser & D. A. Jopling (Eds.), *The conceptual self in context: Culture, experiences, self-understanding* (pp. 13–61). New York: Cambridge University Press.

Miller, J. G. (1997). Theoretical issues in cultural psychology. In J. W. Berry, Y. H. Poortinga, & J. Pandey (Eds.), *Handbook of cross-cultural psychology, Vol. 1: Theory and method* (pp. 85–128). Boston: Allyn and Bacon.

Miller, J. G. (2002). Bringing culture to basic psychological theory—Beyond individualism/collectivism: Comment on Oyserman et al. (2002). *Psychological Bulletin, 128*(1), 97–109.

Morales, A., & Hanson, W. E. (2005). Language brokering: An integrative review of the literature. *Hispanic Journal of Social Sciences, 27*(4), 471–503.

Nisbett, R.E., Peng, K., Choi, I., & Norenzayan, A. (2001). Culture and systems of thought: Holistic versus analytic cognition. *Psychological Review, 108*(2), 291–310.

Ono, H., & Piper, N. (2004). Japanese women studying abroad, the case of the US. *Women's Studies International Forum, 27,* 101–118.

Paludi, M. A. (1998). *The psychology of women.* Upper Saddle River, NJ: Prentice Hall.

Patton, M. Q. (1990). *Qualitative evaluation and research methods* (2nd ed.). Newbury Park, CA: Sage.

Pessar, P. R. (1999). Engendering migration studies: The case of new immigrants in the United States. *American Behavioral Scientist, 42*(4), 577–600.

Phinney, J. S. (1990). Ethnic identity in adolescents and adults: Review of research. *Psychological Bulletin, 108,* 499–514.

Phinney, J., & Devich-Navaroo, M. (1997). Variations in bicultural identification among African American and Mexican American adolescents. *Journal of Research on Adolescence, 7,* 3–32.

Pitner, R., & Sakamoto, I. (2005). Examining the role of critical consciousness in multicultural practice: Its promises and limitations. *American Journal of Orthopsychiatry, 75*(4), 684–694.

Rodriguez, N. P. (1999). Globalization, autonomy, and transnational migration: Impacts on U.S. intergroup relations. *Research in Politics and Society, 6,* 65–84.

Rosenberger, N. R. (1992). *Japanese sense of self.* Cambridge, UK: Cambridge University Press.

Ryder, A. G., Alden, L. E., & Paulhus, D. L. (2000). Is acculturation unidimensional or bidimensional? A head-to-head comparison in the prediction of personality, self-identity, and adjustment. *Journal of Personality and Social Psychology, 79*(1), 49–65.

Sakamoto, I. (2001). *Negotiating multiple cultural contexts: Flexibility and constraint in the cultural selfways of Japanese academic migrants.* Unpublished doctoral dissertation, University of Michigan, Ann Arbor.

Sakamoto, I. (2003). Changing images and common dynamics: Historical patterning of *foreignness* in the social work profession. In R. Saunders (Ed.), *The concept of the foreign: An Interdisciplinary dialogue* (pp. 237–279). Lanham, MD: Lexington Books.

Sakamoto, I., & Pitner, R. (2005). Use of critical consciousness in anti-oppressive social work practice: Disentangling power dynamics at personal and structural levels. *British Journal of Social Work, 35*(4), 420–437.

Sakamoto, I., & Zhou, Y. R. (2004, August). *Cultural negotiation of Japanese and Chinese (im)migrants in North America: A comparative analysis.* Paper presented at the 28th International Congress of Psychology in Beijing.

Sakamoto, I., & Zhou, Y. R. (2005). Gendered nostalgia: The experiences of Chinese new skilled immigrants in Canada. In Agnew, V. (Ed.), *Diaspora, memory and silence—Who calls Canada home?* (pp. 209–229). Toronto: University of Toronto Press.

Shweder, R. A., & Bourne, E. J. (1984). Does the concept of the person vary cross-culturally? In R. A. Shweder & R. A. Levine (Eds.), *Culture theory: Essays on mind, self and emotion* (pp. 158–199). New York: Cambridge University Press.

Strauss, A., & Corbin, A. (1998). *Basics of qualitative research: Techniques and procedures for developing grounded theory* (2nd ed.). Thousand Oaks, CA: Sage.

Swales, J. M. (1997). English as *Tyronnosaurus rex. World Englishes, 16*(3), 373–382.

Tse, L. (1995). Language brokering among Latino adolescents: Prevalence, attitudes, and school performance. *Hispanic Journal of Behavioral Sciences, 17*(2), 180–193.

United Nations. (2002). Number of world's migrants reachers 175 million mark: Migrant population has doubled in twenty-five years. Retrieved December 8, 2005, from http://www.un.org/News/Press/docs/2002/pop844. doc.htm

Valenzuela, A. (1999). Gender roles and settlement activities among children and their immigrant families. *American Behavioral Scientist, 42*(4), 720–742.

Author Index

Subject Index